1994

Towards the end of the nineteenth century many affluent and educated people, influenced by developments in medical, biological and psychiatric sciences, became convinced that destitution, insanity and criminality – even homosexuality and hysteria – were symptoms of the degeneration of the human race, through the determinism of heredity. Such theories seemed to provide plausible explanations for disturbing social changes, and new insights into human character and morality. For a time they achieved extraordinary dominance. William Greenslade's book is the first to investigate the impact of degeneration theories on British culture and on fiction. He traces the difficulties experienced by writers, including Hardy, Gissing, Conan Doyle, Conrad, Wells, Forster and Woolf, in negotiating their own freedom of interpretation in the light of such theories; he pursues the survival of degenerationism in the work of popular writers Warwick Deeping and John Buchan; and he charts the resilience of its tropes through the 1930s, to the holocaust.

DEGENERATION, CULTURE AND THE NOVEL
1880–1940

DEGENERATION, CULTURE AND THE NOVEL 1880–1940

WILLIAM GREENSLADE

University of the West of England, Bristol

CAMBRIDGE
UNIVERSITY PRESS

1994

Published by the Press Syndicate of the University of Cambridge
The Pitt Building, Trumpington Street, Cambridge CB2 1RP
40 West 20th Street, New York, NY 10011-4211, USA
10 Stamford Road, Oakleight, Melbourne 3166, Australia

First published 1994

Printed in Great Britain at the University Press, Cambridge

A catalogue record for this book is available from the British Library

Library of Congress cataloguing in publication data

Greenslade, William P.
Degeneration, culture, and the novel, 1880–1940/William Greenslade
p. cm.
Includes bibliographical references and index.
ISBN0-521-41665-5 (hc)
1. English fiction – 20th century – History and criticism.
2. English fiction – 19th century – History and criticism.
3. Literature and society – Great Britain – History.
4. Degeneration in literature.   I. Title.
PR888.D373G74   1994
824′.809355–dc20 93-25373 CIP

ISBN 0 521 416655 hardback

*To Stella, Basil, Karen, and Isabel
and in memory of John Goode 1939–1994*

Contents

ix

Illustrations

Acknowledgements

I owe an enormous debt of gratitude to the late John Goode, my one-time Ph.D supervisor, for his expert advice, critical insight and his unflagging belief that my subject was worth pursuing. His generous and unequivocal response to my first, half worked-out, research proposal was of inestimable value. Numerous other post-graduate students and colleagues at Warwick, and at Reading and Keele, owe similar debts to a man of rare critical gifts and radical courage.

In John Stokes I have been most fortunate to find an exemplary guide, critic and friend whose comments on my manuscript at the various stages of its composition never failed to hit the mark. My thanks also to Kate Fullbrook, Rosemarie Bailey, and my friend of longstanding, Keith McClelland – each of whom gave generously of their time and wisdom.

I also gladly acknowledge the help given to me, in different ways, by Steve Attridge, Michael Bell, Oliver Bennett, Jeremy Bennett, Bernard Bergonzi, Marion Doyen, U. A. Fanthorpe, Nicole Foster, Giles Foster, Brian Gibbons, John Goodman, Basil Greenslade, Lynne Hapgood, Loveday Herridge, Robin Jarvis, Tom Jeffery, the late Michael Katanka, Anthony Kearney, Mary Langan, John Lucas, Ludmilla Jordanova, Keith Maiden, Michael Mason, Karl Miller, Evelyne Muller, Michael Neve, Kathleen Knapp, Geoffrey Pearson, Kate Petty, Deborah Philips, John Reid, David Shewell, Jenny Bourne Taylor, Kevin Taylor, David Trotter, Tom Wakefield, Eddie Wainwright, Frank Warren, Paul Weindling, Richard Wilson, Michael Wheeler, Kevin White, and Polly Wright.

I would like to thank the library staff at the following libraries and institutions for their assistance: the British Library, the London Library, the libraries of the Universities of London, Warwick, Manchester, Bristol, Bath, and the UWE, Bristol, S. Martin's

College of Higher Education, Lancaster, the Wellcome Institute, London, and the Royal College of Physicians.

I should like to thank the Trustees of the British Library, the Trustees of the Thomas Hardy Memorial Collection in the Dorset County Museum, Dorchester, and the Sheffield City Library, for permission to quote manuscript material in their possession.

An earlier version of Chapter Seven first appeared in *Victorian Studies* 32 (4) (Summer 1989): 502–523 and a version of the first three sections of Chapter Eight first appeared as 'The Lure of Pedigree in Hardy's *Tess of the D'Urbervilles*', *Thomas Hardy Journal* 7 (October 1991): 103–115; my thanks to both editors. I am grateful to Macmillan for allowing me to draw on some of the material contained in my essay 'Fitness and the Fin de Siècle' in John Stokes (ed.) *Fin de Siècle/Fin du Globe* (Macmillan, 1992), 37–51, for Chapters Two, Three and Nine.

I am grateful to the following for permission to reproduce illustrations in their possession: The Museum of London for 'Little Collingwood, Bethnal Green'; Hulton Deutsch for 'Prehistoric Iguanondon'; Punch Publications Ltd for 'The Nemesis of Neglect' and 'Quite Unnecessary Question'; Bridgeman Art Library for 'Motherhood' and Barnaby's Picture Library for 'Hitler at the "Degenerate Art" Exhibition'.

Introduction

I

In *The Fifth Child* (1988) Doris Lessing deploys a concept of degeneration which she makes account for the anomalous nature of a strange and horrifying child – from his gestation through to his adolescence. Ben is a monster, and the serviceable myth of degeneration, in one of its common manifestations – atavism, offers a rational structure for his inexplicability, capturing and fixing him as if definitions must needs bend to accommodate and stabilise the rush of violent emotions aroused within his family. It is Ben's mother who finally invokes the myth of a degenerate 'type', when she sees in her son an atavistic throwback: 'she felt she was looking through him at a race that reached its apex thousands and thousands of years before humanity, whatever that meant, took the stage'.[1]

The feelings of incredulity, anger, resentment and fear aroused by this encounter with a reversionary embodiment, provide Lessing with a workable but dubious typology. For she allows Ben to be labelled quite unironically. Her implied revulsion from the barbarism of the 1980s rests on a schema which permits her to fix on Ben's reverted 'nature' as the reason why at the end of the novel, Ben is an expectant recruit-in-waiting to a global army of teenage vandals and delinquents, as viewed, apocalyptically, on television, in the major cities of the world. Lessing's novel is a work of science fiction, offering a parable for our time, but its mythic component hails from a now discredited family of ideas, active in the late nineteenth and early twentieth century. These ideas and the different ways they were assimilated and deployed by British writers of fiction in this period is the subject of this book.

The idea of degeneration was an important resource of myth for the post-Darwinian world. The late Victorian establishment and the

I

propertied classes generally harboured anxieties about poverty and crime, about public health and national and imperial fitness, about decadent artists, 'new women' and homosexuals. The loose assemblage of beliefs which can be marked out as 'degenerationism', especially when these beliefs claimed the ratification of empirical science, offered a displacement and transference of guilt, and of fear of the uncontrollable and baffling energies of material existence. Degeneration offered boundless scope for both attacking the irrational and sustaining it. Late nineteenth century 'learned men', with their 'inclination ... to frighten themselves and their audiences', as Peter Gay puts it, 'dreaded spectres that they themselves had painted on the wall'.[2]

Such fears at the *fin de siècle* were at work shaping institutional practices – medical, psychiatric, political – and their assumptions. Degeneration facilitated discourses of sometimes crude differentiation: between the normal and the abnormal, the healthy and morbid, the 'fit' and 'unfit', the civilised and the primitive. Degeneration was at the root of what was, in part, an enabling strategy by which the conventional and respectable classes could justify and articulate their hostility to the deviant, the diseased and the subversive. At times when the social order was under particular pressure (London in the mid-1880s is an example, or much of Europe after 1917) the pathological element in the discourses of social panic was pressed into service to undermine the intentionality of the oppositional voice, by rendering it as irrational or 'sick' – whether it was the voice of organised labour, Jewish immigrants or psychoanalysis. In the rhetoric of establishment anxieties (which extends to doctors, politicians, novelists, feature and leader-writers) there are, at times, striking and tenacious continuities which it is one aim of this book to trace.

As is by now well recognised, the work of Michel Foucault has been most instrumental in directing attention to such fields of discourse embodying whole 'ensembles' of beliefs, and traceable to quite discrete origins – despite their apparent contiguity. Such a 'discursive field', for Foucault, is psychopathology. Here assumptions about the human subject and institutions form a frame around discrete 'objects' of that discourse: the criminal, the 'feeble-minded', the neurotic woman, the hooligan, the artist. Degeneration is one 'surface of emergence' of that discourse in late nineteeth and early twentieth-century Europe.[3]

These discursive relationships, Foucault argues, are not passively reflected, but actively elaborated, asserted – even defined – through the forms of language itself: for this is one way the exercise of power happens. Power is not to be solely identified with a monolithic state apparatus, it is disseminated through many and varied discourses, institutions and institutional contexts. In Foucault's terms, degeneration is discursively activated to produce, for example, typologies of 'inclusion' and 'exclusion'. Regulating morality or sexuality entails not only repression (or indifference) but the active production of categories and distinctions. The prostitute or the hooligan are defined in terms of their variation from a posited ideal or norm – the womanly woman, the manly ideal: the same is true of the neurotic woman, the homosexual or introspective adolescent. As the authority of norms falters, so the regulation through categories becomes more necessary.

Foucault has much to offer the literary historian for whom the literary text engages with, battens on to, yet can defy and move beyond the discursive. But to illustrate what novelists can do with the idea of degeneration, I want to use Frank Kermode's distinction between the function of myth and that of fiction as a starting-point. For Kermode, the mythic component of a concept and practice such as degeneration lies in the absence of a sense of its fictiveness, its constructedness. 'Myth', Kermode has written, 'operates within the diagrams of ritual, which presupposes total and adequate explanations of things as they are and were; it is a sequence of radically unchangeable gestures.' Fictions, on the other hand, 'are made for finding things out, and they change as the needs of sense-making change. Myths are the agents of stability, fictions the agents of change.'[4]

The critical obligation is, as far as possible, to historicise the claims that degeneration makes to 'truth', to show how it might mythologise history, or, as R. P. Blackmur put it when thinking of those positivist synthesisers – Comte, Buckle and Nordau – how it represents 'history' as the 'science of thought'. This is not 'truth', for Blackmur, it is 'drama' – even melodrama.[5] The writers featured in this book, Thomas Hardy, George Gissing, H. G. Wells, Joseph Conrad, E. M. Forster, Virginia Woolf and others, dealt in different ways with this noisy, intrusive, public discursive practice: to listen to them addressing the world is to listen to how they dealt with its rhetorical configurations.

On better acquaintance, it does become possible to talk about a text, 'arguing with the past', in Gillian Beer's phrase. This involves trying to recreate something of what Beer calls the 'hermeneutic circle of novel and first readers, the complexity of whose relations is written into the work'. For Beer, 'the presence of those voices (arguing, repeating, refusing, diversifying the range of the book's linguistic community)' makes for a 'fuller, more specific, and often more disturbing resonance to our reading now'.[6] In the reading and rereading of texts those voices reverberate, often unpredictably. To face head on the activity of degeneration in this period allows a way of testing the particular, local effectivity of these voices, and so of registering the pressure of that 'linguistic community'.

Historicising the text helps to reconstruct the effort writers make at writing within, alongside or, often, against the terms of discourse, consciously or unconsciously. While the question of 'influence' is rarely straightforward, I acknowledge the importance to writers of particular sources, the identification of which may help to clarify an interpretative question in the text. But of course influence can easily elude this empirical appeal to precise source and authority. In Beer's words 'profound habits of mind often leave only the slightest fossil traces within writing'.[7]

To hear the voices of influence in a text is to engage with its 'network of resistances', as Dominic LeCapra has it.[8] And of course within the network there may be a resistance from the author; the play of a polyvalent idea such as degeneracy can help to suggest what the author is repressing and how much can be allowed to show, or let slip. John Goode extends the point from poetry into history: like poetry, history 'needs to be *read*, transitively, like a dialogue'. But Goode goes on to say that 'its marks, its signs, like the signs motivated in literary texts, are veiled by the obscurity not merely of time but of domination and assimilation'.[9] To attend to the dialogue over degeneration in the text reveals both its resistance and its capitulation to the ideological engines which drive degenerationism into the utterance of 'truth', rather than 'myth'.

II

Gissing is an interesting example of a writer whose novels capitulate (more wholeheartedly than one would like) before the forces of assimilation. Despite his insight into how the late Victorian cultural hegemony was sustained and how mainly marginal social groups were subjected to the processes of ideology (from his own marginal, unintegrated position), Gissing none the less holds out for models of biological essentialism which turn on his considerable investment in the 'natural'. For him, social classes are divided by 'natural antipathies'[10] (the phrase is from *Demos*), and in the psychopathology of Max Nordau spliced with Herbert Spencer, Gissing finds a convenient and serviceable short cut to the unresolved question of female 'nature' by reproducing, with considerable imaginative force, the teleology of the woman as index of a whole societal 'condition'.

There were few writers of the late nineteenth and early twentieth century, who were not vulnerable to the explanatory lure of forms of biological determinism. But Britain had little that could match the programmatic fictions of degeneration by naturalist writers on the continent. In France, the plots of Zola's *Rougon-Macquart* novels were structured to demonstrate the power of inherited effects of pathologies acquired from the environment: alchoholism and mental disease led to crime and prostitution.[11] In Germany, authors like Voss and Kirchbach wrote plays about the 'ill-effects of degenerate parental behaviour'. Hauptmann's *Vor Sonnenaufgang* (*Before Dawn*) (1889), was a naturalistic study of the pathological degeneration of a peasant family – 'the first major statement in Germany on racial biology'.[12]

But scientific positivism did find its way into British fiction in much writing of the 1880s and nineties, drawing on the conventions of theatrical melodrama and sensationalist fiction. These works took on other kinds of shocking subject matter – mental instability, moral insanity, venereal disease and their threat to the sanctity and purity of marriage and family.[13] Writers such as 'Lucas Malet', R. L. Stevenson, Sarah Grand, Emma Frances Brooke assimilated the melodramatic and the hyperbolic for characteristically British didactic ends. The play of hyperbole, which, as Peter Brooks notes, makes 'the world morally legible, spelling out its ethical forces and imperatives in large and bold characters', has considerable relevance for the narratives of anxiety and fear, both in fiction and discursive writing, in the post-Darwinian period. For what is now 'legible' is the evidence of hereditary contamination, no less moral for being viewed through the lens of scientific rationalism. Science now competes for the right to display what Brooks calls 'the grandiose moral terms of the drama' in which 'gestures within the world constantly refer us to another, hyperbolic set of gestures where life and death are at stake'.[14]

Gissing, Wells and Conrad, in their different ways, gained from post-Darwinian science resources for articulating consciousness under modern pressures. Hardy, as his notebooks show, was acutely attuned to the scientific debates and controversies from the 1870s to the late nineties. He was exceptionally sensitive to questions of heredity and its profounder mysteries, such as the interplay between the determining 'germ', and the indices of creative variability, playing through not just the lineaments but the character and destiny of the human subject. He worked both with and against the grain of these explanatory myths.

At the same time he accepted (albeit with increasing reluctance) the constraints placed upon him by editors, and resorted to strategies of subterfuge which allowed his texts to address controversial and sensitive themes – now advancing into dangerous territory, now withdrawing to more familiar ground – within the stages of composition and revision of the same novel, as he did in the writing and rewriting of *Tess of the D'Urbervilles*. Hardy subjects his characters to all the forms of determinism needed to bring them into conformity with the contemporary discourse of heredity, without closing down the possibility of alternative readings by those who might understand the strategy of his writing: in both *Tess* and *Jude* determinism is ironically and painfully treated – internalised by his characters to offer an explicable myth for the inexplicability of their lives.

Hardy's achievement and challenge in his late fiction is to recuperate, from dominant discourses, alternative vantage-points from which the mythic component of these discourses can be weighed, so that from 'Mixen-Lane' in *The Mayor of Casterbridge*, we see what was withheld or repressed in the 'darkest', 'outcast' London of the 1880s. Country and city, respectable and unrespectable, integrated and abject, 'fit' and 'unfit', 'nature' and 'society' – Hardy negotiated these oppositions through strategies of indirection, and yet (given the hegemony and power of the remit of these discourses of appropriation and control in the 1880s and nineties) the extent of Hardy's resistance commands considerable respect.

The fictional resources which Wells brought to evolutionary speculation in the last decade of the century prompt an extension or refinement of Kermode's distinction between myth-maker and fictionalist; Wells is so obviously an ambiguous, if rewarding, test-case. His 'fictions' of the nineties are never without their mythic element, and his 'myths', crystallised from new biological science and sociology, are neither pure science nor pure myth, and can only be, in a highly qualified sense, 'agents of change'. Wells understood with devastating clarity how post-Darwinian science was being used as a vehicle for what Lord Rosebery called the 'competition of the universe'. *'The Time Machine* was his response to the facile progressivism and imperialism of the nineties. His use of degeneration, or of alien invasion, offers a speculative instrument for the penetration of late Victorian complacencies, but, at the same time, he colluded with the reader's understandable fascination with these bio-social myths – with his eye on the market-place.

Like Hardy, Conrad inhabits a post-Darwinian frame of reference, and was widely read in contemporary science; but his involvement with degeneration is paradoxical. He is attracted by the typologies of reversion and atavism, and by the strains of the pathological and criminal. Conrad sought out such ideas to arm himself with an authoritative scientific repertoire to explicate those states of mind which both fascinated and appalled him, but which precisely defied rational explanation. He sought a psychopathological clue to the inexplicable fact of the irrational, the trangressive, the evil.

In pursuit of the 'dark places' of the psyche, Conrad finds in Max Nordau's 'ego-mania' a serviceable idea which offers a provisional clue to the seductive plausibility of the men of defective 'nature'. With their powerful delinquency, their tenacious and charismatic malignity, they witness to what he called the 'eternal fitness of lies and impudence'.[15] These degenerate energies are reviled as 'other', because Conrad knows that they inhabit the civilised psyche too. The butcher and the criminal are uncomfortably close to home, even scandalously a requirement of the state with its evolving technologies of surveillance, control, law and order. This is a real advance towards the deconstruction of the *hubris* of turn-of-the-century apostles of progress, empire and conquest. But of course it is now a repertoire which he eventually, with precise irony, turns on the perpetrators of this positivism: in *The Secret Agent* it becomes the quarry in a supremely confident display of ironic gamesmanship: the game is cat and mouse, and the degenerationists are caught in the trap which the author neatly springs.

So pervasive and seductive was the terminology of degeneration in this period that it was all but impossible to avoid: writers could be forgiven for resorting to its terms, even though, in other respects, their work serves notice on the value of its typologies. D. H. Lawrence, who is not a degenerationist but a primitivist, none the less keeps in circulation the small change of psychopathological diagnosis.[16] And Forster, even as he is contesting incorporation into the terms of degenerationist reductionism, uses a third-person narrator, or author-commentator, to pass off an unproblematic stock of commonsense, not liable to critical challenge.

The lure of degeneration sparkles in Forster's cult of uncorrupted yeoman stock, or in the 'morbidity' of a psychologically disturbed character like Helen Schlegel (a more complex creation than he realises). Yet Forster registers that those who pronounce on morbidity do so to keep their 'feminine' feelings at bay. It is – as for Conrad – a mask, to be worn against the suspicion of introspection and a besetting fear of consciousness, and mental breakdown. Forster's sure-footed exposure of the patriarchal fortress which harbours the imperial type (an underrated achievement of *Howards End*) brings out into the open the values of the Edwardian ruling-class male, and, for the first time, asks how the discourses of appropriation come to be wielded and why. Like Conrad before him and Woolf after him, Forster anticipates the Foucauldian idea that discourses of diagnosis are formidable coercive instruments of cultural and sexual power. Like Conrad, Woolf in *Mrs Dalloway* subjects a discourse of control, as explained by her fictional doctors Holmes and Bradshaw, to corrosive irony. In their different ways, Conrad, Forster and Woolf permit the reader a resistant anger at the sufferings of victims of these late Victorian systems of containment. There is a clear line from Stevie to Helen Schlegel to Woolf's Septimus Smith; the doctors who oppress them symbolically represent systems of thought now suddenly rendered antiquated by war. But by 1925 the degenerationist way of looking at things was fast losing claim to serious attention. *Mrs Dalloway* is the first to fully comprehend and objectify the myths of degeneration: it is the last, in that no subsequent sophisticated fictional account could or would take degeneration seriously. By *Point Counter Point* (1928), Aldous Huxley allows it, po-faced, to play as one out of a cocktail of ideologies. It now offers only the insignia of an intellectual conviction, a rhetorical position to be taken up no more seriously than any other.

A notable absentee from this study is Lawrence. In the context of degenerationism an important line has been crossed. The persistent grip of degeneration on late nineteenth-century culture derived ✗ essentially from the fear of what was repressed. It is the absence of that fear that marks Lawrence out as singular. This separates him from a major emphasis of degeneration – from the discourses of reversion and atavism, the 'up-cropping' of the 'bestial', the fear of the 'other' – which so preyed on the first and second generation of post-Darwinians. By embracing, in more or less idiosyncratic ways, the activity of the unconscious, the instinctual, the body, the primitive, Lawrence defused those particular sources of the 'other'. In these respects he is unlike Hardy and Conrad, both of whom had more invested in late nineteenth-century positivism and Darwinism. Lawrence had less to lose, and so, perhaps, there was more that he could find. Conrad read primitivism from 'within the stand-point of a moral civilization', facing, but recoiling from the 'destruction of the civilized self', as Michael Bell puts it. But for Lawrence these were starting-points, which were developed in his later work: the primitive was not to be feared, but welcomed as permitting the 'expanding and enriching of the ... emotional life'.[17]

Yet there were also, less importantly, but more intractably, his negotiations with the typologies of race (from Gobineau and Housten Chamberlain), with an attendant anti-semitism; his vision of 'dissolution', extinction and apocalypse, which, if eventually modernist property, had their origins in turn-of-the-century fears and phobias of decline and invasion.[18] On the other hand, there is his Spencerian commitment to creative evolution,[19] his radical invasion of the territory of social Darwinist 'force', where (with Forster and Woolf) he pin-pointed its ideological foundations in industrialism, imperialism and patriarchy; above all, his diagnosis of the failure of vitality in the English body, not buried in the genes but in the 'mechanical'.[20] Had Lawrence been writing a generation earlier, might not Clifford Chatterley have been a syphilitic, not a cripple, with Connie suffering the anxiety of hereditary taint, and Mellors her sympathetic 'nerve-doctor'? Lawrence's targets, twenty years later than Gissing and Hardy, were not so much biological as cultural and 'spiritual'.

Woolf's *Mrs Dalloway* can be read as penetrating so finely the primal error of degenerationism, in her treatment of the fate of Septimus Smith, as to prompt my hazarding that this novel is the 'first and last fiction of degeneration'. In comparison with Woolf, Lawrence's treatment of degeneration, centrally in *Women in Love*, belongs to a different imaginative dimension: the condition is absorbed into the larger prophetic theme of death and rebirth. The apocalyptic subsumes and transmutes the biological and hereditarian essence of degenerationism. But that *Women in Love* accommodates and develops 'degenerationist' typologies and plots is amply demonstrated by David Trotter in his recent study.[21]

It is through the prism of historically and discursively embedded evidence that a way can be found of not ducking judgements about the resonance and sophistication of less canonical texts. While I did not start from this position, I have been confirmed in the view that what a particular writer does with an available discourse can constitute a test, not only of the defining angle of vision, but of its 'truth'. I believe there is evidence enough to claim for the novelist, in this period, a role as critical, combative humanist – in the sense of having the insight to place certain values over others; of witnessing to the complex right of individuals to be themselves without having recourse to publically available labelling strategies with their simplistic appeal; of challenging the 'typologising' scientism of the sociologist or Darwinian propagandist.

In the fictions of Hardy, Conrad, Forster and Woolf, which, in various ways, take up the cudgels against the myths of degeneration, there is a commitment both to the complexities of human experience and to a concern with those sources of ideological power which shape the possibilities open to individuals: determinisms, not merely of biology, of course, but of money, class, status, education. By Kermode's test, certain popular genre writers examined in this study, such as Warwick Deeping and John Buchan, do not measure up since they are not principally committed to using fiction to 'find things out'. Theirs is another project: to reassert the conventional by the tried and trusted routes to readerly approval. While recent critics of genre fiction have been properly sceptical of reading off a whole set of beliefs or ideological programmes from such fictions,[22] the very transparency of such texts allows particularly direct access to a bedrock of ideology or of myth – whether of race, class or gender – active in a particular historical situation. We can hear in these fictions rhetorical strategies which, with narrative encouragement, re-present the tones and preoccupations of significant numbers of readers. No matter if this advances the argument out of literary into cultural criticism, there is significant evidence here of the larger distribution of the idea – which is one index of its meaning.

III

Within the time span of sixty years or more, it was virtually overnight that degeneration metamorphosed, after the full realisation of the meaning of the holocaust and what had led to it, in the 1940s. A repertoire of easy commonplaces had been transformed into a myth, horrifically sacrificed to by a mad positivism. With the knowledge of its consequences, what had been more or less easily lived with in an unvexed present now became the matter of history. The gestures of this acknowledgement came in various ways after 1945 as the myths which drove the holocaust were eventually seen for what they were – the logical extension of fear and anxiety, underpinned by a misappropriation of the laws of biological inheritance; a positivism masquerading as rationality, but offering, all the while, its antithesis.

In its ultimate manifestation as 'negative eugenics' degeneration, at any rate as a scientific category, was thoroughly discredited. The 1935 edition of the American *Encyclopaedia of the Social Sciences* entered the concept. It was gone from editions after 1945.[23] A current *Dictionary of Psychiatry* renders 'Degeneration theory' as 'obsolete'.[24] In 1963 the Professor of Eugenics at University College, London could tolerate his title no longer, and had his chair re-named the chair of 'human genetics'. Degeneration needed to become an object of critical enquiry and scholarly reconstruction. From the late 1940s studies began to surface which brought a much needed historical perspective to the concept, tracing its post-Darwinian origins.[25] By the mid-fifties an article 'What Became of the Degenerate: A Brief History of a Concept' suggested both its growing remoteness and an impetus to begin, again, at the beginning.[26]

Against a background of mounting interest in Darwin and Darwinism (which was helped by the attendant activity around the centennial of the publication of *The Origin of Species* in 1959) it was perhaps only a matter of time before degeneration was again subjected to scrutiny. But the major studies did not appear until the 1980s. It was tracked into French political culture by Robert A. Nye in *Crime, Madness and Politics in France; The Concept of National Decline* (1984) and German science and politics in Paul Weindling's *Health*,

Race and German Politics 1870–1945 (1989).[27] J. E. Chamberlain and Sander Gilman's collection *Degeneration: The Dark Side of Progress* (1985) was the first volume devoted to the topic. The essays reflected with a proper eclecticism the manifold presences of degeneration in sociology, biology, sexology, racial theory, theatre. Daniel Pick's *Faces of Degeneration* was the first monograph treatment to give the organisation the topic needed. Pick examined the French, Italian and British contexts, from the work of French psychiatric positivism in the 1850s to 1918. As an historian of ideas he has placed the protean quality of the idea in firm discursive contexts, and is alive to the permutations and metamorphoses of the concept with their representation in some fictions of degeneration, notably Zola's *Rougon-Macquart* series and *Dracula*.

This is certainly a timely focus, since the projections of fear and fantasy at the turn of the nineteenth century are once again addressed from within the current *fin de siècle* in *Fin de Siècle and its Legacy* (1991), edited by Mikulas Teich and Roy Porter, *Fin de Siècle/Fin du Globe* (1992), edited by John Stokes, Stokes's own *In The Nineties* (1989), Elaine Showalter's *Sexual Anarchy* (1991) and Judith Walkowitz's *City of Dreadful Delight* (1992).

In pursuing this subject a range of disciplines has been explored – social history, sociology, politics and demography, the history of science, medicine and sexuality, feminist scholarship and criticism and interdisciplinary work in science and literature – but inevitably that exploration has been selective. Among studies in these disciplines which have proved invaluable are: Gareth Stedman Jones, *Outcast London* (1971); H. J. Dyos and Michael Wolff (eds.), *The Victorian City* (1973); Anthony Wohl, *The Eternal Slum* (1977); Geoffrey Pearson, *The Deviant Imagination* (1975); Bernard Semmel, *Imperialism and Social Reform* (1960); G. R. Searle, *The Quest for National Efficiency* (1971); Michael Freeden, *The New Liberalism* (1978); Richard Soloway, *Demography and Degeneration* (1990); Greta Jones, *Social Darwinism and English Thought* (1980); Daniel Kevles, *In the Name of Eugenics* (1985); Pauline Mazumdar, *Eugenics, Human Genetics and Human Failings* (1992); Loren C. Eiseley, *Darwin's Century* (1959); Peter Bowler, *Evolution: a History of an Idea* (1984); Stephen Jay Gould, *Ontogeny and Phylogeny* (1977) and *The Mismeasure of Man* (1981); Nikolas Rose, *The Psychological Complex* (1985); Vieda Skultans, *Madness and Morals* (1977); W. F. Bynum, Roy Porter and

Michael Shepherd (eds.), *The Anatomy of Madness* (1985–8); Andrew Scull (ed.), *Madhouses, Mad-Doctors and Madmen* (1981) and his *The Most Solitary of Afflictions* (1993); Elaine Showalter, *The Female Malady* (1985); Janet Oppenheim, *'Shattered Nerves'* (1991); Sheila Rowbotham and Jeffrey Weeks, *Socialism and the New Life* (1977) (on Carpenter and Havelock Ellis); Jeffrey Weeks, *Sex, Politics and Society* (1981); Bernard Bergonzi, *The Early H. G. Wells* (1961); John A. Lester, *Journey through Despair 1800–1914* (1968); Patrick Parrinder, *H.G.Wells* (1972); Tom Gibbons, *Rooms in the Darwin Hotel* (1973); Cedric Watts, *A Preface to Conrad* (1977); John Goode, *George Gissing: Ideology and Fiction* (1978); Roger Ebbatson, *The Evolutionary Self* (1982); Peter Morton, *The Vital Science* (1984); Gillian Beer, *Darwin's Plots* (1985); R. B. Yeazell (ed.) *Sex, Politics and Science in the Ninteenth Century Novel* (1986); J. A. V. Chapple, *Science and Literature in the Nineteenth Century* (1986); Jenny Bourne Taylor, *In The Secret Theatre of Home* (1988).

Of works which first prompted my interest in this topic, two in particular stand out: Samuel Hynes's *The Edwardian Turn of Mind* ҃ (1968) and Raymond Williams's *The Country and the City* (1973). Hynes's title is symptomatic of what now dates it – its original attempt at synthesis is no longer so easy to sustain, since it is the proliferation of discontinuous 'Edwardian' voices with discrete and complex discursive trajectories which interest us and which challenge the periodisation 'Edwardian', even as we read their testimony more attentively through the laundry lists of 'new historicism'. Yet Hynes offered both insights and empirical evidence (he was the first to enlist the statistics of turn-of-the-century unfitness) by which an investigation of the working of 'efficiency' and its 'other', 'degeneracy', might be taken forward.

The influence of what is, I think, Raymond Williams's most significant work was and is considerable. Without recourse to Foucauldian terminology, Williams showed how both 'country' and 'city' were discursively organised through representation, over centuries, by a cultivation of a required myth of a golden age, which in persistent literary representations, and their appropriation by a developing literate culture, simplified and dissolved the truth of 'history' into the terms of a (still seductive) 'myth' – with its rhetorical strategies and figures. This was the evidence for that post-structuralist enterprise, a genetic history – Foucault's 'archaeology'.

For an ideologically committed critic Williams's notable open-mindedness and hospitality are prized qualities – no less needed today. No one currently writing about literature, culture and society can fail, in some measure, to be in his debt.

CHAPTER I

De-generation

I

The growth of degeneration into fully fledged explanatory myth, with widespread applications, in the latter half of the nineteenth century, is bound up with the huge economic, social and cultural changes which took place in the major industrialised European states – Britain, France, Germany and Italy. These changes, above all in the urban environment, were new in kind to large sections of the European population, and they were momentous. Rapidly expanding populations in larger cities where extremes of wealth and poverty were concentrated as never before, gave rise to new forms of social organisation and new patterns of mobility and access. The scale and speed of these developments were unprecedented, their psychological and behavioural consequences profound. Religious belief, moral codes, attitudes to class, to sexual roles, to sexuality itself underwent seismic disturbance and shock, as well as subsidence and erosion. And the world emerging from the ruins of the old was baffling as well as new. There was a paradox to be explained, and it was, in simple terms, the growing sense in the last decades of the century of a lack of synchrony between the rhetoric of progress, the confident prediction by the apostles of *laissez-faire* of ever increasing prosperity and wealth, and the facts on the ground, the evidence in front of people's eyes, of poverty and degradation at the heart of ever richer empires.

The belief in the existence of degeneration, or even a suspicion that it existed, fostered a sense that what might really be happening to civilisation lay somehow hidden, buried from sight, yet graspable through patient observation of the contours of the surface. There was a negative energy which was both all pervasive and never fully explicable. Bafflement and disillusionment found release in a theory which seemed to identify the sources of rot.

The discourses of degeneration provided such a structure of explanation inscribed within the ambiguity and instability of the term itself, within its twin interlocking semantic properties. 'Degeneration' represented the boundless capacity of a society to 'generate' regression: on the one hand, generation and reproduction, on the other, decline, degradation, waste. The remarkable grip which the idea secured suggests a sense of a permanent secularised 'fall' from grace, a structure for feelings of extreme disappointment with the state of things for which the traditional religious sanctities offered little help. Instead degeneration installed an alternative myth which spoke to this 'dark side of progress'.[1] Founded on the Darwinian revolution in biology, and harnessed to psychological medicine, the idea of degeneration spread to social science, to literature and art. In its scientific and rational practices it offered to diagnose the agencies of the irrational component threatening the orderly progress of the society. The practitioners of medicine and science found in forms of determinism powerful diagnoses of the enormity of the problems which they suddenly confronted.

The crucial intellectual component of ideas of inherited and transmitted pathology can be traced back to the influential mid-nineteenth-century school of French psychiatry. For Bénédict Augustin Morel (1809–73) degeneration was a morbid deviation from a perfect primitive type – a deviation subject to a law of 'progressivity' which compounded deviation through the generations: 'Les dégénérations sont les déviations maladives du type normal de l'humanité héréditairement transmissables et évoluant progressivement vers la déchéance.'[2]

Morel believed that the environmental horrors to which Europeans were exposed were both the symptoms and the causes of a civilisation infected by degeneration which, as a disease, produced three categories of symptoms: physical deformity, perversion of the organism and disturbance of the emotional faculties. What was novel was his belief that civilisation could progress or decline over time through hereditary transmission: it is this teleological component that pathologists fastened on to, to produce superficially plausible accounts which might explain the perpetuation of disease or neurosis, and also thereby provide a diagnosis of the lamentable state of human affairs. Morel conceded that forms of social health might check pathology, but nevertheless he foresaw progressive decline working through the generations. As one commentator has put it, 'the first generation of

a degenerate family might be merely nervous, the second would tend
to be neurotic, the third psychotic, whilst the fourth consisted of
idiots and died out'.[3] Since nineteenth-century society appeared to
manifest these degenerate symptoms in ever increasing profusion,
civilisation itself could be on the verge of extinction.[4] Urban living,
its diseases and pathologies, were leaving metropolitan men and
women vulnerable to fatigue and debility from prolonged exposure
to the pressures of the very environment which had formed them.

Built into Morel's model was the idea, associated with the biologist Jean Baptiste Lamarck (1744–1829), of use-inheritance:
changes in heredity took place because of the 'effort of the organism
to adapt to the changed conditions in its environment'.[5] For social
theorists and Darwinian popularisers like Herbert Spencer, the
Lamarckian idea that the characteristics of an organism could be
acquired from the environment and then passed on had considerable appeal: if social behaviour obeyed the laws of natural selection,
'useful' social characteristics would survive as would 'useful' physiological characteristics.[6] In the event, Lamarckianism had itself to
adapt in order to accommodate the gloomier apocalyptic visions of
the *fin de siècle*.

Heredity offered, it seemed, a sufficiently all embracing explanation
for all that mattered and all that could not be resisted. It was precisely
attuned to uncover what was hidden and unavailable to reason, what
was deaf to the efforts of social control or told against official, and
predominantly middle-class standards in morality, and taste in art
and literature. If all that was irrational, injurious and disturbing was
encoded in the determinism of heredity, it meant that the irrational
was preserved as mystery, whose secrets only the high-priests of science
could understand. In fact, the human subjects who became the objects
of scientific surveillance had projected on to them the loss of control
and sources of fear and unreason which they aroused: they became the
'other' of a social order which had apparently much to gain from
re-asserting control, order, clarity and reason.

In a passage from *Entartung* (1892), translated into English as
Degeneration (1895), the journalist Max Nordau identifies something
of an early psychopathology of everyday life, of how living in a
modern city was like living on the edge of nervous collapse:

If he do but read his paper ... he takes part, certainly not by active inter-
ference and influence, but by a continuous and receptive curiosity in the

thousand events which take place in all parts of the globe ... all these activities ... involve an effort of the nervous system and a wearing of tissue. Every line we read or write, every human face we see, every conversation we carry on, every scene we perceive through the window of the flying express, sets in activity our sensory nerves and our brain centres ... the perpetual noises and the various sights in the streets of a large town, our suspense pending the sequel of progressing events, the constant expectation of the newspapers, of the postman, of visitors, cost our brains wear and tear.[7]

In terms appropriate for the *fin de siècle* Nordau knits 'close ties between biological behaviour ... social conduct, technology and psychology', as John Stokes puts it.[8] Here in the late nineteenth-century city was a territory of immanent breakdown, where the contours of that territory and the map which described it were conflated. Symptoms of the city 'condition', such as neurasthenia and hysteria, have been inherited, and so have become determinants of the 'condition' from which they have been bred. Both symptoms are observable states of disorder and generalised symptoms of the prevailing urban condition.

The reasoning is circular: the diagnostician of degeneration is vigilant in alerting the reader to the threatening proximity of the city condition, which may, at any time, manifest itself in the unsuspecting city-dweller. Social groups and deviant types are tactically dispatched to a 'safe' zone of abnormality; this renders them innocuous and deprived of the power to challenge the dominant order. The referents are manifold: men of genius, anarchists, lunatics, hooligans, prostitutes are all dealt with by this expedient of attributing to them symptoms of a pathology, congenital criminality, hysteria or neurasthenia. Any cultural or political challenge from such marked-out groups was neutralised by the charge of degeneracy. Degeneration established the necessary boundaries in a period in which 'the longing for strict border controls around the definition of gender, as well as race, class and nationality, becomes especially intense'.[9] Fear and anxiety extended to sexuality, particularly fear of female sexuality by men. This took extreme forms as in Otto Weiniger's polemics, or the misogyny of Schopenhauer and the paranoia of Strindberg. Images from art and literature at the *fin de siècle*, gathered in Bram Dijkstra's *Idols of Perversity* (1986), show how fear of loss of control led to distorted projections of attraction and threat in the destructive figure of the vampire or parasite. Images of reversion to lower states of animality signified the uncontrollable mystery of female desire.[10]

These signs are on display in Arthur Conan Doyle's 1894 story *The Parasite* which tells of the tenacious hold exerted by Miss Penelosa, a crippled mesmerist, over Gilroy, a young Professor of Physiology, who relates in a diary narrative the woman's power for evil, her invasion of his being and her domination of his will. This 'gentleman' and 'man of honour', engaged to 'one of the sweetest girls in England', is overtaken by 'reasonless' erotic desire: 'had I stayed another minute in her presence I should have committed myself'. Gripped by sexual longing for which he finds a vocabulary of atavism, he casts himself as the brute primitive: 'was it the sudden upcropping of some lower stratum in my nature – a brutal primitive instinct suddenly asserting itself?' And he reaches for a biological image of degeneracy in his effort to expunge her through discourse: she is 'a monstrous parasite' who can 'project herself into my body and take command of it'. She both attracts and repels: 'I loathe her and fear her, yet while I am under her spell she can doubtless make me love her.'[11] His hatred of her, as a monster, represents his transference of his own internalised guilt and self-hatred: he rids himself of it by constructing her as an evil 'other'. In the same year George Gissing found a devolutionary figure for the alarming, but no doubt erotic spectacle of brawling lower-middle class women in *In The Year of Jubilee* (1894): 'now indeed the last trace of veneer was gone, the last rag of pseudo-civilisation was rent off these young women; in physical conflict, vilifying each other like the female spawn of Whitechapel, they revealed themselves as born – raw material which the mill of education is supposed to convert into middle-class ladyhood'.[12] 'Female spawn' succinctly conflates the biological and the class origins to which Gissing cannot resist delivering them. Natural-istically, he grounds their unrespecting lower-middle class chal-lenge in the biological terms of atavism which inscribes their otherness. Such tactics of reversion, and their manifold uses, are examined in chapter four.

The evolutionary naturalism of Spencer and the pathological model of Morel were lent support by the French psychiatrist, Théo-dule Ribot, who showed how individual aptitudes 'reflected the environmental experience of the entire race and species ... passed onto later generations in the genotype'.[13] Take the case of the apparently large increase in mental pathologies. For Ribot, as Robert A. Nye puts it, 'the lower passions and instincts had a prior adaptive role in human evolution than the qualities of reasoning and self-control and so were more firmly rooted in contemporary mental structure'. Mental disease could be explained as the failure of the controlling 'higher' over the 'lower' levels of the nervous system, but its prevalence could be understood as an 'adaptive pathology' which became fixed in the organism as an inheritable trait. The weakened capacity for resistance made the individual progressively vulnerable to disease or a degraded environment whose moral effects expressed themselves as a pathology of the will, an inability to resist the lure and temptations of easy sensualism or crime.[14] So that a pathology like insanity, according to Charles Mercier as late as 1910, is an expression of evolutionary regression: 'it is a traversing of the path of development in the reverse direction. It is a peeling off of those superimposed layers of development which have been laboriously deposited by the process of evolution.'[15]

II RACES APART

In his book *Crime, Madness and Politics in Modern France* Nye has identified a process of 'medical bi-polarity of the normal and the pathological' which enabled scientists and doctors from the 1870s onwards to appeal from science to 'life' through the powerful persuasion of this polarity as common-sense and common experience. Few areas of living seemed untouched by it since this normal-pathological duality was 'conceptually isomorphic' with 'so many other binary terms that regulate the perception of social life: moral-immoral, criminal-honest, sane-insane, violent-passive'. Medicine gained its 'social power' because 'experts shaped a medical discourse that spoke to all those problems in comprehensible language, which appeared to many contemporaries to be an accurate portrayal of the world'.[16]

Degeneration, in its medico-psychological emphasis, offered explanatory, totalising myths which were hostile to the (ironic) claims of the decadent writer. By such diagnoses, 'any cultural manifestation of "exception" comes to be seen as a crisis or a symptom of disease',[17] and this included the exponents of decadence and decadent art, such as Wilde and Beardsley. The terms 'decadent' and 'degenerate' were intentionally elided since the self-destructive way of life cultivated by figures like Ernest Dowson could be 'written up to make them fit the myth [of decadence] even more exactly'.[18] The 'decadent' artist was stigmatised as unhealthy 'other', the carrier of a prevailing cultural sickness.

Decadent art was ironic, playful and subversive of late Victorian systems such as positivism: it was the temporary and evanescent rather than the immanent that mattered. Oscar Wilde took on 'morbidity' – a key term for the degenerationists – and re-presented it as no more than fashionable talk, the higher gossip. But degenerationism faced squarely in a different direction, and after the Wilde trial in 1895, with his conviction on 25 May, both events and opinion seemed to point the same way.

Bio-social models assume that the rules governing the structure of organisms hold good for social groups, societies and civilisations. These assumptions were very widespread and had been used in the work of Auguste Comte (1798–1857), the founder of positivism, and by Spencer, Mill and others.[19] It was not until the inter-war period that there was a significant shift from biological to cultural interpretations of social ills (when hereditary determinism is replaced by population studies, degeneracy by demography).

The place of racial biology and the uses of the terminology of 'race' in underpinning the bio-social assumptions of the normal-pathological are critical. By the mid-nineteeth century racial biology had mapped out a 'science of boundaries between groups and the degenerations that threatened them when those boundaries were trangressed'.[20] In the eighteenth century all human races tended to be seen as belonging to a common species, but subject to environmental influence which produced different varieties. In Buffon's *Histoire Naturelle* (from 1749) the degeneration of races was a recognition of change between species: 'each family, as well in animals as in vegetables, comes from the same origin ... all animals are come from one species, which, in the succession of time, by improving and degenerating, has produced all the races of animals which now exist'.[21]

A century later things had changed. Races were no longer seen as available to environmental influence and were placed, more pessimistically, within a hierarchical typology of evolutionary development. In contrast to industrious 'historic races' of northern

Europe,[22] certain races were cast as degenerate types. The biologist
Cuvier identified the negro race as 'the most degraded human race
whose form approaches that of the beast'.[23] Within the ideology of
the progress, it was imperative to establish a hierarchy of racial
difference. 'The savage races are without a past', said F. W. Farrar
in 1861.[24] 'The highest places in the hierarchy of civilisation will
assuredly not be within the reach of our dusky cousins', was the view
of T. H. Huxley in 1865.[25] For the major race theorist of the
nineteenth century, Comte de Gobineau (1816–82), such was the
necessity of keeping the races apart, that miscegenation and race-
mingling would inevitably lead to degeneration and the extinction
of civilisation.[26]

For many race theorists, including Robert Knox and Charles
Kingsley in Britain, the degenerate races were best off dead.[27] Such
racial ideas offered serviceable metaphors for the 'otherness' of the
threatening classes: 'a race of whom we know nothing, whose lives
are of a quite different complexion from ours', wrote the *Saturday
Review* of the Bethnal Green poor in 1864.[28] These metaphors helped
to organise the zones of respectability and of foreign 'otherness'
within the metropolis itself. As the threat of new class formations
became more powerful in the last decades of the century, so the
boundaries were drawn ever tighter. As Nancy Stepan puts it: 'the
urban poor, prostitutes, criminals and the insane were being constructed as "degenerate types" whose deformed skulls, protruding
jaws, and low brain weights marked them as "races apart", inter-
acting with and creating degenerate spaces near at home'.[29] Where
there was movement across boundaries, where there was mingling
on them, differences of speech, manners, dress and cleanliness could
not be mistaken, as 'race' met 'race'. Fear and resentment were
inseparable from these encounters. Proximity also brought the risk
of pollution. The biologising of class differences was encouraged by
the fear of contagion and infection.

It was exceptional for the underlying political and economic
causes to be publicly acknowledged. The American writer Jack
London went down into the 'abyss' – the slums east of the Bank of
England – and living as one of the slum-dwellers, honestly
attempted to report what he found in his *People of the Abyss* (1903),
including the 'cash-nexus' at the root of it. 'Every worn-out, pasty-
faced pauper', he wrote, 'is hungry because the funds have been
misappropriated by the management.' But we also find him, in the

same work, distancing himself (now dressed like a gentleman) from his experience of the abyss, describing the East End crowd as a 'breed of city savages ... the slum is their jungle'.[30] In Britain, as numbers of the casual poor rose dramatically from the late 1870s, a theory of urban degeneration was invoked to explain the inherited recalcitrance of the 'residuum', yet at the time of the first world war, the casual poor, according to Gareth Stedman Jones, were shown to have been 'a social and not a biological creation'. With regular employment available, "the unemployables" proved impossible to find. In fact they had never existed, except as a phantom army called up by late Victorian and Edwardian social science to legitimize its practice.'[31]

All sorts and conditions of human manifestation or social organisation were susceptible to socio-biological construction. The biologising of the city, with its pressure of people, its ever more visible crowds, was expressed in J. J. Izoulet's *La Cité moderne* (1894) (a work which interested Gissing at the end of the century). Izoulet proposed that the city was the third of three 'étages de l'animalité', – 'cellules, animaux, cités': the city is 'un agrégat d'animaux'. Activated by the fear of eviction of the élite classes by the crowd, Izoulet naturalises, typically for the period, the class-fear into a biological fact.[32]

Indeed, early crowd psychology was heavily indebted to this organicist socio-biology, loaded with popular Darwinian rhetoric and figures. In the work of Gustave Le Bon, Gabriel Tarde and Scipio Sighele, the crowd was assimilated to figures of the bestial, regressive and atavistic. Le Bon's *La Psychologie des foules* (1895) went through twelve printings by 1920, influencing literary figures of the political right, such as Wyndham Lewis and Dean Inge.[33] The crowd was seen as regressive in evolutionary terms since, as Daniel Pick says, 'instead of individual development, it tended towards homogeneity'. For crowd theorists, social revolution was a regression to barbarism; socialism was tarred with the same brush.[34]

A further boundary between the normal and the abnormal was the medicalisation of sexuality. There is evidence to show that the category of homosexuality became effective as a boundary at the end of the century. Medical investigation detailed certain sexual practices as deviations from a prescribed model of normal behaviour. Along with Féré and Moll, Krafft-Ebing was the most influential writer on the subject. *Psychopathia Sexualis* (1886) was translated into

English in the 1890s, and identified in homosexuality 'a hereditary
neuropathic or psychopathic tendency'.[35] From the nineties, homosexuality travelled through discourse in a coercive code. 'Criminal
degenerate', which netted artists like Verlaine in the nineties, was
perhaps the most perfected term of degenerationist abuse, encoding
sexual perversion, promiscuity and the 'unspeakable'. In the late-
thirties Cyril Connolly could still, albeit ironically, label Wilde as a
'criminal degenerate', one of the 'few bad boys' in English poetry
'we do not speak about'.[36]

The threat posed by the condition of mental instability, and by
the growing numbers of mental defectives, was dealt with by turning
away from mid-century practices of 'moral management' to a deterministic model of insanity – deployed by the medical profession in
the expanding County Asylums (the numbers in 1900 were thirteen
times those at their mandatory establishment in 1845). New objects
of the emerging technologies of measurement, specialisation and
segregation were invented.[37] The range of pathologies now
expanded to cover conditions, not previously thought serious
enough for incarceration, such as the category of the 'feeble-minded'
which came into view from the last two decades of the century.

In 1918 Rose, a rape victim from the West Midlands, gave birth
to an illegitimate child. Under legislation eventually passed in 1913,
she was diagnosed as 'hereditarily feeble-minded' (she was herself
illegitimate), and sent to a mental institution which successfully
contained her perceived eugenic threat until the late 1950s – when
the legislation was repealed. Rose was by then over sixty.[38]

Concern for the incidence of particular pathologies within families, and their reproductive consequences, can be seen in an extreme
form in the frequency with which the deviant Jukes family appears
in writing on degeneration over a period of at least thirty years. This
drama of familial perversion, written up in a study of 1877, offered
an epic of degeneracy which only a Zola could emulate.[39] Jukes, a
colonial frontiersman, had married into a defective family, which
had resulted in 709 descendants, 181 of them prostitutes, 106 of
illegitimate birth, with 142 beggars and 70 convicted of criminal
offences.[40] The case of this extraordinary family was taken up as a
cause célèbre by hereditarians, particularly from the nineties, prompting wide-ranging calls for 'racial hygiene' by Havelock Ellis and
others.[41] Both the case of the Jukes and that of another 'degenerate'
family, the New Jersey Kallikaks, were widely cited in Weimar
Germany, where racial hygienists expressed keen interest in the

sterilisation policies which twenty-eight American states had implemented at the end of the 1920s (some 30,000 'defectives' had been sterilised on eugenic grounds by 1930).[42] Such repeated allusion and invocation is likely to have helped fix and sustain the idea of the disastrous racial consequences of degenerate fecundity.

Degeneration extended its remit into the heart of the urban nightmare in its concern with a pathology of crime and criminality. The effort to identify and fix a born criminal 'type' with its physiognomatic idiosyncracies, and then remove that type from society, evolved into the considerable, if not uncontroversial enterprise of 'criminal anthropology', primarily associated with the Italian positivist Cesare Lombroso, whose influence is discussed in chapter five.

Doctors and alienists like Daniel Hack Tuke (1827–95) and Henry Maudsley (1835–1918), who were wedded to an organic conception of the relation between body and mind, believed that from the 'outward defects and deformities' they could read those 'inward and invisible faults which will have their influence in breeding'.[43] They pursued their investigations with an appetite for empirical observation which stemmed from their belief in positivistic science: here was a 'faith', opposed to idealism speculation and metaphysics. The nature of human evil they explained as organic anomaly, a deviation from the evolutionary norm, which, under pressure of adaptation to new conditions, revealed an unbalanced organisation.

An example of this redrawing of the map of ideas of good and evil is offered by the libretto of one of the great operas of the 1880s, Verdi's *Otello*, where, at one decisive point of character presentation, the presiding influence is more that of a Morel or a Moreau de Tours than the metaphysic of Shakespeare. Arrigo Boito, the librettist, makes his nihilist Iago proclaim: 'Dalla vilta d'un germe o d'un atomo / Vile son nato' ('From baseness in the seed, or from some vile atom I was born').[44] In 1887, in the Italy of Lombroso, the use of the terms 'germe' and 'atomo' bore witness, as we shall see, to a deeply symptomatic act of translation.

III 'FACING THE WORLD AS IT IS'? THE WRIT OF POSITIVISM

Contemporary critics of the materialism and godlessness of nineteenth-century science were well aware of the formidable scope and influence of the instititution they were attacking. When the

conservative essayist and novelist W. H. Mallock began a critique of
scientific atheism, he made it clear that in applying to it the term
positivism, he was not referring to the system of Comte and his
disciples, but to 'the common views and position of the whole
scientific school' with reference, above all, to Tyndall, Huxley and
Leslie Stephen.[45]

But for the positivist scientist, the scientific method was almost an
article of faith. Francis Galton (1822–1911) announced with awe his
statistical procedures as a providential path to enlightenment: 'I
know of scarcely anything so apt to impress the imagination as the
wonderful form of cosmic order expressed by the "law of Frequency
of Error" ... it reigns with serenity and in complete self-effacement
amidst the wildest confusion. The huger the mob, and the greater
the apparent anarchy, the more perfect is its sway.'[46] The conscious
development and improvement of man by the application of
rational principles was for Galton, and for the race-improvers who
looked to him as a father-figure, in virtually every respect a form of
secularised religion, a 'religion of humanity'. 'Man has already
furthered his evolution very considerably, half consciously and for
his own personal advantage', he said in *Inquiries into the Human
Faculty* in 1883, 'but he has not yet risen to the conviction that it is
his religious duty to do so deliberately and systematically.'[47] It
would take a further twenty years for the wide and public recognition of such a duty to be realised in the science of 'eugenics', first
enunciated in *Inquiries*.

The idealism of positivistic thinkers can be seen in a scientific
populariser like Havelock Ellis (1859–1937): 'we know that
wherever science goes', he said, 'the purifying breath of spring has
passed and all things are re-created'. Associating himself with
Huxley, science, for Ellis, is a source of truth and demystification;
mankind's suffering can only be relieved by using science to face the
world as it is and to strip off 'the garment of make-believe by which
pious hands have hidden its uglier features'.[48]

Such confidence was seen in the traffic of exchange with the lay or
non-scientific public. The late 1880s and nineties, in Britain, saw
new scientific series aimed at the intelligent reader. Titles of *The
Contemporary Science Series* which Havelock Ellis edited for the
publisher Walter Scott (Geddes and Thomson's *The Evolution of
Sex*, Ellis's own *The Criminal*, J. M. Guyau's *Education and Heredity*)
reflect the intermarriage between what Ellis called the 'great and

growing sciences of today ... the sciences of man – anthropology, sociology ... political economy'[49] Another title, *The Science of Fairy Tales*, could hardly have been commissioned by anyone else! Evolutionary ideas were popularised by writers such as Huxley, Galton, Stephen, Ellis, Edward Clodd and H. G. Wells. Journals, such as *Fortnightly Review*, *The Nineteenth Century* and *The Contemporary Review* were widely read by men (and women) of letters, novelists, politicians – a powerful late Victorian intelligentsia. Figures such as Ellis who wrote literary essays, produced editions of Jacobean playwrights, and wrote on criminology, anthropology and – famously – sexual behaviour, or Grant Allen, novelist, writer on anthropology, sociology and folk lore, occupied a key position in the circulation of a scientific culture.[50] Even a minor figure like the Fabian Hubert Bland, played a significant part as a scientific populariser. As 'Hubert' of *The Sunday Chronicle* Bland produced regular essays on popular sociology – 'Brains 1904', 'The Duel of Sex' – and in 'Concerning Heredity' he sets up a debate about the merits of the theory of the inheritance of acquired characteristics, and makes complex arguments come alive through lively dispute.[51]

Late nineteenth-century positivism did not flinch from the role of moral teacher. In the writings of the major scientific proponents of degeneration, concepts and tropes, which affirm traditional classifications of experience into normal and abnormal, right and wrong, are never far from the surface; in fact, more authoritative thinkers like Galton and Maudsley reappropriate traditional pieties for evolutionary science. Maudsley, in particular, was obsessed by the idea of nemesis following the violation of 'natural law'; such 'disobedience ... whether physical or moral, is avenged inexorably in its consequences on earth, either upon the individual himself, or more often, perhaps, upon others'.[52] 'A man struggling against his nature', he wrote in 1895, 'is like the ancient Grecian fighting fruitlessly against the fate foredoomed to him by the oracle; he goes painfully about to fulfill his destiny unwittingly by the very means which he employs to evade it.'[53]

Such gifted publicists sought support for their medico-scientific position from the traditional sanction of divine retribution, but at the same time made themselves into public moralists on the basis of their science.[54] Scientific writing of this period, in fact, claimed authority from commonsense orders of truth, and blatantly smuggled in unquestioned, apparently self-evident, and so ideological, discourses of morality, politics, class and gender. Consider Galton's aims for the science of eugenics. Its purpose, he believed, was to develop qualities 'that everyone except "cranks" would take into account when picking out specimens of his class'. The qualities he took as unproblematic were 'health, energy, manliness and courteous disposition.'[55]

This new generation of scientists and medical men stood aloof from the church – and from some aspects of traditional academic life. They were also no particular respecters of class hierarchy with its unequal distribution of wealth and influence. They were keen to establish their own power base in society as the source of influence on the community – which would later be felt in numerous official reports investigating the health of the nation. The principle of primogeniture, for example, was inevitably regarded with scepticism since it was at odds with the claims of natural ability.[56] Eugenicists championed merit and ability, and so had a vested interest in promoting the interests of a professional middle class against the existing hereditary élites.

For more radical eugenicists the possession of wealth 'operated in a dysgenic way by encouraging idleness and selfish luxury', inimicable to the promotion of 'a healthy racial instinct'.[57] The 'large class of more or less wealthy persons who flee to the sunnier coasts of England, or expatriate themselves for the chance of life', presented a sad dysgenic spectacle for Galton: 'a crowd of delicate English men and women with narrow chests and weak chins'.[58] An influential turn-of-the-century publicist like Arnold White was typical of those who had no time for the products of public schools, while Max Nordau criticised the upper classes and leant his support to the ' "healthy" parts of the population of all classes'.[59]

The forces which coalesced in the early 1900s to promote eugenic proposals on social policy, were propelled by a commitment to the ethic of professional expertise which would cut a swathe through the bulky weight of privilege and inherited power. With a turn of the eugenic key they would open up a brighter future for the nation state – but with the professional, scientific and medical elite very much in control. The desire for professional recognition and influence helps to explain why eugenicists came from the left of British politics as well as from the right. Within the left there was a continuity between the rhetoric of Fabian eugenicists like Shaw and that of libertarian socialists like Edward Carpenter, who spoke dismissively of 'these great clotted and congested centres which call themselves "society", but through which the true life-blood of society does *not* circulate.'[60] Few men of science would have disagreed with the parallel Henry James drew in 1886 between the upper classes and the 'heavy, congested and depraved Roman world upon which the barbarians came down'.[61]

Turning that key, Galton pressed inheritance into the service of mankind's attributes and potentialities in a discursive practice around the concept of 'fitness'. His quest was, in his words, 'to see what the theory of heredity, of variations and the principle of natural selection mean when applied to man'.[62] Chance variations were subject to the law of regression to the average and the law of ancestral contribution to heritage; the child of any deviation from the norm tended to regress towards an average, but it was also the product of its ancestral history.

Individual and familial variation took on a more political significance in the last decades of the nineteenth century, when Galton made the cultivation of stock an index of *population*. These statistical laws produced a practice which could easily convert a concern for quality of a variation into one for quantity. The overall quality of a stock was measured by how differentiated qualities of variation were numerically dispersed through the population and between constituent populations.

The coupling of quantity and quality was the driving force behind the crucial topic of the differential birth-rate – which emerged into social, medical and political discourse at the turn of the century. At its simplest, the less eugenically desirable varieties were out-breeding 'those whose race we especially want to have', as Galton himself put it.[63] And the most vexatious and contested term of the post-Darwinian era, 'fitness', cemented the bond between quantitative and qualitative value, endowing it and 'degeneration' with their suggestive and seductive doubleness.

IV 'THE AGE'

If 'fit/unfit', 'fitness/unfitness', were ambiguous question-begging words – prompting, inevitably, the question 'fit for what?' – the intimately related word-families of degeneration and decadence are similarly alive. 'Degeneration' entails the existence of a norm from which degeneration has occurred. It is an aspect of the subject of this book that the interaction, at a particular phase in European history, of the culture of the city, psychological medicine and Darwinian natural selection authorised a specialisation of the discourse of degeneration not known before. Yet the term and its family never lost their associations of older ideas of decline and fall. When Thomas Carlyle was reported in 1847 to have been 'in great force of lamentation over the degeneracy of our age',[64] he was responding in a time-honoured way to an impulse of blame and praise about the present and the past.

The spirit of Horace's *laudator temporis acti* has been a perennial feature of European civilisation.[65] In the late Renaissance it became a commonplace that the world was getting old and was running out of time – 'this world's spent', in John Donne's words.[66] But for a generation from the late 1880s there was a marked intensification of the sense of the decline of the age – associated with the decline of empires and the disease at their 'heart'. A growth of national and racial self-consciousness accompanied the sense of threat to Britain's industrial and imperial pre-eminence from the United States and Germany. 'On all hands England's industrial supremacy is tottering to its fall, and this result is largely German work', announced an excited journalist for the *New Review* in 1896.[67]

Parallels with the fate of past empires, especially the Roman Empire, never failed to provide lessons for the present.[68] In April 1895, when Wilde was committed for trial, a journalist attacking the 'shocking depravity of the English idle classes' reminded his readers that 'history teaches us that moral corruption has always been the forerunner of the downfall of nations. It was so in Greece, Rome ... '[69] W. R. Inge (later Dean of St Pauls) warned in 1909 that 'the urban proletariat may cripple our civilization as it destroyed that of ancient Rome',[70] and in 1913 H. B. Gray noticed the 'ominous resemblances' in the 'luminous pages of Gibbon': the 'same decay of agriculture ... predominance of town over country life ... deterioration of physique and general health ... growth of luxury and desire for bodily comfort ... distaste for the burdens of married life ... excessive taxation ... decadence in public morals ... demand for unearned bread ... '[71]

These parallels have persisted well into the twentieth century. When the Conservative politician Sir Keith Joseph spoke in October 1974 of 'a watershed in our national existence', in a context, again, of perceived national decline, he had in mind the 'dependency culture' of the welfare state, and foresaw, with an identical trope, the grim consequences of Britain failing to remoralise itself:

The populist leaders of Rome thought they had hit on a fool-proof method of achieving a permanent curb on their patrician rivals, when they created a dependent proletariat relying on them for bread and circuses; but in the end it destroyed the political stability of Rome, and so Rome itself fell, destroyed from inside.

To create dependence among the poor, he said, 'is to destroy them morally while throwing an unfair burden on society'.[72] The rhetorical position of this notorious attack on welfare (and permissiveness) is not essentially different from that mounted against 'decadence' at the turn of the nineteenth century. When a speaker climbs on to the rostrum to call attention to the 'decadence' of the age, he invariably does so in the interests of some mutation of degeneration theory.

CHAPTER 2

Biological poetics

I

In 1880 the zoologist Edwin Ray Lankester (1847–1929) published *Degeneration: A Chapter in Darwinism.*[1] His work on lower vertebrates had convinced him that analysis of the operation of natural selection had been hampered by mistakes in classification. Certain species belonged with higher species in the evolutionary hierarchy and should be reclassified as atrophied or degenerate members of that grouping. The ship's barnacle, the nauplius, for example, hitherto classified with snails and oysters, should more properly be classified as a degenerate crustacean, along with shrimps and crabs: but it was a degenerate variety since its organs of touch and sight had atrophied. Here was one example of the process which Lankester called degeneration: 'a gradual change of structure in which the organism becomes adapted to *less* varied and *less* complex conditions of life'.[2] He contrasted this with 'elaboration' which, conversely, constituted 'a gradual change of structure in which the organism becomes adapted to more and more varied and complex conditions of existence'.[3]

Lankester points to general conditions under which degeneration might occur. An organism seeks out 'less varied and less complex conditions of life' where 'its food and safety (are) very easily obtained'.[4] But conditions of safety and security are hardly conducive to further evolutionary development; rather they usher in the reverse. An organism which fails to take up the challenge of the struggle for existence (as the Eloi failed in H. G. Wells's *The Time Machine* (1895)), will decline into simplicity, parasitism, immobility, reduction in size and the capacity only to consume vegetable matter (the Eloi are indeed vegetarians).

Like other Darwinian scientists of his time (though Darwin

32

himself was *sui generis*), Lankester did not hesitate to suggest an analogy with the human species. The features he observed in the nauplius in its backward evolutionary track also 'disfigure our modern civilisation'. 'Possibly we are all drifting', he said, 'tending to the condition of intellectual Barnacles or Ascidians.'[5] Also in the 1890s the young H. G. Wells saw the imaginative, and the controversial, potential of 'degeneration as a plastic process in nature' in his early essay 'Zoological Retrogression' (1891).[6] Wells welcomed this complication in the assumed teleology of human progress. In a passage suggestive of the imaginative scope of his science fiction he claims that man descends from the mudfish Dipnoi which from the rigours of the open sea has adapted to the more hospitable environment of river mud: 'they preferred dirt, discomfort, and survival to a gallant fight and death'. By a deft reversal, the suppressed becomes the suppressor: 'he it is who goes down to the sea in ships, and, with wide sweeping nets and hooks cunningly baited, beguiles the children of those who drove his ancestors out of the water'.[7]

The ironic curve of the argument, knowingly confident, conjures up a biological apocalypse; the tone of studious understatement offsets the naïvety of the speculation:

there ... is no guarantee in scientific knowledge of man's ... permanent ascendancy ... the presumption is that before him lies a long future of profound modification ... it may be that, instead of this, Nature is ... equipping some now humble creature ... to rise in the fulness of time and sweep *homo* away into the darkness from which his universe arose. The Coming Beast must certainly be reckoned in any anticipatory calculations regarding the Coming Man.[8]

In illuminating man's descent from a degenerate species, Wells questions the assumption that it is mankind which gives evolution its direction and purpose. If evolution can admit retrogression, how certain could mankind be of its ever upward progress?

In 'On Extinction' (1893), Wells reminds the reader that the nineteenth century has witnessed the virtual elimination of one species – the bison: 'The last shaggy bison, looking with dull eyes from some western bluff across the broad prairies, must feel some dim sense that those wide rolling seas of grass were once the home of myriads of his race, and are now his no longer.'[9] One aim of this slight essay is to bring out the stark contrast between barrenness and plenitude, extinction and vigorous life, cold isolation and warm

society. The reader is enjoined to speculate about the future implications for humanity of evolutionary reverse. Wells questions the
teleology at the heart of evolutionary *hubris*. What grounds are there
for human kind to assume that its nature and its achievements are
confirmation enough of assured progress?

This idea threads in and out of his speculative journalism and his
short fiction, in narratives which insist that mankind's hegemony
over lower species and other planetary life cannot be taken for
granted. Mankind needs to look to its own fitness if it is not to be
overtaken by other 'fitter' competitors. Wells articulates what is
unspeakable – imperial man's vulnerability not only to colonisation
but to replacement – as in his invasion story of 1898, *The War of the
Worlds*: its intention and effect is to undermine the hegemony of
mankind as a species.

When Wells writes in 'On Extinction' that 'these days are the days
of man's triumph',[10] he exercises a sleight of hand by ironically
fusing a piece of imperialist rhetoric with an evolutionary commonplace. His intention here is to cast a shadow over this habitual
conflation of science and political dominance, and he does so by
interposing forces which the play of evolutionary discourse itself has
made credible and potent.

While contemporary mankind are 'indisputably lords of the world
as it is',[11] Wells argues in 'The Rate of Change of Species' (1894),
that a sudden change of climate or the 'advance of a fresh glacial
epoch' would leave man powerless to adapt to new conditions'.[12]
And as if to answer critics for whom catastrophe could not possibly
usher in a new biological order, Wells writes in 'The Extinction of
Man' (1894) that it is 'part of the excessive egotism of the human
animal that the bare idea of its extinction seems incredible to it. "A
world without *us*" it says, as a heady young Cephalapsis [a now
extinct species of fish] might have said it in the old Silurian sea.'[13]

These early and deliberately provocative essays by Wells emerged
at a relatively advanced stage in nineteenth-century Darwinian
thought. In the thirty years and more between the publication of
The Origin of Species (1859) and Wells's speculations about the
situation and the future of man in time, in the cosmic prospect,
Darwin's theory, that all organic life underwent modification
through variation and so natural selection, had itself undergone
radical qualification, elaboration and refinement. Inevitably *The
Origin* led to a vast literature of social generalisation, 'invoked to

explain social evolution in general and to support individualism and socialism, competition and cooperation, aristocracy and democracy, brute force and kindliness, militarism and pacificism, ethical pessimism and optimism, creative emergent evolutionism and evolutionary naturalism'.[14]

Gillian Beer reminds us that what emerged from Darwin's 'view of things' were laws which he had not so much 'invented' as 'described'.[15] Nevertheless, they were there, in *The Origin*. Darwin's 'tangled bank' with its bushes, insects and worms had been produced, he said, 'by laws acting around us'. These laws, to which he put capital letters and which were 'taken in the largest sense', were 'Growth with Reproduction; Inheritance, which is almost implied by reproduction; Variability from the indirect and direct action of the external conditions of life, and from use and disuse; a Ratio of Increase so high as to lead to a Struggle for Life, and as a consequence to Natural Selection, entailing Divergence of Character and the Extinction of less-improved forms'.[16]

Darwin's crucial discovery had been the mechanism of natural selection. In its formulation, the law of struggle for scarce subsistence, enunciated by the economist Thomas Malthus in *An Essay on the Principle of Population as it Affects the Future Improvement of Society* (1798), had been critical, and had furnished Darwin with, as Robert Young puts it, 'a convenient natural mechanism for the changes Darwin was studying in the selection of domesticated varieties. It gave Darwin the analogy he needed to move from artificial to natural selection, and this was the essential step in his reasoning: indefinite variation and natural selection could produce new species.'[17] But the inferences drawn from 'nature' to 'society' were not lost on a critic such as Engels. The idea of struggle involved a transference, he said, 'from society to living nature'. 'When this feat has been performed', Engels wrote, 'the same theories are transferred back again from organic nature into history', and so it is claimed that 'their validity as eternal laws of human society has been proved'.[18]

In the 1880s a counter-movement different from, though not unrelated to the objections of Engels, represented by the philosopher D. G. Ritchie, and by William Morris, Kropotkin, Edward Carpenter and A. R. Wallace (the co-founder of natural selection), questioned the simplification inherent in the mechanism of struggle, and proposed that mutual co-operation or voluntarism were just as important elements in the evolutionary process. The human brain was a factor in its modification, they argued. But it was the harnessing of bio-logical science to liberal individualism through the interpreters and popularisers – such as Spencer, Huxley, Lankester and Galton – which dominated late nineteenth-century thinking. And given the power and confidence of the post-Darwinian establishment with its growing professional prestige, it was probably inevitable that the new ideological uses of science would emerge only through con-troversy initiated from within, rather than beyond this hegemony.

In assenting to Spencer's formulation 'the survival of the fittest' in the sixth edition of *The Origin*, Darwin could not have anticipated the transformations which that concept of fitness would undergo, nor the extent to which this process would concentrate such a constellation of fears and foreboding. The 'struggle for life', he assured readers, was, after all, absolved from any charge of harsh-ness 'when we reflect that the war of nature is not incessant ... and that the vigorous, the healthy, and the happy survive and multiply'.[19]

Yet few words in scientific discourse have so soon opened up their stock of unforeseen ambiguity, as was the case with 'fitness' and its derivatives. For Darwin, and for succeeding biologists, 'fitness' corresponded, without value judgement, to a state of adaptation in the process of natural selection. But the value-loaded meanings could not be kept out. With the emergence, in the last twenty years of the century, of various strains of 'social Darwinism', which was the predisposition to 'describe and explain phenomena in terms of competition and conflict',[20] 'fitness' became purposive; it had an end – complete with strategies to direct the conduct of individuals, groups, populations, races. Value was being effectively and widely smuggled into Darwinism.

'Fitness' was now available to discursive strategies that used biological concepts to naturalise social and cultural practices. And these strategies were highly ideological. An index of this practice was the making visible of the 'waste' products of the struggle for survival. By the early eighties it was no longer believed that in that struggle the 'unfit' – the 'waste' products – were being successfully weeded out. Writing in 1883, Francis Galton was to the point: 'those whose race we especially want to have, would leave few descendants, while those whose race we want to be quit of, would crowd the vacant space with progeny'.[21] What was increasingly giving rise to alarm was not just the failure of the social organism to eliminate the unfit variety but the differential reproductive success of the unfit. Would the 'weak' inherit the earth?

'I had proved myself fittest by the mere fact of survival. The sole remaining question was, could I adapt myself to my environment? If so, I had fulfilled the whole gospel of Darwinism.' So remarks the heroine of Grant Allen's novel *The Type-writer Girl* (1897) whose 'energy' and 'promptitude' has enabled her to find and keep a job.[22] The language of popular Darwinism had a critical function in mediating and rationalising these concerns, notably in writers who took up for the nineties the rhetoric of Spencer and social Darwinism, uninhibited by Spencer's reservations over imperial warfare.

'Good is nothing more than the conduct which is fittest to the circumstances of the moment ... failure or success in the struggle for existence is the sole moral standard. Good is what survives.'[23] This was the view of Somerset Maugham, doctor turned novelist, at the turn of the century. His notebook for the late nineties is peppered with references to the ethics of the struggle for survival, and he concludes that unmitigated competition and struggle are indeed in the natural order of things. The most eloquent academic spokesman of this point of view was Karl Pearson, biometrician and future eugenicist, who in 1900 addressed an audience on 'National Life from the Standpoint of Science':

This dependence of progress on the survival of the fitter race, terribly black as it may seem to some of you, gives the struggle for existence its redeeming features; it is the fiery crucible out of which comes the finer metal ... [when wars cease] ... mankind will no longer progress ... [for] ... there will be nothing to check the fertility of inferior stock; the relentless law of heredity will not be controlled and guided by natural selection.[24]

And in Benjamin Kidd's *Social Evolution* (1893) (an enormously popular study which quickly went into several editions) 'the law of life has always been the same from the beginning, – ceaseless and inevitable struggle and competition, ceaseless and inevitable progress'. By the mid-nineties it is a commonplace that not just individuals but whole societies are to be seen as subject to this law of necessary struggle, in which 'winning societies gradually [extinguish] their competitors, the weaker peoples disappear before the stronger, and the subordination or exclusion of the least efficient is still the prevailing feature of advancing humanity'.[25] The

poet and editor W. E. Henley gave this idea a mystical colouring in
'The Song of the Sword' (1892):

> Sifting the nations,
> The slag from the metal,
> The waste and the weak
> From the fit and the strong.[26]

II THE LANDSCAPE OF UNFITNESS

The abysmal fecundity ...
                        (W. E. Henley, 'Song of the Sword' (1892))[27]

The experience, direct or at some remove, of the growth of urban
poverty in the nineteenth century, had always generated a metaphoric energy of response with which to master the enormity of the
experience. From the 1880s it coalesced in the compelling and
powerful image of 'Darkest London'. For William Booth of the
Salvation Army, here was moral darkness. Booth demanded attention for England's urban poor with a precise and effective reattri-
bution to them of conditions reported by the explorer H. M. Stanley
from 'Darkest Africa': 'A population sodden with drink, steeped in
every vice, eaten up by every social and physical malady, these are
the denizens of Darkest England, amidst whom my life has been
spent, and to whose rescue I would now summon all that is best in
the manhood and womanhood of the land.'[28]

There were other components – tracts of sunlessness derived from
earlier representations of the Victorian city, the darkness of fog or of
the seemingly impenetrable alley or court. The metaphoric and the
literal were hideously mingled in a lethal spell of freezing fog, which
lasted from 20 December 1891 to 2 January 1892 during which time
the death-rate rose from 18 to 32 per thousand.[29]

Edward Carpenter saw not so much moral darkness as a
physically distorted population of city-dwellers, 'puny white-faced',
'a thin-legged slouching apathetic population', 'white-faced girls'.[30]
The condition of urbanism was such that only the etiolated, the
'bloodless', could survive.

The post-Darwinian city was imagined not merely as a city of
moral darkness and of outcasts. Here were tracts of new degenerate
energies, menageries of sub-races of men and women. Down in the
darkness, the struggle for life was producing new species of mankind

which signalled an all too successful adaptation. Biological and zoological writing had already established that the unfit species survives in a less demanding environment which, in turn, permits it a degenerate life.

So far from entailing extinction, these creatures of the biologically degenerate underground were the tenacious, perverse, and ambiguous fit/unfit, with an appropriately dark future ahead of them. Wells's Morlocks brilliantly figure the prospect. The Time Traveller in *The Time Machine* (1895) sights the parasitic Morlocks at different times, but each of his sightings registers a biologically lower-order being, glowing white in the darkness: 'a solitary white ape-like creature', 'a small, white ... creature, with large bright eyes ... like a human spider', 'a bleached ... nocturnal Thing'.[31] If Carpenter lamented the ill-nourished body of the factory girl, her eyes, 'washed-out small',[32] Wells chooses to put degradation in the unsentimental terms of social Darwinism: the eyes are a striking index of 'fitness', of successful adaptation.

Such degraded fitness is robustly exemplified by Clem Peckover, in George Gissing's precisely titled *The Nether World* (1889). A 'rank, evilly-fostered growth'[33], her tenacious degenerate life is founded on naturalistically conceived biological tropes: adaptation, parasitism (she preys on and strangles the life of those around her) and, as we shall see in chapter four, on atavism. Gissing began composition of *The Nether World* on 19 March 1888. During the previous four days he had been reading Thomas Hardy's recently published novel *The Woodlanders* (1887).[34] It seems certain that Gissing's presentation of the enclosed subterranean density of urban Clerkenwell was influenced by passages in *The Woodlanders*, though these fictional worlds were, on the face of it, so distinct. But Hardy, in his turn, was keenly aware of the problem of the city, and of the degenerationist frame of reference within which the blight of the contemporary city was discussed.

In *The Woodlanders*, Giles Winterbourne, Grace Melbury and her father are described making their way through the woodlands. Yet their human presence is all but crowded out by the very plenitude of organic life:

They went noiselessly over mats of starry moss, rustled through interspersed tracts of leaves, skirted trunks with spreading roots whose mossed rinds made them like hands wearing green gloves; elbowed old elms and ashes with great forks, in which stood pools of water that overflowed on rainy days and ran down their stems in green cascades. On older trees still than these, huge lobes of fungi grew like lungs. Here, as everywhere, the Unfulfilled Intention, which makes life what it is, was as obvious as it could be among the depraved crowds of a city slum. The leaf was deformed, the curve was crippled, the taper was interrupted; the lichen ate the vigour of the stalk, and the ivy slowly strangled to death the promising sapling.[35]

The subject 'they' is soon buried beneath a cluster of natural objects, with the verbs of motion – 'went', 'rustled', 'elbowed' – pushed to the head of each clause, allowing the vivid, anthropomorphic life of the woodland full play. The focus shifts to the older trees. The key simile, the 'lobes of fungi' as 'lungs', brilliantly heralds the common deformation of human and vegetational life in the 'Unfulfilled Intention' of degeneration. Here, then, Hardy taps the topical moral and biological meanings of the discourse of 'darkest' London. Fungus and 'city slum' are both subjected to the process. And the intrusion, in this woodland scene, of an image of debased urban life effectively seals off the natural object from appropriation by any conventional pastoral conceit of rural innocence.[36] Yet within the picture of dissolute growth there are variations: the elaborate and ornate moss is parasitic but harmless, whereas the combative, throttling lichen and ivy have for their victims the 'stalk' and 'promising sapling'. Each object, whether ornately decadent or rapaciously efficient, parades its degeneracy as an index of struggle for existence in conditions of oppressive and gloomy futility. The woodland is like an inner sanctum of the vast edifice of the natural world, its objects monuments only to their own deformed existence.

In an earlier scene the struggle for existence is graphically anatomised in a brief descriptive aside, where with economy and intensity the organic intrudes on the man-made. The ivy, with its promiscuous and destructive quest for purposeless life, is the subject. In the sunless gloom of early morning, a blaze of firewood lights up Melbury's outhouse:

In the hollow shades of the roof could be seen dangling and etiolated arms of ivy which had crept through the joints of the tiles and were groping in vain for some support, their leaves being dwarfed and sickly for want of sunlight; others were pushing in with such force at the eaves as to lift from their supports the shelves that were fixed there.

Drawing on Zola (he was reading and making notes from *Germinal* and *La Faute de l'Abbé Mouret* between 1885 and 1887),[37] by a naturalistic mode of representation Hardy makes the biological process available to perception by speeding up the film of the evolutionary struggle. Deep inside 'one of those sequestered spots outside the gates of the world' are images of organic nature, pointless, despairing, futile. The contemporary discourse of urban blight, so crucial to Gissing, was also sharpening Hardy's perception of the deformation and degeneration of nature.

III URBAN DEGENERATION

One guessed him as the third generation grandson to the shepherd or ploughboy whom civilization had sucked into the town; as one of the thousands who have lost the life of the body and failed to reach the life of the spirit.

(E. M. Forster, *Howards End* (1910))[38]

'Nearly half a million of fresh-bodied units ... arrive in our great Babylon every year. They settle down, marry, and for a time stay the degenerative process by the infusion of healthy life ... two or three generations of London life see them out and as extinct as the dodo itself.'[39] This was the *Illustrated London News* in June 1889. From the late 1870s the city was depicted as a 'vortex', a 'whirlpool', which remorselessly sucked in the 'fresh-bodied' from the country, using up their 'infusion of healthy life', and inducing in them progressive and inevitable deterioration. The urban 'unfit' were represented as preying on their 'fit' country cousins, reducing them to their level of physical torpor, denuding them of their country colour: 'country-born labourers in the prime of life', wrote Arnold White in 1901, 'are now white-faced workmen living in courts and alleys'.[40] The predatory Morlocks of *The Time Machine* are never far from view.

This was the essence of urban-degeneration theory, which fused degradation and 'generation' into a condition which was inexorable, because inherited, and thus transmitted; a pathology which, according to Galton, was sucking out the lifeblood of the imperial body. Galton claimed that the struggle for existence was not improving the British race but spoiling it. The full title of Darwin's *The Origin* referred to 'Favoured Races in the Struggle for Life'. What were now 'most favoured' appeared to be 'the classes of coarser organisation' who 'survive to become the parents of the next'. Galton and others believed that the 'fittest', in the sense of 'healthiest' stock – the countrymen – were less able to adapt, and so were ill-equipped to survive the special exigencies of urban life. The theory of urban degeneration was at hand. 'Sickly-looking and puny residents in towns', wrote Galton, 'may ... be better knit and do more work and live longer than much haler men imported ... from elsewhere'.[41]

But if the native of the city had this degenerate vigour to survive, Galton had difficulty in squaring such a proposition with one of his earlier findings which showed that families in rural Warwickshire were more fertile than their counterparts in urban Coventry.[42] The solution to this conundrum was to argue that the fitness of the rural stock, as measured by their reproductive advantage, would be damaged if they bred with town-dwellers. The vigorous but degenerate city-dweller, through reproduction, inexorably dragged down the level of fertility of country dwellers and diminished their 'stock' of nobility, sobriety and honesty.

The proliferation of commentary from the turn of the century onwards, about measures for the eugenic improvement of the nation's stock had its origins in studies initiated a generation earlier. Galton, who had first coined the term 'eugenics' in 1883, achieved a new eminence late in life. In 1903, at the age of eighty-one, he wrote to the national press on 'Our National Physique : Prospects for the British Race: Are We Degenerating?'[43]

James Cantlie was another figure whose early concern about urban degeneration brought him belated recognition. In 1906 he produced *Physical Efficiency: A Review of the Deleterious Effects of Town Life upon the Population of Britain with Suggestions for their Arrest*, with a preface by Sir Lauder Brunton and a foreword by Sir James Crichton-Browne, both of them eminent physicians. They paid tribute to Cantlie's proposals for improving the quality of the urban race. Crichton-Browne pointed out that while twenty years earlier Cantlie was 'little heeded', now 'his warnings are being justified by events and ... the market-place is agog for guidance'.[44] Cantlie's original lecture 'Degeneration amongst Londoners' was delivered in 1885, and at the time attracted little more than a satiric riposte from *Punch* to his scheme for bringing ozone-intensive air into towns via pipes.[45] He was among the first to seek, in the fitness of the urban working class, the key to the fitness of the nation and the imperial race, in its struggle for survival.

Level-headed advice about health here alternates with an emotive rhetoric which was to be endlessly reproduced for a generation. Cantlie found unmistakable evidence of urban degeneration in the fatal ease with which man had adapted to a diseased and abnormal environment: 'the close confinement and foul air of our cities shortening the life of the individual, and raising up a puny and ill-developed race'.[46] By 1904, when the Inter-Departmental Committee on Physical Deterioration reported amid a plethora of surveys and speculation about the physical and moral fitness of the imperial stock, in the wake of the Boer War, Cantlie's rhetoric of the mid-eighties must have seemed, in retrospect, strikingly prophetic.

Another doctor, J. P. Williams-Freeman, took up a frequently aired theme among doctor-commentators. The city, he thought, was not an especially efficient instrument of natural selection, for the race was only 'slowly adapting itself to more complex conditions'.[47] The more the city sucked in the country-bred to interbreed with city dwellers the more likely it was that breeding might cease altogether because of the high infant mortality rate (which for children under five in central London in the 1880s could rise to 30%). This was a proposition which derived from a traditional view of the innate robustness and superior health of the countryman – 'bigger, heavier, slower, more plethoric in temperament, and requiring far more physical exercise to keep him in health'.[48]

Rural virtue was an essential element in the Edwardian mythology of nature. E. M. Forster in *Howards End* (1910) shows this clearly enough. As Leonard Bast makes his early morning journey through the Hertfordshire countryside he passes men whose hours are 'ruled not by a London office, but by the movements of the crops and sun'. While conceding that 'only the sentimentalist' could celebrate them as 'men of the finest type', Forster nevertheless sentimentally embraces them as 'England's hope. Clumsily they carry forward the torch of the sun, until such time as the nation sees fit to take it up.' Contaminated by progress they may be – 'half clodhopper, half board-school prig' – but, for all that, they can lay claim to what is for Forster a superior organic rootedness: 'they can still throw back to a nobler stock and breed yeomen'.[49]

From Galton's calculations of the differential birth-rates between rural and urban families, Williams-Freeman argued, apocalyptically, that 'physical degeneration and diminished increment in a population point unmistakably to eventual extinction ... of the race'.[50] The perception of the inexorable loss of healthy breeding power was the source of the degenerationist's nightmare in the *fin de siècle*. That 'the pick of youth' were deserting the rural districts, leaving 'the second-rate ones ... to supply the future generations' was, for Williams-Freeman, a travesty of 'natural law, a survival of the unfittest by elimination of the best'. 'It seems impossible', he said, 'to exaggerate the importance of the question.'[51] Yoking together those moral and political attributes of the working class which were most threatening to middle-class opinion, he deplored the degenerate Londoner who 'finding himself at a disadvantage in competition with the immigrant', refused to submit to 'extinction' without 'forcible protest on his part'. He passes through 'many stages before he is finally eliminated. Irregular labour, odd jobs, sweaters' dens, prostitution, subsistence on charity, agitation, "demonstrations" and riots are only some of the struggles of the dying Londoner before he pays the debt of nature.'[52] The confusion of the urban degenerationist's thesis is evident enough: on the one hand the Londoner reproduces prolifically, on the other he threatens to die out. Natural selection is made to operate both to the disadvantage of the city-dweller *and* against the natural order of things by denuding the agricultural economy of its healthy stock.

Gareth Stedman Jones has argued that the phenomenon of urban degeneration is best understood within a 'complex of middle class beliefs' which arose from a constellation of anxieties: 'the agricultural depression, the rural exodus, the growing predominance of urban England, the increase in working-class discontent, fears about foreign competition and doubts about free trade'.[53] Each of these concerns is visible in the crude rhetoric such fears gave rise to during these years. One figure caught up in the casuistries of the urban degenerationists' special pleading was the predominantly Jewish 'alien' immigrant, arriving in Britain from the pogroms of Eastern Europe from the 1880s and in larger numbers at the turn of the century. The alien quickly became identified with the horrors of the rediscovered abyss of the imperial city. The Earl of Dunraven exploited biological determinism in his campaign against immigrants when he argued that the immigrants were dangerous, not only because they were poor and numerous, but because of their victory in the battle of survival, through their successful adaptation to the 'demands of urban life'.[54] 'They can feed off the offal of the streets, and live in conditions, in respect of indecency, dirt and overcrowding, incompatible with existence to an Englishman ... It is the superiority of the lower over the higher order of organism – the comparative indestructability of the lower forms of animal life.'[55]

The immigrant is offensively hybridised into a form of sub-man or scavenging beast. The 'habitat' of the immigrant differs little from the fantasy, aired by *The Daily Telegraph* in 1859, of a breed of scavenging black pigs reputed to be running wild in the sewers of Hampstead: a similar story was conveyed to Henry Mayhew.[56] The rapacious, predatory rodent, breeding in the 'sewers' of Europe, was, of course, a standard figure of anti-semitic rhetoric under the Nazis.

As the vulnerability of Britain's imperial mission became more pronounced in the 1890s, commentators like W. H. Wilkins and the indefatigable Arnold White drew on paradigms of the decline and fall of empires in their anxiety to warn against the degenerative threat which the alien posed. Rome had 'welcomed all nationalities', said Wilkins, 'it was a sign of the canker which in time ate away the heart of the Empire. So, too, England in the Victorian era – an era of prosperity unequalled even by Imperial Rome – throws open wide her arms to receive the destitute, the criminal and the worthless of other lands ... '[57]

Hostility to the alien continued well into the Edwardian period, fuelled by an increasing paranoia about foreigners, particularly Germans, reflected in popular spy novels such as William LeQueux's *Spies of the Kaiser, Plotting the Downfall of England* (1909) and E. Phillips Oppenheim's *The Secret* (1907) in which the hero observes an East End crowd of aliens who are frustrating the publication of a German invasion plan. 'This is what comes ... of making London the asylum for all the foreign scum of the earth', he remarks.[58]

According to Rider Haggard, by 1902 the self-selection of the fittest country people for urban life had left a depleted rural landscape bereft of all but 'dullards, the vicious or ... wastrels ... because they are unfitted for any other life'. 'It is this indifferent remnant', he complained, 'who will be the parents of the next generation of rural Englishmen.'[59] The same year C. W. Sorensen remarked that for lack of capital 'the land has gone back to pasture, the farmer has given his space to the grazier, the labourers have been packed off to the factories, while the landlord continues to have his rent sent to him to spend in London or Paris, and the nation goes on its way towards moral, social and physical degeneration'.[60] And in evidence to the *Royal Commission on the War in South Africa* (1903), the Inspector-General of Recruiting declared that the rural supply of 'healthy' (and so deferential) personnel was fast drying up: 'the population in the country is getting smaller, and that is rather an unfortunate thing for us'.[61] It would be 'disastrous ... to the quality of the race', said the physiologist, John Berry Haycraft, 'if the most prudent and capable are bred out of and eliminated from the community'.[62]

While the absolute growth of the British population – 'the number of our citizens' – was seen as a dependable index of racial resilience, fears about the only too successful proliferation of the city population and the city 'type' continued to gather momentum. It was precisely this contradiction which Edwardian race-improvers would try to resolve, with their policies of 'positive' and 'negative' eugenics. To save the nation from degeneration they sought to encourage the breeding of 'fit' stocks and to bring the breeding of the 'unfit' to a halt, once and for all.

CHAPTER 3

Degenerate spaces: the urban crisis of the 1880s and 'The Mayor of Casterbridge'

I NOT SENTIMENT BUT SEDIMENT

Earlier in the century, the physical and moral condition of the urban poor had been the cause of much comment and reproach, especially in the 1840s and 1850s, when the health, way of life and moral state of the poor of the towns were the subject of a flood of reports. Novels of the period by Kingsley, Dickens and Gaskell conveyed a similar perception of urban destitution. Again and again in reports from observers like William Farr, Scott Alison, Thomas Beggs not only poverty but degradation, physical and moral, are described and deplored.[1] And a discourse of degeneration is resorted to, expressing the observer's sense of physical deterioration, of a falling-off of morality and conduct, a 'sinking down to the level of brute tribes', as one 1844 report had it.[2]

By the early 1880s the political, social and intellectual contours had shifted in the direction of a new pessimism and a more systematically applied determinism affecting the outlook of the governing class. Whereas reformers like Farr and Beggs tended to believe that sanitary reform would in time check or ameliorate the physical and moral damage caused by chronic poverty,[3] there was now a more general apprehension about the threat to the nation and the race. The consequences of degradation were becoming fixed as inexorable and invisible.

Commentators of the eighties were burdened by the inescapable facts of mass poverty. Schemes for sanitary improvement, undertaken a generation earlier, had not proved adequate to the task. With the onset of longer cycles of industrial recession, particularly from 1882–3 onwards, it seemed that a fast approaching urban crisis was in the making. Yet the underlying economic and structural causes of the urban crisis, with its fast rising unemployment, were not, on the whole, addressed. Instead, relief from acknowledging the intractable realities of the system was sought in the great bogey of the period and by the bio-social discourse invented to dramatise it – the residuum, the recalcitrant hard-core of urban unemployed, usually seen as unemployable, feckless, violent and incurably criminal. The term 'residuum' was powerfully freighted to secure the dehumanising of the human and to absolve those who might contemplate involvement.

The residuum was, in every sense, a standing and offensive rebuke to a society which had still to expunge the appalling record of slum development so well publicised in the 1840s. These areas of London, Manchester and other growing cities remained *terra incognita* for the late Victorian middle class. But complacency was disturbed by the most talked about pamphlet of the 1880s, *The Bitter Cry of Outcast London: An Enquiry into the Condition of the Abject Poor* (1883) by Congregationalist minister, Andrew Mearns. He drew on a range of well-established images when he helped to delineate for a generation to come the idea of 'outcast London'. Mearns found the slum courts of London's East End 'reeking with poisonous and malodorous gases arising from accumulations of sewage and refuse scattered in all directions, and often flowing beneath your feet: courts, many of them, which the sun never penetrates, which are never visited by a breath of fresh air, and which rarely know the virtues of a drop of cleansing water.'[4] In the following year George Gissing wrote in his novel *The Unclassed* of a court where there were 'very few houses in which the air was at all tolerable; in many instances the vilest odours hung about open door-ways. To pass out of Elm Court into the wider streets around was like a change to the freshness of woods and fields. And the sources of this miasma were only too obvious.'[5]

Attempts were made during the eighties to tackle the problem of urban overcrowding by encouraging emigration – to evacuate the city's 'waste' by exporting it. Yet those who emigrated were not those at the bottom of the heap, but rather the 'flower of the population', as one commentator put it. The residuum, tenaciously, threateningly, stays at home 'corrupting and being corrupted, like the sewage of the metropolis which remained floating at the mouth of the Thames last summer, because there was not scour sufficient to propel it into the sea'.[6]

In the representation of the residuum as sewage there is a persistent elision of object and referent. 'There were few communities, rural or urban', writes Anthony Wohl, 'without heaps of accumulated excrement as an all-too apparent feature of their topography'[7] – figured by Dickens in the 'dust heaps' of *Our Mutual Friend*. The hierarchy of the human body, for Peter Stallybrass and Allon White, is 'transcoded through the hierarchy of the city'.[8] Within its moral topography the residuum had drifted to the low points, surrounding and surrounded by the river, the cloaca and the sewer which stood in a metaphorical and metonymic relationship to the residuum. The lowest of the urban poor were figured as shit, which in literal terms overwhelmed the efforts of sanitary reform of the nineteenth-century city. The residuum was the city's excrement, inhabiting the body's 'nether' regions, its 'privy' areas.[9] 'The medical metaphors of disease, degeneration and filth coalesced in the rhetorical creation of 'cesspool city', about to be submerged in a tide of excrement.'[10]

For writers of the 1880s, such rhetorical figures were very well established in the writing of social outrage of the earlier period. The 1840s saw much debate around the subject of contagion and miasma, the epidemic consequences of fermenting waste matter, and the generation of deadly air-borne poisons.[11] Evidently the emotive utility of the potential of miasma was recognised, long after its threat as a source of pestilence had passed.

So the residuum of unemployables came to represent, as Nikolas Rose suggests, 'all those anti-social forms of conduct and vices which threatened good order and public tranquillity'.[12] To be unemployable was to have failed a test set both by the labour market and by respectable morality, for it implied modes of conduct – vagrancy, prostitution, crime – which were 'the outward and visible signs of an inward state of character'.[13]

These concerns can be detected in Charles Booth's epic social enquiry *Life and Labour of the People in London*, the research for which was initiated in 1886 at the height of the panic about the threat of social unrest. Booth was dismayed to discover that around 35% of the London population was still living in a state of poverty. What is interesting about this work of ostensibly objective research is the reiteration in the margins of the enquiry of contemporary degenerationist assumptions and categorisations about the London poor.

Informing Booth's categorisation of the poor was a concept of 'fitness', which, deployed metaphorically, reaffirmed an 'existing linkage between pauperism, crime, indigence and social danger'.[14] Booth used a concept of a norm, and deviations from it, derived from

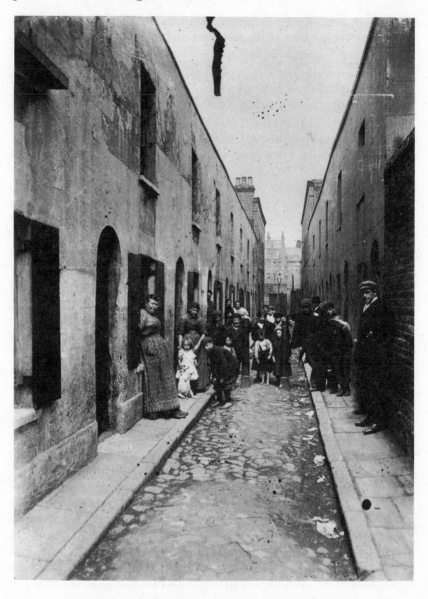

1 'Little Collingwood Street, Bethnal Green, London'.

Galtonian population statistics. Adopting the classes E and F as together 'truly representing the standard of life in England',[15] this classification offered a grid across which individuals could slide and fall: D, small regular earners; C, intermittent earners; B, casual earners; and A, the lowest class.

Class B (a relatively large group) is described as 'not ... a class in which people are born to live and die, so much as the drift from other classes'. At first glance this is a mobile class, frequently changing in composition. But, 'here in class B', Booth suggests, 'we have the crux of the social problem. Every other class can take care of itself, or could so, if Class B were out of the way. Those unfortunate people form a sort of quagmire underlying the social structure, and to dry up this quagmire must be our principal aim.'[16] These are not quite paupers but 'rather the material from which paupers are made'.[17] Despite its transitional status, class B in fact takes on the appearance of a fixed class; this is enforced by the ambiguous physicality of the vehicle 'quagmire' (a metaphor for both mass and fluid), to be dried up before it seeps upward, like rising damp, into the solid fabric constituted by the classes above it.

Class A, the lowest class, comprising 'some occasional labourers, street-sellers, loafers, criminals and semi-criminals', has staked out a discrete, autonomous space which, Booth believes, is 'hereditary to a very considerable extent'.[18] And as a degenerate class it proliferates its degradation. The life of its members 'is the life of savages, with vicissitudes of extreme hardship and occasional excess ... they render no useful service, they create no wealth: more often they destroy it. They degrade whatever they touch, and as individuals are perhaps incapable of improvement'.[19] They harbour the threat of social disruption, being 'the ready materials for disorder when occasion serves'.[20]

While Booth and his co-workers, such as Herbert Llewellyn-Smith, were anxious to make precise and sensible differentiations among the poor, their descriptions and definitions of the residuum and of the class of casual employed are shot through with degenerationist assumptions. The criminal is in 'a hereditary class', apparently unaffected by the lack of opportunity offered by the labour market which the findings themselves copiously illustrate. The unemployed are engulfed by an inexorable degeneracy which sucks down those skilled artisans who have moved from the country into the city in seach of work. While Llewellyn-Smith does acknowledge the impact of 'industrial dislocations', he none the less explains the downward passage from labourer to pauper as the result of 'personal "unfitness" '.[21] The over-determining effect of the town is virtually biological. The artisan's strength is sapped through the generations. 'The shiftless, the improvident . . . are deposited every year from the ranks of labour, and form a kind of sediment at the bottom of the social scale.'[22]

Such a piece of 'sediment' is the monstrous man-beast Slimy in George Gissing's early novel *The Unclassed* (1884), perhaps the first representation in fiction of a specifically biologically-degenerate urban space. Slimy is a stark emblem of the polluting residuum:

Leaning on the counter, in one of the compartments, was something which a philanthropist might perhaps have had the courage to claim as a human being; a very tall creature, with bent shoulders, and head seeming to grow out of its chest; thick, grizzled hair hiding almost every vestige of feature, with the exception of one dreadful red eye, its fellow being dead and sightless. He had laid on the counter, with palms downward as if concealing something, two huge hairy paws.[23]

Subsequent references by Gissing to 'monster' and 'creature' ensure his objectification as a bestial grotesque. He is also a repository of pollution: he carries the smallpox which, emanating from the effluvial slime of the tenements, kills, with retributive 'selectiveness', the slum landlord Woodstock.[24] Slimy himself lives in one such tenement, Litany Lane, and at one point assaults the main protagonist, Waymark, who is collecting rents on behalf of Woodstock.

Slimy embodies all the disruptive and transgressive potential of disease as a defining characteristic of a degenerate and dangerous class formation. He inhabits a tract of degeneracy which is characteristic of other representations of urban space in the social realism of the eighties – the slum enclave, part of the total urban picture but cut off from its 'civilized face'. Writers now make central these marginal borderlands: 'darkest London', fast becoming a 'conventional epithet'[25], is now lit up by a writing which will reveal the obscurity of the subject matter and the real limits of knowing it.

The light which Gissing shines on these enclaves invariably casts doubt on their being reformed at all. *The Unclassed* points up an interesting and provocative contradiction between Woodstock's official public role – his contacts at Westminster, his interest in public affairs – and his dereliction of duty as a landlord. Litany Lane, the worst slum, is deliberately set in Westminster, in the shadow of the national legislature. Woodstock's late conversion to charitable work is a decidedly unconvincing afterthought in the edition of 1884; even so, it would have been better had Gissing retained Woodstock's devotion to 'Blue-Books' in the 1895 text – on which the modern edition is based.

II *THE MAYOR OF CASTERBRIDGE*: URBS IN RURE

The urban question gained a new prominence through publicity. Magazine articles such as 'How the Poor Live' by George Sims (in *The Pictorial World*), hinted at 'nameless abominations which could only be set forth were we contributing to the *Lancet*'.[26] Walter Besant's novel of 1882 *All Sorts and Conditions of Men* and Mearns's *The Bitter Cry of Outcast London* led the way in exposing the squalor and deprivation in 'darkest London'. Mearns's revelations (excerpts were published in Stead's *Pall Mall Gazette*) caused, in the words of *Reynolds Newspaper*, 'a tremendous sensation and thrill of horror throughout the land' when they were published in October 1883.[27] In the light of this activity of revelation and commentary about the urban poor, it is not surprising that Hardy invoked the 'depraved crowds of the city slum' in *The Woodlanders*, nor that he should have chosen this time to contribute to *Longman's Magazine* an essay on 'The Dorsetshire Labourer' in July 1883.

Hardy was contributing to a lively debate. In the same month the *Fortnightly Review* carried an editorial, written by T. H. S. Escott, 'The Future of the Radical Party'. It endorsed a speech made by Joseph Chamberlain in Birmingham on 13 June, urging landlords to 'provide better accommodation for the working classes in town and country'.[28] Hardy read reports of that speech. A fortnight later he wrote with evident satisfaction to John Morley that 'my description … harmonizes with what was said at Birmingham',[29] sending him a copy of his article, with another to Gladstone.[30]

Hardy focusses on the 'incertitude and precariousness' of the lives of the agricultural poor. Whereas a generation before 'the majority remained all their lifetime on one farm', now 'the labourers … look upon an annual removal as the most natural thing in the world'. The relation between landlord and tenant is changing; benevolent paternalism is being superseded by an impersonal relationship in which tenants now exercise direct authority over others: 'the labourer has not even the stability of a landlord's tenant; he is only tenant of a tenant'.[31]

Working relationships on the land increasingly resemble the regimen of the factory. Agriculture is becoming a new site of antagonism between capital and labour, more characteristic of manufacturing industry, as farm management itself becomes neo-industrial. Labourers are more conscious of their commodity value and thus their expendability within the labour process. Hardy explicitly draws these rural and urban perspectives together when he compares the 'painless passivity' induced by the monotony of field work to the 'drudgery in the slums and alleys of a city' which induces 'a mood of despondency which is well-nigh permanent'.[32] Female labourers, in their enforced mobility, have now 'acquired the rollicking air of factory hands'.[33]

In calling attention, albeit obliquely, to the interconnectedness of the urban and agricultural questions Hardy had placed himself, briefly, in the van of this short-lived radical liberal formation. Moreover, this essay offered unmistakable evidence of a fast-evolving and distinctive mode of social awareness. The consequence for Hardy's fiction was immensely important. The idea of a 'native' rural life now underwent a subtle reconstruction through a kind of radical 'archaeology'.[34] In *The Mayor of Casterbridge* (1886) and the novels which followed it, a complex landscape, new to Victorian fiction, made the 'urbanising' of rural life show through.

It is a landscape shaped by a construction of difference; by a magnification of divisions between the normative and the 'other', marking out boundaries between the healthy and the polluted, the respectable and disreputable, between the 'official' and subversive class formations and social groups, and the prospect of these boundaries being trangressed. Such meanings shape Hardy's representation of the social space of 'Casterbridge', his *urbs in rure*.

Midway through the novel, Michael Henchard, the unemployed hay-trusser who has risen to prosperous corn factor and town mayor, is descending a steep slope of economic decline. Declared bankrupt, he stands at the lower of the two bridges which Hardy precisely distinguishes as gravitation points of two very different groups of social and economic failures. Henchard falls into the category of '*misérables* ... of a politer stamp',[35] – the glance at Hugo is deliberate.[36] These include 'bankrupts, hypochondriacs, persons who were what is called "out of a situation" from fault or lucklessness, the inefficient of the professional class ... The eyes of this species were mostly directed over the parapet upon the running water below' (248). Farfrae, now in every way Henchard's vanquisher, drives up and Henchard takes the opportunity of reminding him of the social symbolism of the situation:

> I am going where you were going to a few years ago, when I prevented you and got you to bide here. Tis turn and turn about isn't it? Do ye mind how we stood like this in the Chalk Walk when I persuaded 'ee to stay? You then stood without a chattel to your name, and I was master of the house in Corn Street. But now I stand without a stick or a rag, and the master of that house is you. (250)

That earlier Chalk Walk meeting at the top part of the town is recalled: 'The young man's hand remained steady in Henchard's for a moment or two. He looked over the fertile country that stretched beneath them, then backward along the shaded walk reaching to the top of the town' (94). As the men shake hands, the configuration of the landscape offers, in a moment of poise, the possibilities for both of them. Hardy's use of place resonates with personal and social significance. Henchard's descent, when mayor, back down into Casterbridge with Farfrae is proleptic of his passage from the pros- perity of Corn Street down to the low-lying bridge. Excluded from the town houses higher up, he stands incongruously within the slum domain at Durnover, the parish which contains Mixen Lane, 'a back slum of the town', as Hardy puts it, 'the *pis aller* of Casterbridge domiciliation'.[37] And Henchard's re-employment of the morally bankrupt Jopp, who has gravitated to the Mixen Lane community, is itself a 'last resort' to wrest back from Farfrae his financial hegemony.

Mixen Lane constitutes a memorable and vividly realised social space in the novel.

> Mixen Lane was the Adullam of all the surrounding villages. It was the hiding-place of those who were in distress, and in debt, and trouble of every kind. Farm-labourers and other peasants, who combined a little poaching with their farming, and a little brawling and bibbing with their poaching, found themselves sooner or later in Mixen Lane. Rural mechanics too idle to mechanize, rural servants too rebellious to serve, drifted or were forced into Mixen Lane.
>
> The lane and its surrounding thicket of thatched cottages stretched out like a spit into the moist and misty lowland. Much that was sad, much that was low, some things which were baneful, could be seen in Mixen Lane.

Vice ran freely in and out certain of the doors in the neighbourhood; recklessness dwelt under the roof with the crooked chimney; shame in some bow windows; theft (in times of privation) in the thatched and mud-walled houses by the sallows. Even slaughter had not been altogether unknown here. (278)

This is indeed where the 'refuse' of the community is consigned. A 'mixen' is a dungheap, and so this nomenclature enforces the identification between these down-and-outs with the nether regions of town, social order, and human body – all that is rejected, disposable, repressed: it finds a graphic synecdoche in Henry Mayhew's description of the inmates of an 'Asylum for the Houseless' in *London, Labour and the London Poor* where the visitor 'is overcome with a sense of the vast heap of social refuse – the mere human street-sweepings – the great living mixen – that is destined, as soon as the spring returns, to be strewn far and near over the land, and serve as manure to the future crime-crops of the country.'[38]

Yet Hardy gives us a more variegated and clear-sighted picture. His dispossessed are not reducible merely to the waste matter of the social order, we have rather a diversity of types and of their motivation. While there is certainly degraded behaviour – 'vice', 'shame', 'theft', 'slaughter' – there is also the diversity of circumstances which makes people vulnerable to the social process – 'debt', 'brawling and bibbing', a refusal to conform to the disciplines of work and conduct. Hardy's allusion to the cave of Adullam is surely meant to elicit sympathy for the plight of those who like David (and those that sought his company in their trouble) have fled to the cave for solace from Saul's anger.[39]

Mixen Lane also harbours a more respectable class which has fallen on hard times: 'families from decayed villages ... of that once bulky, but now nearly extinct, section of village society called 'liviers' or lifeholders – copyholders and others' (279). While both are consigned to the same disreputable territory, Hardy distinguishes between the respectable tradesmen, uprooted from a traditional and legally sanctioned way of life, and the small-town proletariat with their deviant culture. If the respectable inhabitants wanted to move on and out, there is little sign that the rest would wish to do so, since they have evolved their alternative traditions, based on a cunning mutual aid. The 'rusty-jointed executors of the law' (304) prove to be no match for this efficiently organised sub-culture whose members can finely judge how far to step outside the law without incurring its penalties. Mixen Lane is literally lawless.

The idea of the 'no-go' area, with its long history, has consider-able imaginative appeal for Hardy. These areas were traditional sanctuaries for those perceived by the authorities to be a source of threat – the destitute poor, beggars and vagrants. But these 'no-go' areas were also means of containment – the only form of control where the rule of law was either unenforceable or tacitly suspended. Such areas – 'suburbs' or 'rookeries' – were from mediaeval times beyond the reach of corporation authority. Indeed up to the eighteenth century the city 'fed harassed thieves into 'sanctuaries' which sometimes gave freedom from arrest'.[40] The early nineteenth-century city still had such sanctuaries, Angel Meadow, for one, 'the lowest, most filthy, most unhealthy and most wicked locality in Manchester', according to the *Morning Chronicle* of 1850,[41] or 'China' in Merthyr Tydfil, described in an 1847 report as 'a mere sink of thieves and prostitutes such as unhappily constitutes an appendage to every large town' and a 'Welsh Alsatia'.

The sanctuary of 'Alsatia' (like Alsace, debatable land) had originally been a precinct for law-breakers and debtors in Whitefriars in London. But as one observer recorded in 1860, 'the city of cadgers is not what it was ... the introduction of a police station in the immediate vicinity' changed the lawless character of this once notorious district: 'formerly its boundaries were lawless like Alsatia ... it was a refuge for the desperate, the thief, the cadger and the prostitute'.[42] Mayhew, in the 1860s, also noted St Giles and its decline over twenty years.[43] With a unified police force established in London by 1839, and county forces made obligatory in 1856, these areas of sanctuary were being steadily reduced.[44] As the metropolis developed so did its moral topography. According to Dyos and Reeder, the term 'slum', originally a room of low repute, was extended by Pierce Egan in 1821 to 'back slums' which now comprehended 'low, unfrequented parts of the town', and thence to 'everyday use'.[45] The massive schemes of slum clearance, involving elaborate road building programmes from the 1860s (many of them designed precisely to open up and destroy the rookeries) aggravated the slum problem, by driving the poor out to other areas of the city.[46]

But testimony from Charles Booth would suggest that in the London of the 1880s the 'sanctuary' was still a powerful, if more efficiently policed, presence. Among his class A (the lowest) there were those who resisted 'the efforts of philanthropy or order'. Their 'instinct of self-preservation seeks some undisturbed sanctuary where they can still herd together, and, secured by the mutual protection of each other's character for evil, keep respectability at bay'.[47] Allowing such a class to colonise a territory was to be avoided at all costs: 'no sooner do they make a street their own', says Booth, 'than it is ripe for destruction and should be destroyed'.[48]

The emotive potential of the 'Alsatia' is mobilised in a novel by Lucas Malet (Mary Kingsley, 1852–1931), *Colonel Enderby's Wife* (1885), which explores the disruptive effects of inherited degeneracy on an established county family. One scene describes the philanthropic Mrs Farrel venturing into the dangerous slum:

[She] took her way by back streets to a quarter of Tullingworth that lies across the river, along the low ground between the canal and a range of dreary brickfields. This region presented a marked contrast to the rest of the smart, pleasure-loving little town. It is a moral Alsatia, to which, by the law of social gravitation, all the human refuse of the place finds its melancholy way. Mean one-storied houses open on to narrow, black wharves and ugly cinder-paths, where bargemen and labourers loiter at dreary corners, and ragged shrill-voiced children angle for sluggish minnows in the slimy water, while the smoke and stench of the burning bricks fill the thick air. Dirty little shops maintain a feeble existence, with an attenuated show of attraction behind the panes of their dim windows. Only the public-house rises prosperous, cheerful, defiant above the dingy squalor of unpaved streets and lanes. Such places are altogether too common on the outskirts of even flourishing well-to-do places like Tullingworth for it to be incumbent on one to make much fuss over them.[49]

Here is a clearly demarcated setting out of social and moral space. It turns on a simple binary opposition, 'a marked contrast' between normative and 'other', between the 'smart pleasure-loving town', and a region of 'human refuse'. A standard figure of popular Darwinism, exploiting the language of fitness, informs the opposition. The 'dirty little shops' maintain a 'feeble existence', on the outskirts of the 'flourishing' town; only the morally questionable pub offers an ironic degenerate fitness. The promise of life and energy is everywhere foreshortened – the offerings of the shops 'attenuated', the minnows 'sluggish'.

But this vision of marked contrasts is equivocal, in that both the healthy and the diseased find their symbolic inversion. Just as the 'region' is degenerately fit, so the morally and socially normative

Tullingworth is made sick by its organic relationship with its degenerate suburb. Moreover the spatial relationship between the two is uncertain. At the opening of the description the danger posed by the *terra incognita* is strongly marked (as it has to be in the standard rite of passage of the urban explorer), the slum appears distant and separate from the town out of which Mrs Farrel walks. Yet by the end of the passage this region's proximity is foregrounded with the admission that such a parasitical relationship with prosperity is 'altogether too common'.

Hardy, too, is caught up in the contradictions offered by the idea of urban degeneration when he invokes a truly Spencerian organic image to describe Mixen Lane's relationship to the body of Caster-bridge. It is, he remarks, 'a mildewed leaf in the sturdy and flourishing Casterbridge plant' (278). The hold exerted by such organic tropes is tenacious indeed, and here rather leads Hardy astray, since the Casterbridge he actually renders offers a different way of seeing. Many of the denizens of Mixen Lane bear witness to the fact that Casterbridge does not flourish for everyone. This Spencerian Darwinism is caught napping by the clarity of his social vision, which pulls against the naturalistic determinism. For the passive, intransitive way in which the blighted are seen by this ideology is actually contested within the text itself: there is an alternative ethic available to Hardy, self-determining, anarchic and resistant to such naturalistic incorporation.

None the less the homologies between these descriptions from two novels, published within months of each other, are quite striking. In both we find the blighted leaf on the 'flourishing' town: an area morally tainted on the outskirts of a town on low ground, cut off here by a river. The river in *The Mayor* marks the dividing line (which the poacher has to cross between 'moor' and 'tenements') where the process of gravitation (we recall Hardy's river image in the 'Dorsetshire Labourer' essay) figures the economic and moral descent of 'human refuse', as if being swept down by, and further polluting, an already dirty stream.

As an image and repository of degeneracy, the polluted river has a central place in nineteenth-century writing about the city. In *The Condition of the Working Class* Engels had described the 'coal-black stinking' river Irk, 'full of filth and garbage' which it deposits on the 'lower-lying bank . . . out of whose depths bubbles of miasmatic gases constantly rise' to 'give forth a stench that is unbearable'. The river takes 'the total entirety of the liquid wastes from nearby tanneries, dye-works, bone mills and gasworks' together with contents of 'the adjacent sewers and privies'.[50]

Rivers, notes Anthony Wohl, were an 'easy solution' to the mounting problem of 'human and industrial filth' of this kind, which reformers saw as the major cause of death.[51] In Gissing's *Demos* (1886) the stinking Regent's canal which runs through north London *'maladetta e sventurata fossa* – stagnating in utter foulness',[52] marks a boundary (so important for the post-Darwinian city) between areas of respectability and of ill-repute: it divides the 'mean and spirit-broken leisure of dwelling houses' to the north, from the 'region of malodorous market streets ... factories, timber yards' to the south. Here the pavements are trodden by 'working folk of the coarsest type, the corners and lurking-holes showing destitution at its ugliest'.[53] Gissing's previous novel *A Life's Morning*, written the previous year, 1885 (but not published until 1888), offers a stream derived from 'an impure source' as one index of a pervasive blighted landscape – which is the more striking because it is rural heathland.[54] The dividing river cuts off the 'official' world of the authorial observer from the *terra incognita* in which the values of order, propriety and respectable morality are symbolically inverted, beyond the terms of civilisation, but not beyond its discourses of appropriation. The hideous fascination of the 'other' at the same time sustained the comfortable sense of civic virtue.

III

The threat from unofficial space in its symbolic configuration, imaged in terms of heights of a city terrorised by the depths, is recalled by the Victorian circus showman and celebrity 'Lord' George Sanger. As an old man he looked back to the 1840s to tell of a destructive raid on his father's circus troupe, camped on the heights of Lansdown outside the city of Bath, by a gang of roughs from 'Bull Paunch Alley, the lowest slum in the cathedral city, where no policeman ever dared to penetrate'. The gang is led by 'a red-headed virago, a dreadful giantess of a woman known as "Carroty Kate" ... a big brutal animal, caring nothing for magistrates or gaol' and long 'the terror of every respectable person in Bath'.[55] Despite his itinerant status as a member of a travelling circus, Sanger's view is from social as well as topographical high ground, confirmed by his encounter with low, 'outcast' Bath. In 'the lowest slum ... where no policeman ever dared to penetrate' is the rhetoric of social panic, constructing both the spectacle of society's lamplight and the dark purlieus beyond its reach.

In the narratives of Malet and Gissing outcast London remains, in Mearns' epithet, 'abject'. But in *The Mayor* the inhabitants of Mixen Lane, in their sly way, fight back; there is rebellion as well as contagion as their disruptive influence works back up to the official, public, high ground of the town. In Casterbridge this is first given shape in the spread of 'scandal': 'The ideas diffused by the reading of Lucetta's letters at Peter's Finger had condensed into a scandal, which was spreading like a miasmatic fog through Mixen Lane, and thence up the back streets of Casterbridge' (290). Casterbridge's residuum will act like Victor Hugo's 'ditch of truth' in *Les Misérables* (1861) which 'at times flowed back into the town giving Paris a taste of bile ... The town was angered by the audacity of its filth, and could not accept that its ordure should return.'[56] As Stallybrass and White suggest, 'Hugo imagines a social "return of the repressed" in terms of the city's topography.'[57] So does Hardy.

One of the things repressed in *The Mayor* is the past. It falls to the figure of the furmity woman, in court on a vagrancy charge, to reveal what Henchard has kept hidden, his participation in the illegal wife-sale. In helping to precipitate his fall from grace, she symbolically becomes a principal agent of retribution. And it is through active retribution – in the form of the skimmington ride – that Mixen Lane, to which she gravitates, will assert itself. The root of Mixen Lane's grudge is economic, and in the experience of the furmity woman Hardy condenses its causes.

Her decline is mirrored in the decline of the traditional fair, a reliable index of the economic health of the countryside. When Susan passes through Weydon-Priors with Elizabeth-Jane, eighteen years after she was sold there, she notices that it has lost its former vitality: 'The new periodical great markets of neighbouring towns were beginning to interfere seriously with the trade carried on here for centuries. The pens for sheep, the tie-ropes for horses, were about half as long as they had been' (53). The furmity woman now serves a markedly inferior brew to the 'nourishing' 'Good Furmity' which Susan and Henchard had gratefully consumed. When later Henchard revisits Weydon-Priors he finds that the fair has disappeared altogether.

Hardy's factual source for the decline of the fair which pauperises the furmity woman was a report from the *Dorset County Chronicle* of 15 October 1829, which he intended to stand as an index of deteriorating economic conditions in the Dorset of the late 1820s: '*Weyhill Fair* – By 12 o'c only 40 wagons had passed through Andover gate – in former abundant years, 400 have passed it by same hour.'[58] Such 'facts' (which include three wife-sales and countless examples of family tragedy, crime and 'rough justice') testify to a world penetrated by developments more usually associated with the growth of large cities: greater centralisation, more efficient law-enforcement and increasing accessibility (made possible in the late 1840s by the coming of the railway). Even when Hardy was a young man, the town of Dorchester was acquiring, in miniature, some of the characteristics of a large city. Merryn Williams points out that while the population of surrounding small towns and villages like Cerne Abbas fell in the period 1841–1901, the population of Dorchester rose steadily through the century, and especially in the parish of Fordington – the 'Durnover' of Casterbridge. After 1850 the town prospered, but it also attracted a growing population of paupers as did any city. Fordington was, Williams suggests, 'the nearest thing Dorset had to an industrial slum'.[59]

Hardy was driven to recreate the old, unregulated world, of which Henchard in *The Mayor* is the epitome. The years around the date of his birth, 1840, marked a watershed between this primitive culture and the world of his youth when social change was fast rendering that culture obsolete. This impoverished and disaffected underclass speaks directly to the 'outcast' London of the period of the novel's composition: Hardy's way of seeing Casterbridge is moulded both by this unassimilated, resistant culture and the language of contemporary commentators.

In a crucial sequence of chapters (36–9) official and unofficial Casterbridge intersect: the visit of a 'Royal Personage' to Casterbridge collides with the skimmington ride. It is a conjuncture which Laurence Lerner claims, quite unaccountably, 'sets off no ideological or class conflicts in Casterbridge'[60]. The reverse is true. Chapter 36 records how the love letters between Henchard and Lucetta, which Jopp has let fall into the hands of Mrs Cuxsom and the company of Peter's Finger, serve as the 'good foundation for a skimmity-ride' (264). In the next chapter Hardy describes the visit to Casterbridge by the 'Illustrious Personage', the unexpected climax of which is Henchard's Brechtian upstaging of the mayoral duty, which Farfrae, his vanquisher and rival, 'performs'. This precipitates their confrontation and physical struggle in the following chapter (38). Chapter 39 describes the skimmington ride itself, and its fatal consequences for Lucetta, its target.

The bizarre juxtaposition of the royal visit and the skimmington ride is seen by Mixen Lane as an opportunity for defiance not to be missed. Jopp voices the general feeling: 'as a wind-up to the Royal visit the hit will be all the more pat by reason of their great elevation today' (291). It is a piece of agitprop theatre which mimics the official play in which Lucetta, sitting at Farfrae's side as the mayor's wife, has a leading role, and to which Henchard's performance is the merest ironic counterpoint.[61] The ceremonious official 'play', with its echoes of the speeches at the *comices agricoles* in Flaubert's *Madame Bovary* (1857), attempts to involve the community of Casterbridge (not, though, the 'lowest social stratum', who hear of it by accident, rather than by design) in its ritualised display. The town Corporation thanks the 'Royal Personage' for his services to 'agricultural science and economics by his zealous designs for placing the art of farming on a more scientific footing' (285). What are those made jobless by such developments, we are encouraged to ask, to make of that?

The answer is the symbolic act of charivari.[62] Any pretended consent which the inhabitants of Mixen Lane might display, by their presence at the ceremony, is made laughable. The Corporation claim to speak for the whole community and are ridiculed for their pains, and the whole solemn show is reduced to farce. And the masque requires – and precipitates – its anti-masque. As law and order are reasserted, 'effigies, donkey, lanterns, band, all had disappeared like the crew of *Comus*' (304).

Of course the denizens of Mixen Lane represent the 'undeserving', not 'deserving' poor, the distinction affirmed in Booth's sociology.[63] Hardy gives us an image of this distinction (so necessary to Victorian philanthropy) in his characterisation of the clientele of the two inns – Peter's Finger, and higher (symbolically) up the High Street, the more respectable Three Mariners where Farfrae made his first favourable impression in Casterbridge.[64] The dispossessed residuum – Nance Mockridge, Mother Cuxsom and Charl (later drawing in Jopp and the furmity woman) – gather in the lower; in the higher the 'philosophic party' of small tradesmen, Longways,

Coney, Buzzford, Billy Wills. Hardy makes explicit both the difference and the possibility of slippage from one social category to the
other: 'the company at the Three Mariners were persons of quality
in comparison with the company which gathered here; though it
must be admitted that the lowest fringe of the Mariner's party
touched the crest of Peter's at points' (280).

The morning of the royal visit finds the clientele of the Three
Mariners displaying their respectable credentials: 'there was hardly
a workman in the town who did not put a clean shirt on'(286–7);
these drinkers 'showed their sense of occasion by advancing their
customary eleven o'clock pint to half-past ten' (287). Later that day,
once the full implications of the skimmington ride become clear,
Hardy calls on an explicitly Darwinian figure at the moment of
gathering social and moral crisis: 'this mixed assemblage of idlers . . .
[including Coney, Buzzford and Nance Mockridge] . . . fell apart
into two bands by a process of natural selection, the frequenters of
Peter's Finger going off Mixen-Lane-wards, where most of them
lived, while Coney, Buzzford, Longways and that connection
remained in the street' (290). And their next action, a worthy
attempt to mitigate the consequences for Lucetta of the skimmington ride by removing Farfrae from the scene of humiliation, sets
them even further apart from the unsentimental subversives of Mixen
Lane.

The clarity with which a social and cultural structure finds its
symbolic landscape is, to my mind, a major achievement of Hardy's
novel. The topography of Casterbridge, with its keenly observed
configurations, encodes the polarisations which incessantly inflect
writing about the late nineteenth-century city. Family distress and
degradation, class antagonism, fear, censoriousness were inscribed
in the demarcations of the town's social space. In the real Dorchester's Top of Town and low-lying Fordington there was a model to
hand. But unlike other contemporary writers on the urban poor,
Hardy cannot be relied upon to deliver these demarcations in
strictly degenerationist terms. Slipping in and out of contemporary
discourse, he is able to offer his outcast types the possibility of a
subversive, if crude, resistance to the terms of incorporation and
exile held out by the dominant social order. In this, as in all the
things that mattered to him, Hardy was his own man.

CHAPTER 4

Reversionary tactics

I

In Conrad's *Heart of Darkness* (1899/1902) Marlow opens up to his sceptical audience of crewmen the scandalous possibility of imperial man's kinship with the 'savage'.

No, they were not inhuman. Well you know, that was the worst of it – this suspicion of their not being inhuman. It would come slowly to one. They howled and leaped, and spun, and made horrid faces; but what thrilled you was just the thought of their humanity – like yours – the thought of your remote kinship with this wild and passionate uproar. Ugly. It was ugly enough; but if you were man enough you would admit to yourself that there was in you just the faintest trace of a response to the terrible frankness of that noise, a dim suspicion of there being a meaning in it which you – you so remote from the night of first ages – could comprehend.[1]

Rather than repress this affiliation in the interests of difference, power or fear, Conrad has Marlow offer atavism as a constituent part of a common heritage and a common experience. It is an insight which marks a decisive shift away from the hierarchical assumptions which late nineteenth-century positivism underpinned and which issued in imperialist conquest and suppression. It marks a step on the road of modernist reaction when writers from Lawrence to Jung would embrace the 'primitive' as a necessary constituent of a libertarian view of the modern psyche.

A generation later, D. H. Lawrence would invoke the 'strange dark continent' of the self in what is, in effect, a retrospective acknowledgement of Conrad's creative singularity, in his time, in facing the relationship between the civilised self and the 'other':

The *cause* in man is something we shall never fathom. But there it is, a strange dark continent that we do not explore, because we do not even allow it exists. Yet all the time, it is within us: the *cause* of us, and of our days.

And our feelings are the first manifestations within the aboriginal jungle of us. Till now, in sheer terror of ourselves, we have turned our backs on the jungle, fenced it in with an enormous entanglement of barbed wire and declared it did not exist ...

Yet unless we proceed to connect ourselves up with our own primeval sources, we shall degenerate.[2]

William Morris's anti-capitalist utopianism was another reaction to the hegemony assumed by western civilisation. He invoked a radical barbarism: 'how often it consoles me to think of barbarism once more flooding the world, and real feelings and passions, however rudimentary, taking the place of our wretched hypocrisies'.[3] 'Civilisation' and 'barbarism' were terms which he always employed with ironic inversion, drawing, in part, upon the inheritance from Carlyle and Ruskin, and his commitment to mediaeval, pre-capitalist modes of life. To 'become barbarians' alarmed Morris not at all. 'Civilisation' (he wrote to Georgie Burne Jones in May 1885) 'I *know* now is doomed to destruction.'[4]

In *Civilisation; Its Cause and Cure* (1889) the socialist, Edward Carpenter, effects an ironic reversal of the civilisation-barbarism couple: it was a vision which entailed an acceptance of primitivism in the manner of Thoreau. By using the language of the degenerationists, Carpenter apes their manner, as he undermines their assumptions. Civilisation 'founded' on 'property' produces a corruption which duly causes mankind to '*break up*' the 'unity' of their 'nature':

He deliberately turns his back upon the light of the sun, and hides himself away in boxes with breathing holes (which he calls houses), living ever more and more in darkness and asphyxia, and only coming forth perhaps once a day to blink at the bright god ... he ceases to a great extent to use his muscles, his feet become partially degenerate, his teeth wholly, his digestion so enervated that he has to cook his food and make pulps of all his victuals, and his whole system so obviously on the decline ... And so with this denial of Nature comes every form of disease; first delicateness, daintiness, luxury; then unbalance, enervation ... [5]

The stunted denizen of the dark is a familiar figure in the polemics of urban degeneration, but whereas, conventionally, it is the urban working class who are marked out, Carpenter here extends the image to civilised society as a whole. Man deteriorates because he is cut off from primitive conditions, but unlike the primitive imperialists, with their anti-urban fantasies, Carpenter resurrects a struggle for existence not in competition with other men, cultures or states, but with nature. His holistic and anti-capitalist simple-life culture witnesses an attempt to redraw the map of civilised life. This cultivation of simplicity and barbarism is specifically a counter to what was seen as the corpulent, stuffy degeneracy of a complacent civilisation.

As late as 1931 Jung was having to rebut the assumption that the primitive was regrettable evidence of degenerate reversion – a state to be feared rather than embraced. He accepted the 'archaic' in man's psyche, and so rejected the scientific positivism which had designated reversion as an anomalous state: 'It is not only primitive man where psychology is archaic. It is the psychology also of modern, civilized man, and not merely of individual "throw-backs" in modern society. On the contrary, every civilized human being, however high his conscious developement, is still an archaic man at the deeper level of his psyche . . .'[6]

II

In 1885, the physician and visiting Medical Officer to the York Retreat, Daniel Hack Tuke, wrote of a patient: 'Such a man as this is a reversion to an old savage type, and is born by accident in the wrong century. He would have had suffcent scope for his bloodthirsty propensities, and been in harmony with his environment, in a barbaric age, or at the present day in certain parts of Africa.'[7]

This is the utterance of a distinguished man of medical science, a specialist reporting to other specialists on a case. If the defect of his patient is, as the title of the paper claims, 'moral', it is also 'congenital': medical science is the assumed privileged area of this discourse. Yet, in 'an old savage type', 'a barbaric age', 'certain parts of Africa' – phrases which make for a kind of eloquence – we hear something else: the note of a powerful discourse of reversion and atavism, part of a loose assemblage of post-Darwinian beliefs, which in degenerationism will find a resilient ideology for at least half a century. With this and more in the pages of the *Journal of Mental Science*, it would be possible to foresee how reversion could make its way from a mental hospital in York to the public sphere, accruing a rhetorical force as it went. The heart of darkness is already coming into view.

Darwin had drawn attention to reversion as an element of the vexed question of inheritance – how species received and passed on characteristics from and to each other. Drawing on data about the breeding of both plants and animals, he observed in *The Variation of Plants and Animals Under Domestication* (1868), that reversion usually occured either when an uncrossed species had lost, through variation, characters it had formerly possessed, or, more dramatically, when a species had 'at a former time been crossed with a distinct form, and a character derived from this cross ... often having disappeared during one or several generations, suddenly reappears'.[8] In *The Descent of Man* (1871), he observed cases among men of 'arrested development' which he first distinguishes from reversion, but then notes that the arrested structure can continue to grow 'until it closely resembles a corresponding structure in some lower and adult member of the same group'.[9] So that 'it may in one sense be considered as a case of reversion'. In endorsing research which found 'muscular variations' in certain men which clearly resembled 'muscles proper to various kinds of apes',[10] Darwin lends his support to the idea that these anomalous survivals shows that an 'unknown factor' is operating in the evolution of man, a 'reversion to a former state of existence'.[11]

Darwin's evident tentativeness with regard to shared characteristics of higher and lower species is evinced in a reluctance, not shared by many of his popularisers, to stray beyond analogy. Did the resemblance of one structure to another necessarily show that evolutionary development was being thrown into reverse; what was implied by drawing analogies between plants, lower-order organisms and man himself? Those who most vigorously put forward one proposition habitually deployed the other, contending that the survival of anomalous characteristics signalled a sudden onset of degeneration.

Various current biological explanations were available, such as the theory of recapitulation, to explain anomalous characteristics in mankind. In Arthur Conan Doyle's 'The Adventure of the Empty House' (1903), Sherlock Holmes lectures Doctor Watson on the theory of recapitulation, claiming it, wholly improbably, as his own. Here he explains how it serves to account for the deviant and his propensity to crime:

There are some trees, Watson, which grow to a certain height and then suddenly develop some unsightly eccentricity. You will see it often in humans. I have a theory that the individual represents in his development the whole procession of his ancestors, and that such a sudden turn to good or evil stands for some influence which came into the line of his pedigree. The person becomes, as it were, the epitome of the history of his own pedigree.[12]

The person in question is an Oxford-educated, game-hunting Colonel who has 'gone wrong' (581). He is now 'the second most dangerous man in London' (580). Recapitulation (*pace* Holmes) was a biogenetic idea associated primarily with the German biologist, Ernst Haeckel. In his *General Morphology of Organisms* (1866), he had suggested that the life-history of a species member – the ontogeny – recapitulated the phases of the whole evolutionary development of that species – the phylogeny.[13] Recapitulation enabled, say, a case of arrested brain development in the insane to be categorised as an instance of incomplete transition from a lower to a higher evolutionary state. Although it is not possible to divine this from Doyle's Holmes, recapitulation had become a pathological and psychiatric commonplace by the 1870s. 'When we reflect', wrote Henry Maudsley magisterially,

that every human brain does, in the course of its development, pass through the same stages as the brains of other vertebrate animals, and that its transitional states resemble the permanent forms of their brains ... [and] ... that the stages of its development in the womb may be considered the abstract and brief chronicle of a series of developments that have gone through countless ages in nature, it does not seem so wonderful ... that it should, when in a condition of arrested development, sometimes display animal instinct.[14]

Recapitulation offered a plausible explanation for defective structure, in terms of incompletion and insufficiency, and had immense appeal for a scientific culture which prized biological success and feared the unknown consequences of failure. Furthermore, by placing the evolution of a particular structure in such a clear micro-macro relationship with the whole history of evolution itself, recapitulation could permit a quite cavalier traffic of association between any biological structure belonging to any species of any kind. By this theory it was a small step from lower-order species to man himself, and to a view of the human animal, prompted by an organicist obsession with structure.

The obvious example of human incompletion is the child, who is, wrote Havelock Ellis, 'naturally, by his organisation, nearer to the animal, to the savage, to the criminal, than the adult'.[15] The child and the criminal (and their perceived fusion in the figure of the homosexual) were aligned together at a low point on the two-tier scale of ontogeny and phylogeny, marking a kind of evolutionary under-achievement from which the criminal could not recover. But recapitulation offered a neat circularity. Those who were beyond civilisation's help, for whom nothing or little could be done, were cast beyond its reach because of the limitations of their biological organisation. A criminal or an idiot lived out, as if in a vast and unpenetrated silence, a permanently estranged relationship to his civilisation – a piece of jetsam in an evolutionary sea, without moorings or direction. Not for nothing did the Marquess of Queensbury, at the height of his battle with Wilde, send to his daughter-in-law, Lady Douglas, an illustration of an iguanodon, with its leadenly-offensive note: 'Perhaps an ancestor of Oscar Wilde.'

'The step-children of nature' was Maudsley's telling familial metaphor for these human anomalies which suffered 'the tyranny of bad organization'.[16] For pathologists like Tuke and himself, the abnormal type would always be placed outside and away from the family – that acceptable agency of mediation between nature and civilisation. For the scientific naturalists the synchrony between 'nature' and 'civilisation' was so total – allowing for so little in the way of cultural determinants – that recapitulation could, on occasion, obliterate ludicrously all other differences in the interests of an all-comprehending biologism. Ellis fell into this trap in 1894 when he sought to position man on the axes of 'verticality' and 'horizontality'. Whilst apes are 'imperfect bipeds with tendencies towards the quadrupedal attitude', the 'human infant' is 'as imperfect a biped as the ape; savage races do not stand as erect as civilised races. Country people ... tend to bend forward, and the aristocrat is more erect than the plebeian. In this respect the women appear to be nearer to the infantile condition than men.'[17] Apes, infants, savage races, country people, plebeians and women are all to be seen fumbling in some evolutionary egg-and-spoon race, yards from the finishing-tape.

But the wider cultural meaning of reversion cannot be attributed alone to the prestige enjoyed by the practitioners of positivism and psychiatric Darwinism. Reversion was a constituent of a troubling myth about origins. For many Victorians the point about evolution was not, as Darwin perceived it to be (in Gillian Beer's words), 'the restoration of familial ties, the discovery of a lost inheritance',[18] but

2 'Prehistoric Iguanodon' an engraving by Alice B. Woodward, sent by The Marquess of Queensberry to his daughter-in-law, Lady Douglas, 1895.

its confirmation both of mankind's separateness from the beast and its sovereignty over it, expressed in triumphalist narratives of development.[19] An atavistic survival, a 'throwback' or the 'upcropping' of a savage 'sport' in the midst of what was deemed to be a highly evolved civilisation might be rationalised as the inevitable fall-out in the struggle for existence, with its accompanying discursive strategies. Still for the late Victorians such a discovery could be a source of shock and scandal.

The shock lay in the intensified awareness of the contiguity of barbaric or lower-order species with the civilisation which had assumed an unquestioning 'natural' hegemony over them. If, by some quirk of the evolutionary process, an uncalled-for deviant variety could co-exist with the planet's most developed species, then, in spite of optimistic voices such as Herbert Spencer's, the teleology of that prized alliance of evolution with necessary progress might be badly shaken. This was the basis of the pessimistic and scandalous biological poetics of Wells's essays and fictions of the nineties. What was shaken was a sense of control: racial, political, psychological, social, sexual. The deviant type mediated, in various ways, these anxieties about control in which, as Sander Gilman has argued, conflict between self and 'other' was central:

When the sense of order or control undergoes stress, when doubt is cast on the self's ability to control the internalized world it has created for itself, an anxiety appears ... we project that anxiety onto the Other, externalizing our loss of control. The Other is thus stereotyped, labelled, with a set of signs paralleling (or mirroring) our loss of control.[20]

III

It was a conflict which was frequently represented in writing by the figure of the 'secret sharer' or 'double' which inhabited, obsessed or preyed upon the human subject.[21] The doubled or mirrored identity, where subject and 'other' are brought into troubling relationship, proliferated in the literature of the period: we need only think of Holmes and Moriarty, Van Helsing and Dracula, Marlow and Kurtz, Heyst and Jones. And the idea of two identities inhabiting the single subject, Jekyll and Hyde, stands as a commanding figure of the divided self.

The secret sharer was emblematically figured for a post-Darwinian culture as the beast in man. Fear of the hidden presence

of a 'monstrous' and disruptive energy was experienced and articulated as the surrendering to that influence. Age-old hierarchies,
which had assumed unquestioned relations of authority and subordination – civilised and brutish, higher and lower, mind and body,
reason and instinct – were under pressure as never before. The fear
of atavism, of reversion to a lower state, offered the perfect medium
for the expression of these worrying questions. Peter Brooker and
Peter Widdowson suggest that fear of reversion is an important
component in the threat to 'the wholeness of the civilised subject
which come from below the waist of prohibitive morality'. The
'unease these fictions register', they suggest, 'stems from encounters
with a dangerously internalised "other", whether sexual, racial,
criminal or supernatural in aspect; provoking thus a fear of reversion
to some lower point on the psychic or social or evolutionary
scale'.[22]

Reversion offered the writer a rich field of sensational subjects and
effects, particularly in the revelation and discovery of new, hitherto
unrecognised, feelings or affiliations. The recognition of kinship with
the degenerate 'other' fitted well with long-established conventions
of melodrama. Unlikely as it may seem, Henry Maudsley drew on
such tropes of melodramatic revelation when he explained how the
civilised subject might coexist with a 'throwback' who is

caught momentarily as a transient gleam, unfamiliar and unexpected, on
particular emotional occasions that stir the being to its depths. Now and
then a person may detect in his own face in the looking-glass a momentary
flash of expression of the sort which he will find formal in the portrait of an
ancestor or perhaps of some living relative, near or remote. In the same
way silent memories of strange feeling shall startle and move him. Beneath
every face are the latent faces of ancestors, beneath every character their
characters.[23]

The unmasking of vice beneath the hitherto civilised surface, or the
moment of glimpse, glance or gaze, by a witness to it, drew on a
poetics with a long history, but it was now envigorated with the
spectacle of the devolutionary and degenerating self. The shock of
recognition, or anagnorisis, delivers, according to Terence Cave,
both the 'recovery of knowledge' and the 'disquieting sense, when
the trap is sprung, that the commonly accepted co-ordinates of
knowledge have gone awry'.[24]

Writers responded to the typology of reversion because they could
have it both ways: it offered to place the 'other' in a reassuring

framework of scientific authority, while exploring the uncontrollable and transgressive, in encounters betwen the subject and 'other'.
Gissing, Stevenson, Wilde, Doyle, Conrad and H. G. Wells all
explored the scandalous possibilities of new affiliations and new
objects of knowledge in fictions in which a poetics of recognition
formed a key writerly tactic.[25] Stevenson's *The Strange Case of Dr
Jekyll and Mr Hyde* (1886) exploits the indeterminate relationship
between subject and threatening 'other', by showing how fatally
that relationship might be inverted. And a 'scientific' fable, such as
Wells's *The Island of Dr Moreau* (1896), explores the sensational
possibilities of reversion by annihilating the dividing line separating
man and beast through the empowering hubris of vivisection. An
ambitious fiction like Conrad's *Heart of Darkness* and a popular story
like Conan Doyle's *The Hound of the Baskervilles* (1902) ('a surprisingly comparable story')[26] both explore the boundaries between
knowledge of the familiar and the unknown, the conventional and
the transgressive.

In *The Hound of the Baskervilles*, the task of taming the criminal and
atavistic 'other' for civilisation tests the legendary omniscience of the
detective 'to the limit. Sherlock Holmes is up against the cunning of
Stapleton who adopts, for those who wander on to the asocial,
'natural' terrain of the moor, the pose of artless butterfly collector.
Stapleton's monstrous hound acts out his master's hidden criminality. Holmes must in turn disguise himself as a primitive hut-
dweller[27] in order to meet, in defense of civilised society, the threat
of Stapleton's atavism. Stapleton eventually sinks into the primeval
Grimpen Mire into which he has hoped to lure others; he is 'mired in
his own past' to use a phrase of Lombroso's to describe the incom-
pletely recapitulated criminal type.[28]

Holmes's competing intelligence prevents a crime, but on this
occasion cannot bring the miscreant before the bar of society:
civilisation has not managed to assert itself against the threat of
barbarism. By drowning in the Mire, Stapleton works out the
consequences of his own reversion. Self-regulating nature is the best
that can be hoped for. This is not a case that Holmes can fully claim
to have won.

While the escaped convict Selden is offered as a true atavism,
Stapleton, on the other hand, recapitulates the criminality of an
ancestor. He is not a 'primitive', but the higher type 'gone wrong',
with the status of master criminal. From the nineties writers were

prompted by a new interest in a causal relationship between criminality and 'genius' which was given currency by the criminal anthropology of Lombroso and his school. Increasingly the idea of reversion would be used to explore the predicament of men of secure social standing – the dubious flowers of a decadent civilisation.

While Doyle's narratives simply enact the processes of control, by maintaining the authority of the subject in the face of the threatening 'other', a more speculative writer like Conrad questions whether such a normative authority for bringing the 'other' to book, could be defended in the name of the civilisation for which it offered to speak. Such writers explicly confronted the complacent alliance of evolutionary theory and the belief in the ever upward progress of mankind.

IV

Our civilization is nothing but a thin film or crust lying over a
volcanic pit.
(William Hale White, *Mark Rutherford's Deliverance*, 1885)[29]

The Savage of Civilisation whom we are raising by the
hundred thousand in our slums is quite capable of bathing
his hands in blood as any Sioux who ever scalped a foe.
(*Pall Mall Gazette* 8 September 1888)[30]

More intensively than most of his major contemporaries, and more than might have been expected of a major novelist, George Gissing embraced the potentialities of evolutionary discourse of his day. Medical and social science sharpened his perception of the malfunctioning of men and women in a social order about which he was deeply ambivalent. But, like other fiction writers of the 1880s, he also felt the attraction of the exciting, dangerous – even erotic – stereotypes of atavism and reversion.

In Clem Peckover, in his novel *The Nether World* (1889), he creates a degenerate figure from current discourses of class and gender in an exercise in literary naturalism. The name is obviously emblematic of a hierarchical 'pecking' order among the working class, where to survive means pecking before being pecked.[31] Yet while Gissing finds in Clem's barbarism an extreme image of the social reality of hand-to-mouth existence, she is not by any means representative of a social formation.

For Clem's atavism is a function of her deviation from conventional womanhood. She is explicitly presented as a variation on the biological norm. She has 'masculine' and explicitly erotic features: 'her forehead was low and of great width; her nose was well shapen, and had large sensual apertures'.[32] Later she is described as 'in the prime of her ferocious beauty ... her shoulders spread like those of a caryatid; her arm with which she props her head is strong as a carter's and magnificently moulded. The head itself looks immense with its pile of glossy hair' (120). An inversion of the ideal type of late Victorian woman, she transgresses the feminine. 'Cruel', 'fierce', 'crafty', she is a sexual hybrid, a blend of 'female' and 'male' characteristics which recalls Darwin in *Variations*: animality is not a purely feminine or masculine trait, but is accompanied by secondary sexual characters which 'exist in a latent state ready to be evolved under certain conditions'. Darwin uses the example of the hen 'which had ceased laying, and had assumed the plumage, voice, spurs and warlike disposition of the cock; when opposed to an enemy she would erect her hackles and show fight'.[33] Clem's 'warlike disposition' is certainly on display in the mock-heroic Bank Holiday scene where fierce sexual competition precipitates violence. Pennyloaf, her rival, is the first to display her 'erected nails'. But Clem responds effectively: 'in an instant she had rent half Pennyloaf's garments off her back, and was tearing her face till the blood streamed' (112).

While other tags of barbarism apply to Clem (she is literally lawless – beyond civilisation, which 'could bring no charge against this young woman; it and she had no common criterion' (6)) within the sunless 'nether world' she is figured as a peculiar strain of stunted plant: 'a rank, evilly-fostered growth'. Gissing comments that 'the putrid soil of that nether world yields other forms besides the obviously blighted and sapless' (8). Clem is a living hybrid; she is both diseased *and* fit, repellent and attractive, an ambivalent and transgressive figure. Gissing knew about female violence at first hand; it both intrigued and appalled him. He found little difficulty in admitting it into his fictional world, committed realist that he was, but the deterministic codes of reversion offered him a diagnostic language with which to channel his disgust and by which he could objectify the phenomenon.

A run of fictions through the 1880s channelled the social and political unease felt by a middle-class readership. The contaminating

3 'Among the Savages' from J. F. Sullivan, *The British Working Man*, 1887.

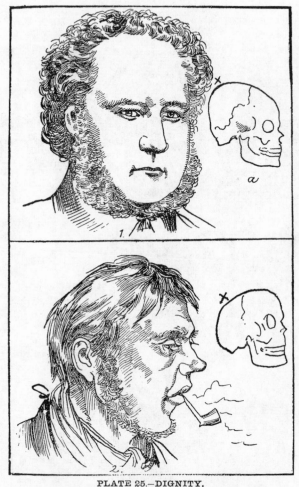

PLATE 25.—DIGNITY.
Large—Rev. Joseph Parker, D.D.   Small—A street loafer without self-respect.
Figs. a and *b* represent the difference in outline of the heads of a dignified and
undignified character.

4   'Dignity' from Gustav Cohen, *Modern Self-Instructor in Phrenology, Physiology and
Physiognomy: or the People's Handbook of Human Nature*, 1884.

slum product, Slimy, of Gissing's early novel *The Unclassed*
(1884), has been encountered in the previous chapter. Although he
is a grotesquely stark emblem of the threatening residuum, Gissing
endows him with a kind of biological authenticity, derived from
reversionary discourse (T. H. Huxley acknowledged the phenom-

enon as 'notorious', not 'mythic').[34] But Slimy's physiognomy is not only figurative; it is literally the physical manifestation of atavism, calculated to induce terror in the visitor from the other parts and zones of the city. 'Sensory and bodily signifiers', as Gill Davies has suggested, 'are very powerful elements in the discursive making of the English working-class.'[35] This East End Polyphemus is a source of generalised panic. On revising the novel in 1895, Gissing watered down some of the more sensational details of polluting animality; he excised examples of the impersonal pronoun 'it' for 'him', and deleted the following passage from the 1884 edition: 'its clothing, if the word can be used, was a huddled mass of vilest rags. Its presence was pollution to all the senses; the air grew foul around it, as it breathed with the heavy snorting of a beast.'[36]

I have already described how the slum enclave, cut off from the 'civilised' face of the city, constituted a powerful influence in the construction of an 'outcast London' of the 1880s. In *The Unclassed* these enclaves are peopled not merely by the poor, but by the biologically inadequate and pathologically abnormal. A deleted passage from the 1884 edition shows, in a small detail, Gissing's interest at this time in the psychological and topographical border-land.[37] The barmaid of the pub is a girl 'whose look suggested feeble-mindedness, if not idiocy. She smiled constantly in a vacant manner, and moved her head about fantastically.'[38] A further deleted extract has Harriet Smales, the egoistic wife of the sensitive but hapless Julian Casti, suffer a convulsive fit while drinking at the pub. Gissing has graphically created a townscape with deviants, mental inadequates and biological sports.

What Gissing's later revisions pointed up is the sensational realism of the 1884 edition. He may have thought that he had applied the squalor too thickly: by the mid-nineties perhaps it was no longer so appropriate. With London still his subject, Gissing clearly was feeling the gravitational pull of the West End. His female emblems of degeneracy were likewise going across town and up-market. Each edition of *The Unclassed* is very much of its time.[39]

It would be difficult to find a novel of these years more explicitly committed to ideas of reversion than *Demos* (1886), Gissing's most propagandist work. As Adrian Poole suggests, this text is an 'overt parable about the moral and cultural incapacity of the working class to use power for anything other than selfish ends'.[40] Gissing was writing at a time of mounting middle-class anxiety about working-

5 '"Here They Come!" – The Mob in St James's Street' (London), *The Graphic*, 13 February 1886.

class insurrection. Engels wrote optimistically in November 1886 that 'we can almost calculate the moment when the unemployed, losing all patience, will take their own fate into their own hands'.[41] Gissing's response was to deploy biological determinism to discredit working-class aspiration.

This was scarcely a new tactic. In the wake of the Paris Commune of 1871, Walter Bagehot linked atavism with social revolution.

Such scenes of cruelty and horror as happened in the French Revolution and has happened more or less in any great riot, have always been said to bring out a secret and repressed side of human nature. And now we see that they were the outbreak of inherited passions long repressed by fixed custom but starting into life as soon as that repression was catastrophically removed.[42]

'Have you ever looked into the faces of an East End mob? Have you ever realized what an appalling sight they are?', asked W. H. Mallock's Mrs Harley in *The Old Order Changes* (1886). She reports the view of the French Ambassador that 'England ... [is] ... in a most critical and dangerous condition, and that the savage and sullen spirit fermenting throughout the country now is just what there was in Paris before the great Revolution.'[43]

In *Demos* Gissing demonstrates the impossibility of class mobility through the personal inadequacies of the socialist artisan, Richard Mutimer. By fabricating an experiment in social transition he delivers for the reader a predetermined result. At first Mutimer is a heroic figure of radical energy; he seems fitted to lead an Owenite experiment in enlightened industrial organisation. Fortune endows him with wealth and power. But the hero and the heroic plan are ruthlessly undermined as is his political idealism. The privileged world of his wife, Adela, emerges morally enhanced through Gissing's insistent comparison of her integrity with Mutimer's innate brutality. What is at work here is not simply the convention of proletarian boorishness, but an ideological assumption which makes coarseness of feature and behaviour a 'natural' function of class origins.

By exposing Mutimer to the determinants of an inherited taint, Gissing gives us, in effect, a case study of biological degeneracy. Here we have, as Rod Edmonds has shown, a striking instance of how biological determinism could be turned to ideological advantage.[44] At first Gissing conceals this determinism, by endowing

Mutimer with the potential for moving on and up – for adaptation. This is the 'natural' outcome of his hybrid inheritance:

Richard represented – too favourably to make him anything but an exception – the best qualities his class can show. He was the English artisan as we find him on rare occasions, the issue of a good strain which has managed to procure a sufficiency of food for two or three generations. His physique was admirable; little short of six feet in stature, he had shapely shoulders, an erect well-formed head, clean strong limbs, and a bearing which in natural ease and dignity matched that of the picked men of the upper class.[45]

Insistently, physical qualities denote 'pedigree'. The 'lower order' class (physically as well as socially) in which Mutimer is an 'exception', is represented by his friend, Daniel Dabbs: 'the proletarian pure and simple. He was thick-set, square shouldered . . . a man of immense strength, but bull-necked and altogether ungainly – his heavy fist, with its black veins and terrific knuckles, suggested primitive methods of settling dispute'(34). That hand is an index of a primitive type, rather than of what we might anticipate from a 'proletarian' – his manual labour. The 'bull' neck, according to Mary Cowling, is conventional physiognomatic shorthand for at best 'stolidity, tenacity and strength of purpose' but at worst 'ruthlessness and a tendency to violence'.[46] Dabbs, as it turns out, is morally the better man.[47] But Gissing needs to commend Mutimer early on since he must deserve the respect of his fellow London socialists. In the event Mutimer fails the test Gissing sets; his nature is against him. And his defective personality is uncovered layer by layer to reveal the degenerate bedrock of his class.

His reversion to type is strikingly staged in two set-piece scenes, both of which aspire to that melodramatic intensity which accompanies the spectacle of uncompromising scandal which reversion precipitates. Mutimer's dissolute nature reveals itself in drunken sexual desire:

He turned, propped himself against the dressing table, and gazed at her with terribly lack-lustre eyes. Then she saw the expression on his face change; there came upon it a smile such as she had never seen or imagined, a hideous smile that made her blood cold. Without speaking, he threw himself forward and came towards her. For an instant she was powerless, paralysed with terror; but happily she found utterance for a cry, and that released her limbs. (285)

What seems to concern Gissing most 'about this unholy alliance', as John Lucas has observed, 'is the possibility of miscegenation'.[48] At the site of marital intimacy, working-class male sexuality is figured as a source of pollution. Gissing draws on sensational clichés to theatricalise Mutimer's metamorphosis into barbarism: from 'lacklustre' to the lust-filled 'hideous smile' (connoting the unspeakable presence of sexual desire), exposing the baseness which is his 'nature'. The lineaments of his degeneracy are perceived through the eyes of Adela, emphatically the normative touchstone of sympathetic integrity in the novel. In a scene during a train journey, she glances across the carriage at her sleeping husband:

His lips were sullenly loose beneath the thick reddish moustache; his eyebrows had drawn themselves together, scowling. She could not avert her gaze; it seemed to her that she was really scrutinising his face for the first time, and that it was as that of a stranger. Not one detail had the stamp of familiarity: the whole repelled her. What was the meaning now first revealed to her in that countenance? The features had a massive regularity; yet . . . she felt that a whole world of natural antipathies was between it and her. It was the face of a man by birth and breeding altogether beneath her. (349–50)

Gissing's uncritical endorsement of the naturalistic correlation of physical and moral characteristics is striking. Through Adela's scrutiny of his face, class difference is translated into 'a whole world of natural antipathies'. For a moment the passage registers the activity of Mutimer's alien force, in the frisson of his wife's recognition of her husband as 'other' – as 'stranger'. But in this passage his otherness is inscribed, not in his metamorphosis into beast, but in the buried contours of that 'countenance' which are thrown into relief in a state of sleep, beneath the control of consciousness. Mutimer's reversion to type is all too clear. A deeply conservative ideology dissolves differences of class into 'blood', 'breeding' and 'natural antipathies'.

R. L. Stevenson's *The Strange Case of Dr Jekyll and Mr Hyde* was published only three months before *Demos* appeared, in December 1885. It gives direct access, unlike the realist fiction of the period, to a radical uncertainty about the notion of a unitary identity, and to a perplexing coexistence of competing psychic and bodily states – the 'multifarious, incongruous and independent citizens' which, according to Henry Jekyll, will henceforward comprise the 'polity' of mankind.[49] The trope of metamorphosis, drawn both from ancient sources and from evolutionary science, is, in this fiction, a literal practice:

He put the glass to his lips, and drank at one gulp. A cry followed: he reeled, staggered, clutched at the table and held on, staring with injected eyes, gasping with open mouth: and as I looked, there came, I thought a change – he seemed to swell – his face became suddenly black, and the features seemed to melt and alter – and the next moment I had sprung to my feet and leaped back against the wall ... my mind submerged with terror.[50]

Stevenson gives a developed somatic form to the process of the dissolution of Jekyll's identity and the emergence of a hidden identity or 'double' – Hyde – which is congruous with the transformation of Mutimer in Gissing's novel from civilised to brute: in each case the recognition (by the normative Lanyon and Adela) is of a physical metamorphosis, marking a trangression across the boundaries (established by physical and psychic identity and by breeding), which induces terror and repulsion in the observer. Another such moment of recognition, where Utterson and Enfield glimpse the Hyde in Jekyll at the window, offers further parallels with Gissing:

... the words were hardly uttered, before the smile was struck out of his face and succeeded by an expression of such abject terror and despair, as froze the very blood of the two gentlemen below. They saw it but for a glimpse, for the window was instantly thrust down; but that glimpse had been sufficient, and they turned and left the court without a word.[51]

Jekyll's smile gives way to 'terror', Mutimer's 'lack-lustre' expression transmutes to a 'hideous smile'; the blood of the gentlemen freezes, and Adela's goes 'cold'.

Gothic narrative, as David Punter has suggested, is more than usually eloquent about the unspeakable: here it is the fear of evolutionary reversion which resides in that silent recognition ('without a word'), that an English professional man – the epitome of civilised development – should harbour within himself the type of lower animal which he has supposedly superseded.[52] *Jekyll and Hyde* provided a timely myth. Along with other typologies of reversion, such as those in Gissing's fictions, it helped to coalesce into the moral and class panics of the later 1880s.

The murder of six prostitutes in London's East End in 1888 found the atavistic 'man-beast' assimilated to monstrous 'sex-beast'. The typology of reversion explicitly shaped contemporary accounts of the 'Ripper' murders through the convention of a hidden bestial identity, established by Stevenson's fiction. Indeed, a play, based on the story, happened to have been staged in London at the height of the crisis.[53] The untraceable murders in Stevenson's narrative, solved, as it were, by our recognition of Jekyll's criminal 'other', Hyde, helped to give the fiction a peculiarly prescient resonance. What could be solved in fiction could not, as it turned out, be solved in fact.

Yet everyone had a solution to the unfolding murder story; everyone required a culprit. The *Pall Mall Gazette* argued (in what could only be interpreted as a rebuke to the arguments of libertarian socialists and anarchists) that mankind had proved that it had not outgrown the need for the apparatus of restraint, and drew explicitly on Stevenson's myth to target its readership of Henry Jekylls: 'This renewed reminder of the potentialities of revolting barbarity which lie latent in man will administer a salutory shock to the complacent optimism which assumes that the progress of civilisation has rendered unnecessary the bolts and bars, social, moral, and legal, which keep the Mr Hyde of humanity from assuming visible shape among us.' 'There seems to be a tolerably realistic impersonation of Mr Hyde at large in Whitechapel'[54], the *Gazette* journalist concluded, with an unmistakable glance at that other 'impersonation' in town – at the Lyceum.

That 'salutory shock', which the writer was keen to see administered by the shocking revelations of the murders, is very much in the conservative-radical spirit of Conrad's deconstruction of civilised complacency in *Heart of Darkness*. After all, it is Marlow who needs to remind his crewmates that the 'bolts and bars' on barbarism, not available in the Congo, are the unspoken institutional witnesses to man's lack of progress: 'You can't understand. How could you? – with solid pavement under your feet, surrounded by kind neighbours ready to cheer you or to fall on you, stepping delicately between the butcher and the policeman, in the holy terror of scandal and gallows and lunatic asylums.'[55] The forms which the Ripper took in the public imagination, the Hydes of late Victorian society, constituted the projections of such internalised terrors – anarchists, Jewish immigrants, artists; or, more subtly perhaps, the cohabiting Jekylls – top physicians, aristocrats or even members of the royal family.

The anomalous deviant, the internalised and repressed 'other',

THE NEMESIS OF NEGLECT.

"THERE FLOATS A PHANTOM ON THE SLUM'S FOUL AIR,
    SHAPING, TO EYES WHICH HAVE THE GIFT OF SEEING,
INTO THE SPECTRE OF THAT LOATHLY LAIR.
    FACE IT—FOR VAIN IS FLEEING!
RED-HANDED, RUTHLESS, FURTIVE, UNERECT,
'TIS MURDEROUS CRIME—THE NEMESIS OF NEGLECT!"

6   'The Nemesis of Neglect', *Punch*, 29 September 1888.

was daily paraded in the national press, as a subhuman beast. Even socially concerned sensationalism could not avoid the pathological trap. The intention of a notorious *Punch* cartoon (29 September 1888) was to suggest that the Ripper was a slum-dweller, the inevitable 'nemesis of neglect' as it was captioned. It depicted 'a phantom on the slum's foul air' in the form of dagger-wielding, man-beast degenerate: 'red-handed, ruthless, furtive, unerect'.[56] And the stereotypes of the lower, primitive and bestial races were invoked; the *Pall Mall Gazette* was not exempt: 'We should have to go to the wilds of Hungary or search the records of French lower peasant life', it wrote, 'before a more sickening and revolting tragedy could be told'.[57] Here was an echo of a racist trope which was to sound again through English culture.

When anti-German feeling was at its height in 1915, the social psychologist Wilfred Trotter called up images of the wolf-pack and 'lupine herd suggestion'.[58] Anti-German sentiment was shamelessly milked by popular writers of spy fiction, such as Valentine Williams (1883–1946). His 'Clubfoot', a devolved simian chief of the Kaiser's secret service, appeared in a run of novels from 1918 into the 1930s (a *Clubfoot Omnibus* was published in 1936). In *The Man With The Clubfoot* (1918) Clubfoot is observed by the normative, upstanding English officer who has insinuated himself into enemy Germany: 'his rapid change of moods was fascinating, now the kindly philosopher, now the Teuton braggart, now the Hun incorporate'.[59]

As he limped across the room ... I studied him ... Altogether, there was something decidedly simian about his appearance ... his squat nose with hairy open nostrils, and the general hirsuteness of the man, his bushy eyebrows, the tufts of black hair on his cheek-bones and on the backs of his big, spade-like hands. And there was that in his eyes, dark and courageous beneath the shaggy brows, that hinted at accesses of ape-like fury uncontrollable and ferocious'.[60]

In these years of uneasy peace after 1918, the fear of violent social unrest spreading anarchy from Bolshevik Russia would, once again, bring on a remaking of the discourses of atavism, placed at the service of defensive ideological tactics.

CHAPTER 5

Criminal degeneracy: adventures with Lombroso

I

In Jaroslav Hasek's *The Good Soldier Svejk* (1921–3), the eponymous anti-hero is interrogated by 'a gentleman with a cold official face and features of such bestial cruelty that he might have just fallen out of Lombroso's book, *Criminal Types*'. That it is the state interrogator who actually resembles the criminal type is welcome evidence of a joke at Lombroso's expense, which to be effective needs the reader to be familiar – even over-familiar – with the demonology of the Italian criminologist.[1] Yet the spirit of Hasek's comic ridicule seems to have permeated few of such imaginative adventures with the great criminologist and his methods: most of the evidence points towards po-faced – if fascinated – encounters; some of them depressingly and damagingly credulous.

The 'science' of criminal anthropology held out a strange popular appeal well into the 1920s. A generation after Lombroso's academic reputation had gone into decline, he was still being called up as a familiar and legitimised source of criminological authority – whether by the authentic or by the bogus sleuth. Bogus, certainly, in Edgar Wallace's 1927 novel *Terror Keep* in which a crook, Daver, posing as a hotel-keeper with a hobby of criminology, tries to dupe the detective J. G. Reeder by masquerading as 'a humble disciple of Lombroso and of those other great criminologists who have elevated the study of abnormality to a science'[2] That Reeder does not see through the ploy is not the only point. Wallace can count on the non-specialist reader – hoteliers included – registering Lombroso's evident proverbial status. By this test he is something of a legendary figure for the large readership on whom Wallace and other crime-writers could depend.

Not surprisingly, the Lombrosian criminal type found its way to audiences of the post-war silent cinema – particularly the early horror film. In F. W. Murnau's *Nosferatu* (1922), the vampire figure Orlock was played by the actor Max Schreck as a 'bald, snaggled-toothed fiend with pointed ears and huge claws' – at some variance from the polished original of Bram Stoker.[3]

In R. Austin Freeman's *A Savant's Vendetta* (1920), the reader is invited into the crazed world of Challenor, a scientist, who devotes his life to tracking down the burglar who murdered his wife. One after another he tempts burglars to his house; his clues are fingerprints and a tuft of biologically suspect hair clutched in his wife's hand. He murders them and puts them on display. His one triumph is to have netted a specimen who presents 'the orthodox stigmata of degeneration': 'his hair was bushy, his face strikingly asymetrical, and his ears were like a pair of Lombroso's selected examples; outstanding with enormous Darwinian tubercles and almost devoid of lobules'.[4]

Convinced that his wife's murderer is a degenerate, at large in London's East End, he proceeds to purge the streets of violent criminals, of invariably foreign extraction. The criminal–scientist now threatens to become a morally normative figure, perversely so, given that policemen and innocent children are the victims of ever more gratuitous acts of armed violence. While the frame narrator eventually ensures that Challenor is a curiosity not to be taken seriously, there is a disconcerting sense that the identification of the born criminal is a precondition for ridding the streets of their vermin, and that Challenor's anthropological expertise is an increasingly prized commodity in a London menaced into nervous panic by 'Russian Poles' and 'frenzied' Slav criminals (174). Observing a particularly dramatic Whitechapel shoot-out, Challenor becomes captivated by the real thing: 'here at last was the real Lombroso criminal, the sub-human mattoid, devoid of intelligence, devoid of the faintest glimmering of moral sense, fit for nothing but the lethal chamber; compared with whom the British "habitual" was a civilized gentleman. Without a specimen or two of this type, my collection was incomplete' (175).

The discourse of Lombrosian criminal anthropology here services a racial requirement to expunge the post-war social order of its pollutants, with Challenor, the scientist–murderer, as momentarily its normative spokesman. By a reversal, the criminal 'other' is now the degenerate foreigner, quite beyond the pale of civilised interest;

his fit destination, chillingly, the 'lethal chamber'. Indeed it may be said that the shocking *termini* of degenerationism – criminal, psychiatric, sexual, artistic – were the chambers of Dachau. To travel at length with Lombroso is to find that perception of shock qualified by a sobering sense of inevitability.

II 'A VAST PLAIN UNDER A FLAMING SKY'

The popularity both of the Lombrosian criminal type and the notorious stigmata by which that type might be recognised, can be attributed to an enduring fascination for translating the threat posed by the criminal into the palpable evidence of deviancy. Long before Lombroso attempted to correlate physical stigmata with behavioural predispositions on a systematic basis, physical abnormality had been linked to 'more commonplace attitudes about misfits and the "dangerous classes" '.[5] Henry Mayhew in 1850 had identified street-folk as abnormal by their 'high cheek-bones and protruding jaws'.[6] The dangerous classes, it was frequently observed, had a particular physical appearance of deformity. Nineteenth-century representations of insanity reproduced these assumptions. The asylum physician Alexander Morison (1779–1886) noted that 'the appearance of the face ... is intimately connected with, and dependent upon, the state of mind',[7] and studies of the insane reinforced well-established conventions of physiognomic representation.

Deformity without had always signalled deformity within – and vice-versa. Physiognomy, in which the forms and features particularly of the head and face are taken to give perceptual clues to inward states, dates back to Aristotle. At the end of the eighteenth century Johann Caspar Lavater's influential *Essays on Physiognomy* (1775–85) systematically demonstrated how the features of the face cohered into a symbolic system of types with culturally normative meanings.[8] Victorian science, with its inductive methods derived from observation, devoured Lavater as physiognomy became a corner-stone of anatomy, physiology and anthropology. And, as Mary Cowling has shown in her study of how Victorian art and illustration reproduced the cultural imagery of physiognomy, the subject was of consuming interest to the Victorians and was 'all but universally believed in'.[9] The artist, the scientist, the man in the street subscribed to the system of class and moral differentiation nuanced to an extraordinary degree by the detail of physiognomatic representation. When in Italy in the 1870s Lombroso underlined such stereotyping with his particular display of statistical remorselessness, he was doing no more than proving for a more scientifically exacting era what had long been held to be self-evident in the faces and gestures of people in the lanes, on the streets and behind the closed doors of the asylum.

Post-Darwinian criminal anthropology rapidly assimilated an armoury of evolutionary phenomena – reversion, atavism, recapitulation. By the mid-1870s these concepts had become commonplaces of the psychiatric Darwinism of prolific and influential pathologists like Henry Maudsley, Lombroso's exact contemporary, and alienists like Daniel Hack Tuke. Much of the impetus for Lombroso's researches derived from the perceived limitations of received ideas about the nature of insanity – particularly the condition of 'moral insanity' which criminals also manifested. Although initially developed by Esquirol and other pupils of the French psychiatrist Philippe Pinel, it was first propounded in this form by the English ethnologist James Prichard in 1833: it became established as an orthodoxy alongside the reforming strategy of 'moral management' of the insane.[10] But like Maudsley, Lombroso wanted to move beyond 'moral management' by deploying, in a spirit of scientific positivism, the practices of measurement and identification, drawn from observing asylum patients, in order to distinguish a particular criminal type.

Criminal anthropology came to Lombroso not merely as an idea, but as 'a revelation'. In his prison visits he had made the acquaintance of a 'famous brigand Vilella', a man of 'extraordinary agility', who 'openly boasted of his crimes'. Performing a post-mortem at his death, Lombroso discovered a depression in the skull precisely in the middle of the occiput – 'as in inferior animals'. This evidence constituted for Lombroso empirical proof of atavism – the *fons et origo* of his whole science of criminal anthropology by which he sought to redirect the course of penal theory and policy. Ironically, he announced this triumph for positivism in terms of the overwhelming experience of a religious conversion:

At the sight of that skull, I seemed to see all of a sudden, lighted up as a vast plain under a flaming sky, the problem of the nature of the criminal – an atavistic being who reproduces in his person the ferocious instincts of primitive humanity, and the inferior animals. Thus was explained anatomically the enormous jaws, high cheek-bones, prominent supercilliary arches, solitary lines in the palms, extreme size of the orbits, handle-shaped or sessile ears found in criminals, savages and apes, insensibility to pain, extremely acute sight, tattooing, excessive idleness, love of orgies, and the irresistable craving for evil for its own sake, the desire not only to extinguish life in the victim, but to mutilate the corpse, tear its flesh, and drink its blood.[11]

Lombroso's overriding concern was to establish a distinctive criminal type. By shifting attention away from the nature of the crime to the nature of the criminal, the Lombrosian school was placing itself in the van of reform. If a criminal could be identified early, then he need not be condemned to a life of crime – that is, if he were isolated from society for good. Segregation would follow from recognition.

But by the turn of the century not just the criminal, but the genius, the artist, the political revolutionary, the prostitute were all branded with the notorious physical stigmata of degeneracy. Writers of various narratives – social reformers, polemicists and novelists – increasingly assisted the normalisation of these recalcitrant indices of abnormality, by their construction through the medium of rational 'scientific' discourse. In the wider culture it was, above all, the degenerate criminal type who most effectively embodied the 'other' – in a double bind of attraction and disgust.

The corner-stone of Lombroso's work was the exhaustive display of statistical findings correlating physical characteristics with deviant behaviour or predisposition. In *L'Uomo delinquente* (1876), translated as *Criminal Man* (1891), he enumerated the recurrence of cranial anomalies in skulls of criminals which were 'deviations from the normal type of man', in B. A. Morel's celebrated definition of degeneration,[12] and which recalled animals of the lower type. The physiognomy of the several thousand criminals researched by Lombroso and his industrious co-workers confirmed the presence of deviations and abnormalities: 'in general, many criminals have outstanding ears, abundant hair, a sparse beard, enormous frontal sinuses and jaws, a square and projecting chin, broad cheekbones'.[13] The criminal was born with these characteristics; they were inherited traits to be understood through the evolutionary categories of reversion and atavism. The born criminal was by his nature a reversion to a distant ancestral primitive type.

What for Henry Maudsley was an article of faith was, for Lombroso, empirically established fact. The Lombrosian deviant had a

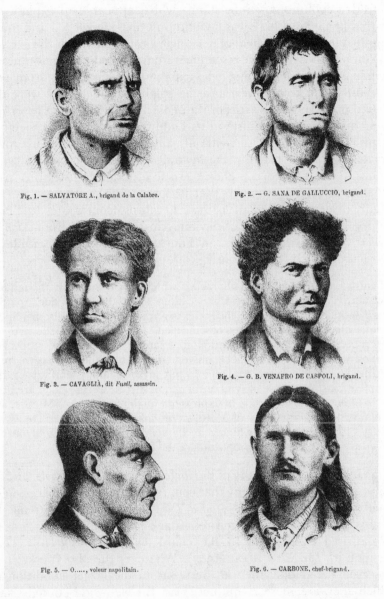

Fig. 1. — SALVATORE A., brigand de la Calabre.

Fig. 2. — G. SANA DE GALLUCCIO, brigand.

Fig. 3. — CAVAGLIÀ, dit *Fusil*, assassin.

Fig. 4. — G. B. VENAFRO DE CASPOLI, brigand.

Fig. 5. — O....., voleur napolitain.

Fig. 6. — CARBONE, chef-brigand.

7 'Six Criminal Types' from Cesare Lombroso, *L'homme criminel*, 1895.

defective evolutionary inheritance which appeared to explain his asocial behaviour; here was civilisation's unacknowleged and unintegrated 'other'. This field of deviancy was peopled with the exotica of Lombroso's exhaustive researches: from protruding membranes to criminal slang, everything was capable of assimilation from one deviant group to another, and the stigmata of deviancy were the shared property of the artist or the genius, the female offender or the anarchist. Degenerationism in its Lombrosian form yoked together 'signs of difference ... without any recognition of inappropriateness'.[14] In this respect the procedure corresponds to what Foucault has argued is a characteristic of nineteenth-century psychiatric discourse, which is that it 'forms objects that are in fact highly dispersed'. We can see how Lombroso contributes to establishing a discursive field of deviancy in this passage from *Man of Genius* (1891), which offers, in Foucault's words, a plenitude of 'objects of which [the discourse] can speak'.[15]

Alienists have noted certain characters which very frequently, though not constantly, accompany these degenerations ... on the moral side, apathy, loss of moral sense, frequent tendencies to impulsiveness of doubt, psychical inequalities owing to the excess of some faculty (memory, aesthetic taste) or defect of other qualities (calculation, for example), exaggerated mutism or verbosity, morbid vanity, excessive originality, and excessive preoccupation with self, the tendency to put mystical interpretations on the simplest facts, the abuse of symbolism and of special words which are used as an almost exclusive mode of expression. Such, on the physical side, are prominent ears, deficiency of beard, irregularity of teeth, excessive asymmetry of face and head, which may be very large or very small, sexual precocity, smallness or disproportion of the body.[16]

Here is a catalogue worthy of Burton's *Anatomy of Melancholy*, and in his unawareness of the irony that could be directed at his excesses, of Swift's hack writer in *A Tale of a Tub*. The reductive reference to genius putting 'mystical interpretations on the simplest facts' was to be satirised by Conrad in the character of the anarchist Tom Ossipon in *The Secret Agent* (1907). Whatever the idiosyncracies of observed behaviour, they all derive from the larger condition of which they are mere symptoms. Cast the net wide enough, and anarchists, epileptics, poets can all be caught, enmeshed and indiscriminately flung on the slab. So, from data on the skull, Lombroso can conclude, by a false syllogism, that artists are in fact insane: 'the capacity of the skull in men of genius, as is natural, is above average,

QUITE UNNECESSARY QUESTION.

Newly-appointed Magistrate. "Any previous Convictions against the Prisoner?"

8 'Quite Unnecessary Question', *Punch*, 22 February 1896.

by which it approaches what is found in insanity'.[17] *Man of Genius*, together with a plethora of works of the late 1880s and early nineties which treated genius and, in particular, artistic genius as a species of insanity and criminality, helped to create the necessary conditions for the noisy reception of Max Nordau's *Degeneration* when it appeared in England in 1895.[18] Nordau properly acknowledged his debt by dedicating his text to his 'Dear and Honoured Master Cesare Lombroso'.

He did so knowing that Lombroso's reputation had been the subject of mounting controversy among criminologists since the mid-1880s. Indeed, according to Robert A. Nye, the influence of the Italian school of Lombroso, Ferrero and others actually peaked at the First International Congress of Criminal Anthropology held in Rome in 1885. At that, and subsequent congresses, opposition from doctors, jurists and criminologists (predominantly from France) fastened on the biological determinism underlying the 'born' criminal type. The idea of the atavistic nature of the criminal was ridiculed by those who believed that it was environment, not heredity, which disposed people to become criminals.[19] Even as Lombroso's influence spread from conference proceedings outwards over the next two decades, the status of atavism was being gradually adjusted to take account of the opposition it had aroused.

Most vulnerable to attack was Lombroso's claim that tattooing was proof of atavism. His critics asserted that criminals and other deviants tattooed themselves for a culturally acquired reason – to be fashionable – not because of some biological drive: it followed that Lombroso was a covert Lamarckian. Lombroso was driven to reply that a malign environment could be a factor in exerting pathological pressure on the organism. But in spite of such modifications, the born criminal type could no longer be argued for in specialist circles. Charles Mercier argued in 1910 that Lombrosian doctrine was 'entirely wanting in proof'.[20] And the publication of Charles Goring's *The English Convict* (1913) buried the empirical foundations on which the Lombrosian project had rested.[21]

Yet throughout the period during which the criminal was the object of such professional scrutiny, Lombroso had paradoxically managed to fix the born criminal type into the popular imagination – quite in defiance of the drift of expert opinion and the empirical evidence. Even in a work which attacked the defects of the penal system, the stereotypes of born criminality are still present. In making the case for the recidivistic rather than the reforming effects of prison on the criminal, John Galsworthy in *Justice*, his play of 1910, has recourse to those familiar tell-tale signs of the born criminal in the 'funny eyes' of the convicted clerk, Falder, and the 'outstanding bat's ears' of the perpetual offender, Moany, who moves around his cell 'like an animal'.[22] While the intention of the play was 'progressive' in its (successful) assault on the use of solitary confinement for punishment, Galsworthy still reproduces the familiar Lombrosian representation of the criminal.[23] The case for Falder's defence relies heavily on the 'peculiar, uncanny' look of the felon's eyes which indicates that he is a pathological case and so must be 'acquitted of criminal intent and treated as a patient'. The plea is unsuccessful, since Falder must be convicted to become the victim of the penal system which is the play's over-determining concern. But in delivering Falder into the solitary cell, Galsworthy finds in Lombrosian criminology a convenient aetiology (allowing him to side-step questions about the social order which drove Falder to steal from his employer), which renders Falder a hapless victim – both of 'justice' and his own pathological organisation.

III

The working out of these controversies was on display, symptomatically, in the influential criminological writings of the polymath Havelock Ellis. Ellis's doubts about the labelling of criminals as atavistic throwbacks had already surfaced in the first edition of *The Criminal* (1890). He had been happy to use the concept of atavism, but claimed the freedom to employ it as analogy or metaphor. Ellis saw criminals as essentially anti-social, which in the evolutionary discourse of his day he interpreted as *pre*-social: 'by some defect of heredity or birth, or training, he belongs, *as it were*, [my emphasis] to a lower and older social state than that in which he is actually living'.[24] He follows with a significant qualification: 'it thus happens that our own criminals frequently resemble in physical and psychical characters the normal individuals of a lower race. This is an "atavism" which has been so frequently observed in criminals and so much discussed.'[25]

By the third edition of 1901, Ellis had shifted his ground and now argued that criminal behaviour was pathological in origin, and so was susceptible to individual treatment. Atavism was now accommodated as part of a pathological condition: for 'if we regard pathology as the science of anomalies', he wrote, 'it certainly includes the phenomena of atavism'.[26] Environmental pressures, he thought, could produce atavistic behaviour 'common to primitive peoples' in children, criminals and women; the ties of domesticity, for instance, might be the reason for some womens' savage-like behaviour.

While he acknowledged Lombroso's achievement (adding *The Man of Genius* (1891) in his own translation to his Contemporary Science Series for Walter Scott and Co.), Ellis questioned the lengths to which Lombroso had taken the idea of the criminal as a degenerate type. So by 1901, he was arguing that parallels between the criminal and the pre-social savage no longer stood up:

That the criminal often acts like a savage who has wandered into a foreign environment – it is scarcely necessary to remark that a savage in his own proper environment is not an anti-social being – is true. But we must be cautious in arguing that this necessarily means a real atavistic revival of savage ancestral traits. The criminal acts like the savage ... because a simple and incomplete creature must inevitably tend to adopt those simple and incomplete modes of life which are natural to the savage. It is not a real atavism, but mainly, it is probable, only a pseudo-atavism.[27]

Now the criminal is merely a 'pseudo-atavism'; the term has virtually become a metaphor for deviant behaviour. As proof of degeneracy it no longer carries conviction. Ellis asserted that the term was simply too general to be of further diagnostic use:

> That the criminal is often a 'degenerate' might readily be granted were it not that 'degeneracy' has become so vague and meaningless a term of popular use that it means little or nothing; Lombroso and others were undoubtedly well inspired when they sought to give greater definitiveness to the conception of the criminal by dividing the vague 'degenerate' class into groups and seeking to discover criminal types. That we cannot use the term 'type' in this connection with the same precision that we use it in racial anthropology is now generally accepted.[28]

In the light of growing environmental and hereditary evidence, the days of criminal anthropology were obviously numbered.

Yet given his substantial indebtedness to Lombroso, Ellis needed to distance himself from him on other fronts, which was no easy matter. No better evidence of Ellis's ambivalence about Lombroso could be found than what he wrote in a letter to J. A. Symonds (with whom he was collaborating on *Studies in the Psychology of Sex*) in 1892 – two years after the first appearance of *The Criminal*: 'Nothing too severe can be said of Lombroso's lack of critical judgement, historical insight and accuracy; one forgives it all because he has opened up so many lines of investigation and set so many good men to work.'[29]

Even so, Lombroso's lingering influence on Ellis allowed his judgement to go badly astray on the question of a link between criminality and artistic genius. Phyllis Grosskurth is right to claim that Lombroso's *Man of Genius* led Ellis to 'the unshakeable belief that the criminal and the genius were complementary forms of degeneration'.[30] Ellis devoted five pages of a chapter on 'Criminal Literature and Art' to Verlaine and other 'criminal' poets:

> A living poet of some eminence, M. Paul Verlaine, furnishes an interesting example of the man of genius who is also distinctly a criminal. M. Verlaine is the chief of the so-called 'decadent' school ... at his best he excels in delicate passages of vague and mystic reverie, in sudden lines of poignant emotion. His style, a curious mixture of simplicity and obscurity, is studied with words borrowed from the criminal's argot.[31]

This is almost identical to the position taken by Max Nordau in *Degeneration*. Yet ten years later, in the 1901 edition, we find that these five pages have been omitted altogether. In their place are extracts from autobiographies of an American and an Australian criminal. By 1901, then, Ellis had totally severed the connection between the criminal and the genius: and an endorsement of Lombroso's work was pointedly absent.[32] Late in life, in a reconsideration of Nordau's work, Ellis went out of his way to exonerate Verlaine from degeneracy and to reaffirm his 'primitive emotional temperament of genius'.[33]

IV

That Lombrosian criminal anthropology continued to compel was due, in part, to an insatiable interest in the spectacle of abnormal states, deviant types and their characteristics. As the 'case' of the 'Elephant Man' showed in the 1880s, physical deformity, with its enticing spectacle of horror, could be counted on to provide sensational copy within the popular culture of late nineteenth-century Britain. Photographic images, culled from professional practice, helped to bring organic anomalies into the visible foreground. Psychiatrists and criminologists, including the Russian, Pauline Tarnowsky, and Lombroso himself, made systematic use of photography: the 'mug-shot' highlighted the prominent abnormalities of the degenerate type by displaying them from different angles.[34]

In England the physician to the female department of the Surrey County Lunatic Asylum, Hugh Diamond, was among the earliest doctors to apply the technique of photography to the physiognomy of the insane, presenting a paper to the Royal Society 'On the Application of Photography to the Physiognomic and Mental Phenomenon of Insanity' in 1856.[35] James Crichton-Browne, Medical Director of the West Riding Asylum at Wakefield from 1866–76, was also a keen amateur photographer of the insane.[36]

For readers of Lombroso and Ferrero's *La donna delinquente: La prostituta e la donna normale* (1893) (translated with extreme caution into English as *The Female Offender* (1895)), the deviant nature of fallen womanhood or maternal delinquency was reinforced by crude and graphic representations of physical deformity, designed to show and tell all: this was positivism as pornography.[37] Susan Sontag has suggested that photographic display constitutes a means of 'surveillance and control'[38], exercised in the first instance by the medical practitioner, and assimilated thereafter by the lay reader. It was held to be axiomatic by these practitioners that prominent physical traits could offer essential clues to types of degeneracy. This meshed with the popular interest, sustained throughout the nineteenth century, in physiognomy and phrenology. There was no reason why scrutinising the face or reading the body might not be a game that anyone could play – even as late as the mid-nineties.

The 'People we hear about' column of *Cassell's Saturday Journal* for 1895 offers an example of this obsession: it is a fascination not merely with the great and the good, but with their build and height, the shape of their lips and the size of their boots. There was no telling what clues to German foreign policy or to the British class system might not be gleaned from close inspection of a nation's leading protagonists: 'Prince Bismark is very proud of his prominent lower lip ... he says it is a sign of perseverance, and that his moustache has prevented the proper appreciation of it.'[39] Cassell's noted the 'remarkable fact' that in Parliament A. J. Balfour 'enjoyed the distinction of wearing the largest and longest boots in the House', whereas the plebian Labour member John Burns was 'remarkable for possessing very small feet', since 'it is generally supposed that small hands and feet constitute a token of blue blood and ancient lineage'. Indeed readers of the Christmas 1895 edition received a piece of gift-wrapped gossip (from 'one who knows him well') about 'Professor Cesare Lombroso, the famous criminologist', who though a man of 'powerful memory and vast learning', was not at all distinguished in appearance: 'in fact he is short and rather stout'![40]

In *The Hound of the Baskervilles* (1902) Arthur Conan Doyle tapped this widespread and irresistible fascination with physiognomy when he details the *curriculum vitae* of a Dr Mortimer, who is learned in anatomy and has come to see Holmes about the mysterious death of Sir Henry Baskerville. The doctor's professional credentials are quickly established through the dependably degenerationist tenor of his published papers – 'Is Disease a Reversion?', 'Some Freaks of Atavism' and 'Do We Progress?'[41] His function is to underwrite the plausibility of the narrator's extensive use of degenerationist and reversionary discourse – extending primarily to the two degenerate criminals – Stapleton, the higher intellectual, and Selden, the escaped convict.

Doyle deploys the habitual tropes associated with the unexpected discovery and fleeting recognition of atavism. By candlelight, in the darkness, the convict Selden momentarily displays 'a terrible animal face, all seamed and seared with vile passions. Foul with mire ... it might well have belonged to one of those old savages who dwelt in the burrows on the hillsides ... like a crafty and savage animal' (102–3). Later Holmes holds up his bedroom candle to illuminate a portrait hanging in the banqueting room at Baskerville Hall which reveals to Dr Watson's gaze that the face of Stapleton the naturalist is a 'throwback' to the murderous Baskerville ancestor in the seventeeth-century painting.

On both occasions Doyle has created conditions analogous to those of flash photography: the 'flash' of recognition of degeneracy is precisely the effect that the Lombrosian practice of decoding facial stigmata (extended to the photographic image of the criminal mug-shot) is intended to convey. The snapshot serves both as literal practice and as a metaphor which facilitates a translation of positivistic typology into popular narrative – a narrative here dominated by an extensive repertoire of physical (and thus moral) snapshots.

It is of course part of Sherlock Holmes's stock-in-trade to reveal, from trivial or hidden clues, data which, usually to the astonishment of the reader–surrogate, Watson, will lead the detective all the way to the solution of the crime. Thus at the inception of their partnership (in *A Study in Scarlet* (1887)) Holmes astonishes Watson (in his second sentence) by observing: 'You have been in Afghanistan, I perceive.'[42]

Doyle makes considerable play with skull sizes and cranial development, the small change of sub-phrenological magazine gossip. (In 'The Blue Carbuncle' (1892) Holmes fixes the characteristics of a man from the size of his hat, observing that the head on which it habitually sits 'must have something in it'.)[43] In *The Hound of the Baskervilles*, Mortimer interprets the skulls of his acquaintances as nonchalantly as Holmes draws inferences from traces of mud on boots: 'A glance at our friend here [Baskerville] reveals the rounded head of the Celt', and on first acquaintance he praises Holmes's 'well-marked supra-orbital development' (12). In 'The Adventures of the Final Problem' (1893) Moriarty, the genius-villain, whose own forehead 'domes out in a white curve', is less impressed: 'You have less frontal development than I should have expected', he tells Holmes.[44]

These narratives of diagnosis and discovery, which betrayed little in the way of psychological depth, but which insistently assumed the authority to speak for the whole man, reflected and contributed to the cultural hegemony which contemporary pathology and its practitioners commanded and which popular fabulists, like Conan Doyle, reinforced. The 1895 edition of *The Pathology of Mind* (a substantial re-working of the original study *The Physiology and Pathology of Mind* (1867)) found Henry Maudsley urging prospective husbands to scrutinise their future wives for 'physical signs ... which betray the degeneracy of the stock ... any malformations of the head, face, mouth, teeth and ears. Outward defects and deformities are the visible signs of inward and invisible faults which will have their influence in breeding.'[45] In effect, Maudsley was urging men to become amateur detectives of the salon and the drawing-room, enjoining them, bizarrely, to identify clues to the 'inward and invisible' mystery of degenerate female sexuality – a subject on which late nineteenth-century men were hardly reliable guides. Doyle's fictional register and contemporary pathology have much in common. Both invite a wholehearted response to narratives of control, where the inspected deviant subject is appropriated by an equally confident display of diagnostic acumen.

Contradiction is more or less unthinkable. A Maudsley or a Doyle is largely untroubled by the arbitrary relationship of stigma to condition. Doyle's narratives endow Holmes with power over any data that come to hand, so that he can complete and close his case and relieve the narrative of its mystery. Yet Doyle's fiction does allow the degenerate some degree of unpoliced freedom of movement before he is eventually brought into the sphere of social control by Holmes's competing intelligence. The higher criminal can threaten and disturb; his unstable chemistry of intellectual potency and savagery poses an unsettling challenge to the rationality of the detective's procedures.

Both Lombroso and Nordau had reported the emergence of a new figure for the early nineties: the 'higher degenerate'. Nordau noted the work of contemporary experts on this type and remarked: 'As regards their intellect, they can attain to a high degree of development, but from a moral point of view their existence is completely deranged', adding that the higher degenerate 'just as he occasionally exhibits gigantic bodily stature or the disproportionate growth of particular parts, has some mental gift exceptionally developed at the cost ... of the remaining faculties, which are wholly or partially atrophied'.[46] While Valentin Magnan conjured up the *dégénéré supérieur*, Lombroso promoted the 'mattoid'. The scene was set for the entrance of the 'higher' criminal, the degenerate genius. He stalked the pages of popular narrative, in particular the work of Doyle, John Buchan and 'Sapper', and he was a powerful influence on Conrad, as he sought paradigms of turn-of-the-century man's defective psyche.

Sherlock Holmes's arch-rival, Professor Moriarty, is a precise embodiment of the criminal 'higher degenerate' out of Lombroso, Legrain and Magnan. Moriarty is a dangerous figure precisely because his intelligence is placed at the service of his criminal intentions. It is through Holmes's eyes that he is marked out as the 'Napoleon of crime', so encouraging a reading of him as Holmes's double. Holmes recognises in Moriarty an 'antagonist who (is) my intellectual equal'(540). The struggle which ends sensationally above the Reichenbach falls, as Doyle kills off his creation – now grown monstrous – is the culmination of the 'thrust and parry' work in which both men shadow the other through the story. "One would think that we were the criminals", exclaims Watson as they play cat and mouse with Moriarty south from London to the continent (548). Moreover, in order to outwit him, they must anticipate his movements and so in a sense become him; to neutralise his degenerate influence they have to live it. Watson's comment unintentionally betrays that element of identification which the author requires of the reader in the very transgression which the detective is trying to bring to book.

For Holmes to get the measure of his higher degenerate opponent he requires that compromising knowledge of the underworld, to which the higher criminal belongs: 'there is no one', he says, 'who knows the higher criminal world of London so well as I do' (539). From the moment when he is first presented as decadent scientist and *flaneur* in *A Study in Scarlet* (1887) (he spends his time between the 'chemical laboratory', the 'dissecting room' and 'long walks' which take him 'into the lowest portion of the city')[47] Holmes gives his readers, through the eyes of Watson, a vicarious glimpse of an ambiguous lifestyle. It tantalises with glimpses of the shocking (his addiction to cocaine) and the irregular (his expertise in burglary in 'Charles Augustus Milverton' (1904)). But these lapses are reassuringly countered by the very exercise of these ambiguous gifts in clearing the streets of yet another threat to private and public order. So that in 'The Adventure of the Bruce-Partington Plans' (1908)

Holmes receives the ultimate establishment accolade – a gift from the Queen for having foiled a dangerous plot against the state. Doyle continually indulges his readers with the thrill of the forbidden, while keeping them fundamentally reassured.[48]

Moriarty is a gifted man tainted by a defective inheritance. According to Holmes he has 'hereditary tendencies of the most diabolic kind. A criminal stain ran in his blood' which is intensified by 'his extraordinary powers'(539). Holmes's hyperbole runs on: 'He is a genius, a philosopher, an abstract thinker. He has a brain of the first order. He sits motionless, like a spider in the centre of its web. But that web has a thousand radiations, and he knows well every quiver of each of them. He does little himself. He only plans' (540). Abnormal and anomalous both in biology and mental capacity, Doyle's Moriarty anticipates the clever villains who would cross the path of Richard Hannay and Bulldog Drummond of the next generation of crime thrillers. In fact the idea of the protean criminal intelligence, in all its atavistic colouring, would survive with surprising persistence into the inter-war period. One of the first of John Buchan's numerous criminal types, Marker, makes his debut in *The Half-Hearted*, published in 1900, so making him a near-contemporary of Doyle's Moriarty. Marker has the hallmarks of the civilised genius–criminal – a cultivated manipulator who is in league with anti-British tribes on the Indian frontier, threatening military conquest. For Buchan's hero, Lewis Haystoun, he is 'a man of uncanny power and intelligence beyond others', with an 'iron will' and a face 'sharp, eager, with the hungry wolf-like air of ambition'.[49]

In 'The Adventure of the Final Problem'(1893), Moriarty embodies a generalised sense of threat and a precise anxiety of Holmes: 'I have continually been conscious of some power behind the malefactor, some deep organising power which forever stands in the way of the law . . . for years I have endeavoured to break through the veil which shrouded it, and at last the time came when I seized my thread' (539–40). Catherine Belsey has argued that 'the project of the Sherlock Holmes stories is to dispel magic and mystery, to make everything explicit, accountable, subject to scientific analysis'[50], but as with other paradigmatic realist texts, the stories 'push to the margins of experience' whatever positivism 'cannot explain or understand'.[51]

'The Adventure of the Final Problem' is a story in which Doyle dispenses with the usual project; for what is habitually suppressed is here made unusually explicit: Holmes's scientific mastery is systematically undermined by Moriarty's counter-intelligence. Holmes's sense of a 'deep organising power' in the land reveals an uncharacteristic sensitivity to the mysterious force of a man so obviously Holmes's equal, and a living proof of the uncertainty of the detective's positivistic methods; he is constructed as undetectable. Despite Holmes's elaborate arrangements to put him off the scent, Moriarty virtually intercepts them at Victoria station and then charters a special train to pursue the pair down to the coast. Holmes and Watson, having alighted short of Dover to elude him, witness the train: 'A minute later a carriage and engine could be seen flying along the open curve which leads to the station. We had hardly time to take our places behind a pile of luggage when it passed with a rattle and a roar, beating a blast of hot air into our faces' (549). There are unmistakably supernatural and diabolic overtones here. Although foreseen by Holmes, Moriarty's commandeering of the train is a strictly fantastic image of boundless mobility which has much in common with the disembodied degeneracy of Count Dracula in Bram Stoker's fantasy of 1897. Dracula's capacity to instil horror derives, in part, from his habitual breaking of the constraints of time and place, which conventionally set the limits to mimetic realism. While this image of Moriarty verges on the absurd, he still transmits an inexplicable, disturbing force.

Doyle uses images of overreaching power in a particularly explicit way in this tale. Holmes's London presents itself here as a *paysage moralisé* penetrated by the struggle between good and evil. Superimposed on the habitual metonymic depiction of London as the realistic world of the stories is a mystical – even apocalyptic – vision of chaos. Holmes speculates that Moriarty is the 'organiser of half that is evil and of nearly all that is undetected in this great city' (540). Yet Doyle characteristically has it both ways. Holmes takes immodest pride in his clean-up rate: 'If my record were closed to-night, I could still survey it with equanimity. The air of London is sweeter for my presence. In over a thousand cases I am not aware that I have ever used my powers upon the wrong side'(551). Of course Doyle's readership required that Holmes be reinvented, and this meant reinventing something criminally interesting in the city. Brought back from the dead, Doyle had Holmes strike his more customary world-weary note when he observes that 'from the point of view of the criminal expert ... London has become a singularly uninteresting city since the death of the late-lamented Professor Moriarty'.[52]

V

'Going wrong' is what degenerates do and it is the direction which a degenerate energy must take. Degenerate energy is unsettling since it precipitates dissolution and transgression: it produces the unproductive, reproduces the sterile and generates the degenerate. It is this unstable coexistence of incompatible features which compelled the paradoxical imagination of Joseph Conrad. Conrad's characterisation of the protean face of disorder and irrationality in such figures as Donkin in *The Nigger of the 'Narcissus'* (1897), Kurtz in *Heart of Darkness* (1902), the Professor in *The Secret Agent* (1907) and Jones in *Victory* (1915) has a powerful source in the paradoxical discourses of degenerationism, as handed down through Lombroso and Nordau. To isolate Conrad's use of degenerationist discourse spotlights his familiar preoccupations: a deep pessimism about man's capacity to ameliorate the social and political order, a political conservatism, a disenchantment with man's ethical capacity, and a scepticism of the claims of rational – particularly scientific – thought.

Conrad was impressively well read in contemporary science. As Ian Watt suggests, he derived two main inferences from natural science: that the 'heartless secrets which are called the Laws of Nature', as he put it in his preface to *The Nigger of the 'Narcissus'*, were irrelevant to the 'deepest human concerns', and that scientific determinism undermined man's individual and political aspirations[53]. Outwardly Conrad looked turn-of-the-century science in the face, and found confirmation of his worst fears. But his negotiations with contemporary popular science were complex. Conrad habitually mobilised scientific and pseudo-scientific ideas precisely to isolate what indeed defied rational enquiry.

Given his unbelieving yet persistent sense of man's fall from a state of grace, perhaps it was not possible for Conrad to shrug off the totalising jeremiads of certain degenerationists. Yet did he find in their zeal a kind of doomed Faustian (or Kurtzian) mission – to cast the light of science on those aspects of human nature most resistant

to explanation? Conrad evidently made extensive use of degenerationist concepts, yet, unlike the positivists, he used them to question
the very rationality of 'civilized normality' which the mainstream
positivist habitually invoked to prove the evidence of the degenerate
type.

Although Conrad nowhere openly acknowledges his reading of
the degenerationists, he turned to them for some corroboration of
mental and psychological states which he found disturbing and
compelling. Strong echoes of both Lombroso and Nordau have been
noted in his texts by several critics, but his only known direct
comment on Nordau, made in 1898, registers an amused reponse to
Nordau's 'expounding attitude', presumably in *Degeneration*.[54]

Conrad appears to have retained his belief that the concept of
degeneration could account for extreme psychological states,
including unaccountable acts of 'bad faith'. In 1908 he reacted
positively to reading the manuscript of John Galsworthy's *Fraternity*
(1909). Conrad praised the truthful presentation of the amoral
behaviour of Hilary Dallison, but commented, 'I don't think ... you
have realized the harrowing atrocity of his conduct ... He is a
degenerate who is completely satisfied with the last scene with the
girl ... morbid psychology, be it always understood, is a perfectly
legitimate subject for an artist's genius. But not for a moralist.'[55]
Nevertheless, the 'technology' of reversion and degeneration seemed
to offer a highly serviceable pseudo-psychological repertoire, which
gave him points of access to extreme and pathological states of mind
which he had conceived imaginatively. The typologies of degeneration helped him to write about them. But degeneration also gave
him an armoury of defensive irony, which, donned as necessary, lent
protection against the psychologically disturbing implications he
had opened up.

It may have been the very religiosity at the heart of contemporary
positivism which drew from Conrad such adverse judgements; he
found the positivists *truly* offensive. As the high priests of a faith, they
claimed an unmerited access to a higher form of truth. Conrad's
response was not that of the defensive believer – he had little time for
traditional religious sanctities – but of the thoroughgoing sceptic
who saw (more clearly than the orthodox believer) how the spiritual
was being hijacked by the peddlers of a quack religion. For Conrad
the degenerationist credo was as much a dead end as any other.

Yet what activates his scepticism about the irrationality of 'rational' science is a lack of belief in the perfectibility of man, in the development of a better self, and a profound political conservatism – ideas which were reflected in one strain of degenerationism. There was, as we have already seen, a confluence of discourses in the 1880s and nineties about social and political disturbance, urban degeneration and racial decline, couched in social Darwinism, which found an echo in Conrad's view of the condition of contemporary Europe.

In *The Nigger of the 'Narcissus'* (1897), Conrad turned to this component of degeneration for some psychopathological clue to the nature of his first developed criminal. In this novella the sailor Donkin is, in almost all respects, morally and psychologically representative of a vicious type. But with the insertion, unobtrusively, of certain key significant details, Conrad places the type, displaces its received 'universality', and locates it in a complex ideology of degeneracy, which for him, as for his contemporaries, inevitably exacts a response as to an energy gone wrong. Donkin is both born and made. His inherent criminality is signalled by an explicit reference to the Lombrosian ear: 'his big ears stood out, transparent and veined, resembling the thin wings of a bat',[56] as over the heads of the crew Conrad invokes Lombrosian physiognomy for a readership apprised, he assumes, of its signs. Yet Donkin is also the product of quite precise environmental factors, turning on a familiar conceit of the nineties – a functional relationship between a Darwinian adaptation to environment and efficiency or success in life: good, in social Darwinism, is what survives. There is also a negotiation in the text about energy, based around a recurring *fin de siècle* duality: the decadent, or 'soft', counterpoised against the disciplined and self-contained. It is Conrad's most Wellsian text, with its preoccupation with the paradoxes of 'fitness'.

Donkin, obviously, presents the criminal face of the survival of the unfit. But it is the specifically urban discourse of degeneration which powers this paradoxical type. His origins are in the slums of the East End of London, and these are discursively regulated by the tropes of conventional conservative rhetoric we have met earlier. As Jeremy Hawthorn points out, Conrad reads Donkin from within the same ideological frame which he establishes in an important early letter of December 1885.[57] Conrad writes that 'the whole herd of idiotic humanity' are moving to the left at the 'bidding of unscrupulous rascals and a few sincere, but dangerous lunatics'.[58] Showing a 'classic conservative fear of the spread of socialist ideas',[59] Conrad extends the terms of the political in his novella by assimilating it to a psychopathological diagnosis permitted by degeneration. For social-ism is not merely a threat to the social fabric, it is an emanation of an unforgivable decadence: it is both an indulgence, a variety of egoism, and the dubious source of the crew's factitious deliverance from the privations of their lot. It is a sentiment anticipated in the 1885 letter: 'the International Socialist Association are triumphant, and every disreputable ragamuffin in Europe feels the day of univer-sal brotherhood, despoliation and disorder is coming apace, and nurses day-dreams of well-plenished pockets amongst the ruin of all that is respectable, venerable and holy'.[60]

In *The Nigger* these 'day-dreams' are peddled by Donkin: 'inspired by Donkin's hopeful doctrines they dreamed enthusiasti-cally of the time when every lonely ship would travel over a serene sea, manned by a wealthy and well-fed crew of satisfied skip-pers'(90). There is a straight line from these ideas to the anarchist doctrines spreading from Europe to the streets and parlours of south London in *The Secret Agent*. And Donkin is indulged by the social reformer; he is the 'pet of philanthropists ... the sympathetic and deserving creature that knows about his rights, but knows nothing of courage, of endurance' (21). Conrad turns to degeneration in the service of a conservative ideology which insists on counterpoising qualities of fortitude *against* political awareness; endurance *against* the consciousness of injustice. These prevailing hard/soft, austere/decadent, efficient/inefficient antinomies are absolutely of their time, of course, and inflect much writing of the nineties, from the counter-decadent work of Henley, Kipling and the idealists of Empire, to Wells's evolutionary poetics.

Donkin, then, is not so much a criminal type, naturalistically formed by his environment (Conrad is not that kind of writer), rather he is framed to exemplify, in his depravity, the ethical hollowness of a nature capable of adaptation to a low form of existence, the potential for which exists in any social situation. We notice that he is the 'independent offspring of the *ignoble freedom* of the slums' (20). The slum environment offers not stultification but a degenerate vitality, which, in the text, is pitted against the 'austere servitude of the sea'. His natural habitat is not that of the heroic seafarers, but an environment which supplies conditions to which defective nature can readily adapt, and where man's 'natural', non-ethical instincts are not suppressed. He is an 'ominous survival' who testifies to the 'eternal fitness of lies and impudence'. With biological fitness ironically juxtaposed with moral unfitness, he perfectly embodies the paradox of the man 'gone wrong'. Donkin has energy and vitality but it is thoroughly degraded: 'his picturesque and filthy loquacity flowed like a troubled stream from a poisoned source'. That source is the degenerate city.

In stealing from the dying black sailor Jimmy Wait, Donkin is actively parasitic. Shirking work (and so in Conrad's terms scandalously offending against one of the sanctities of life at sea) he accrues around him predatory images of lower forms of life; he is 'venomous and thin-faced', he is called 'a sick vulture', with an 'inefficient carcass' (20), a rat and a cur who shows 'yellow teeth'. And he is a bird of prey: 'a sick vulture with ruffled plumes' (109), his 'shoulders were peaked and drooped like the broken wings of a bird' (20).

What is undeniably disturbing about Donkin is his capacity to wreak havoc through his seductive plausibility. Conrad understands both the psychology of the transgressive criminal type and that of the group on which it thrives. Donkin, like Jimmy Wait and Kurtz, Moriarty and Dracula, creates a field of influence which irresistibly drags people into its plots. What should be an enclave of sea-going efficiency, embodied in the self-reliant ethic of the old sea-dog, Singleton – 'a lonely relic of a devoured and forgotten generation' (31) – turns into a scene of contagious inefficiency, offering prospects of ease and delight which answer to the 'narcissus' in each man's character. Wait, too, has this effect: by 'being all extremity'(67) he produces confusion in the ranks, inspiring, alternately, hatred of his 'malingering heartlessly in the face of our toil' (67) and, elsewhere, devotion and what Conrad sees, in his social-Darwinian way, as a dangerous tenderness: 'through him we were becoming highly humanized, tender, complex, excessively decadent: we understood all the subtlety of his fear, sympathized with all his repulsions, shrinkings, evasions, delusions' (117).

By holding to an ethic which appears to transgress the norm the degenerate generates his potent and destructive influence. Wait's shamming of an illness to mask his impending death is a benevolent counterpart to Donkin. But the actions of both men infect the delicately poised polity of the ship since, in the terms which Conrad has adopted, the crew is forced to work at a lower level of efficiency. The proof of its corruption is that the crew are blind to the source: the fact of Donkin being the immediate cause of Wait's death is never generally known. His degenerate criminality is now the shared property of the crew who take on the role of guilty transgressors: 'There could be no greater criminal than we, who by our lies conspired to send the unprepared soul of a poor ignorant black man to everlasting perdition' (121).

VI

As part of the preparations for his journey into Africa, Marlow in Conrad's *Heart of Darkness* is interviewed by a doctor who asks to measure Marlow's head, getting 'the dimensions back and front and every way, taking notes carefully'. The passage continues:

'I always ask leave, in the interests of science, to measure the crania of those going out there,' he said. 'And when they come back too?' I asked. 'Oh, I never see them,' he remarked; 'and, moreover, the changes take place inside you know.' He smiled, as if at some quiet joke. 'So you are going out there. Famous. Interesting, too.' He gave me a searching glance, and made another note. 'Ever any madness in your family?' he asked, in a matter-of-fact tone. I felt very annoyed. 'Is that question in the interests of science, too?' 'It would be,' he said, without taking notice of my irritation, 'interesting for science to watch the mental changes of individuals, on the spot, but ... 'Are you an alienist?' I interrupted. 'Every doctor should be – a little,' answered that original, imperturbably. 'I have a little theory which you Messieurs who go out there must help me to prove. This is my share in the advantages my country shall reap from the possession of such a magnificent dependency. The mere wealth I leave to others ...'[61]

Here is a complacent, tunnel-visioned doctor, with his narrow cult of scientific facts, set against the superior consciousness of the narrator, Marlow, who regards his questions as both inappropriate and insensitive. There is an ominous quality to the interchange – a sense that it would not be at all surprising if, during his journey up the Congo, Marlow were to 'go wrong'. The heads of other adventurers, after all, have evidently passed through this doctor's hands even if he 'never sees them' on their return. And the sinister 'quiet joke' is that the unspoken changes that might 'take place inside' the man who ventures out of civilisation, would, of course, defy measurement. Satirising the contemporary fad for measuring skulls, as a means of establishing a client's propensity to deteriorate under stress, Conrad has Marlow suspect that the doctor is a fraud (a 'harmless fool'). Yet later, when confronting physical danger, en route for the outer station, Marlow recalls the doctor's words: 'I remembered the old doctor, – "It would be interesting for science to watch the mental changes of individuals on the spot." I felt I was becoming scientifically interesting. However, all that is to no purpose' (49).

At this crisis point (he has to contemplate reprisals, having just stumbled on a recently ambushed caravan), Marlow toys with seeing himself as the object of the doctor's diagnostic practice, and he is tempted to apply the doctor's procedure to himself. Yet sensing that he might be losing rational control, he is struck by its sheer irrelevance to his situation, and dismisses the thought. But rather than allow himself to become introspective he blocks the way of consciousness by submitting once more to the imperatives of action and the ethic of duty – we know of course that introspection will continue to tighten its grip on him. Moreover, it is a kind of Darwinian folly. In *Victory* the scrupulosity of the super-civilised Axel Heyst becomes a liability amid the 'primitive' Far East and the suitably adapted denizens of Schomberg's bar. Tony Tanner reminds us of Darwin's crucial observation from the *Descent of Man* that 'under very simple conditions of life a high organisation would be of no service'.[62] Marlow is learning just how 'simple' these conditions are; a retrogressive nemesis awaits the man who thinks.

Conrad, it seems, could not easily ignore the diagnostic seductions propounded by positivistic doctors like the Belgian. The post-Darwinian findings of Lombroso and Nordau (and those of other pathologists and alienists, whose work they gutted) offered Conrad explanations for states of mind which persistently fascinated him – states of obsession, of irrational force and moral transgression. Nordau's term was 'egomania'.[63]

Both *Heart of Darkness* and *Lord Jim* exemplify the tendency of modernism to privilege 'consciousness' over external reality – the Paterian 'sense of fact' over 'fact'. In both texts the knowledge of objective 'fact' is made problematic. In *Lord Jim* ' "facts" become a specific literary target'.[64] Jim complains at his trial about the facts required from him 'as if facts could explain anything'.[65] And it is within this frame of reference that we can also situate the positivistic cult of fact in the late nineteenth century.

Marlow's distrust of the doctor brings out a more sceptical component in Conrad's negotiations with degenerationism. Marlow can detach himself from the lure of facts – of thinking himself 'interesting'. But does this mark a victory for consciousness, for the 'sense of fact', over 'fact'? Conrad suggests, of course, that 'consciousness' can usher in unsought knowledge of an order far removed from the knowledge of facts. It overlays the perils of Marlow's physical journey with psychic pitfalls, which is why Marlow so readily invokes the imperatives of work and duty: 'duty' as Michael Levenson puts it 'is an antidote to consciousness'.[66]

In the hands of positivistic science, consciousness is occluded by a reversionary paraphernalia which forecloses its exercise but, at the same time, prefigures its representation. Conrad seems to have wanted to exploit positivist science, tactically, but then to face away from the reductive and limiting psychology which it posited. In this respect, he is like Hardy – a transitional figure. In so far as he is post-Darwinian he conceptualises with the available discourses of determinism, but as he is a modernist he urges the claims of 'consciousness' against that determinism. He anticipates, both on this issue and in their hostility to degenerationism's social-Darwinian face, Forster and Woolf.

Conrad was also well versed in the notion of the higher degenerate type, derived from Lombroso, or from Nordau's summarising of Lombroso, Magnan, Legrain and others in *Degeneration*.[67] In *Heart of Darkness* one of the strains of ideology which go into the making of Kurtz is the idea of crazed genius, where a high intelligence in the obsessional service of an abstract idea is driven by forces beyond conscious control in an unstable, fatal mix. The popular euphemism for the downward trajectory of this type, used by Doyle, is serviceable for Conrad too. As Marlow puts it, 'his – let us say – nerves, went wrong, and caused him to preside at certain midnight dances ending with unspeakable rites' (86).

Conrad almost certainly drew closely on Nordau's summary, in *Degeneration*, of the characteristics of the higher degenerate. Kurtz's physical size (Marlow thinks 'he looked at least seven feet long' (85)) has a source in Nordau, who, as we have seen, noted that 'the higher degenerate . . . occasionally exhibits gigantic bodily stature'. Kurtz's 'lofty frontal bone' denotes conventionally high intelligence; Nordau reports that this type 'has some mental gift exceptionally developed'. But the sentence continues: 'at the cost, it is true, of the remaining faculties, which are wholly or partially atrophied';[68] the price paid for this prodigious development is a dangerous imbalance – characteristic, it seems, of the higher degenerate type.

Lauded by the station manager as a 'universal genius' (40) Kurtz is both idealist and transgressor, prodigiously successful in generating an aura of godliness and wealth. And like all higher degenerates he is immensely productive, but the production indeed goes 'wrong': he becomes a monster of exploitation. Kurtz acquires the negative aspects of his proferred identity, so that his 'surplus of civilizing zeal', in Chris Baldick's phrase,[69] de-generates a barbaric loss of restraint. The unstable, contradictory nature of the degenerate type offers Conrad a pathology which produces the ironic double. The higher-degenerate Kurtz both compels and appals Marlow because he lives out, *in extremis*, oppressive dilemmas, and residual conflicts, which inhabit the civilised, turn-of-the-century mind. Conrad's deconstruction of that mind here yields a simple but crucial insight, quite outside the limited imaginative scope of degenerationist pathology: the man 'gone wrong' is not 'out there' to be labelled by positivist science, he is, of course, the man within. Kurtz embodies the atavistic 'other' because Marlow has internalised Kurtz's 'exalted and incredible degradation'(107).

'All Europe contributed to the *making* of Kurtz'(86). Marlow is one of Europe's 'emissaries of light', but is aware both of the dark coexistence of civilised and barbaric, the aspiration to imperial godhead and its lapse (the sense of a fall, secularised, is real enough). In this sense Marlow creates Kurtz, as the crew of the 'Narcissus' create Donkin and Jimmy Wait. And without intending it, Doyle has Sherlock Holmes require Moriarty; the suppressed criminality of the detective feeds on the competing intelligence of the criminal. Less innocently, and altogether more disturbingly, in Conrad's *The Secret Agent* the establishment, in the person of Chief-Inspector Heat, will require the continuing existence of the anarchists. To the world at large, the policeman is cleansing the streets of vermin, but Conrad shows the actual covert collusion. The anarchist is necessary for the smooth running of law and order. The degenerate can be totem and scapegoat – a figure both idolised and reviled.

VII 'SAINT' LOMBROSO

By the time Conrad came to compose *The Secret Agent* in 1906, it seems that he had become the master rather than the servant of the degenerationists. There are 'degenerates' in plenty in this novel, but Conrad's scepticism about the scientific credentials of the degenerationists constitutes a major development. One wonders to what extent the views of a modernist like Edward Garnett (so acutely cynical about Nordau) were responsible for shifting Conrad's point of view and whether the decline in the reputation of these last upholders of positivism hastened Conrad's evident disenchantment.

In *The Secret Agent* Conrad addressed, more explicitly than hitherto, the deterministic pathology of Lombroso and Nordau. The result is a devastating and brilliant demolition job on an ideological edifice within which Conrad himself had sheltered. Lombroso becomes an explicit reference point in this novel; it is his tendentious theories which are debated by the anarchists grouped around Adolph Verloc's fireplace. While they talk, Stevie, Verloc's retarded young brother-in-law draws circles at the table 'with his soul's application to the task'.[70] One of the conspirators, Ossipon, pronounces on the drawings: they are 'very characteristic, perfectly typical' of 'this form of degeneracy'. But before he elaborates, Conrad satirically tells us that Ossipon is 'nicknamed the Doctor, ex-medical student without a degree'.(77) Ossipon is a fraud, the ideology he peddles is bogus, and his audience are his dupes. He is a 'wandering lecturer to working-men's associations upon the socialistic aspects of hygiene'(76), in other words, a eugenicist. When he resumes in the first person, in reply to Verloc's question, we register the gathering weight of irony: 'That's what he may be called scientifically. Very good type, too, altogether of that sort of degenerate. It's good enough to glance at the lobes of his ears. If you read Lombroso – ' (77).

Conrad is now playing a confident game with the 'scientific' status of Lombrosian pathology, for it is by no means clear, at first, just how steeped in irony the narrative is.[71] We see the discourse exposed in Conrad's insistently ironic juxtaposition of the anarchists' use of scientific authority in the interests of positivism, with their own 'degenerate' characters. Some of them are drawn as unashamedly Lombrosian 'types': Ossipon's mouth is 'cast in the rough mould of the Negro type'(75), and the Professor, who espouses an extreme eugenicist creed, has 'large ears, thin like membranes', which stand 'far out from the sides of his frail skull'(263) – we recall that Donkin in *The Nigger of the 'Narcissus'* is (unironically) endowed with 'big ears' which 'stood out, transparent and veined'. A third terrorist Yundt, for whom 'Lombroso is an ass' (77), declares that the 'law' not 'teeth and ears' marks the criminal. But this, says the narrator, is the posturing of an 'actor on platforms, in secret assemblies, in private interviews. The famous terrorist had never in his life raised personally as much as his little finger against the social edifice'(78). Yundt's social conspiracy theory is no more endorsed than is Ossipon's pontificating – both are rooted in a bogus humanitarianism. The savage mockery with which this appallingly inert exchange is infused by Conrad drags the whole Lombrosian doctrine deeper and deeper into disrepute.

Late in the novel, in the conversation between Ossipon and Winnie on the station platform, the play of degeneration precipitates an ironic and lethal deconstruction. Conrad's impersonal narrative points up the ironies of the mask of spurious concern that Ossipon presents to the deluded Winnie. It exposes both Ossipon's moral bankruptcy and the hollowness of the scientific discourse he speaks. The episode recalls the earlier diagnosis of Stevie as a 'degenerate' at Verloc's; for Stevie is the subject around whom the scene is framed.

Following her murder of Verloc, Winnie has told Ossipon that the man blown up in the park was Stevie, her brother. Ossipon responds with a reflex diagnosis of Winnie herself: 'He was excessively terrified of her – the sister of the degenerate – a degenerate herself of a murdering type ... or else of the lying type'(254). Having planned his desertion of Winnie, and having also relieved her of all her money, he receives the benediction of the desperate woman on the station platform, prior to boarding the boat-train. The scene is worth quoting in full:

'You'll get me off, Tom?' she asked in a gust of anguish, lifting her veil brusquely to look at her saviour.

She had uncovered a face like adamant. And out of this face the eyes looked on, big, dry, enlarged, lightless, burnt out like two black holes in the white shining globes.

'There is no danger,' he said, gazing into them with an earnestness almost rapt, which to Mrs Verloc, flying from the gallows, seemed to be full of force and tenderness. This devotion deeply moved her – and the adamantine face lost the stern rigidity of its terror. Comrade Ossipon gazed at it as no lover ever gazed at his mistress's face. Alexander Ossipon, anarchist, nicknamed the Doctor, author of a medical (and improper) pamphlet, late lecturer on the social aspects of hygiene to working men's clubs, was free from the trammels of conventional morality – but he submitted to the rule of science. He was scientific, and he gazed scientifically at that woman, the sister of a degenerate, a degenerate herself – of a murdering type. He gazed at her, and invoked Lombroso, as an Italian peasant recommends himself to his favourite saint. He gazed scientifically. He gazed at her cheeks, at her nose, at her eyes, at her ears ... Bad! ... Fatal! Mrs. Verloc's pale lips parting, slightly relaxed under his passionately attentive gaze, he gazed also at her teeth ... Not a doubt remained ... a murdering type ... If Comrade Ossipon did not recommend his terrified soul to Lombroso, it was only because on scientific grounds he could not believe that he carried about him such a thing as a soul. But he had in him the scientific spirit, which moved him to testify on the platform of a railway station in nervous, jerky phrases.

'He was an extraordinary lad, that brother of yours. Most interesting to study. A perfect type in a way. Perfect!'

He spoke scientifically in his secret fear. And Mrs Verloc, hearing these words of commendation vouchsafed to her beloved dead, swayed forward with a flicker of light in her sombre eyes, like a ray of sunshine heralding a tempest of rain.

'He was that indeed,' she whispered, softly, with quivering lips. 'You took a lot of notice of him, Tom. I loved you for it'.

'It's almost incredible the resemblance there was between you two', pursued Ossipon, giving a voice to his abiding dread, and trying to conceal his nervous, sickening impatience for the train to start. 'Yes, he resembled you'.

These words were not especially touching or sympathetic. But the fact of the resemblance insisted upon was enough in itself to act upon her emotions powerfully. With a little faint cry, and throwing her arms out, Mrs Verloc burst into tears at last. (259–60)

The passage works through two structures of irony, exposing the duplicity of Ossipon's tactics (as Winnie's total belief in his sentiments of concern testify) and the spurious language in which it is couched. The first irony is directed at Ossipon's bogus diagnostic role which is a reiteration of the earlier exposure. The repetition of his scientific pretensions is there, as is his charlatanism – 'nicknamed the Doctor'; his lecturing career is noted again, for added ironic emphasis, as the dry narrative restatement invokes the false credentials which Ossipon repeatedly offers to those around him. This irony precipitates another: the complete misreading by Winnie of the significance of Ossipon's gestural and verbal utterance – a kind of sign system, coherent and fraudulent. Such is Winnie's desperate confusion that she is painfully susceptible to any proferred image of comfort and authority.

Comically, Ossipon is by turns a grotesque priest-figure, lover and doctor, while Winnie is constructed as suppliant, lover and patient.

And this disjuncture between appearance and reality is registered through the silent stupidity of the gaze. We notice how the passage is framed by Winnie's uncovering of the veil to reveal her eyes – and at the end her purgative tears; it is as if she has undergone confession. Just as Conrad invokes Lombroso, who would innocently be Ossipon's saint, were he not so 'scientific', so Lombroso would unproblematically rule, saint-like, over the passage – were it not for the demystifying instrument of the author's irony.

Ossipon's gaze is both holy and scientific for Winnie; she feels it to be 'full of force and tenderness'. Her devotion, figured in the relaxation of her rigid expression, appears to match his. We then register his gaze, returned in the guise of the lover who gazes as 'no lover ever gazed'. This brilliantly conveys Winnie's infatuation and also speaks to our sense of incongruity and incredulity. The detached tone and the increasingly detailed examination of the features of her face combine now to expose the utter banality of the Lombrosian stigmata system itself – especially as Ossipon proceeds to inspect her features in the name of that science: 'He gazed scientifically. He gazed at her cheeks, at her nose, at her eyes, at her ears ... Bad .... Fatal.'

His fraudulence is actualised and revealed in his gaze, which Winnie interprets in her reciprocating gaze as promising her salvation. From now on our view of Ossipon, as the spokesman of bogus science, is assimilated to Winnie's deluded reading of him. Now Ossipon's character ceases to retain even the autonomy of a curiosity-piece, subject to Conrad's scepticism about the Lombrosian 'scientific spirit'. Ironic and tragic depths are increasingly sounded as language itself lies and fabricates. It is particularly disastrous for Winnie, because at this moment of crisis language is the sole negotiable commodity left to her, now there is nothing more to negotiate.

When Ossipon speaks, commending Stevie's uniqueness, he voices a scientific detachment heard earlier. But Winnie reads his attribution of uniqueness – 'Perfect'- as Ossipon's *appreciation* of Stevie, and misguidedly returns to him what she blindly takes to be a compliment to her brother – 'You took a lot of notice of him, Tom.' In view of the ambiguity of Ossipon's medical gaze, this is ironically just. Then playing on her extreme emotional vulnerability, he reiterates Winnie's dangerous degeneracy, as sister to Stevie: 'It's almost incredible the resemblance there was between you two.'

While this remark is intended to strike Winnie with the note of authority, it actually serves to screen Ossipon's now rising terror. Although to Winnie Ossipon's statements appear to be those of a concerned man, the concern is, inhumanly, with cold fact. Stevie is 'unique' only because he is the uniquely privileged provider of empirical confirmation of Ossipon's 'scientific' method. And as we register that Ossipon's cult of the dispassionate and the rational is actually a mask for the paralysing horror welling up in him, so the nature of Conrad's exposure of the discourse becomes transparent. The deterministic ideology, whilst appearing to rescue deviants from the tendentious grip of moral censure, in fact exposes them to a more sinister practice. Characteristics of individuality, the indices of a person's unique identity, become the very means by which the deviant is objectified and reduced to a category of degeneration. The diagnostician, Ossipon, is left untouched by the hideous fatuity of his own theories as, with his ready explanation to the bystanders, he picks himself up unscathed from his last-minute jump from the train which carries Winnie off to her death.

CHAPTER 6

Max Nordau and the 'Degeneration' effect

I

Max Nordau (1849–1923) was the high priest of the creed of degeneration. His book *Entartung*, first published in Berlin in 1892, was its sacred text. Of Austro-Hungarian, Jewish origins, Nordau studied medicine and then settled in Paris as a journalist, and a polymathic one – not for him the narrow role of the specialist. Through the 1880s and early nineties Nordau became the era's great assimilator, reading as much as anyone might be expected to read in science, medicine, literature and the arts – in a number of languages.[1]

Capaciousness and remorselessness are the hallmarks of his procedures and of his text. Aggressively compendious, his book produces the effect of having being written not so much by a shaping intelligence as by the idea itself, with Nordau its secretary, recording the very rhythms and cacophonies of the late nineteenth-century metropolis.

No other writer was as successful as Nordau in goading the leading critics of the day into addressing the idea of degeneration, even if for the most part they roundly condemned him for it. *Entartung* was a sensation in Germany, and, shortly after, it reached Italy as *Degenerazione*. It was translated as *Dégénérescence* in France the following year, and as *Degeneration* in 1895 in America and England, where it ran to seven editions in six months and was the most spectacular of a clutch of literary successes of that year.[2] Yet within two years *Degeneration* was the subject of lengthy critiques and vigorous denunciation, and in due course its fate was ironic dismissal. The Nordau episode appeared to produce its own pathology – in a double movement of assertion and denial, of excitement and ennui – which Nordau repeatedly attributed to the culture of the *fin de siècle* itself.

Degeneration was a wholesale denunciation of tendencies in modern art – particularly in literature. Nordau's targets included Wagner, Nietzsche, Ibsen, Tolstoi, Zola and the French Symbolist poets. It constituted one of the most extraordinary examples of a book which was at once intellectually risible and strangely compelling, methodologically absurd and yet a logical extension of positivistic thought. Both in its highly derivative and unique character this strange book may be seen as the last positivistic epic – or to put it less charitably – as positivism run mad.

Nordau's central thesis concerns the pathology of artistic production. The artist produces his art as if the brain emitted vapours; both the act of production and the work manifest the pathological condition. Works of art are interpreted as, in Allon White's phrase, 'transcriptions of the fantasy life of psychically disturbed patients'.[3] Nordau forces texts into the realm of the author's subjectivity, while the author is ruthlessly objectified as unwell – and unaware, for he omits to credit the artist with intentionality, awareness of form, aesthetic distance or any grasp of the ironic or ambiguous resources of language. Nordau seeks evidence of degeneration not only in the individual works of writers (he appears to have read Ibsen's entire dramatic output), but in particular passages, lines and images from them.

Baudelaire, for Nordau, is a case of 'ego-mania' whose life 'showed all the mental stigmata of degeneration'.[4] For confirmation he raids over twenty poems from *Les Fleurs du mal*. He treats 'Le Gouffre', for example, as a poem where Baudelaire 'suffers ... from images of perpetual anguish'. He quotes an extract, the first line of which is 'Tout est abîme – action, désir, rêve.' Nordau shows little interest in Baudelaire's imaginative apprehension of an emotional state, rather he seizes on the image of the abyss as a literal manifestation of the poet's unconscious disorder, and so diagnoses a pathological condition, traced back to an 'obsession of degenerates which is called "fear of abysses" (cremnophobia)' (292–3). Odd lines from other poems, 'La Rêve d'un curieux', 'Spleen', 'Le Vin du solitaire', 'Le Crépuscule du soir', 'La Destruction', are strung together to prove Baudelaire's attraction to 'the morbid, the criminal and the lewd' (290). The highly selective choice of evidence in the hands of a skilled and remorseless analyst yields a certain numbing authenticity; a single point is hammered home in an endless series of proliferating syllogisms; Nordau beats the reader into critical submission. The project was certainly a brilliant vindication of the conventional and philistine attitude to art and the artist. What price the claim of the avant-garde to tell the truth of their seeing, when 'literary genius was characterised as a form of abnormality'?[5]

Abnormality could also be fixed as 'criminal', as in Nordau's notorious treatment of Verlaine. 'In this man', he remarks, 'we find, in astonishing completeness, all the physical and mental marks of degeneration' (119). But Nordau deploys science as straight abuse: Verlaine is 'a repulsive degenerate subject with asymmetric skull and Mongolian face, an impulsive vagabond and dipsomaniac' (128). Of course Verlaine's poetic style confirms this 'mental debility': 'the combination of completely disconnected nouns and adjectives which suggest each other . . . through a senseless meandering by the way of associated ideas . . . "a slow landscape" . . . "a slack liqueur (jus flasque)" ' (126).

Nordau finds degeneracy, to give another example, in the detailed realism of Zola. His descriptions of 'women's linen', the sight of which 'produces a peculiar excitation in him', confirms the novelist as a 'sexual psychopath' (500). Meting out reassurance and threat in equal measure, Nordau concludes darkly that 'this effect of female linen on degenerates affected by sexual psychopathy is well known in mental therapeutics' (500).

There are times when the characteristic tendencies of a culture are most accurately perceived by those most hostile to them. This was arguably the case with Nordau who identified and then attacked the seminal movements of the age: philosophical relativism and the aesthetic experiment of modernism. For Nordau the direction of progress could only be in the opposite direction, towards the 'contraction of the unconscious', 'the weakening of impulsion', 'the repression of reckless egoism' (554). 'Whoever worships his "I" ', is, for Nordau, 'an enemy of society' (560). Yet perversely such traces of the Nordau world-picture survived not only the turn of the century, but the late Edwardian encounter with modernism and the first world war.

II

Nordau's *Die conventionellen Lügen Der Kulturmenschheit* (*Conventional Lies of our Civilisation* (1883) was well received,[6] but his subsequent work – particularly in the theatre – had been less successful and, understandably enough, Nordau wanted another triumph. In an exhaustive account of the reception of *Degeneration*, Milton P. Foster has advanced a persuasive reason for its notorious success: 'To many English and American readers in 1895 Nordau must have seemed like a true prophet. He had written *Degeneration* during 1892 and 1893 and at that time called attention to pathological aberrations in Oscar Wilde's character. The English translation appeared just two months before Wilde was sentenced.'[7] A celebrated review of *Degeneration* in June 1895 by Hugh E. M. Stutfield – 'Tommyrotics' – connected Nordau's description of Oscar Wilde's apparent degeneracy with his conviction for homosexuality in the last week of May; the innuendo is brilliantly contrived in his reference to 'the direct intellectual progenitors of our aesthetes, whose doctrines Dr. Nordau examines at quite unnecessary length ... recent events, which shall be nameless, must surely have opened the eyes even of those who have hitherto been blind to the true inwardness of modern esthetic Hellenism, and perhaps the less said on this subject now the better.'[8]

Extraordinarily, in July 1896, Wilde petitioned the Home Secretary for his release, on the grounds that his homosexuality was a degenerate 'sexual madness' of a type peculiar to 'the literary and aesthetic temperament', and that it belonged to a class of 'diseases to be cured by a physician, rather than crimes to be punished by a judge'.[9] This accorded precisely with Nordau's studies of 'degenerates', one of whom was Wilde himself. Wilde could remind the Home Secretary that Nordau had 'devoted an entire chapter to the petitioner' (it was, in fact, three pages of one chapter). As John Stokes notes, on his release from Reading gaol Wilde was 'free to mock the spurious diagnosis he had formerly espoused': 'the fact that I am ... a pathological problem in the eyes of German scientists is only interesting to German scientists'.[10]

To stigmatise artists with the marks of insanity was not, of course, a new phenomenon. There was a long line of speculation from Plato and Aristotle down to the Romantics, which associated inspiration with states of insanity and madness. It was only in the mid-nineteenth century that the idea of genius, particularly the artistic genius, became gradually medicalised; the revered Romantic figure was displaced by the post-Romantic deviant. But by the late 1880s, there had developed a newly focussed fascination with the artist as a deviant subject.[11] J. F. Nisbet, drama critic of *The Times*, saw in a whole swathe of literary figures 'the long suspected relationship of genius and insanity' in *The Insanity of Genius* (1891) (it ran to a second edition that year and a further four up to 1912).[12] Francis Galton's second edition of *Hereditary Genius* (1892) took account of Lombroso's influential *L'uomo di genio* (1888), which appeared in Havelock Ellis's translation in 1891. And it was Ellis who, as we have already seen, perpetuated the link between Verlaine and the condition of criminal degeneracy in *The Criminal* (1890).

For Nordau individual artists were the most dangerous spokesmen of the world of the *fin de siècle*. And they were nourished and cultivated by a neurotic audience who besottedly fed the artist's delusions. Both artistic producer and consumer are caught up in a whirligig of the same condition – the disease of civilisation. The physician, 'especially if he has devoted himself to the special study of nervous and mental maladies', is well placed to recognise 'at a glance'

in the *fin de siècle* disposition, in the tendencies of contemporary art and poetry, in the life and conduct of the men who write mystic, symbolic and 'decadent' works, and the attitude taken by their admirers in the tastes and aesthetic instincts of fashionable society, the confluence of two well-defined conditions of disease, with which he is quite familiar ... degeneration ... and hysteria, of which the minor stages are designated as neurasthenia. These two conditions of the organism differ from each other, yet have many features in common. (15)

Wagner's and Ibsen's audiences, the readers of Zola and Wilde, are part of the hysterical condition which the degenerate artist both trades on and inflames. Just as intentionality is not a part of his equipment so discrimination is not a characteristic of his audience – which is prone, degenerately, to 'emotionalism' and susceptible to 'imitation'. Nordau sees this audience as pathologically infected by industrial society – its degenerate effects, compounded by a Lamarckian inheritance of degenerate variations, were acquired through the generations.

III

One effect of *Degeneration* was to draw into the open a range of writers and a bewildering number of opinions on the state of contemporary art' music and literature. Among them was Chekhov ('I read fools like Max Nordau with considerable distaste'),[13] Shaw, Henry Adams, Israel Zangwill, Andrew Lang, H. G. Wells, and later, T. S. Eliot.[14] Almost without exception those who welcomed *Degeneration* used the publication of the book to stoke the fires of antipathy to current aesthetic literary trends. W. J. Courthope, Professor of Poetry at Oxford, joined Nordau's attack on the 'wilful' confusion of genres in poetry,[15] and there was W. R. (later Dean) Inge, at the foothills of his own career as jeremiah, attacking the mysticism of contemporary art, as he continued to do into and through the 1920s.[16]

Both for traditionalists and for the exponents of the new there was clearly much at stake. Shaw's early denunciation 'A Degenerate's View of Nordau' (1895) (later reprinted as *The Sanity of Art* (1907)) was almost certainly provoked by Nordau's extensive treatment of Ibsen and Wagner, artists in whom Shaw had invested much of his credibility as a critic. In fact it was as a 'relief to the Wagner and Ibsen booms' that Shaw believed Nordau had spotted 'a good opening for a big reactionary book'.[17] Shaw had much fun with *Degeneration*, seeing off Nordau's denunciation of Wagner in two effective pages. Together with other of Nordau's most perceptive critics, Shaw accused him of falling prey to the very condition he was condemning in others, and invited him to 'tell us frankly whether, even in the ranks of his "psychiatrists" and lunacy doctors, he can pick out a crank more hopelessly obsessed with one idea than himself'.[18] B. A. Crackenthorpe cleverly mocked Nordau as that 'prince of graphomaniacs'. Nordau had described 'graphomania' as 'the restless repetition of one and the same strain of thought', allegedly manifested by Ibsen. Crackenthorpe thought this 'by far the best bit of criticism (all unconscious though it is) of Herr Nordau's *Degeneration* that has yet appeared.'[19]

Nordau's work also achieved the distinction of becoming a familiar and early point of psychological and criminological reference within contemporary fiction. In Bram Stoker's *Dracula* (1897) Mina Harker cites Nordau and Lombroso as evidence that 'the Count is a criminal and of criminal types Nordau and Lombroso would so classify him'.[20] And in Wells's *The Plattner Story* (April 1896), Nordau has clearly gained an ironically definitive status: Plattner is described as 'quiet, practical, unobtrusive, and thoroughly sane from the Nordau standpoint'.[21]

Wells was particularly adept at the casually insinuating and sceptical allusion to the vogue for Nordau. In his comic novel of 1895, *The Wonderful Visit*, a satire on English moral parochialism,

Nordau is indirectly mocked in the person of the local physician Doctor Crump. An angel descends on the village of Siddermorton. Its innocence of mortality and ignorance of physical deterioration and the division of labour provoke this doctor to pronounce it a deviant in the manner of Nordau:

A mattoid. An abnormal man. Did you notice the effeminate delicacy of his face? ... many of this type of degenerate show this same disposition to assume some vast mysterious credentials. One will call himself the Prince of Wales, another the Archangel Gabriel, another the Deity even. Ibsen thinks he is a Great Teacher and Maeterlinck a new Shakespeare. I've just been reading all about it – in Nordau.[22]

Wells wittily points up a tactic of degeneracy-peddlers – the use of a scientific diagnosis to stigmatise the inexplicable and to fix abnormal behaviour as a deviant form – here the mad genius. Lady Hammeryellow believes the angel is a genius but then has to censure him when he shows amorous interest in a servant. In the figure of Doctor Crump Wells's exposure of small-time earnestness sounds a more sinister note when he tries to get rid of the disruptive angel by certifying it as insane. Crump also comically voices the personal frustration of a diagnostician, soaked in Lombroso and Nordau, who looks in vain for a single suitable degenerate patient among the 'thoroughly sane people' of the village: 'I wish Nordau or Lombroso or some of these Salpetrière men could have a look at you. Down here one gets no practice worth speaking about in mental cases.'[23] Another parish doctor comes in for satiric treatment some years later when in *The Food of the Gods* (1904), Wells has him speaking eulogistically of Nordau: ' "A most gifted and celebrated philosopher, Lady Wondershoot. He discovered that the abnormal is – abnormal, a most valuable discovery, and well worth bearing in mind. When I come upon anything abnormal, I say at once, this is abnormal." His eyes became profound, his voice dropped, his manner verged upon the intimately confidential.'[24]

With Zola and Ibsen long accepted in literary circles, and Nietzsche's work promoted by a growing number of enthusiastic critics, it was not difficult to demonstrate the flimsiness of Nordau's views on art and civilisation. Besides Shaw's attack, two other lengthy studies of Nordau took Nordau to task: William Hirsch's *Genie und Entartung, eine Psychologische Studie* (1895) translated into English as *Genius and Degeneration: A Psychological Study* (1897) and E. A. Hake's *Regeneration: A Reply to Max Nordau* (1896).

For Havelock Ellis, writing with the hindsight of thirty years, Nordau was simply 'a clever German journalist in Paris, who had the journalist's flair to concoct in a popular shape the not very scientific doctrine of "degeneration" then floating in the air and applying it to contemporary men of letters and art'.[25] While Ellis incorporated degeneration in his studies of criminal anthropology and sexual deviation, he rejected its application to artists. Indeed one of his singular achievements was to promote a favourable, early response to writers whom Nordau specifically attacked; Nietzsche (one of the earliest British evaluations), Huysmans and Ibsen.[26] In the curious absence of a direct riposte to Nordau, Ellis's essay 'The Colour Sense in Literature' must stand as his indirect reply.[27]

Degeneration drew perhaps the most analytically penetrating critiques from two philosophers of the pragmatic school, William James (1842–1910) and F. C. S. Schiller (1864–1937). James pointed out ✓ that the fallacy of Nordau's approach in 'his bulky book'[28] resided in his attempt to apply indiscriminately pseudo-scientific terms like 'degeneracy' and 'morbidity' to what were in fact distinct conditions of being:

The trouble is that such writers as Nordau use the descriptive names of symptoms merely as an artifice for giving objective authority to their personal dislikes. Medical terms become mere 'appreciative' clubs to knock men down with. Call a man 'mad' and you've settled his social status. Call him a 'degenerate' and you have grouped him with the most loathsome specimens of the race, in spite of the fact that he may be one of its most precious members.[29]

And Schiller condemned the 'semantic unreliability' of Nordau's use of the term degeneration. It was 'pseudo-scientific humbug' to take 'some prevalent technical term' and make 'a great stir by giving to it a vague and indefinite extension of meaning'. He went on to point out:

In biology the term 'degeneration' has a definite reference to the past history of an organism, and indicates that organs and structures which it formerly possessed have decayed or disappeared. Or, morphologically, 'degeneration' may be used to designate any change in the direction of less complexity, when progress has been defined as a process tending towards greater complexity. But in neither case is any slur cast on the organism . . . by saying that in some respects it is degenerate.[30]

Whether it is used in its biological or morphological sense, there must be a state from which the object of inspection – civilisation, poet, criminal – has degenerated, says Schiller: 'this is what Nordau assiduously avoids doing – lest it should appear that "degeneration" in some form or other is coeval with some form of humanity itself, and that the "type" to which his reasoning logically conducts him must be some providentially extinct form of ape'.[31] It is an essential insight. Schiller and James were among the very few (Shaw was another) who effectively broke down the synthesis of biological and metaphorical components in the term.

Paradoxically, Nordau's very polemical success helped undermine the status of degeneration as a serious diagnostic category, particularly in the area of mental pathology. Doubts had been voiced within the profession: 'Is it useful in the understanding of mental illnesses?', asked a French doctor in 1895. Fewer people seemed to know what the concept meant: 'the quarrel turns as much on the words as on their contents; nobody agrees to speak the same language'.[32] By the turn of the century, as we have seen, Havelock Ellis had come to the same conclusion.[33]

But if the diagnostic value of the concept was shrinking in the eyes of specialists, it stubbornly refused to surrender its value as generalising shorthand currency. In 1908 Wilfred Trotter ruefully reflected that degeneration was just an all-purpose 'catchword' which was seriously inhibiting investigation into the 'real meaning' of what he took to be the 'steady increase' of 'the mentally unstable'. 'That question', he wrote, 'has been seriously begged by the invention of the disastrous word "degenerate". The simplicity of the idea has charmed modern speculation.'[34]

Freud had also come to view degeneration as a nuisance. Back in the mid-nineties he had expressed reservations about how the 'French school of psychiatrists' would diagnose the symptoms shown by his hysterical patients. Whereas it would uncover 'stigmata of neurotic degeneracy' Freud believed such symptoms to be 'adequately determined by traumatic experience'.[35] Degeneracy had ceased to have any use for Freud, although he still called on heredity to explain sexual abnormalities in the family, the new focus of his enquiries.

Twenty years later he claimed that degeneration theory was still in currency among European psychiatrists. The sexual aetiology which he had evolved to account for the precise working of the 'concealed motives which have often remained unconscious'[36] had made little headway in psychiatry, which was still wedded to what he saw as an anachronistic and moralistic symptomology:

Psychiatry gives names to the different obsessions but says nothing further about them. On the other hand it insists that those who suffer are 'degenerates'. This gives small satisfaction; in fact it is a judgement of value – a condemnation instead of an explanation . . . we are supposed to think that every possible sort of eccentricity may arise in degenerates. Well it is true that we must regard those who develop such symptoms as somewhat different in their nature from other people. But we may ask: are they more 'degenerate' than other neurotics – than hysterical patients, for instance . . . Once again, the characterization is evidently too general. Indeed, we may doubt whether there is any justification for it at all, when we learn that such symptoms occur in distinguished people of particularly high capacities.[37]

Freud is frequently illuminating about specific works and artists, but on the subject of the psychology of the artist and the reception of art his views partook of the very judgmental reductionism he had imputed to the psychiatry of his time. If Nordau had spoken of degenerate compulsions, Freud spoke of neurotic ones. Art, for Freud, was a form of sublimation, artistic works the gratification of unconscious wishes. Burdened by strong instinctual needs, the artist is compelled to withdraw from unsatisfactory reality.[38] The public for art was also suspect. 'Art affects us', he said, 'but as a mild narcotic and can provide no more than a temporary refuge for us from the hardships of life; its influence is not strong enough to make us forget real misery.'[39] This positivism sits far too comfortably alongside those inheritors of Nordau's jeremiads against artistic experiment and modernity, whose strident voices could still be heard well into the inter-war period.

IV

Looking back from the early 1920s to the origins of the modernist novel, Virginia Woolf famously asserted in 'Mr Bennett and Mrs Brown' that 'in or about December, 1910, human character changed'.[40] As Samuel Hynes noted, she was alluding with this ostentatiously precise dating to Roger Fry's first Post-Impressionist exhibition 'Manet and the Post-Impressionists', which ran at London's Grafton Gallery from 8 November 1910 to 15 January 1911.[41] The exhibition was itself a landmark in the British acceptance of modernist art.

Yet human 'character' had changed very little to judge by the reaction of some critics to paintings by Cézanne, Van Gogh, Gauguin and others. 'It was a relief to breathe the petroleum-laden air of Bond Street', confided Sir William Richmond, on emerging from the 'suffocating tomb' of the exhibition. 'For a moment there came a fierce feeling of terror lest the youth of England ... might be contaminated here. On reflection I was reassured that the youth of England, being healthy in mind and body, is far too virile to be moved save in resentment against the providers of this unmanly show.'[42] Here was a strong aftertaste of familiar arguments and tropes. While the exhibition was not lambasted as thoroughly as Woolf believed (she could only recall one supportive press review)[43], Fry's exhibition drew out the avatars of a still resilient degenerationist mentality: critics such as Richmond, T. B. Hyslop, Robert Ross, E. Wake Cook and C. J. Weld-Blundell collectively showed that the school of criticism founded on principles laid down by Lombroso and Nordau was alive and well and living in Georgian England.

It was perhaps understandable that critics of this cast of mind should want to go on the offensive, since, together with the second Post-Impressionist exhibition, this was an avowedly polemical event. Desmond MacCarthy, who composed the introduction to the exhibition catalogue, and Roger Fry, in articles for the *Nation*, published as the exhibition was in progress, certainly understood it as a key event in the imprinting of modernism on the British consciousness.

Relishing the controversial nature of the material, Fry readily conceded that the Post-Impressionists had jettisoned the 'tempered realism' of post-mediaeval artistic representation and the 'photographic vision' developed during the nineteenth century, not for a 'barbaric art', but for the 'necessary' task of rescuing art from 'the hopeless encumbrance of its own accumulations of science' in order that it might 'regain its power to express emotional ideas'.[44] MacCarthy made clear the anti-empirical, anti-materialist basis of Post-Impressionism, in his objection to the traditional equation of 'truth' with the ideal of the 'close representation of nature'. Instead he proposed an art which transmitted the 'emotional significance which lies in things': this was 'the most important subject matter of art'.[45]

Bloomsbury's claims for the event were probably fair, if not exactly modest: 'it is impossible', wrote Vanessa Bell, 'that any other single exhibition can ever have had so much effect as did that on the rising generation'.[46] By the same token, to certain sections of the art establishment the exhibition indeed represented a powerful provocation. Here, as S. K. Tillyard notes, was 'degeneracy, lunacy and gross subjectivism' flying in the face of 'natural truth and scientific fact'.[47]

It was, inevitably, the work of Van Gogh which signalled these defects most acutely. Robert Ross (a director of the Carfax Gallery in London) dismissed the claims of the subjective and followed Nordau's 'scientific' procedure of analysing the art work as an emanation of a pathologised imagination: 'the emotions of these painters (one of whom, Van Gogh, was a lunatic) are of no interest except to the student of pathology and the specialist in abnormality'.[48] Even so, Van Gogh was the 'typical mattoid and degenerate of the modern sociologist'.[49] According to *The Athenaeum*, in Van Gogh's paintings 'the churned up paint moves ... spasmodically: beside the well-controlled stroke of the great masters this is the twitch of the paralytic'.[50] The *Daily Express* talked of an 'epileptic landscape by Matisse'.[51]

These were indeed the simplistic strategies that Nordau employed in *Degeneration*. Once again it seemed a straightforward matter to assimilate the terms of the life to the work. Van Gogh's *Jeune fille au bluet* 'was evidence of mental and physical collapse'.[52] And given the subtitle 'The Mad Girl in Zola's *Germinal*', for those who recalled Nordau's demolition job on Zola, what more was there to be said? As Tillyard comments, 'the critics' correlation between abstraction and insanity was apparently verified by Van Gogh's acknowledged madness, Gauguin's rejection of the civilized world and Cézanne's reclusive habits'.[53] A household name in the 1930s, Van Gogh and his *Sunflowers* still attracted the pronouncement: "mad" '[54].

The labelling system of the nineties was still in good order. These artists were subversive political extremists, or at least 'amiable anarchists', as Ebenezer Wake Cook called them. He had first enunciated this view in 1904 in *Anarchism in Art and Chaos in Criticism*. Progress in art meant maintaining existing standards and raising them by 'progressive evolution', not having them 'overturned by a French Revolution which shall begin by guillotining Academicians and other guardians of law and orderly development'.[55] Assaults on the artistic establishment (symbolised by the

Royal Academy) back in 1895 'were mainly in the interests of the
New English Art Club, and the foreign Bolshevicks of the International Society'.[56]

The association between criminality and the artist had been
discredited at the turn of the century, yet Ross seemed keen still to
insinuate it: 'at Broadmoor there are a number of Post-Impressionists detained at his Majesty's Pleasure', he remarked.[57] Or the idea
of reversion was invoked: these artists, said the *Connoisseur*, had 'gone
back to simple and primitive forms of expression, those of children
and savage races'.[58]

Here was a hall of mirrors in which the degenerationists by their
production of distorted images, in the name of scientific moralism, so
nearly got it right. Look at the way, they said, Fry carried on: 'with
his talk of Van Gogh as a visionary who had seen God'[59] – Fry's
proseletysing certainly had a religiose colouring. It was perhaps
inevitable that he and other advocates of the new art would select
the imputed 'degenerate' features for the highest praise'.[60]

Of course for degenerationist critics, the very enthusiasm with
which the exhibition was greeted by the avant-garde was itself proof
of the degeneracy of the enterprise and its fashionable, gullible
acolytes. The physician T. B. Hyslop (1864–1933) was one such
critic who, like Wake Cook, pursued a long and sustained campaign
against what he saw as unhealthy and insane degenerate art. A
practising artist (he had exhibited at the Royal Academy) he
believed that good art was 'true to nature'. The views of Hyslop,
Wake Cook, Richmond, Ross and others lead along an undeviating
path back to Nordau. His 1911 article 'Post-Illusionism and Art in
the Insane' was based on a lecture given some months earlier, at
which Fry was present. Virginia Woolf recalled in her biography of
Fry that Hyslop 'gave his opinion before an audience of artists and
craftsmen that the paintings were the work of madmen'. His conclusions 'were accepted with enthusiastic applause.'[61] Attacking the
public for its enthusiastic reception of the exhibition, Hyslop pro-
ceeded to arraign the event as a manifestation of the pathological
condition which had engulfed the artists. 'Degenerates', he wrote,
following Nordau, 'often turn their unhealthy impulses towards art,
and not only do they sometimes attain to an extraordinary degree of
prominence but they may also be followed by enthusiastic admirers
who herald them as creators of new eras of art'.[62] Success,
'prominence', 'admirers', had to be explained away as deplorable

symptoms of a child-like, regressive public. The circularity of the argument against degenerate art was complete.

A year later, in 1912, at the height of public discussion about the best means to legislate against the 'feeble-minded', Hyslop showed himself to be a true 'eugenicist of art',[63] when he chillingly claimed that necessary eugenic measures, designed to weed out mental defectives, were being now hampered by soft-hearted attitudes which indulged the rights of this group:

In the history of every prophylactic measure adapted for the benefit of the greatest number there has ever been much opposition and delay owing to *fetish worship of the liberty of the subject* (my italics) and ... in spite of the overwhelming evidence of much evil inheritance that tends to destroy the vital energies of the nation, there are many who will raise their voices in indignant protestation.[64]

Hyslop is a striking case of a professional physician who, in the style of men of an earlier generation, had no inhibitions in publicly pronouncing on matters outside his field of competence. The eugenic frame of reference, as we have seen, sought to mark out as degenerate all that was deemed injurious to the health of the nation and its 'stock' – and that included psychoanalytic as well as artistic experiment, 'subjectivism' and mysticism.

At the end of the first world war in which the 'vital energies of the nation' had been expended beyond imagining, Hyslop once more had artists and writers in his sights accusing them of creating an unsettling climate of neurosis. He delivered a paper cataloguing instances of neurosis and degeneracy in artists from Giorgione to Rubens and from Reynolds to Fuseli.[65] And like Arthur Conan Doyle, who bracketed Nietzsche, the Post-Impressionists and the Futurists as part of a 'wave of artistic and intellectual insanity',[66] Hyslop revived the connection between the artist genius and a pathology of morbidity and insanity. Max Nordau's legacy – the *Degeneration* effect – was not, after all, quite spent.

CHAPTER 7

Women and the disease of civilisation: George Gissing's 'The Whirlpool'

I

Four months before he began *The Whirlpool* (1897), Gissing read Herbert Spencer's *Education* (1861), in which the opening chapter contains this confident pronouncement: 'Nature is a strict accountant; and if you demand of her in one direction more than she is prepared to lay out, she balances the account by making a deduction elsewhere.'[1] Spencer's 'nature' was the process of reproduction in which women find their 'natural' role. Spencer defines and limits women according to their function to bear and nurture children. Activity at any level of intensity unconnected with this function is an unnatural source of pressure, producing a deleterious 'tax' on the female system. As Spencer put it: 'assuming the preservation of the race to be a desideratum, there results certain kinds of obligation to pay this tax and to submit to this sacrifice'.[2]

Women are thus abstracted and positioned within a grand process of reproduction, for which an appropriate rhetoric emerges from the concepts of economics and accountancy. A similar trope, conveying a comparable message, occurs in an influential essay of 1874 by Henry Maudsley: 'The energy of a human body being a definite and not inexhaustible quantity, can it bear, without injury, an excessive mental drain as well as the natural physical drain which is so great at that time [pregnancy]? ... When Nature spends in one direction, she must economise in another direction.'[3] For Maudsley, as well as for Spencer, 'nature' has to balance the books, and consequently the taxes levied by motherhood leave women with little capital to invest elsewhere.

An alternative model for the female system is implicit in Maudsley's assumption of a finite quantity of energy in the human body – the description of the nervous system as subject to the laws of physics. From the 1850s Joule and Helmholtz (and earlier Dubois-Reymond) had been formulating the laws of the conservation of energy.[4] Nervous organisations came to be thought of as energy systems which, like batteries, expended energy only in proportion to their capacity to store it via a dynamo. When energy had been overexpended there would be signs of 'dimming', and the system would be unable to recharge.[5] Experiments which showed that nerves had an electric potential and responded to electrical stimulation lent credibility to this mechanical model.[6] Thus by the 1870s the medical profession was tending to treat nervous organisations very much as dubious or even failed mechanisms. Notoriously, electrical treatment was administered, often quite indiscriminately, to the brain cortex.[7]

From the persistent application of these positivistic models of woman's 'natural' state – where all wasteful expenditure of energy, outside the apparent calm of home, hearth and nursery, brought its inescapable penalties – emerged the concept of the neurasthenic woman. The American George M. Beard was the first to use the term 'neurasthenia', a disease which he claimed was a response to the accelerating growth of large cities after the Civil War. He believed nerve weakness to be the inevitable consequence of overtaxing the nerve supply by the frenetic pursuit of wealth through business and commerce.[8] According to optimists like Beard, nervous fatigue was the inevitable fallout of a dynamic, forceful society. And it comes as no surprise to find that this analysis intersected with the evolutionary optimism of Herbert Spencer who had, in any case, gained a far wider hearing among American intellectuals and business people than he had received from their counterparts in England.[9] As Charles Rosenberg suggests:

Neurasthenia was a concept exactly suited to the interest, particularly evident in America, in Darwinian and Spencerian notions of biological and social evolution and degeneration. Primitive man was protected from many of the mental diseases of civilised man by his natural state [whereas] civilised man ... through his evolutionary progress was subject to 'dissolution' – a sort of collapse of the evolutionary gains.[10]

If women demanded too much in the way of cerebral activity and independence then 'nature' would exact its price and neurasthenia or hysteria would result. The cure was to abandon celibacy for the 'natural' exercise of the reproductive faculties. According to Spencer: 'The not infrequent occurrence of hysteria and chlorosis shows that women, in whom the reproductive function bears a larger ratio to the totality of the functions than it does in men, are apt to suffer grave constitutional evils from that incompleteness of life which celibacy implies.'[11]

Women became doubly bound to this evolutionary and teleological view. While they were deemed essential to the evolutionary struggle of the race, they were also, in increasing numbers, diagnosed to be suffering the stresses and strains resulting from the struggle. This 'hysterization' of women, to use Foucault's term,[12] became more pronounced as the need to regulate fecundity in the interest of racial progress gathered force from the *fin de siècle*. And it is in this period that among other writers – Sarah Grand in *The Heavenly Twins* (1893) and Thomas Hardy in *Jude the Obscure* (1895) – George Gissing directs a discourse of specifically female pathology at the female protagonist of his novel *The Whirlpool* (1897).

II

By the early nineties Gissing had established himself as a novelist and short-story writer of critical although not popular significance. Crucial for that recognition was his having laid claim to a distinctive fictional world – the territory of marginality, assigned to the 'unclassed' poor, the displaced intellectual, the unintegrated 'odd' women, or the aspiring lower-middle class.[13] Gissing's most assured works, *The Nether World* (1889), *New Grub Street* (1891), *Born in Exile* (1892), *The Odd Women* (1893) and *In The Year of Jubilee* (1894), represent all these marginal groups.

The Whirlpool (1897) unquestionably joins the ranks of these novels, and yet it marks the development of a new phase in Gissing's work. For he writes now, not of the rim, but of the hub itself – fashionable, moneyed London, the epicentre of the *demi-monde*. It is as if (superficially) the ambience were that of George Meredith's *One of Our Conquerors*(1891)[14] or of Henry James's *The Awkward Age* (1898). Yet marginality remains Gissing's preoccupation. The marginal territory is not now a social but a psychopathological borderland, assigned predominantly to female neurosis.

Why should Gissing, at this stage in his career, have recourse to this psychological strategy? The fact is that his difficulties with woman's 'nature' were long-standing. His problem was to square his genuine respect for the intelligence of women with his aversion to what he took to be their destructive emotionalism. The mid-nineties saw Gissing in retreat from the feminist implications of his own fine study of the quest for female autonomy, *The Odd Women* (1893). By 1894 he was writing (somewhat prematurely) that 'people are getting very tired of the "woman question" '; he did not want his novel of that year, *In The Year of Jubilee*, 'to be regarded in that light'.[15]

The disclaimer is understandable. *In The Year of Jubilee* does treat (however unconvincingly) the highly topical 'marriage question'. It also offers a Spencerian case of the harmful 'tax' which intellectual effort imposes on women, notably in the figure of Jessica Morgan, whose periodic hysterical outbursts and eventual nervous break-down are the result of her 'cramming' for university examinations.[16] Gissing would seem to be in retreat from the view that woman's incapacity is open to a merely cultural explanation, and is resorting to a more thoroughgoing biologistic model, derived from the ortho-doxy of Darwinian positivism.[17]

But the novel announces another theme, the infusion of the energies of contemporary materialism into national aspirations. No wonder, then, if within four months of the publication of *In The Year of Jubilee* Gissing found himself influenced by Nordau's *Degeneration*, which had just been published in English.[18] Here was a psycho-pathology which linked those materialist energies to the city, the menacing repository of a disease of civilisation. The neurasthenic and hysteric state, which Gissing already assumed to be the sign of woman's nature under stress, was now assimilated into an embrac-ing degenerate condition. While Gissing conceded that *Degeneration* contained 'a great deal of exaggeration,'[19] coming when it did it was too serviceable a text for him to resist. Like Hardy's Sue Bridehead in *Jude the Obscure* (1895), Gissing's Alma Rolfe in *The Whirlpool* is, in Ian Fletcher's words, 'a new type of woman, the *névrose*, the modern hysteric.'[20] She is also the marked-out representative of the forces signified by the title of the novel itself – 'the vertigo and whirl of our frenzied life', as Nordau puts it.[21] The image of the whirlpool[22] was used in the same month in which *Degeneration* appeared in English in an article for the *Contemporary Review*, 'Nervous Diseases and Modern Life'. Its author, the pathologist Clifford Allbutt, pointed the finger with an insinuating rhetorical flourish to 'hysteria, to neurasthenia, to the fretfulness, the melancholy, the unrest due to living at high pressure, to the whirl of the railway, the pelting of telegrams, the strife of business, the hunger for riches, the lust of vulgar minds for coarse and instant pleasures ... '[23]

Allbutt's title could well stand as the subtitle of a Gissing novel. Both in Nordau and Allbutt the locale in which the 'nervous' condition flourished was the city. Alma is not the only victim of the metropolis in the novel, but her case is the most fully worked out from the materials of a predetermined and coherent discourse: the availability of these materials gives Alma's career its curious authenticity. Her own condition fuses with the overdetermined condition of this ambitious novel. Not for the first time, Gissing turns psychological deadlock into a compelling study of obsession.

From H. G. Wells onwards, commentators on *The Whirlpool* have usually placed the quest by Alma's husband Harvey Rolfe for a meaningful pact with the compromising metropolitan world at the centre of the novel's concerns.[24] This male-centred response has certainly been encouraged by Gissing's own interpretation, which emerged in a frank exchange with Wells.[25] Gissing made it clear to Wells that Rolfe was rescued from cynicism and egoism by the experience of fatherhood. At first a pragmatist and social Darwinist, embracing the 'fighting future', Rolfe becomes feminised by the experience of sacrifice. We can place this transformation in positivistic terms, as the traditional cure for self-regard by altruism – a movement which informs the very ideology of parenthood whose obligations Alma will refuse.

Against this dynamic, Rolfe's consciously experimental marriage to Alma is only insubstantially realised; indeed it hardly gathers momentum at all. While the marriage is predicated on the choice of a simple life-style as an explicit counter to the false sophistication of the London way of life, it is left as a gesture towards that style. We do not learn how they might live out the experiment. Late in the novel Rolfe concludes, 'how much better for him and for her if they had never met ... he with his heart and mind set on grave, quiet restful things, hating the world's tumult ... she, her senses crying for the delight of an existence that loses itself in whirl and glare'.[26]

Yet this is not merely a question of bad judgement on Rolfe's part, or a lack of compatibility between him and Alma. Gissing cannot allow Alma and Rolfe to confront their differences in a realised form because their relationship is programmatically regulated by the requirements of an ideology of female nature. Throughout the various phases of the marriage (each signalled by a change of environment: the move from fashionable London to rural Wales, and then to the London suburbs), Alma brings with her a condition of urban anxiety. What results is the undermining of that trust which both parties have deemed essential for the success of their marriage experiment. Gissing clearly blames Alma for this failure of trust. The narrative is cleverly structured to intensify misunderstanding into mistrust, establishing Alma through various ethical motifs – integrity, altruism, the commitment to children – on the wrong side of a line dividing moral from lawless behaviour.

Early in the marriage Alma nurses a suspicion that Rolfe has a hidden understanding with another woman, Mary Abbott. Mary has undertaken the welfare and education of two children deserted by a mutual friend, who later commits suicide after his investments in a company, owned by Alma's father, crash. Rolfe does the decent thing and puts up half the money for the childrens' maintenance; but on marrying Alma, he refrains from telling her of this arrangement. This rather curious lack of candour attracts no comment from Gissing. Instead he stresses Rolfe's magnanimity: while not free of money worries, he unfailingly meets Alma's needs and distances himself from financial matters as far as he can.

The consequences of his evasiveness become visible in an important episode, early in the second section of the novel, when Mary Abbott pays a visit to the Rolfes, now settled in North Wales. The 'Carn Bodvean' episode shockingly expresses the gulf that separates Alma from authorial sympathy. Rolfe and Mary Abbott are on the mountainside 'airily discussing the education of children and the "whirlpool way of life" '[27], as Patrick Parrinder puts it, while Alma is down in the valley, converting her jealousy into angry physical assertion: she takes out a horse and trap to meet Rolfe and Mary and impetuously decides to drive for the first time herself.

Alma's behaviour seems to confirm that she is suffering from the very whirlpool condition which Rolfe is describing to Mary Abbott on the mountainside: 'the whirlpool of the furiously busy. Round and round they go; brains humming till they melt or explode. Of course, they can't bother with children' (157). Alma's revolt finds immediate expression in a miscarriage, brought on in the wake of a fit of hysteria, which expresses the condition of nervous women of the *fin de siècle*.[28]

Just before Alma faints on the return to the house we glimpse Gissing's authorial position through Rolfe's interpretation of his wife's loss of control. From marks on the wheel of the trap he realises that Alma had also lost control of the horse over a considerable distance: 'Without doubt, she had had a very narrow escape. Her anger seemed to be the result of nerves upset and mortified vanity; she wished to show Mrs. Abbott that she could drive – the explanation of the whole matter. Harvey was vexed at such a piece of childishness'(159). Rolfe's diagnosis of Alma's irrational behaviour carries the stamp of authorial approval. No counter-diagnosis is made available, no alternative centre of authority which could mediate between husband and wife at this crisis. The nameless doctor attending Alma is merely functional, and Mary, herself faint with agitation and weariness, is virtually silent. Could it be Gissing himself who is the honorary physician here, voicing through the unironised Rolfe his objectification of Alma as a patient?

And Rolfe's own responsibility in the matter is left uninspected. He fails to reassure Alma with the necessary facts about his own selfless project; the gulf of silence is as wide as ever. Yet his silence is surely irrational – as irrational as the hysteria which Alma displays in her conversion of her silenced utterance to physical form. He responds to Alma's effusive apologies and self-abnegation after the event by evading the source of her difficulty through his half-joking, half-admonishing bedside manner: 'The way to please me is to get some colour into your cheeks again, and snub me for my ignorance of music, and be your own arrogant self'(165). To see (with Gissing) Rolfe as wishing to accommodate Alma here, is to miss the point. What is more at issue is the reassertion of male control, with Rolfe in full command of the discursive field which exacts feminine subjugation to the male speaker. The incident serves to confirm Alma as neurotic and irrational, viewed from the value-free perspective of the healthily sane male.

Another significant crisis erupts in the third section of *The Whirlpool*. Alma's suspicion of a secret relationship has not been allayed and she opens a letter addressed to Rolfe acknowledging the receipt of his regular cheque. She now concludes that the children are Rolfe's by a previous liaison and that Mary Abbott is party to the cover-up. But out of feelings of resentment and because, as her musical interests take root, she is increasingly committed to the whirlpool socialite world of Felix Dymes, Cyrus Redgrave and Mrs Strangeways, Alma suppresses her feelings of grievance.

Months later, after her debut concert and after she is the involuntary witness of the murder of Redgrave, her paranoia is fuelled by Rolfe's suggestion that they move from one suburb of London to another to be nearer Mary Abbott who will undertake the future education of their son. Now in a more advanced state of nervous weakness, Alma begins to break down. Rolfe assumes that Alma, who is ill-disposed to the move, wants to avoid seeing Abbott. Instead of confronting her anxiety, Rolfe now questions her right to decide what to do with the boy. At this point Gissing introduces the blooming mother of four, Mrs Morton, whom Rolfe and Alma visit. And full of the fecund and harmonious atmosphere of the provincial backwater of Greystone, Rolfe now asserts his paternal idealism and appropriates the moral authority for deciding about Hughie's future, supposedly with the assent of the reader, as Mrs. Morton is clearly meant to form an attractive contrast in the reader's mind to Alma's maternal inadequacy. The climax of the scene is convincing; yet the perspective the reader is expected to take is a disturbing one:

'Why do you behave as if I were guilty of something – as if I had put myself at your mercy? You never found fault with me – you even encouraged me to go on –.'

Her choking voice made Harvey look at her in apprehension, and the look stopped her just as she was growing hysterical.

'You are right about my letter', he said, very gravely, and quietly. 'It ought to have been in a kinder tone. It would have been, but for those words you won't explain.'

'You think it needs any explanation that I dislike the thought of Hughie going to Mrs Abbott's?'

'Indeed I do. I can't imagine a valid ground for your objection.'

There was a word on Alma's tongue [presumably,liar] but her lips would not utter it. She turned very pale under the mental conflict. Physical weakness, instead of overcoming her spirit, excited it to a fresh effort of resistance.

'Then', she said, rising from the chair, 'you are not only unkind to me, but dishonest.'

Harvey flushed.

'You are making yourself ill again. We had far better not talk at all ...'

... Rolfe hesitated. Believing that her illness was the real cause of this commotion, he felt it his duty to use all possible forbearance; yet he knew too well the danger of once more yielding, and at such a crisis. The contest had declared itself – it was will against will; to decide it by the exertion of his sane strength against Alma's hysteria might be best even for the moment. (355–6)

In describing how Freud undermined the intellectual defenses of his hysterical patients, Elaine Showalter writes that late Victorian nerve doctors 'saw themselves locked in combat with their hysterical patients in a contest for mastery'.[29] Rolfe's subduing of Alma can plausibly be interpreted in these terms; she can be seen as his 'patient' who carries the overdetermining condition of mental and nervous weakness. And in his 'duty to use all possible forbearance' and his 'sane strength', his rational authority is leant authorial support. Once more the narrative voice ratifies the ideology of male power. We notice, for instance, how Alma's feelings are filtered through Rolfe's diagnostic vision of her. The awakening of the reader's expectation that Alma will be in charge of her own destiny is frustrated as Rolfe reads off her surface behaviour as if it was the key to her state of mind. And while there is a hint that Gissing qualifies Rolfe's diagnosis – we see his flushing hesitation, and the uncertainty conveyed by '*Believing* that her illness was the *real* cause of this commotion', it is Rolfe's viewpoint rather than Alma's which is privileged. Alma is left to draw attention to herself through physical behaviour – the female subject is again on display but only in its objectified form. The historian of science, Carroll Smith-Rosenberg, is helpful here when she suggests that while 'hysteria as a chronic, dramatic and socially accepted sick role could ... provide some alleviation of conflict and tension ... the hysteric purchased her escape ... only at the cost of pain, disability, and an intensification of woman's traditional passivity and dependence.'[30]

The upshot of this crisis for Rolfe is to confirm a stereotype of female behaviour, rather than to provoke questions about the cause of Alma's neurosis. Her crisis keeps Rolfe as far away from understanding as ever. When Alma's fears do spill out, in the form of an accusation, Rolfe has no difficulty in dismissing it, as he can explain that 'it is I who support those children and pay for their education' – and her question as to why he has kept this information secret, he answers with 'burlesque gravity'. He then meditates, not on the implications of the male ethic to 'keep secrets from ... wives,' but rather (without, I think, attracting authorial irony) 'on Woman' (359).

Rolfe's behaviour is judged to be little more than an allowable male lapse. Unrestrained by the interposition of a sceptical point of view, Rolfe is very much a free subject, whereas Alma is bound to the pervasive discourse governing neurasthenic women. In the 'hysterization' of Alma, any sense of her personal history, her origins, is virtually absent. Indeed, shortly after his meditation Gissing has

Rolfe put this question to himself: 'His thoughts wandered over all he knew of Alma's life. He wished he knew more, that he might better understand her. Of her childhood, her early maidenhood, what conception had he?' (359). Alma really is a closed book – both to Rolfe and the reader. Early on Alma's step-mother informs Rolfe that Alma's mother was 'handsome, and had some natural gifts, especially a good voice,' that her education was rudimentary, and that 'she died suddenly, after an evening at the theatre, where, as usual, she had excited herself beyond measure' (136), but apart from this information Rolfe and the reader have little to go on.

Gissing has structured Alma as a case of the deleterious effects of the whirlpool existence on the female constitution, rather than as an individual whose past and inner life are available for utterance. Whereas Rolfe is characterised by rational and moral deliberation, Alma is by contrast in control of very little – she is instead moved by irresistable waves of energy and is magnetically drawn to the sophis-ticated irrationality of the rentier's metropolis.

Towards the end of the second section of the novel the prepar-ations for Alma's concert are described. The day before Alma is due to perform, Rolfe's impetuous friend Carnaby, believing a rumour that the aesthete Redgrave is having an affair with his wife, dashes over to Redgrave's bungalow and, seeing him with a woman in the shadows, strikes him down, killing him. Out of the shadows emerges not Carnaby's wife Sybil, but Alma – who begs him to conceal the fact of her presence. Alma is now caught between her supposed infatuation with the murdered Redgrave – her influential musical backer – and the need to maintain appearances to her husband. What keeps her awake at night, driving her nearer the final overdose of morphine, is the continuing memory of that moment of unfulfilled desire which she now converts into jealousy of Sybil Carnaby, whom she believes stole Redgrave's affections from her.

Again, Gissing does not allow these feelings rational access. There is no mode of utterance in the novel which takes the reader closer to Alma, other than the outward signs of her 'nature' in revolt. Indeed, under the extreme psychological pressure induced by these unresolved conflicts, her nature appears to reveal something darker; it is, in terms of a strain of degenerationist discourse available to Gissing, the stigmata of criminal degeneracy. An American reviewer, Greenough White, detected this taint in Alma's behaviour; he referred to 'the depth of degeneracy in a wife and mother, a regret that she had not, in her salad days, profited by Redgrave's dishonourable proposal'.[31]

For White, the significance of the novel 'inheres in the degeneracy of a woman's character' which is 'exhibited by a few infallible signs'.[32] One such sign is 'her opening a letter addressed to her husband and the unfounded and degraded suspicions excited by something she had read in it'.[33] It is likely that the publicity surrounding Ibsen's Nora in *A Doll's House* (1888), who reads a note to her father and forges his signature, ensured that a similar action in a novel of the nineties would also be regarded as infamous.[34] Yet Gissing draws his own distinctly menacing conclusions from Alma's transgression:

At this point in her life Alma had become habitually suspicious of any relation between man and woman which might suggest, however remotely, dubious possibilities. Innocence appeared to her the exception, lawlessness the rule, where man and woman were restrained by no obvious barriers. It was the natural result of her experience, of her companionship, of the thoughts she deliberately fostered. (252)

If there is a specific source for the criminal and sexual innuendo in the novel, as detected by Greenough White, it may well be Lombroso's and Ferrero's *The Female Offender* (1895) which Gissing read in August 1895, some eight months before beginning *The Whirlpool*.[35] The degenerate female criminal lacks maternal impulses, exhibiting 'masculine obsessions', being 'excessively erotic, weak in maternal feeling, inclined to dissipation, astute and audacious ... Added to these virile characteristics are often the worst qualities of woman: namely, an excessive desire for revenge, cunning, cruelty, love of dress, and untruthfulness.'[36]

As with Nordau's catalogue of degenerate characteristics among artists, such stigmata can bear little detailed attention, yet Gissing need not have read Lombroso uncritically in order to have his idea of female lawlessness confirmed. Alma is blemished by the strong sense of malevolence which suffuses the whirlpool world, and which disfigures the socialites, Sybil Carnaby and Mrs Strangeways – particularly in their feuding in the wake of Redgrave's death. When Alma calls on Mrs Strangeways, the suffocating atmosphere turns 'her thoughts to evil' (264), and Felix Dymes later confides memorably to Alma that 'I draw a line for women. Mrs Strangeways goes a good bit beyond it' (408). Mrs Strangeways in fact generates an atavistic hatred in Alma when she importunes her for money:

'Looking at her elaborately plaited yellow hair, her thin neck, her delicate fingers just touching the long throat, Alma felt an instinct of savagery; in a flash of the primitive mind, she saw herself spring upon her enemy, tear, bite, destroy' (428).

The modern reader of Gissing has little difficulty in imagining how differently Alma's story might have been structured. But as is clear from the reviews, the late Victorian reader was as likely to be as far from entering Alma's consciousness as Rolfe himself – given Gissing's programmatic insistence that we stay safely with Rolfe at the edge of the whirlpool. While the reader is invited to feel relatively comfortable in Rolfe's company as he makes his periodic dives for solitude, Alma, exposed and adrift amid the salon jackals, is far removed from the companionable narrator's encouragement and solicitude. As a neurotic she bears her neurosis alone, confirming indeed the ideological power of the discourse of degenerationism. Degenerates or deviants, including hysterical women, are by their very nature unconscious of the forces which are deemed to govern them.

III

One component of the late Victorian ideology of woman's 'nature' which merits attention is motherhood, or 'maternalism'. This ideological formation positioned the mother as the double of the unmarried, emancipated, nervous woman. By 1894 the 'new woman' had found fictional representation in such works as Sarah Grand's *The Heavenly Twins* (1893) and George Egerton's *Keynotes* (1893), and was becoming a catch phrase for a complex challenge to the submissive and dutiful role played out by many Victorian women.[37] In that year Grant Allen, one of the Aldeburgh circle which by then included Gissing himself and the evolutionist Edward Clodd, was arguing for a 'new hedonism' through which sexual relations were to be remodelled. But it was probably Allen's elevation of 'responsibility in parentage' that most interested Gissing. Allen asserted, with a eugenic emphasis, a 'moral obligation to fatherhood and motherhood [by] the noblest, the purest, the sanest, the healthiest, the most able among us'.[38]

This could well have been the source of Lionel Tarrant's advice to Nancy in *In the Year of Jubilee* (written January-April 1894), that it is her 'duty to keep out of the beastly scrimmage' and that by devoting herself to her child she proves herself the admirable exception, because 'not one woman in a thousand can bear a sound-bodied child; and not one in fifty thousand can bring up rightly the child she has borne.'[39] And in Allen's best-selling contribution to the fiction about the new woman, the heroine of *The Woman Who Did* (1895) is distanced not only from the thrall of marital conformity, but from 'that blatant and decadent sect of "advanced women" who talk as though motherhood were a disgrace and a burden, instead of it being as it is, the full realisation of woman's faculties, the natural outlet for woman's wealth of emotion. She knew that to be a mother is the best privilege of her sex.'[40] By Allen, Gissing and many other late Victorians, the capacity to be a good mother was identified with womanliness, health and purity.

In the face of the challenge by the new woman, motherhood was above all the test of normality. A reviewer of Grand's *The Heavenly Twins* eagerly sought to re-establish the primacy of motherhood, pronouncing the imminent demise of the 'new woman' who

ought to be aware that her condition is morbid, or at least hysterical ... [she] is destined to excite notice, to be admired, criticised and forgotten. The liberty which she invokes will be fatal to her ... The age of chivalry cannot die, so long as woman keeps her peculiar grace, which is neither rugged strength nor stores of erudition, but a human nature predestined to Motherhood.[41]

'Motherhood' was also gaining momentum as a test of solicitude for the future of the nation and the nation's stock.[42] In the same year in which this review appeared, Karl Pearson made the connection between woman's role as mother and child-rearer and the destiny of the state: 'The race must degenerate if greater and greater stress be brought to force woman during the years of child-bearing into active and unlimited competition with men.'[43] While Pearson's rhetoric found powerful echoes among *dirigiste* new liberals, socialists and eugenicists over the next twenty years, the sentimental novelist Marie Corelli voiced a more common essentially Ruskinian view of woman's natural, sacrificial role. In an article of 1899 on 'Mother-Love' she took up the notion of women's 'rights'. Why, she asked, do women 'unsex themselves by appearing on public platforms and prating of their Rights? Surely their rights are manifold. With them rest the strength, goodness and greatness of the next generation, in the influence they exercise on their children.'[44]

In *The Whirlpool* these widespread expressions of concern for the primacy of motherhood and the healthy family are reflected in Gissing's description of the old-fashioned household of Basil Morton. Gissing offers a comfortable and comforting version of family life from which Rolfe feels his son is being excluded, due to Alma's neurosis and the crisis in their marriage. Inscribed within this organic ideal of a stable, unchanging backwater – unruffled by the whirlpool – is the reconstituted ideal of late Victorian motherhood; a standard by which Alma's maternal unfitness is to be judged. Mrs Morton is introduced as a paragon of good health as well as of 'home' and 'homeliness': 'Mrs. Morton had the beauty of perfect health, of health mental and physical. To describe her face as homely was to pay it the highest compliment, for its smile was the true light of home, that never failed' (324). Good health, in the terms of the prevailing degenerationist discourse, signals a desirable condition of life and invests the children of such a mother with the sound qualities of racial strength. Mrs Morton is indeed eugenically desirable in her fertility:

Four children she had borne – the eldest a boy now in his twelfth year, the youngest a baby girl; and it seemed to her no merit that in these little ones she saw the end and reason of her being. Into her pure and healthy mind had never entered a thought at conflict with motherhood. Her breasts were the fountain of life; her babies clung to them, and grew large of limb. (324)

Alma, we recall, would like to give milk but is prevented by her doctor from doing so. And again, in contrast to Alma, Mrs Morton 'would have felt it an impossible thing to abandon her children to the care of servants' (324).

That Mrs Morton does bypass her servants – she 'conceived her duty as wife and mother after the old fashion' – makes her paradox-ically a woman of the future. Within his idealised portrait of her, Gissing captures that enlightened, leisured, self-sufficient woman who, by the mid-nineties was forming the ready readership for the burgeoning encylopaedias of child-care, medicine, domestic manangement and health and beauty. Partly a response to the accelerating demise of the servant, the independent mother – as opposed to the new woman – signalled a redefinition of the role of motherhood in a national movement for the regeneration of racial vigour.

Such rhetoric in praise of healthy motherhood and families drew on, among other sources, Herbert Spencer's *Education* (1861), an

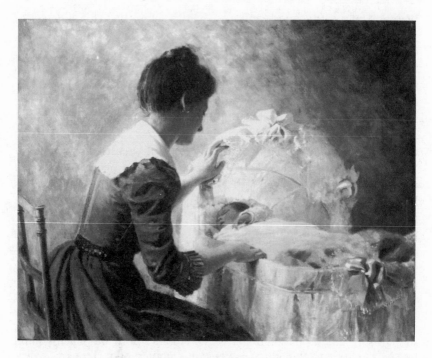

9   'Motherhood' by Louis (Emile) Adan, 1898.

influential text for Gissing and a textbook for the late nineteenth-century middle class. According to Spencer, it is in the family that the highest stage of human development can be witnessed. Spencer exhorts his parent-readers:

Morally you must keep in constant exercise your higher feelings, and restrain your lower ... It is a truth yet remaining to be recognised that the last stage in the mental development of each man and woman is to be reached only through a proper discharge of the parental duties ... That it cannot be realised by the impulsive, the unsympathetic and the short-sighted, but demands the higher attributes of human nature, they will see to be evidence of its fitness for the more advanced states of humanity. Though it calls for much labour and self-sacrifice, they will see that it promises an abundant return of happiness, immediate and remote.[45]

It is as if Gissing had set out to show in *The Whirlpool* that parent-hood was fit *only* 'for the more advanced states of humanity'. While Rolfe finds in his son a means of solace and self-development, Alma draws a broad line of demarcation between nursery and drawing-room: 'it was seldom she felt in a mood for playing with the child, and she had no taste for "going walks". But Harvey could not see too much of the little boy'(383). The son, Hughie, bears the heredity of his parents in his nervousness: 'He had no colour in his cheeks, and showed the nervous tendencies which were to be expected in a child of such parentage'(383). The inference is that it is Alma's degenerate endowment which is decisive.

Shortly afterwards, three incidents occur in quick succession to underline her maternal and domestic inefficiency, in a lurch towards breakdown and the abyss. Rolfe discovers Alma's addiction and now he has 'a most uncomfortable sense of strangeness in his wife's behaviour; it seemed to him that the longer he lived with Alma, the less able he was to read her mind or comprehend her motives' (387). Because of Alma's growing indifference to domestic management, she is unable to undertake finding a replacement for the cook who has just resigned. Shortly afterwards, Alma gives birth to a 'lamentable little mortal with a voice scarce louder than a kitten's' (387). Yet her tenderness towards the baby does not prevent its early death, the result of which is to harden her further against her son: 'Harvey had thought she would ask for her little son, and expend upon him the love called forth by her dead baby; she seemed, however, to care even less for Hughie than before' (394).

IV

Recent criticism of Gissing has had little difficulty in drawing attention to his Janus-faced, even confused depiction of women.[46] An early witness, the *Bookman* reviewer of *The Whirlpool*, remarked that while 'no novelist has taken more pains to understand the condition of the average woman's life today . . . the best of his women are not women at all, but illustrations out of a treatise of the times'.[47] One of Gissing's trademarks as a novelist is indeed to give programmatic expression to the processes of contemporary ideology – 'a treatise of the times' – and to enact the drama of the individual's subjection to it. Alma is the authentically realised casualty of the metropolis, but that authenticity is bought at the expense of her subjection to the condition both of civilisation and her own 'nature.' In exposing Alma to the forces of the whirlpool, Gissing drew on the full range of contemporary anti-feminist discourses which underscored a conservative and passive view of woman as victim of her own 'nature'. Alma's rebellion against her 'natural' role and her demonstrable unfitness for motherhood are heavily freighted with contemporary opinion. By 1897 any moderately well-read woman or man would have understood. Alma's neurosis is the inevitable 'tax' she must pay for spending her energies recklessly in the public sphere. And the authorial point of view endorses a male-centred diagnostic reading of her behaviour which continually closes down the possibilities of her rational assertiveness. Gissing inteprets her breakdown not only in terms of the irrationality of woman's 'nature', but in terms which are placed beyond her possible resistance to them.

Confronted by the overwhelming determinism which powers Gissing's characterisation of Alma, there is little option but to respond to the novel against the grain: bearing witness to Gissing's partiality, to the insistence with which Rolfe is commended as the rational touchstone. Late in the novel, Gissing allows Rolfe the experience of self-education, yet we are forced to lodge against this an extended plea on Alma's behalf: Rolfe's enhanced concern as parent has rarely extended to his role as husband to Alma, or to learning how to live within marriage.[48] So while Alma is seen as the flaw in Rolfe's marriage, he is hardly at all seen as the flaw in hers. The marriage 'experiment' is, in truth, a foreclosing 'proof' of the unfitness of defective female 'nature' for marriage and parenthood.

The burden of Gissing's indebtedness to late-nineteenth century biological and psychopathological determinism falls on Alma, not Rolfe. Two of his most complex protagonists therefore inhabit separate discursive worlds. In response to this realisation there is the need, I think, to rewrite the fiction – imagining Rolfe no longer unbalanced by the authorial insistence on his freedom and Alma spared from her nervous breakdown. And in effect this would be to move the novel beyond the 'aesthetic dead end' of fin-de-siècle 'biological essentialism'.[49]

CHAPTER 8

The lure of pedigree and the menaces of heredity in 'Tess of the D'Urbervilles' and 'Jude the Obscure'

I

In the afternoon by train to Evershot. Walked to Woolcombe, a property once owned by a – I think the senior-branch of the Hardy's ... The decline and fall of the Hardys much in evidence hereabout ... I remember when young seeing the man – tall and thin – walking beside a horse and common spring trap, and my mother pointing him out to me and saying he represented what was once the leading branch of the family. So we go down, down, down.

(Thomas Hardy in 1888)[1]

Why had he not known the difference between these things? In the latter aspect her d'Urberville descent was a fact of great dimensions; worthless to economics, it was a most useful ingredient to the dreamer, to the moralizer on declines and falls.

(Thomas Hardy, *Tess of the D'Urbervilles*)[2]

Thomas Hardy was preoccupied with the decline of his own family. He was far from alone in this obsession. Narratives of the rise and fall of established families were pervasive at all levels of late nineteenth-century British culture, reflecting changes in the patterns of ownership of land and property, all of which were of particular interest to the new inheritors, the families of the late Victorian middle class. One of Hardy's own novels *A Laodicean* (1881) has Paula Power, the daughter of mid-Victorian engineering capital, bailing out the established aristocratic family of the de Stancys, now fallen on hard times. Such families with their long, often chequered, histories had both a deep romantic attraction and imaginative potential for Hardy, which surfaced in his stories for the *Graphic, A Group of Noble Dames* (1891) (which appeared as he was working on *Tess of the D'Urbervilles*.) As Hardy makes Paula Power observe: 'that notion of being a family out of date is delightful to some people'.[3]

The sense of a connection with the past was experienced as Hardy felt it to be – a kind of intolerable loss, which might be resolved through a very late Victorian mode of appropriation, a tracing back of origins. Establishing family connections through records and documents was a thriving activity. A guide of 1889, *How to Trace Your Own Pedigree or a Guide to Family Descent*, showed that 'genealogical works and M. S. S. are more consulted than any other class of literature', and claimed that 'legitimate family pride is on the increase'.[4] But concern for the fate of families was being generated in quite a different quarter in this period. Francis Galton, statistician and cousin to Darwin, pioneered research into the question of which families were 'naturally fated to decay and which to thrive'. In a *Fortnightly Review* article in 1883 (the same year in which he first put forward the science of 'eugenics') he proposed the opening of medical family registers which might 'throw light on the physiological cause of the rise and decay of families, and consequently that of races'.[5] Galton's exhaustive demonstrations exploited the ambiguity of 'pedigree'. It was a descriptive term, representing a genealogy, but it was also an evaluative one, an index of quality. Like the word 'stock', 'pedigree' delineates a peculiarly British conflation of history and ideology which has assisted the exponents of national and racial essentialism, even to the present day. And the part played by the family, that mediating institution between the individual and the state, is always critical.

The nineteenth-century interest in the survival of family traditions, in the rise and fall of particular families, and the quality of its 'stock' tracked through generations is observed by Michel Foucault. In his view there had always been an 'aristocratic obsession with caste'; but for the nineteenth-century bourgeoisie, this obsession took the form of 'biological, medical, or eugenic precepts'. By this analysis the positivism of Galton handsomely serviced the values and interests of the middle class. Foucault argues that:

the concern with genealogy became a preoccupation with heredity; but included in bourgeois marriages were not only economic imperatives ... but the menaces of heredity; families wore and concealed a sort of reversed and sombre escutcheon whose defamatory quarters were the diseases or defects of the group of relatives – the grandfather's general paralysis, the mother's neurasthenia, the youngest child's phthisis, the hysterical or erotomanic aunts, the cousins with bad morals.[6]

Foucault here permits us a glimpse of a whole apparatus of familial involvement in hereditary degeneration which is highly relevant to Hardy's treatment of pedigree and heredity in *Tess* and *Jude*. Foucault's play on the emblematic 'escutcheon' – the symbols of nobility now being superseded by the stigmata of familial degeneracy – almost exactly characterises Hardy's exploration of the dangerous ambiguities of 'pedigree' in *Tess*. A 'concern for genealogy' is inscribed in the very title Hardy eventually gave his novel.

The topic of ancestry and pedigree is raised briefly in Hardy's novel of four years before, *The Woodlanders* (1887). George Melbury's attitude to the ancestral history of Fitzpiers is respectful, but, as with much else in the isolated backwater of Little Hintock, it is seen by the author as old-fashioned and innocent. Hardy comments: 'That touching faith in members of long-established families as such, irrespective of their personal condition or character, which is still found among old-fashioned people in rural districts, reached its full perfection in Melbury.' But the cosmopolitan Mrs Charmond has no interest in such matters: 'Whatever mysterious merit might attach to family antiquity, it was one which her adaptable, wandering, *weltburgerliche* nature had grown tired of caring about – a peculiarity that made a piquant contrast to her neighbours'.[7]

While Melbury's innocence on this subject is harmless enough, in *Tess of the D'Urbervilles* the 'facts' of ancestral connection assume, all too easily, an overwhelming importance. John Durbeyfield is susceptible to the authority of the 'antiquary', Parson Tringham. Indeed, the 'touching faith' which the Durbeyfields show in the status of pedigree proves to be a source of damaging mystification in the novel. In 'hunting up pedigrees for the new county history'(32), Parson Tringham is lured by the boundless attractions of antiquarianism which promise the chance to discover a new affiliation, even if it is to a family line which is extinct. Confessing that 'impulses are too strong for our judgement sometimes'(33), he none the less passes on knowledge which, though 'useless', may 'disturb'. But the Durbeyfields will transform this 'useless' knowledge connecting them with the dead into serviceable information by which they hope to make a better life. And, of course, for them, pedigree is a lure, precisely because the family is so vulnerable to fecklessness and poverty (Melbury is at least protected by a modest prosperity). In an unstable world neither their credulousness nor their fatalism is affordable. And the myth of pedigree to which the Durbeyfields blindly adhere, in the hope that it will be their deliverance, hastens their disintegration. In contrast to Hardy's earlier treatments of the idea of pedigree, in *Tess* it is a 'corner-stone in the structure of the novel'.[8] It kicks the narrative into life, and downhill to tragedy.

II

The worlds of *Tess of the D'Urbervilles* and *Jude the Obscure* are both permeated by ossified assumptions about law and custom and their operation. Among these are deeply held conventions about the working of ancestry and heredity. And these apparently common-sense ideas will be, in effect, exposed by Hardy as ideological. The subject of the decline of family fortunes, for example, so susceptible to the patronage of the educated contemporary reader, becomes transformed in *Tess* from an object of sentiment to an object of knowledge. In the contradiction between common-sense orders of truth (whether generated by the privileged, educated Angel Clare or the struggling, native Joan Durbeyfield) and Tess's actual experience, lies Hardy's critique of the social order which deforms Tess by the 'truth' of its discourses.

The terms in which both the native and educated point of view deal with the status of lineal descent, of pedigree, become undermined by what Ian Gregor has called the 'calculatedly ambivalent play on 'nature' which runs through the novel'.[9] In *Tess* any definition of 'nature' invites both qualification and scepticism. Hardy's sustained ironic treatment of this subject has the effect of pointing up the partiality and ideological limitations of any single interpretation. But behind him are J. S. Mill's *Essay on Nature* and T. H. Huxley's essays, particular those published during the period in which Hardy was preparing the novel.

Hardy almost certainly had read Huxley's 1888 essay 'The Struggle for Existence: A Programme', the first of a group of essays anticipating the argument of Huxley's celebrated lecture 'Evolution and Ethics' (1893). In his essay Huxley proposed a distinction between the province of man which was subject to ethical and moral control and the province of man which was not. Following Mill, Huxley argued that 'nature', at its broadest, could represent 'the sum of the phenomenal world' so that 'society like art, is therefore a part of nature'. But he then distinguishes between 'those parts of nature in which man plays the part of immediate cause as something apart; and therefore, society, like art, is usefully to be considered as distinct from nature'. For Huxley 'society differs from nature in having a definite moral object'. He saw 'non-ethical man – the primitive savage, or man as a mere member of the animal kingdom' as carrying on the struggle for existence to the bitter end. Ethical man, on the other hand, 'devotes his best energies to the object of setting limits to the struggle'.[10]

The Malthusian law of population is crucial, as it is for Darwin, to Huxley's view of the non-ethical face of nature. It was, he said in his 1890 essay 'On the Natural Inequality of Man', 'the real riddle of the sphinx to which no political Oedipus has as yet found the answer. In view of the ravages of the terrible monster, over-multiplication, all other riddles sink into insignificance.'[11]

There are certainly moments when Hardy finds 'ethical man' defeated by the process of reproduction and its personal and economic consequences. Tess's own child, Sorrow, 'that bastard gift of shameless Nature who respects not the social law' (124), signifies this disruption, as of course do the children in *Jude* (they are 'too menny'). The 'half-dozen little captives' of the Durbeyfield ship likewise embody the 'riddle' of the lack of synchrony between reproductive instinct and social arrangements. Hardy is led to question here the 'holy plan' of nature in Wordsworth's conception. But the plan might also be interpreted as the chaotic but inevitable outcome of Malthusian law. As Tess begins to 'see how matters stood', Hardy has her feel 'quite a Malthusian towards her mother for thoughtlessly giving her so many little sisters and brothers'(62).

Yet Hardy is sceptical of Huxley's dualism, taking instead a position which is both more pessimistic and more radical. In Chapter 41, Tess mourns for the dying pheasants. Hardy describes the hunters who have wounded them as part of the phenomenal world of nature in spite of their being 'quite civil persons'. The birds are 'their weaker fellows in Nature's teeming family' (302). The society-nature couple is sidestepped. Tess's shame at the onset of her gloom, provoked by the suffering of the wounded pheasants, is based, suggests Hardy, 'on nothing more tangible than a sense of condemnation under an arbitrary law of society which had no foundation in Nature' (303). The law from which she suffers is both chaotic and non-ethical: the very reverse of Huxley's ethical claims for society against the non-ethical barbarism of nature. What Tess, and still more the reader, reads into the pheasant episode is a function of the radical questioning which Hardy develops in *Tess*, and still further in *Jude*.

So Hardy puts questions to the social order which Malthusian law cannot explain away and which cast doubt on there being any simple rule governing the relationship between natural and social existence. Indeed, how can barren Flintcomb Ash be spoken of in the same terms as the world of the dairy at Talbothays? Yet, in one respect, both crystallise images of the natural order. What Hardy seems to resist is any simple sanction or law which would lend stability to the relationship between human purpose and that order. Neither Spencer's evolutionary naturalism, nor Galton's laws of 'natural' inheritance, nor Huxley's recasting of evolutionary ethics is adequate to Hardy's purpose.

Hardy's epistemology is relativistic. Just as Talbothays is negated by Flintcomb Ash, so Tess's perceived 'natural' qualities are negated by her defiling. It follows that the question of Tess's 'purity' is put, on the title page, relativistically; how 'a pure woman' is interpreted depends on the reader's angle of vision. As the marked out object of the discourses which invoke these laws and fixed ways of seeing, she is appropriately subjected to an aesthetic design which enables her to be viewed, as John Goode has put it, 'from all the angles that are possible'.[12]

When Tess arrives home, pregnant by Alec, her mother observes, 'Tis nater, after all, and what do please God' (111). For the Durbeyfields, 'nature' expresses a faith in a providential force and a fatalistic resignation to the workings of human biology. The family name has come, they believe, 'by nature' (64). By contrast, Angel Clare takes himself to be a representative of educated opinion on the question of pedigree and ancestry. Yet he is unaware that part of him is a 'slave to custom and conventionality' (290). Early on he despises 'increasingly' 'the material distinctions of rank and wealth' (144). Dairyman Crick remarks of Angel that 'if there's one thing that he do hate more than another 'tis the notion of what's called an' old family' (154–5). When Angel speaks of Tess's lineage to his father, as he prepares the ground for his parents' acceptance of her as his wife, he argues that 'politically I am sceptical as to the virtue of their being old ... but lyrically, dramatically, and even historically, I am tenderly attached to them' (195). And having assured Tess, shortly before the marriage, that pedigree means nothing to him, once Angel knows of her ancestral connection he openly avows that this will help to expedite his parents' approval of her; yet later he turns her possession of that advantage against her, accusing her of being 'the belated seedling of an effete aristocracy' (259). It is not until it is too late that he realises the mystification involved in this designation: 'Why had he not known the difference between the political value and the imaginative value of these things? In the latter aspect her d'Urberville descent was a fact of great dimensions; worthless to economics, it was a most useful ingredient to the dreamer, to the moralizer on declines and falls' (364–5).

The damage has, of course, been done. Angel the 'dreamer' and 'moraliser' has continually spoken for her. Tess has become an object of his naming, whether what he calls her is romantic or fanciful. His definitions of her are misreadings emanating from the romantic spectator who had praised Tess, near the onset of the 'Rally' phase: 'What a fresh and virginal daughter of Nature that milkmaid is' (148). In one sense he unconsciously anticipates his shock at Tess's fall from a state of grace and of nature when he later tells her that it is Alec who is 'your husband in nature, and not I' (268). But both these perceptions, one during 'The Rally', the other after Tess's confession, express an appropriating patronage with its idealising view of the 'essence of woman': 'I thought', Angel says, 'that by giving up all ambition to win a wife with social standing ... I should secure rustic innocence as surely as I should secure pink cheeks' (263–4).

Tess senses her appropriation in Angel's terms of endearment: 'He called her Artemis, Demeter, and other fanciful names half-teasingly, which she did not like because she did not understand them. 'Call me Tess', she would say askance; and he did (158).[13] But while she contests Angel's patronage of her when he speaks about her past, she fails, fatally, to disabuse him of his idealisation of her:

> 'But my history. I want you to know it – ... '
> 'Tell it if you wish to, dearest. This
> precious history then. Yes, I was born at
> so and so, Anno Domini – '
>
> I was born at Marlott', she said, catching
> at his words as a help ... (216)

Here is an ironic reversal of Angel's fondness for legends, stories and ancestral history. For as Tess's own history comprises a personal story which she needs to tell, Angel's instinct is to reduce that 'history' to the dry data of a biographical entry in an unwritten annal of the desperate rural poor. Angel's 'history' is her 'story'. And what she goes on to tell him encapsulates her difficulty, as she prises out her story from within the shell of the ancestral connection. But in relation to that ancestry she is only able to utter meaningless and mythical history which, of course, by another ironic twist, has become a part of the unexpressed story of her life. So Angel's reaction is partly explicable, given the terms of his patronage, to which he expects Tess to conform: ' "A d'Urberville. – Indeed. And is that all the trouble, dear Tess?" "Yes", she answered faintly' (216).

The 'trouble' is both his and hers, of course – what she has suffered by that 'title' and Angel's romanticising of her identity. Her confession gives Angel the opportunity to affiliate Tess's 'want of firmness' with the proverbial moral degeneracy of the ancient family in decline. He accuses her of continuing to display her ancestry as 'the belated seedling of an effete aristocracy'. She replies to this by contesting the notion of privileged birth and her uniqueness in this respect; she claims an equality with other girls of the district who, like herself, bear traces of historic lineage in their names: 'Lots of families are as bad as mine in that. Retty's family were once large landowners, and so were dairyman Billet's. And the Debbyhouses, who are now carters, were once the De Bayeux family. You find such as I everywhere; 'tis a feature of our county, and I can't help it' (259). Hardy has himself known the attraction of romantic gene-alogy – the building up of fantasies from the chance fact of lineal descent. But all this is deflated by Tess's common-sense rebuttal of the lure of pedigree.

In the passage where Tess responds to Angel's suggestion that she might take up history as a course of study, she tells him:

'What's the use of learning that I am one of a long row only – finding out that there is set down in some old book somebody just like me, and to know that I shall only act her part; making me sad, that's all. The best is not to remember that your nature and your past doings have been just like thousands' and thousands', and that your coming life and doings' 'll be like thousands' and thousands'. (153–4)

This element of defensiveness about her past, real or imagined, can trap critics who want to impose a resigned fatalism on Tess and the intentions of her author. Such is the case with Peter Morton's neo-Darwinian reading of the novel. Morton suggests that despite Tess's refusal to contemplate her history, she is 'forced against her will to remember it' and that this constitutes her 'tragedy' which is 'absolute ... her fine-spirited refusal to submit to the inevitable, merely serves to lime her the more thoroughly'.[14] But it is rather that her spirit revolts against the condition of her life, a life driven by specific discourses of definition, including those which Angel and Alec use to reconstitute the past as a stick to beat her with.

Yet Tess's plea here is *against* the determinism of the continuous effects of the hereditary taint. The point she makes is that in having continually to take the 'part' of inheritor, living feels like acting. Her protest constitutes a revolt against those discourses of definition to which she is subject and which make her 'sad'. Whilst Tess does not openly contest the terms of the determinism (she certainly does her best to evade them – 'the best is not to remember') it is a naïve reading which supposes that she endorses that ideology. Her assertion, in context, constitutes a stand against the prevailing appropriation of her identity, which includes her past, real or imagined. It is a radical affirmation of the autonomy of the self in the face of the stories which the genes are made to tell.

Morton rightly draws attention to the influence on Hardy of the biologist August Weismann.[15] Hardy read Weismann in 1890, and would have known about contemporary biological debates about Weismann's challenge to Lamarckian ideas of heredity, energetically publicised in British scientific circles and beyond, at the end of the eighties. Weismann's most controversial idea that the continuous track of hereditary influence, vested in the germ-plasm, is independent of the life-history of the organism, struck a favourable chord with Hardy; it powered the rather rigid structure of hereditary determinism working through successive generations in his serial story 'The Pursuit of the Well-Beloved' which ran in the *Illustrated London News* in late 1892.

But there are problems with a neo-Darwinian reading of *Tess*. According to Morton, if we are to read the novel from the 'point of view of inheritance theory' we 'must assert the novel's rigid determinism, its total pessimism, and its fidelity to one coherent scientific vision of the world'.[16] Surely this is not adequate to the experience of reading the novel. Neither does Morton comment on the one passage, in the 'Rally' phase of the novel, where Hardy closely incorporates Weismann's germ-plasm theory, but harnessed to a far from reductive view of the reproductive process: 'The season developed and matured. Another year's instalment of flowers, leaves, nightingales, thrushes, finches and such ephemeral creatures, took up their positions where only a year ago others had stood in their place when these were nothing more than germs and inorganic particles' (156). Compare Hardy's poem 'Proud Songsters', first published in *Winter Words* (1928):

> These are brand-new birds of twelve-month's growing,
> Which a year ago, or less than twain,
> No finches were, nor nightingales,
>   Nor thrushes,
> But only particles of grain,
> And earth, and air, and rain.[17]

Here the explicit allusion to Weismann's theory of the germ-plasm only heightens the awesome power of the reproductive cycle. In its sheer randomness, this potent reappearance of life, owing nothing to purposeful Lamarckianism, is, surely, neo-Darwinism at its least reductive, or, one could say, Weismannite biology at its most creative. As Gillian Beer has put it, the idea of 'succession' leads not to reductiveness but the perpetual spectacle of nature's 'renewal'.[18]

III

The composition of *Tess* was bound up, of course, with the obligation to make the novel fit for publication, given Hardy's industrious response to the controversial nature of his subject matter. What is clear is that the determining influence of pedigree and heredity plays a surprisingly critical role in the mediation of this process – a process which enabled Hardy to withstand the pressures making for the novel's still birth. At particular points of the developing text we can see that the lure of pedigree is less a fatal attraction for Hardy than an elaborate authorial strategy. How might we track it?

J. T. Laird claims to detect an 'ur-novel' from the manuscript, which can be identified by five layers of composition. The first two are contained within the ur-novel which Hardy submitted in September 1889 to the publishers Tillotsons, 'Too Late Beloved', which was promptly rejected. The third, fourth and fifth layers are identified in the manuscript after Macmillan's had rejected the novel in November 1889.[19] Hardy explained that he was now engaged in an 'unceremonious concession to conventionality',[20] which entailed modifying and subtracting existing passages. Hardy adopted a marking system which would record deviations made for serial publication, and a system of inking, indicating which passages would be retained for subsequent inclusion in the volume form.

While Hardy claimed in the *Life* that all such passages were subsequently restored, Laird suggests that many of the alterations which Hardy made in that year did in fact become permanent.[21] Of the changes Hardy makes after 1889, among the most important are those intended to sharpen the influence of heredity on character. And significantly these changes first focus on an instrument of biological generation – the father. John Durbeyfield is made to enact his degeneracy as an explicit vestige of a worn-out pedigree. The opening of the novel was remodelled in layer three after November 1889 as follows:

On an evening in the latter part of May a middle-aged

       walking   ward   town

man was ~~riding~~ home from Stourcastle ~~market~~ by a lane
                    ∧
which led into the recesses of the neighbouring Vale

       or Blackmoor. The pair of legs

of Blakemore ∧ ~~He The animal~~ that carried him

were rickety, and there was a bias in his-gait that
~~was a feeble old white pony whose neck protruded from~~

inclined him ⌐ to the left of a straight line ⌐ somewhat ⌐
~~his shoulders like the arm of a gallows an empty~~

He occasionally gave a smart nod, as if in
~~butter basket was strapped up under his arm &~~

confirmation of ~~the~~ some opinion: ~~yet he~~ though he was not thinking
~~speckled worsted stockings~~   ~~covered~~   ~~the small of~~
             ~~that showed~~

over of anything ∧ in particular An empty egg basket
~~his legs where exposed by the rucking~~[22]
was slung upon his arm

Both John Durbeyfield's deference and his love of the bottle are added features here.[23] So too is the debased coinage of his degenerate physiognomy, as interpreted by Parson Tringham:

Throw up your chin
~~Look up at the sky~~ a moment, so that I may catch
the profile of your face better. Yes, that's the
D'Urberville   –a little debased.
~~Turberville~~ nose & chin.[24]

The effete passivity implicit in this attribution of degeneracy in its turn implicates Tess of course. Her 'submission' to separation from Angel is described at the layer five stage as 'a symptom of that indifference to results too apparent in the whole d'Urberville family'.[25] By the one volume edition of 1892 this had become 'that acquiescence in chance too apparent in the whole d'Urberville family'.[26] Crucially Tess's resistance to circumstances becomes toned down in this example; she is made more passive, a victim of the influence of her heredity.

The moment during the threshing sequence shows a further significant alteration in this direction. Tess lashes out at Alec, who has been doggedly pursuing her and is now ready to take advantage of her state of demoralisation and physical weakness. The manuscript has: 'The leather glove was heavy and thick as a warrior's and it struck him flat in the mouth. Alec fiercely started up from his reclining position.' The first edition contains an inserted comment here: 'Fancy might have regarded the act as the recrudescence of a trick in which her mailed progenitors were not unpractised.'[27] And the more sinister aspects of her inheritance are introduced in new scenes. On the wedding night, at the farm-house at Wellbridge, the portraits of the d'Urbervilles on the wall are introduced as a new feature into the serialised version for the *Graphic*. Angel's remark about 'those harridans on the panel upstairs' still appears in the first edition, and the comparison between Tess and the portrait of the woman in the Caroline bodice appears in the second edition.[28]

With the evolution of the text, it was Tess's actions which underwent the most sustained revision. The effect was to objectify her by a discourse of hereditary determinism through which her character and actions could be more acceptably assimilated – both as a victim of forces beyond her control and as a figure of purity. Mary Jacobus has argued that once Hardy's manuscript had been rejected (three times over), he submitted her to a 'sustained campaign of rehabilitation'.[29] This 'campaign' was also directed at strengthening the influence of heredity in order that she be held less responsible for her actions. Tess's parents, then, were not merely feckless but degenerate. And from layer three onwards, Tess was marked more unambiguously as a scion of the decadent d'Urberville family; this inheritance was made to dictate both her moments of aggression and her passivity, and to endow her, too, with more modesty.

Whereas in 1889, in the ur-version of the novel, there is little sign of the determining influence of heredity working through a decayed family, nine months after the first edition of *Tess* was published Hardy gave an interview in which he stated: 'The murder that Tess commits is the hereditary quality, to which I more than once allude, working out in this impoverished descendant of a once noble family.

That is logical. And again, it is but a simple transcription of the obvious that she should make reparation for her sin.'[30] By 1892, Tess appeared to have entered the domain of public reception, almost as a character in her own right. She had created a kind of magnetic field which drew in reviewers, readers, and – to judge from Hardy's comments here – the author himself. Hardy needed to subject the character of Tess to a form of special pleading and to that end he subtly employed the topical, commonsensical, 'logical' discourse of inherited family taint.

Yet, in spite of his concessions to contemporary ideology, Hardy can give us, in Tess, a figure whom ideology cannot fully claim (not even that of the author himself). 'Call me Tess' – her cry to be seen for what she is – is what we are surely drawn back to, in the face of a social order hopelessly addicted to the lure of pedigree. Hardy's radical achievement, I think, is to make us hear Tess's plea and allow us a way of answering it. We want to respond by calling the social order to account for the names it calls Tess, and the myths those names perpetuate, even if her author could not entirely resist their strategic possibilities.

IV

The analysis of heredity was placing sex ... in a position of 'biological responsibility' with regard to the species: not only could sex be affected by its own diseases, it could also, if it was not controlled, transmit diseases or create others that would afflict future generations.
(Michel Foucault, *The History of Sexuality* Vol. 1)[31]

In our modern mythology Custom, Circumstance and Heredity are the Three Fates that weave the web of human life. (May Sinclair, *Audrey Craven* (1897)[32]

'There is indeed a singular fascination, horrible at times as it may be, in the idea that the experience of ancestors survive as the feelings of the descendants', wrote the philosopher David Ritchie in 1889. 'But a great part of the prevalent opinion about heredity', he continued, 'seems to be only mythology or fiction masquerading as science.'[33] Among the scientific fabulists Ritchie may have had in mind was Henry Maudsley. Heredity, for Maudsley, was pathological fate: 'no one can elude the destiny that is innate in him, and which unconsciously and irresistably shapes his ends'.[34] Solemnly intoning the 'inexorable destiny' of heredity, he pointed to the futile struggles of the Grecian heroes to elude its influence, a struggle which 'embodied an instinctive perception of the law by which the sins of the father are visited upon the children unto the third and fourth generations'.[35]

Hereditary retribution produced a pronounced anxiety in the 1880s and 1890s about the subject of syphilis. Syphilis was widely thought to be inheritable, though in fact it is a sexually or venereally transmissable disease. Under the entry 'Surgery' the 1887 edition of the *Encylopaedia Britannica* shows the belief at the time that syphilis could be truly inherited, causing the 'foetus to be syphilitic'.[36] This view was still being put forward in the 1911 edition of the *Britannica*: 'the ... effects acquired by inheritance from either parent' were 'conveyed, along with other inherited qualities in the sperm-elements or in the ovum'.[37]

In *The Pathology of Mind* (1895) Maudsley argued that 'secret illicit amours, quite unsuspected until disclosed by the calamity [of paralysis], were 'pathologically avenged'.[38] The penalties attached to the taking of unwarranted spontaneous sexual pleasure was a commonplace of late Victorian writing on hereditary determinism. Ibsen had explored this mentality in *Ghosts* by treating the tragic consequences of congenital syphilis. In the aftermath of its London premiere in March 1891, the subject of innocents visited by the sins of their fathers (and, crucially, in the play, their mothers) began to find echoes in other literature of the period. Never before or since had heredity lent itself so readily to narratives of concealment and revelation, of virtue upheld and vice unmasked – of purity and pollution.

Indeed the biological inheritance of a future or present marriage partner, was the subject of any number of dramas of anxiety played out in the late Victorian and Edwardian family, with Foucault's 'erotomanic' aunts and 'cousins with bad morals' peopling any number of sub-plots. From her study of ruling-class families in the period 1860–1914, Pat Jalland suggests that 'the state of each partner's health was very seriously considered by the families before agreement to marriage'.[39] For some fastidious women, evidence of hereditary defect and the perceived certainty of its transmission to the child, given the inevitability of childbearing in marriage, led them to voluntary spinsterhood. The poet Charlotte Mew (1869–1928) and her sister were reported as having renounced marriage 'for fear of passing on the mental taint that was in their heredity'. Two of their siblings suffered from insanity. In one of her poems 'On the Asylum Road', a condition of insanity is 'the incarnate wages of man's sin'.[40] A member of the Trevelyan family, Anna Philips, remained unmarried, it was thought, 'because her mother had been slightly defective in mind'.[41]

The spectre of inherited insanity hung over the family of Leslie Stephen. The death and madness of J. K. Stephen (1859–92), Virginia Woolf's first cousin, was compounded by the madness of Laura (1870–1945), the daughter of Leslie Stephen's first wife, Minnie Thackeray. Leonard Woolf was almost certainly convinced that Virginia's periods of madness had an inherited component. Sir George Savage (1842–1921), one of the doctors advising her, and who had attended J. K. Stephen, was the author of a standard medical textbook on the treatment of the mentally ill, *Insanity and Allied Neuroses; Practical and Clinical* (1884), in which he argued that of the causes of insanity 'heredity stands first in importance ... the torch of civilization is handed from father to son, and as with idiosyncrasies of mind, so the very body itself exhibits well-defined marks of its parentage'.[42] Woolf believed that her vulnerability to mental and physical illness – her frequent bouts of influenza – derived from her father's dowry to her: a second-hand nervous system 'used by my father and his father to dictate dispatches and write books with – how I wish they had hunted and fished instead ... To think that my father's philosophy and the Dictionary of National Biography cost me this.'[43]

v

The subject of heredity is inseparable from questions of gender. It was the woman (often in her role as mother) who seemed to have carried the burden of anxiety or guilt on the subject. In Ibsen's *A Doll's House* Torvald tells Nora that it is usually the mother (here the mother as 'constitutional liar') who bears the responsibility for producing 'young criminals', despite his ostensible intention, at this moment, to attack the deception perpetrated by the male Krogstad. Nora subsequently suffers the anguish of contamination: 'Corrupt my children – Poison my home.'[44] By the end of the act the woman and mother has been discursively constructed as both feckless *and* responsible. The male maintains both Olympian detachment and knowing authority, while being responsible for nothing.

But making the man responsible was the explicit programme of 'one of the greatest sensations in literature', Sarah Grand's *tendez-roman, The Heavenly Twins*.[45] It sold 20,000 copies in its first week of publication in January 1893, and was reprinted eight times over the next year.[46] The combined success of Grand's novel and Emma Frances Brooke's *A Superfluous Woman* (reprinted four times between January and April 1894) may have helped to prompt a 'symposium' in the *New Review* in which Grand participated. Its unspoken yet compelling topic was syphilis – not a new subject for readers of a widely read guide to contraceptive techniques, Henry A. Allbutt's *The Wife's Handbook* (1887): 'A young woman may be ruined in health for life, and have her innocent offspring diseased, if she is allied to a man who has disease lurking in his system. I refer to what is called syphilis.' Women or their parents should be able to 'demand a recent certificate of freedom from syphilis from all men proposing marriage. In this matter false delicacy should be dropped.'[47]

Discovering that her husband has contracted venereal disease in his youth, Evadne, the heroine of *The Heavenly Twins*, confides to her aunt: 'Marrying a man like that, allowing him an assured position in society, is countenancing vice, and' – she glanced round apprehensively, then added in a fearful whisper – '*helping to spread it.*'[48] The implications for the woman married to a man 'with disease lurking in his system' is the shocking subject of this novel. 'Vice' scandalises because it is genetically effective; it contaminates at the very site of conjugal intimacy and procreation. Sarah Grand addresses the question of the inherited and inheritable consequences for the innocent parties to male sexual profligacy, and, by implication, the crucial if vexatious question of the double standard in sexual conduct.

For the feminist writers of the nineties the syphilitic male became a primary target. He was seen as the 'carrier of contamination and madness, and a threat to the spiritual evolution of the race'.[49] His profligate sexual habits were encoded in his 'vice' – a term which neatly condenses the suggestion of moral delinquency, physical need and irrevocable bodily contamination.

'There is no past in the matter of vice', Evadne lectures her aunt, 'the consequences become hereditary, and continue from generation to generation' (80). Later she criticises the church for encouraging 'sinners satiated with vice to transmit their misery-making propensities from generation to generation' (340). Evadne is able to theorise

both from her own narrow escape and from the disastrous experience of the unworldly Edith Beale, who fatally contracts syphilis
from her husband, a degenerate naval officer. Edith recalls too late
Evadne's strictures about hereditary transmission: 'The same thing
may happen now to any mother – to any daughter – and *will* happen
so long as we refuse to know and resist' (304).

The diseased product is her child which she is tempted to kill in
order to end the contaminated line. In *The Heavenly Twins, A
Superfluous Woman* and Hardy's *Jude the Obscure*, the child is a
marked-out, monstrous travesty of nature, on whom is inscribed the
marks of degenerate sexuality.[50] In *A Superfluous Woman* the idiot
children that the syphilitic Lord Heriot has given to his wife replicate the circuit of familial contamination: 'on those frail, tiny forms
lay heavily the heritage of the fathers. The beaten brows, the
suffering eyes, expiated in themselves the crimes and debauchery of
generations.'[51] In this novel nature takes its revenge when the
'malicious idiot girl' kills her 'helpless' brother (258), leaving
Heriot without his desired heir, his wife dead, their third child
stillborn.

In *The Heavenly Twins*, Evadne becomes pregnant by her new
husband, the incorruptible Doctor Galbraith, but is still haunted by
an unfounded 'terrible fear' (665) of the onward transmission of
infection. On the point of giving birth she scribbles him a note: 'To
save my daughter from Edith's fate – better die at once' (663).
Although in theory she abjures thought of suicide after Galbraith
intercedes, at the sight of Edith's boy she regresses into wishing that
her 'children had never been born' (677).

It was to Grand's credit that she could show that Evadne's fear
and loathing of venereal infection was a function of knowledge
rather than ignorance, and that a rational response to her own
question (and the central didactic one of the novel) – 'Why are
women kept in the dark about these things?' – becomes impossible
for her. Her feelings cannot cope with what her intellect com-
prehends: she can survive only by suppressing the experience of her
victimisation and others' oppression – 'do not ask me to think', she
tells her husband.

Significantly, the trigger of Evadne's despair is a manual by a
specialist, Sir Shadwell Rock, on the 'heredity of vice': this has the
unwelcome effect of multiplying fears about her passing on the
disease to her, as yet, unborn child. But knowing the facts does not

alleviate Evadne's anxiety; it rather intensifies her doubt. And as she contemplates the prospect of generation in a state of helpless suspension, Grand has Evadne unironically defer to the unquestioned authority of the medical specialist. But whether or not Rock is right is not really the point; for the truth does not make Evadne free. The ideology of hereditary determinism exacts a passive subjection; for while this knowledge of the facts brings her immunity, it also atrophies the will, and attenuates the very spirit of intellectual enquiry which, up to now, has been her salvation.

By contrast, Jessamine Halliday, the passionate heroine of Emma Frances Brooke's *A Superfluous Woman*, is not intended to be a thinking woman. She has no manual, but she does appear to know the facts about the 'greatest catch in Europe', the debauched Lord Heriot with his 'drunken younger brother', his sister 'a microcephalous idiot', his 'father dying of paralysis and ungovernable temper' (116). Under the influence of Dr Cornerstone, whose life's work is to 'rescue others from the moral complications consequent on either poverty or wealth', she quits enervating, fashionable society for the Scottish highlands. The peasant farmer she falls in love with, Colin McGilvray, is everything the degenerate Heriot is not: strong, healthy, manly, noble. Jessamine's bid for a new life and a longed-for healthy child is thwarted when Colin will not make love before marriage, and she discovers that marriage into a puritan and primitive community is too high a price to pay. Overcome with shame that her attempted seduction has lowered her in Colin's eyes, and lured by the glamour surrounding Heriot's public persona, she returns to London to marry him and ends by paying a heavier price, madness and death in childbirth.

Her late, desperate confiding to Dr Cornerstone about her marital hell points up the fact that, unlike Grand's Evadne, Jessamine is denied any chance by Brooke of inspecting the unresolved question of male sexual conduct: this subject is, paradoxically, shut down tight by the *donnée* of the inherited vice which might have permitted that question to be opened up. The 'truth' is revealed to Jessamine in a final delirium when she suffers the agony of 'reproach' by the faces of future, unborn children, 'each had the eyes of her suffering boy; each had the impress of her husband' (275). She dies 'smitten by the eyes of children' (276), an object of pity, not a medium for insight. While Brooke has Dr Cornerstone refer to her 'facile, undisciplined brain' (260), there is no occasion given for re-education.

But in this text knowledge is for confirming what we already know, not for finding things out. Alone with him at dinner, Cornerstone observes Lord Heriot who has fallen asleep:

There was ample opportunity for observation ... All that the tailor and a priceless personal attendant could do had been done to turn Lord Heriot into a reputable figure of a man. If starch, fine cloth, and shaving could have erased the traces of a past, that past would have vanished under the applications as completely as breath on a well-scrubbed mirror. But Lord Heriot's past was a long one; it did not begin with himself ...
In his imagination he took this instance of the unfortunate semi-criminal loafer, and placed him in the position that suited his capacity – subtracting him, that is, from the House of Lords and setting him down in the Casual Ward. (262–3)

Here is an example of the trope of 'recognition' deployed by Gissing, Stevenson and Doyle. Yet the manner of revelation is not sudden, nor the matter shocking; instead there is a soberly observed endorsement of Maudsley's words in *The Pathology of Mind* (1895) that 'beneath every face are the latent faces of ancestors, beneath every character their characters'.[52] The doctor's gaze only delivers confirmation of the determinism of this diagnosis, offering neither to enliven its dullness, nor dislodge its banal *gravitas*.

So unknowable was heredity, said Oscar Wilde, in another context, that it ceased to be an object of knowledge at all: 'We may not watch it, for it is within us. We may not see it, save in a mirror that mirrors the soul.'[53] And this gives a clue to the immense authority which the determinism of hereditary degeneracy commanded in the last years of the nineteenth-century. The evidence lay buried 'within us', but for the 'new doctors', in the mystery of the body – to be inspected, categorised, isolated. This is the new arena in which the old, grim, classical tragedy is played out, now rewritten by the prestige of positivism. Heredity was not quite as Wilde had it, 'Nemesis without her mask'; it was Nemesis donning the mask of science.

VI

To a pre-Mendelian culture, the idea that 'vice' could be inherited was taken to be self-evident. Neither Grand, nor Brooke, in keeping with contemporary orthodoxy, question this assumption, as has been mentioned, or the fact that congenital syphilis is not strictly an inherited condition, but contracted within the infected womb of the mother. The late 1880s and early nineties saw a deluge of textbooks and handbooks aimed at the prospective parent, all of which could have served as a template for the book which disorientated Sarah Grand's Evadne. Allbutt's primer, *The Wife's Handbook*, was joined by J. F. Nisbet's *Marriage and Heredity* (1889), J. M. Guyau's *Education and Heredity* (1891) and S. A. K. Strahan's *Marriage and Disease* (1892). Each of these studies dwelt on the pervasiveness of inherited factors, drawing heavily on doctors and pathologists like Maudsley, Furneaux Jordan, Ribot and Hack Tuke, going back at least twenty years.[54] Many of the anxieties about hereditary transmission, experienced by the women in Grand and Brooke, find their way into what Elaine Showalter has called the 'consummate literary text of late-Victorian psychiatry',[55] Thomas Hardy's *Jude the Obscure* (1895).

Some of the recurring concerns of this psychiatry are amply displayed in Strahan's book of 1892; the danger of close relatives marrying, the effects of a tainted hereditary history, inherited inebriety and child-suicide.[56] He urges that 'young men and women' should be told about 'diseased conditions' such as 'insanity, epilepsy, scrofula, drunkenness', 'transmitted from parent to child', and remarks on 'the terrible responsibility resting upon those who, themselves bearing such brand of unfitness, continue their kind'.[57] Parents of a 'neurotic family should never forget that the safety of their children wholly depends on their choice of partners'.[58] As well as standard warnings to habitual drunkards – 'they have inherited an unstable nervous system which renders them liable at any time to fall victims to this vice'[59] – Strahan notes that 'suicide of children of tender years' has become of late 'so painfully common', where 'fifty years ago' child-suicide 'was almost unknown'. He quotes from an 1886 article by Maudsley from the *Fortnightly Review*: 'if the child's family history be enquired into, it will usually be found that a line of suicide, or of melancholic depression with suicidal tendency, runs through it'.[60]

By the time Hardy came to prepare for *Jude* in 1892, there is ample evidence that he was well up in developments in psychiatric Darwinism. He was, of course, on easy terms with those writers who moved freely between the world of literature, popular science and journalism – ubiquitous men of letters such as Grant Allen, Edmund Gosse and Edward Clodd; few of the subjects touched on in the *Nineteenth Century* or the *Contemporary Review* would have seemed foreign to their interests. But what is less predictable is that among his acquaintances were significant medical and scientific figures such as Clifford Allbutt, Ray Lankester and Sir James Crichton-Browne. All three were among those present at a *conversazione* at *The Royal Society* in May 1893, where Hardy recalled talking about the exhibits.[61]

Allbutt was a Commissioner in Lunacy who in 1891 had conducted Hardy on a visit to a private lunatic asylum. Allbutt considered the cases of insanity with which he was familiar to be 'a result of physical degeneration and hereditary transmission'.[62] But other nervous maladies, such as hysteria and neurasthenia, he attributed to 'the intellectual acuteness of many of these sufferers';[63] this was an insight of importance to Freud's diagnoses of hysterical patients in the early 1890s,[64] and crucial to Hardy's portrayal of the fastidious, intellectual and neurotic Sue Bridehead.

In August 1893, the month in which he began the full-length composition of *Jude the Obscure*, Hardy talked with James Crichton-Brown (1840–1935), now Lord Chancellor's Visitor in Lunacy. Hardy records their discussing the differential brain size of men and women, and types of women whose contrasting sexuality might reveal gradations of development from 'a state of nature' to 'civilised society'. Here is reflected the obsessive interest, in the early nineties, in the nature of female sexuality, couched, inevitably, in evolutionism.[65]

Ray Lankester, the author of *Degeneration* (1880) was considered to be 'the leading British authority in zoology' by the nineties.[66] A few years earlier he had stepped into the limelight of biological controversy because of his anti-Lamarckian stance on the now energetically debated question of the inheritance of acquired characteristics. Hardy, as mentioned earlier, could hardly have missed the echoes of this controversy, which had been in full swing since the publication, from 1889, of Weismann's collected essays in English translation. Two of its leading protagonists, Herbert Spencer and George Romanes, were both members of The Savile Club of which Hardy was also a member.

Hardy's long membership of the Savile (from 1878 until 1909) may have brought him into informal contact with other leading scientific figures such as Maudsley, and the inebriety expert H. D. Rolleston, as well as Ray Lankester and Clifford Allbutt.[67] A member of its committee was the neurologist H. B. Donkin, physician to Eleanor Marx and Olive Schreiner, who had written an essay on hysteria for a *Dictionary of Psychological Medicine*, edited by Allbutt in 1892.[68]

For all these figures, whether Lamarckians or, more likely, supporters of Weismann, heredity was central in determining the behavioural predisposition of men and women. Rolleston, in an essay on alcoholism for the compendious *A System of Medicine* (1905–11), edited by himself and Allbutt , observed that hereditary influence

> may be traced in a very large proportion of alcoholic cases. Drunkenness not only breeds alcoholic tendencies but produces a decidedly neurotic taint and a strong predisposition to insanity; conversely, the offspring of neurotic or insane parents may be particularly susceptible to the effects of alcohol ... thus drunkards beget 'neuropaths' or 'degenerates' and neuropaths again may have drunken offspring.[69]

Hardy himself made a public commitment to the idea of inherited degeneracy when, in 1894, he contributed to the topical debate about the woman question (debates which inevitably converged on marriage and its responsibilities) in a symposium on sex education, 'The Tree of Knowledge', for the *New Review*. Among other participants was Max Nordau who urged (characteristically and predictably) that women should receive 'physiological teaching' in order that they might counteract the defiling of their 'mental purity' by 'wild fictions based upon morbid art, detestable literature, suggestive plays and inconsidered drawing-room and table-talk'.[70]

Hardy was by now in the middle of composing the full-length version of *Jude* which he eventually completed in March 1895. His *New Review* article reveals the extent of his immersion in the marriage question and the wider claims of personal relationships. He was the only contributor to probe the assumption that marriage was the only fit way of organising sexual relationships, and suggested (with an irony which could only be fully savoured in the light of his exposure of the marriage predicament in *Jude*) that 'civilisation ... has never succeeded in creating that homely thing, a satisfactory scheme for the conjunction of the sexes'.[71] On the question of sex education before marriage, Hardy advocated 'a plain handbook on the natural processes', but also 'similar information on morbid contingencies'.[72] A prospective wife, he thought, should also know about 'the possibilities which may lie in the past of the elect man'.[73] Such advocacy of a medical early-warning system for transmissable defects was for the period, enlightened, and anticipated the views of sexologists like Havelock Ellis, and feminists such as Olive Schreiner and Margaret Sanger, who soon would be urging open discussion of sexual relations with truly eugenic zealousness. There was no substitute, in their view, for confronting the possibility of inherited defect with hard biological information: the facts of life had to include the facts of heredity.

VII

With evidence of Hardy's engagement with the literature of heredity and degeneration and of his familiarity with the intellectual society that produced it, it is not difficult to identify *Jude the Obscure* as a determinist, or even eugenist, fiction, a 'tract for the times', nor to pick out Jude and Sue as specific instances of the *fin de siècle* degenerate condition. But as we have seen in the case of *Tess of the D'Urbervilles* no such straightforward relationship obtains, in Hardy's work, between ideology and fictional expression, between what Gillian Beer distinguishes as 'plot' and 'writing'.[74] The configuration of levels of meaning in the novel is deceptively complex: while Hardy could truthfully state that his novel concerned the 'doom or curse of hereditary temperament', this affiliation to contemporary determinism nevertheless provided a mask behind which he found freedom to explore unutterable themes.

Another way of putting this is to isolate a central tension in *Jude* between what Penny Boumelha has called ' "private" experience' and the 'superficial generalisations of the public language which alone is available to articulate that experience'.[75] Denied the consolations of continuity, Jude and Sue are orphaned figures whose unstable identities have to be made and remade discursively through a language which appears to belong to others – other sources of authority, of rationality and power.

Near the opening of the book young Jude is spoken of not as a boy but as a Fawley, stamped with the mark of his family's unhappy history.

The boy is crazy for books, that he is. It runs in the family rather. His cousin Sue is just the same – so I've heard; but I have not seen the child for years, though she was born in this place, within these. four walls, as it happened. My niece and her husband, after they were married, didn't get a house of their own for some year or more; and then they only had one till – Well, I won't go into that. Jude, my child, don't *you* ever marry. 'Tisn't for the Fawleys to take that step any more.[76]

Aunt Drusilla's gossip meanders, rather menacingly, from an innocuous comment on Jude's 'craze', which he shares with his 'cousin Sue', to the suppressed scandal of the family tragedy. Jude's buried past is elicited not through a narrative of lived history but rather as a discrete link in a chain. This is history now disturbingly rewritten as community myth, offering – in its fusion of observation and prescription – a prognosis: her words warning that the family condition will inevitably replicate its suffering, if reproduced. Jude musn't marry, because he musn't breed and generate the Fawley degeneracy. Not only are his origins buried but the terms of this myth deny him the promise of generating new beginnings. It is appropriately nurtured within a rural culture, cut off from its own roots and figured by the 'meanly utilitarian' harrowlines of Farmer Troutham's field, which, as John Goode has noted, deprives the terrain of 'all history'.[77]

The dangerous Fawley inheritance comprises two incidents of marital breakdown. After his parents separated, Jude's mother drowned herself and he is brought up by his father. Sue's mother separated from her father, and brings up the young Sue in London. There is also a more remote story which tells of a Fawley ancestor, gibbeted for attempting to steal the coffin of a dead child of a broken marriage. Not for nothing does Aunt Drusilla ruefully observe, after Jude's marriage to Arabella has broken down, that 'The Fawleys were not made for wedlock: it never seemed to sit well upon us. There's sommat in our blood that won't take kindly to the notion of being bound to do what we do readily enough if not bound. That's why you ought to have hearkened to me, and not ha' married' (94). This ingenious fusion of the languages of folk-wisdom and pathological degeneration will provide the medium Hardy seeks for the discursive encounter with determinism which is at the heart of the novel.

In *Jude* these discourses are presented as diagnoses, by which the lives of Jude and Sue would appear to confirm their innate degeneracy. And Hardy, on the face of it, offers a substantial endorsement of the authority of hereditarian determinism – both in its 'native' and 'scientific' guises. Yet if we place *Jude* alongside *The Whirlpool*, what emerges is a far more complex encounter with degeneration. Gissing's neurasthenic Alma, as we have seen, is allowed no egress from the determinism which binds and gags her. But Hardy resists such a reductive conclusion: he shows his neurasthenic, Sue, struggling to free herself into autonomy and self-awareness. Sue and Jude are permitted to explore the discourses of determinism by which they are defined, and by which they suffer, and so confront the repressive social order which deploys them.

Sue is certainly intended to approximate to the contemporary 'type' of neurasthenic who suffers the disease of modern civilisation. She has been brought up in London, which for Allbutt, Nordau and other observers was the epicentre of the pervasive and contagious nervous condition which characterised the nineties. Her nervous disposition is insisted upon: 'she is of a nervous temperament' (116); 'all was nervous motion' (113). As a child she is diagnosed as a 'pert little thing ... with her tight-strained nerves' (132). She is the anti-type of the marriageable woman and mother: a 'fine-nerved, sensitive girl, quite unfitted by temperament and instinct to fulfil the condition of the matrimonial relation with Phillotson, possibly with scarce any man' (235). In short, with her intellectual independence, her lack of interest in marriage and her 'nerves' she is the type of the strictly contemporary 'new woman'.

It was Sue's 'temperament' rather than Jude's which conveyed the clearest signals to the reviewers – who, by late 1895, had been exposed to two concentrated years of the literature of the 'new woman', and could freely indulge a rhetoric spiced with know-ingness but laced also with persisting incredulity. To Edmund Gosse, a friend of Hardy's, Sue was a 'poor, maimed "degenerate", ignorant of herself and of the perversion of her instincts', her presen-tation a 'terrible study in pathology'.[78] The reviewer R. Y. Tyrell treated Sue as a morbid anti-type of pure womanhood. 'To what end', he asked

is all this minute registry of the fluctuations of disease in an incurably morbid organism? Why dwell on this fantastic green sickness? Marriage laws do not suit Sue's warped and neurotic nature ... She has no sense of the dignity of womanhood and motherhood, and so all her relations with the other sex become impure in her morbid imagination.[79]

Sue's 'pathological' character allowed the text itself to be widely appropriated as a pathological case study. For some critics it was on these grounds that the novel failed as art. Gosse, for one, commented on the intervention of 'the physician, the neuropathist [who] takes the pen out of the poet's hand'.[80] For Tyrell, 'Mr Hardy's powers' had undergone 'a sad deterioration ... or he has determined to try the patience of his public ... [with] ... in lieu of a novel a treatise on sexual pathology'.[81] To invoke the pathological study as an unworthy discourse which violated the stylistic decorum of prose fiction was a standard ploy in the battle with late nineteenth-century naturalism. Havelock Ellis invoked it to express abhorrence of the Father Time murders, which he failed, strangely, to comprehend. But of the presentation of Sue and Jude Ellis had no doubts: 'Mr Hardy by no means wished to bring before us a mere monstrosity, a pathological "case" ', and he perceptively attributed their complexity to the complexities of civilisation itself:

> Jude and Sue are represented as crushed by a civilisation to which they were not born, and though civilisation may in some respects be regarded as a disease and as unnatural, in others it may be said to bring out those finer vibrations of Nature which are overlayed by rough and bucolic conditions of life.
> The refinement of sexual sensibility with which this book largely deals is precisely such a vibration.[82]

Jude's character and behaviour did not always receive such delicate handling. Gosse was lured up the wrong track by the attention Hardy gave to Jude's tainted heredity, and interpreted the figure of Jude as simply degenerate: 'Jude, a neurotic subject in whom hereditary degeneracy takes an idealist turn, with some touch, perhaps, of what the new doctors call megalomania'.[83] Such a reading, not untypical of this period, pathologises the aspirations of working people. Under the stress induced by aspiration to a higher status of life, their defective make-up would be exposed. George Savage had written in 1884 of 'constant examples in Bethlem of young men, who, having left the plough for the desk, have found after years of struggle, that their path was barred by social or other hindrances, and disappointment, worry, and the solitude of a great city have produced insanity of an incurable type'[84].

What Gosse's reading missed was Jude's characteristic facility for scrutinising his own motives. Yet given the conclusions Jude draws, it was not altogether surprising that Gosse and others should have read him in such narrowly diagnostic terms. In the immediate aftermath of the breakdown of his marriage to Arabella, Jude's struggle to make sense of his experience of marriage is a good example of what Ellis had in mind by 'the finer vibrations of Nature ... (being) ... overlayed by rough and bucolic conditions of life'. Struck by the 'fundamental error' of their 'matrimonial union', Jude confronts the inexplicable logic of 'having based a permanent contract on a temporary feeling which had no necessary connection

with affinities that alone render a life-long comradeship tolerable'
(93). Here Jude gains understanding into the lack of connection
between those elements which the ideology of marriage fuses –
'temporary feeling' and 'permanent contract'. But whilst this is a
moment of insight, he is forced repeatedly to confront an alternative
logic, that of the hereditary myth whose determinism frustrates his
efforts to prise open the terms of marriage. At the moment of his leap
forward to a fuller awareness, he is objectified both as a victim of the
family curse and a carrier of degeneracy. Arabella voices it: 'Going
to ill-use me on principle, as your father ill-used your mother, and
your father's sister ill-used her husband? . . . All you be a queer lot as
husbands and wives' (93). He now goes to visit great-Aunt Drusilla,
the only person alive who could connect Jude with the family past
through lived experience, rather than through the superstitious lens
of mythic history. But in Jude's failed marriage she only finds
confirmation of the menace of heredity – 'there's sommat in our
blood' (94).

Denied confirmation of his identity, Jude increasingly contemplates the self with a Schopenhauerian detachment and a Paterian
irony. His pose is part posture, but it permits the subject to confront
its determinants: he contemplates his own suicide with ironic
detachment, and an image of himself as a degenerate inebriate:
'What could he do of a lower kind than self-extermination; what was
there less noble, more in keeping with his present degraded position?
He could get drunk. Of course that was it; he had forgotten.
Drinking was the regular, stereotyped resource of the despairing
worthless. He began to see now why some men boozed at inns' (94).
In his depression Jude voluntarily submits to an image of a stereotype of degeneracy which is to hand in the culture – the inebriate
'despairing worthless'. This is, of course, a cultivated image which,
under the cover of typicality, will insulate him from taking an
impossible reponsibility for his own life – it is too painful for him to
think otherwise. Jude's drunken excesses will confirm him to the
world as a degenerate type. Hardy makes Jude display himself here
as a composition of the discursive structures which objectify him.

In Jude's rhetoric of self-abasement we hear the interrogation and
the laying bare of the causes of his failure in life. After Arabella has
called on Jude at Albrickham, Sue exclaims that Arabella is 'too
low, too coarse for you to talk to long, Jude, and was always'. He
replies:

Perhaps I am coarse too, worst luck. I have the germs of every human infirmity in me, I verily believe – that was why I saw it was so preposterous of me to think of being a curate. I have cured myself of drunkenness I think; but I never know in what new form a suppressed vice will break out in me'. (280)

The 'suppressed vice' is his need for sexual fulfilment. In the next sentence he declares, 'I do love you, Sue, though I have danced attendance on you so long for such poor returns'(280). This curiously abrupt movement of thought can be accounted for by the pressured function the language of degeneracy has to perform. Jude's 'infirmity' is specifically located in the 'germs', an unmistakable reference to Weismann's theory of the inheritance of characters through the track made by the germ plasm. Given that this theory stresses the transference of characters, activated at the point of sexual conjunction (because the nascent inherited factor is renewed by exchange of germ particles), the act of sexual exchange is freighted with a particular anxiety in Hardy's text, since in Weismann's terms the inheritance of characteristics acquired through life or habit will play no part.

Later in the novel he returns to Christminster on 'Humiliation Day' and publicly speaks of his failure to gain admission to a college not only in sociological terms – 'It takes two or three generations to do what I tried to do in one', but also in terms of organic defect: 'my impulses – affections – vices perhaps they should be called – were too strong not to hamper a man without advantages' (336). And later in his peroration he declares that 'I was, perhaps, after all, a paltry victim to the spirit of mental and social restlessness, that makes so many unhappy these days' (336). Such an empty, if conventionally agreeable, diagnosis prompts Sue's swift denunciation: 'Don't tell them that' whispered Sue with tears at perceiving Jude's state of mind. 'You weren't that. You struggled nobly to acquire knowledge, and only the meanest souls would blame you' (336).

Earlier, on leaving Christminster, his academic aspirations now abandoned, he fears that 'his whole scheme had degenerated to, even though it might have originated in, a social unrest which had no foundation in the nobler instincts; which was purely an artificial product of civilisation. There were thousands of young men on the same self-seeking track at the present moment' (149). Jude can easily define himself either as a victim or a product of larger causes beyond his control: here he diagnoses himself (as a Savage, Maudsley or Allbutt would diagnose him) as a symptom of society's disease. By this discourse, individual quest is rendered as 'artificial product', social challenge becomes 'social unrest'.

And yet Jude's exposure of patterns of determinism, even as he seems compliant with them, questions the very logic of heredity itself. At the prospect of taking his and Arabella's son Father Time, he tackles head-on 'the beggarly question of parentage': 'what is it, after all? What does it matter, when you come to think of it, whether a child is yours by blood or not?' (288). What indeed? This comes as close as anything in the novel to a liberating deconstruction of the ideology of familial inheritance, 'sommat in our blood'. In their assault on the tyranny of the blood-relation Jude and Sue here contest the very basis of the ideology to which they have been and will be subjected. There can be few more devastating attacks on the ideology of the family than Jude's declaration that: 'All the little ones of our time are collectively the children of us adults of the time, and entitled to our general care. That excessive regard of parents for their own children, and their dislike of other people's is, like class-feeling, patriotism, save-your-own-soulism, and other virtues, a mean exclusiveness at bottom' (288).

Jude and Sue's utopian logic has in its sights the destruction of the family system. They pinpoint that ideology which elevates parent-child relations and which insists, in this society, that biological and familial functions are locked together. Sue daringly embraces an image of the child, freed from its familial ties, emptied of all the accumulated continuities of its inheritance: she enthusiastically greets the possibility that the child might not be Jude's: 'And if he isn't yours it makes it all the better. I do hope he isn't' (288). To perceive the child as an aestheticised image of pleasure is to have it immunised from the ideology of family membership. Here Hardy voices a contemporary feminist projection of biological tran-scendence, which was strikingly sounded in George Egerton's *Key-notes* (1893) and other feminist utopias of the *fin de siècle*.[85]

Galton's law of ancestral contribution to heritage lies behind Jude's recognition of the impossibility of pure generation. The imaged virgin birth, with Sue, fecund yet unsullied by the male, is debased by exposure to the laws of nature. Through their effort to aestheticise and envision the impossible, Jude and Sue come to understand the enormity of their subjection, both to bourgeois ideology and the infinitely random process of selection which consti-tutes evolution. In the shadow of these massive totalities they self-consciously live out the evolutionary process, painfully conscious of their debased value. Indeed they represent themselves as alloyed currency: by continuing to give life they devalue the coinage; by generating their alloyed inheritance they display a degeneration which becomes self-confirming in the symbolic judgement of Father Times's suicide and his murder of the other children.

It is entirely characteristic of their heroic perversity that, beset by their degeneration, Jude and Sue project themselves as unalloyed beings, untrammelled by moral and scientific determinism: this extends to their cultivation of what respectable society, the morality of Biles and Willis, forces theme into – obscurity and anonymity. It is an existence which corresponds to Sue's wish for an occupation 'in which personal circumstances don't count' (318), and approximates to her earlier dream when, alone with Jude in a shepherd's cottage, she revels in being 'outside all laws except gravitation and germination' (158).

VIII

But while he gets close to it, Hardy is never quite free to find the language for a quest for physical and spiritual wholeness. Frequently he makes Jude and Sue utter a tantalising series of first drafts of that wholeness – a register, perhaps, of their ironic displacement from ideology. But ideology, instead, continually impresses itself through the censoring discourse of hereditary degeneracy, which is invoked at moments of beckoning candour.

At Melchester, for example, Jude and Sue confide to each other the story of their past relationships – Jude's marriage to Arabella, Sue's affair with the undergraduate. Sue, engaged to Phillotson, faces squarely the idea of marrying Jude, despite the obvious obstacle of Arabella. They both invoke their degeneracy by reiterating the rural myth, at the very moment of defining the terms of their relationship. They are poised between sexual union, unlegitimated by marriage, and an acute perception of how marriage could indeed destroy them:

They stood possessed by the same thought, ugly enough, even as an assumption: that a union between them, had such been possible, would have meant a terrible intensification of unfitness – two bitters in one dish.

'Oh but there can't be anything in it', she said with nervous lightness. 'Our family have been unlucky of late years in choosing mates – that's all'.

And they pretended to persuade themselves that all that had happened was of no consequence, and that they could still be cousins and friends and warm correspondents ... (187)

The buried issue here is whether Hardy can allow them to deal with a sexual relationship, burdened with the dubious associations of their cousinship. And this relationship continually signals the degenerate consequences of their sexual and procreative potential. Their sexual passion (and the guilt these feelings produce) is expressed through their consciousness of their own unfitness. The deployment of the family myth shields them from these intolerable feelings. They feel protected from taking responsibility for these feelings by seeing themselves as subject to other determinants.

This is an evident and understandable difficulty for Hardy. The language of this exchange uneasily strains towards sexual explicitness and the subversion of the ideology of marriage. The straining is there in inexplicit phrasing – 'they pretended to persuade themselves that all that had happened was of no consequence' (187). To what does 'all' refer: the family past, their passion, the incident in the market square at Shaston where Sue rejected Jude's physical approach, or their recently recounted past affairs? The narrator here seems to collude with his characters' inability to verbalise these feelings. And the stolidly invoked 'cousins, friends, warm correspondents' only serves to call attention to everything else that has passed between them. The text suggests this experience, but cannot seem to embody it.

But an alternative draft is possible. Jude and Sue could refute the significance of the determinism and appropriate a sense of themselves as subjects, rather than viewing each other so insistently as objects of contemporary discourse. Indeed, they could make their own sexuality the medium of self-definition: the text might then utter what it suppresses but continually intimates. Of course it is anachronistic to ask this of Hardy, writing in the mid-nineties, but he so deploys the discourses of degeneration as to endow his characters with the power of utterance of these questions. And those discourses, as we have seen in *Tess*, allow the production, within received accepted norms, of truly radical fictions.

CHAPTER 9

Race-regeneration

It matters comparatively little what sort of education we give
children; the primary matter is what sort of children we have
got to educate.[1]

(Havelock Ellis (1908))

Major Booth Voysey: Have you thought of the physical
improvement which conscription would bring about in the
manhood of the country? What England needs is Chest![2]

(Harley Granville-Barker, *The Voysey Inheritance* (1905))

I

If we are to hold our own among the nations in the severe
commercial struggle that lies before us the mass of the people
must be physically and mentally efficient. It is the best fed
and the best taught nation that will survive in the long run.

(W.T.Stead)[3]

In 1901 B. S. Rowntree published his pioneering analysis of life in
York, *Poverty: A Study of Town Life*. It revealed that thirty per cent of
the city population lived in a state of poverty, and that over fifteen
per cent fell below a level of minimum efficiency. The journalist
W. T. Stead read *Poverty* in December of that year. His response,
quoted above, represents the inferences drawn by many of his
contemporaries from such sombre findings. By the turn of the
century the fate of the nation and the health of the mass of the
people had come to seem inseparable. The physical and moral
consequences of poverty at home and the threat of imperial weakness abroad were repeatedly spoken of together. The social imperialist Lord Rosebery harped on the theme when he addressed medical
students at Glasgow University in November 1900 – the threat to
empire from the abyss: 'in the rookeries and slums which still
survive, an imperial race cannot be reared. You can scarcely

produce anything in those foul nests of crime and disease but a
progeny doomed from its birth to misery and ignominy.'

To attack the enemy within, it was necessary to recruit a new model
army, whose weapons were those of medical expertise. 'Where you
convert an unhealthy citizen into a healthy one', Rosebery told the
Glasgow students, 'you in doing your duty are also working for the
Empire... Health of mind and body exalt a nation in the competition
of the universe.'[4] The new cult figure was the expert, the quintessen-
tial 'coming man', to whom the poor were served up as objects for his
procedures of identification and inspection.

If so much was invested in the national health, in the Empire's
'competition of the universe', it was little wonder that reports of the
parlous state of health of recruits for military service in South Africa
were received with dismay, even panic. The annual reports of the
Inspector-General of Recruiting were widely and speedily publicised from 1900 onwards. They showed that in Manchester, for
example, only three out of every eleven applicants for military
service were considered fit; and of those, under half had attained a
moderate standard of muscular power.[5] The revelations had both a
metaphoric and a metonymic force; they were a confirming
symptom as well as a constituent episode in the great turn-of-the-
century drama about the fitness of the national body. And for the
modern historian this moment of national crisis – almost too neatly
timed at the century's turn – encapsulates the mentality of the
establishment in its anxiety about Empire.[6]

For the very conduct of the Boer War itself now became the
charged focus of doubts and uncertainties about the future of the
nation and its imperial role, which had been felt for a generation.
An arduous campaign had been protracted for as much as eighteen
months beyond expectations. A public quite unprepared for military reverses was shocked and angered by what they revealed –
incompetence, ignorance, deceit, brutality. At the heart of Empire
lurked the cancer of unfitness.[7]

The re-establishment of the health of the nation in the new century
was to be achieved by state intervention, through what David
Feldman has termed 'a series of inclusions and exclusions concerned
with who would be contained within the nation and on what terms'.[8]
The qualification for membership of the Edwardian nation turned
ever more insistently on the evidence of reproductive 'fitness'.

A policy of social imperialism in response to the crisis began to coalesce around the idea of 'national efficiency'. Rosebery's manoeuvrings at this time, when he was detached from his old Liberal ties and apparently above the party game, show him actively moving influential opinion behind this new drive towards imperial regeneration.[9] Early in 1900 Haldane thought it opportune to arrange a meeting between him and the leading Fabians, Sidney and Beatrice Webb.

The Webbs had recently secured a majority within the society for Shaw's pro-imperialist position on the Boer War. Now they set about campaigning for target levels of minimum efficiency across all social agencies.[10] And in the unaligned Rosebery they saw a potential confederate. In a widely quoted article of 1901, Sidney Webb praised Rosebery's disavowal of the old liberalism, and claimed, rather disingenuously, that the working class wanted to know 'what steps' his supporters were likely to take to 'ensure the rearing of an imperial race'.[11] Proclaiming his own Fabian expertise, Webb proposed that the campaign for national efficiency should be put in the hands of 'a group of men [sic] of diverse temperaments and varied talents, imbued with a common purpose and eager to work out ... how each department of national life can be raised to its highest possible efficiency'.[12] This was a call for a shadow Civil Service – the 'co-efficients'.

The rallying cry of 'efficiency' was sounded in Rosebery's next major speech, again in Glasgow, in March 1902. Efficiency was 'a condition of national fitness equal to the demands of our Empire – administrative, parliamentary, commercial, educational, physical, moral, naval and military fitness – so that we should make the best of our admirable raw material'.[13] This speech also launched the Liberal League, an extra-parliamentary group to promote national efficiency, with Rosebery as President: its main spokesmen were three future major Liberal politicians, Haldane, Grey and Asquith.[14] Asquith had only recently offered a definition of liberty, tailored to match the utilitarianism of the moment. Its pursuit, he thought, entailed 'the best use of faculty, opportunity, energy, life ... everything, in short, that tends to national, communal and personal efficiency'.[15] Eight months later Haldane and Grey received an invitation from Webb to join his 'co-efficients'.

But the high aims of the 'co-efficients' were never actually realised; it was, in effect, little more than a dining club with an agenda for debating 'the aims, policy and methods of Imperial efficiency', as Webb told Wells.[16] Yet what was singular about it was that under the umbrella of 'efficiency' Webb had managed to bring together men of such contrasting political persuasions – from imperialists like Milner, to radical liberals like Charles Masterman and Bertrand Russell (who took the trouble to resign, shortly after joining). The utilitarian socialist Wells was likewise of the party: his portfolio was literature.[17]

'Efficiency', as Nikolas Rose suggests, did not offer the satisfaction of either a 'single concept' or a hidden principle. It stood or fell by its utility value. For this amalgam of politically interested parties, its 'utility' was that it 'conferred a kind of regularity on the discourses of this period' because of the 'variability' which the term allowed.[18] It allowed, discursively, the 'organisation of controversy'.

In this respect 'efficiency' bore more than a passing resemblance to its bulkier, rather discredited elder cousin 'degeneracy'. Coming in from the cold of the *fin de siècle*, the lean and fit family members gather, in the new century, hoping he won't repeat his recent disorderly exploits. They would like to dispense with him, but really don't want him dying on them yet. They might, indeed, be lost without him.

Soldiers, politicians and administrators were mobilised to combat the unfitness of the urban poor. The unfolding of this campaign can be viewed through the activities of an eminent physician, Sir Lauder Brunton (1844–1916), a figure perfectly attuned to the degenerationist spirit of the time and whose medical training and practice had run roughly parallel with that of other better known specialists such as Allbutt, Rolleston, Clouston and Crichton-Browne.[19]

In 1902, as the forces determined to seek out the causes of physical unfitness gathered momentum, Brunton gathered together a group of influential figures to discuss the question of military training in schools; amongst then was Buckle, editor of the *Times*, and Haldane, who was on the point of joining the Liberal League of Rosebery and the 'co-efficients'. Brunton wanted the British love of sport – typified at its most complacent by 'the flannelled fools at the wicket' mocked by Kipling[20] – channelled into a love of military combat: 'let all children be taught at school ... how to handle a gun, how to shoot, and how to manoeuvre'.[21]

National efficiency and national defence had by now become inextricably linked in an offensive designed to deal with the menace to the Empire from the military and economic power of Germany.

The Great Question of the Day,

. . THE . .

Health of the People.

Full Verbatim Report of the Speeches delivered
on June 28th, 1905, at the
Mansion House, the Lord Mayor presiding,

BY

**THE BISHOP OF RIPON,
THE LORD CHIEF JUSTICE,
SIR WILLIAM BROADBENT, Bt., K.C.V.O.,
ALDERMAN & SHERIFF SIR THOS. VEZEY STRONG,
MRS. BRAMWELL BOOTH,
THE RIGHT HON. R. B. HALDANE, M.P.,
SIR JAMES CRICHTON-BROWNE, M.D.,
MR. J. COMPTON RICKETT, D.L., M.P.,**
and
SIR LAUDER BRUNTON, M.D.,

TO INAUGURATE
THE

NATIONAL LEAGUE FOR PHYSICAL EDUCATION AND IMPROVEMENT.

OFFICES :

49-50, Denison House, Vauxhall Bridge Road, S.W.
Telephone: 1210 Victoria.   (Near Victoria Station.)

PRICE ONE PENNY.

10 'The Health of the People', an advertisement of 1905.

The *Manchester Guardian* instituted a debate on National Physical Training. The London editor, J. B. Atkins, enthusiastically reported, in July 1903, a meeting of luminaries, gathered by Brunton, including Clifford Allbutt and Sir Frederick Maurice, who were planning a National League for Physical Education which would assist in implementing the recommendations of the Physical Deterioration Committee once it had reported.[22] (The League was eventually inaugurated in June 1905, after Brunton's vigorous campaigns at numerous meetings of hospital advisers and head teachers' associations.) This meeting (billed as 'The Great Question of the Day, "The Health of the People" ')[23] was addressed by Haldane and many medical authorities. On the executive council sat Brunton, Clouston, Crichton-Browne, Atkins, Maurice, Ernest H. Pooley – just relieved of his work as secretary to the Physical Deterioration Committee – and the cricketers C. B. Fry and Pelham Warner.[24]

Only two months later, Warner, as captain of the England cricket team, packed his bags for a tour of Australia. At the team's embarkation (25 September 1903), Warner received a remarkable public eulogy from his fellow council member, Fry. Invoking, for the readers of the *Daily Express*, Milton's *Lycidas*, Fry urged Warner's men to 'scorn delights – minor delights – and to live laborious – pleasantly laborious days – throughout the tour'. He addressed the team as soldiers, with Warner their military commander: 'the prime condition of success in the game is unadulterated physical fitness. So we need not fear but that they will take the field like "trained men" ... they say that ... you are a lucky Captain: they say that of Lord Roberts also. It is difficult to find the dividing-line between luck and management in war and cricket'.[25] Not for the first time did the spectacle of a national sport and its practitioners offer the perfect medium for an assertion of the bruised imperial spirit. Or as Kipling characterised it in his fantasy of military organisation 'The Army of a Dream' (1904), 'no cricketer no corps': 'County cricket and County volunteering ought to be on the same footing – unpaid and genuine'.[26]

While many of the advocates of compulsory military training came from the political right, prominent Fabians such as Shaw, Hubert Bland and the Webbs also favoured the idea, testifying to the degree to which social imperialism and national efficiency had permeated all sections of the political scene.[27] The eventual emer-

A " Slopper." The boy who apes the man by smoking ; he will never be much good.

A strong and healthy boy has the ball at his feet.

11 'A Slopper' versus 'A Strong and Healthy Boy' from Sir Robert Baden-Powell, *Scouting for Boys*, 1908.

gence of the Boy Scout movement, under the military hero Baden-Powell, was enthusiastically greeted by Wells – as well as by radical liberals like Masterman and J. L. Hammond.[28] This hugely successful movement had its origins in the obsessions, in the early years of the 1900s, with the unfitness and degeneracy of the urban population and particularly of its youth.

From the turn of the century the nation's adolescents were becoming the pronounced object of a medicalising discourse of fitness. Youth, after all, held the nation's future stock of racial health. But it was the children of the poor and the urban masses, spoken of as the 'physical capital of the nation', who were increasingly singled out for treatment.[29] The public schools of Haileybury and Cheltenham might be confident about the physique and habits of their boys, but look, said Dr William Odell, at the cigarette-smoking youth of the 'lower-classes': in the towns they 'lounge about whilst the youth of other nations are exercising and drilling'.[30] The doctor keeps his eyes upon juvenile errand boys. Mrs Pardiggle, in *Bleak House*, with her impertinence and her religious tracts, has been replaced by another sort of snooper, the exponent of fitness and efficiency. There should be 'no overgrown lads standing idly and foolishly at the street corners, gaping after they knew not what, smoking cigarettes', observed an admirer of the Boy Scout movement in 1911.[31]

The Inter-Departmental Committee on Physical Deterioration, whose findings were published in August 1904, had set out to enquire into 'the allegations concerning the deterioration of certain classes of the population – as shown by the large percentage of rejections, for physical causes, of recruits for the Army'. However, its original terms of reference were widened to include the best means of providing data for a 'comparative estimate of the health and physique of the people'; an indication of 'the causes of such physical deterioration as does exist in certain classes', and 'to point out the means by which it can be most effectually diminished'.[32]

The designation of physical 'deterioration' rather than 'degeneration' was validated by the findings of the report which broadly rejected the hereditary factor as a cause of 'degeneracy'. 'The influence of heredity is not a considerable factor in the production of degenerates', it concluded.[33] The report endorsed the post-Weismann arguments of several doctors, one of whom testified that 'inferior bodily characteristics, the result of poverty and not of vice are not transmissable'.[34] Instead the committee favoured the determining effects of the environment; unfavourable 'noxious' conditions made the offspring of the mother more vulnerable to disease thereby sowing the seeds of progressive degeneration. The committee rejected the claims of Karl Pearson that intelligence was not reproducing itself and was being bred out by the less able, more fertile, stock.[35]

The quality of the environment emerged as critical; the causes of deterioration were to be sought in the specific ill-effects of life in the city with its polluted air,[36] its adulterated food and milk[37] and unhealthy work conditions.[38] Victorian moral high-mindedness was displaced by Edwardian arguments of utility and the economic benefits of fitness. In addressing with a special emphasis the problem of alcoholism, the report explicitly rejected the moral standpoint of the temperance movement. Degeneration from drink, it said, would be better checked by 'bringing home to men and women the fatal effects of alchohol on physical efficiency than by expatiating on the moral wickedness of drinking'.[39] And yet, despite the efforts of the committee to avoid the over-general designation of degeneracy, with its hereditarian assumptions, the report was seized on by some as impressive evidence of a progressive national degeneracy. Sir John Gorst, for one, an ex-cabinet minister, and a persistent propagandist of degenerationism, insisted on talking of the 'recent report upon the degeneracy of the race', even as he campaigned tirelessly for compulsory school meals for underfed children.[40]

II

This changing climate of opinion on the questions of degeneracy and efficiency did not, on the face of it, offer opportunities for writers of fiction, but H. G. Wells, for one, seized his chance. In 1903 he published his story 'The Land Ironclads', which was set on an unspecified battlefield in a campaign seen through the eyes of a war-correspondent. This narrator becomes aware that one of the armies is employing not ordinary weapons but large moving guns which, it emerges, are the guns of a 'land ironclad', a prototype tank. Wells's prescience about a military machine, not invented until 1914, nor in active use until 1916, is often taken to be the most memorable feature of this story. But its broader significance lies in the manner in which he draws on topical issues to raise a larger question about the values of modern civilisation and the competing claims of civilised and primitive, of mind and body, and the future shape of human conflict.

Two kinds of fighting men are compared. Early on the correspondent talks to a jocular, complacent lieutenant who is waiting for an enemy attack. The physical differences between the adversaries are pointed up. The lieutenant and his men are confident roughnecks, old campaigners, 'nice healthy hunters and stock men ... rowdy-dowdy cowpunchers and nigger-wackers',[41] their machismo everywhere apparent: 'hard brown skin ... sinewy frame, an open, tireless stride ... a master's grip on the rifle' (136). Their opponents, by contrast, are effete and apparently ineffectual: 'They're a crowd of devitalised townsmen ... They're clerks, they're factory hands, they're students, they're civilised men. They can write, they can talk, they can make and do all sorts of things, but they're poor amateurs at war' (133).

Underpinning this contrast is the contemporary problematic anxiety about two related questions: what kind of man is necessary for victory in contemporary warfare and what is the nature of that warfare? The experience of the Boer War had shaken the belief in the unrivalled supremacy of English troops. A consequence was a wholesale reappraisal of all aspects of military performance. The year 1903 saw the Elgin Commission of Enquiry into the South African War, and the Butler Committee on the Disposal of War Stores was to report in 1905. Behind these investigations lies a prevailing sense that the nation's military incompetence is a symptom of a pervasive degeneracy at the heart of Empire at the century's turn. In the immediate aftermath of the war the military question attracted to it all the wider fears about national degeneration: fears provoked by the existence of under-bred, physically inefficient recruits, and old-fashioned, amateurish and outmoded military commanders. Conservative imperialists believed that the army was a necessary instrument of social control and that the efficiency of the army mirrored the efficiency of the nation. The result was to intensify military consciousness even in peacetime, as the frenetic activity of Lauder Brunton and others shows.

From the start Wells makes the battle sociologically problematic, turning it into a specific object of investigation. His war-correspondent needs to discover what kind of war is being fought in order to be able to write about it. To begin with he takes the assessment of the battle-scarred lieutenant at face value. The civilised enemy is effete and ineffectual. They may be well-fed, articulate and educated men, but they are devitalised – they are, after all, the product of the town, not the outback. Wells here draws on the prevailing discourse of urban degeneration which had informed the numerous recent critiques of the physical condition of the Boer War recruits. But he characteristically inverts it; for these representative products of the city, with their 'purest water-company water' and 'three meals a day' since leaving 'their feeding bottles' (133), are anything but the stunted products of the abyss.

Depressed by these products of civilisation, and disillusioned by war in general, the journalist sets out to compose an article 'Is War Played Out?'. He seems to be resigned to the inevitable victory of the lieutenant's 'cunning, elementary louts', with their 'sentimental patriotic' songs, over the 'townsmen' (136). But soon the correspondent is to discover that the gunfire of the 'elementary' men is woefully inadequate in the face of the 'townsmen's mechanism ... effectually ironclad against bullets' and which can 'cross a thirty-foot trench ... [and] ... shoot out rifle bullets with unerring precision' (148). Wells reveals not simply the extraordinary technological advance but the qualitatively altered relationship between soldiers and their armaments, – men and the machine. The rifleman is now sunk deep inside his armour-plated machine, his will attuned and accommodated to the gadgetry at his command. War is no longer a matter of individual heroics – 'that hysteria of effort which is so frequently regarded as the proper state of mind for heroic deeds' (152) – proper, that is, for the lieutenant's men. The outcome of war will now be determined by technicians – 'alert, intelligent, quiet'.

That it is these 'townsmen' who are in control of such elaborate technology inevitably forces a reappraisal of what a scientifically advanced culture can supply. Technology privileges mind over body, intelligence over 'effort', and places the townsmen at the acme of man's evolution – in whose light the lieutenant's men are a decaying 'elementary' species, and despised as such: 'they regarded these big healthy men ... as these same big, healthy men might regard some inferior kind of nigger. They despised them for making war; despised their ... emotionality profoundly' (152). And it is the faculty of mind which enables this new brand of soldiers to place an ironic distance between themselves and the business of warfare: 'they resented being forced to the trouble of making man-killing machinery; resented the alternative of having to massacre these people ... '(152).

The military engineer is but another variant on one of Wells's favourite types – the 'coming man' – who made his first entrance as far back as 1891, but insistently from 1899.[42] In *Anticipations*, published while the Boer War was still being fought, Wells described the hallmarks of this modern figure: 'the new sort of soldier will emerge, a sober, considerate, engineering man'.[43]. Instead of 'hundreds and thousands of more or less drunken and untrained young men marching into battle – muddle headed, sentimental', there will be 'thousands of sober men braced up to their highest possibilities, intensely doing their best'.[44] As early as 1901, Wells anticipates that warfare will become more impersonal, 'less dramatic', but with huge consequences for mass society: 'a monstrous thrust and pressure of people against people'.[45]

Seeing the defeat of the lieutenant's men by the technologically advanced townsmen, the war-correspondent renames his article 'Manhood *versus* Machinery'. He compares the 'sturdy proportions' of the prisoners to those of 'their lightly-built captors'. 'Smart degenerates', he mutters, 'anaemic cockneydom' (156). Here Wells deftly redraws the received discourse of urban degeneration. The city is not merely a breeding-ground for feeble inadequates, but is, for Wells, a conceptual space in which the application of mind through education, particularly scientific education, can be promoted. He reverses the terms of the discourse which had stigmatised the city-dweller by his bodily characteristics. For Wells, these no longer carry diagnostic value or weight. Instead the city witnesses a suppression of the physical in the face of mental prowess: these are qualities which can be exported by machinery to the battlefields of the world to sub-jugate the primitive, barbaric but physically vigorous types. These urban 'degenerates' are 'smart', since the realm of the physical is no longer the sole means of evaluating man's efficiency.

In the final phase of this heuristic narrative, the last of the journalist's attempts to accommodate the shifting 'facts' of the conflict is gently ironised. Now he sympathises with the lieutenant's men – defeated by unfair odds. 'I'll call my article', he meditates, ' "Mankind *versus* Ironmongery" ' (157). The tanks are only scrap metal, after all. Yet Wells qualifies his spokesman's scepticism with a quizzical afterthought: 'He was much too good a journalist to spoil his contrast by remarking that the half-dozen comparatively slender young men in blue pyjamas who were standing about their victo-rious land ironclad, drinking coffee and eating biscuits, had also in their eyes and their carriage something not altogether degraded below the level of a man' (138). The narrator comments, rather inelegantly, on the journalist's anxiety when confronted by the new reality. The story delivers, in effect, a qualified endorsement of the 'coming man' who represents the triumph of mind over body, intelligence over will, expertise over sentimentality.

III

To judge by the responses of the dozens of medical specialists who had been interviewed by the Inter-Departmental Committee on

Physical Deterioration, the doctrine of efficiency had become the new century's version of a spiritual and moral regeneration. This seemed to be the moment in which the specialist, the expert, had truly come into his own, free to animadvert on the destiny of the country and of the race. The campaign of efficiency, building on a movement which, for a generation, had various types of the unfit in its sights, showed the immense prestige that biological and medical science had won for itself. In the hands of the new priesthood, with its doctrine of utility, its strategies of scientific measurement – involving the new discipline of biometrics – efficiency could now administer to the plight of the imperial body in the confidence that it had replaced the ineffectual salve of religion for good. It was now in the name of science that certificates of 'civic virtue' were awarded, and in its name that the damned were to be marked out and segregated. But, as Joseph Conrad was observing, in outflanking the old priesthood, science aspired to the very authority it had sought to replace; the aspirations of the new order in 'man-making' were indelibly marked with the hubris of the old.

It is a striking fact that the Fabian socialist thinkers of these years were not so much democratic in their instincts as élitist. Although he was a latecomer to the movement, Wells is a notable example of this radical new priesthood. In spite of individual differences, this group shared a belief in its right to plan the future by virtue of its gifts of expertise and intelligence. Wells's exposition of 'the coming pre-dominance of the man of science, the trained professional expert' in *Anticipations* (serialised in the *Fortnightly Review* April-December 1901), was immediately recognised and praised by Sidney Webb, who wrote to Wells as 'a friend of Graham Wallas and Bernard Shaw whom you know'.[46] Even so, Webb thought that Wells saw this type 'too exclusively as an engineer, a chemist or electrician', and urged the claims of the professional administrator: 'all experience shows that men need organising as much as machines, or rather, much more; that the making of such arrangements, and constant readjustments, as will ensure order, general health and comfort, and maximum productivity, among human beings, is a professional art itself'.[47]

Wells had been taken with the idea of an élite group of intelligent men who would lead society forward to an ever more rational and desirable future, for the best part of a decade. Its proving ground had been his science fiction. Images of supra-human, disembodied intelligences were on display successively in *The War of the Worlds* (1898), *When the Sleeper Awakes* (1899) and *The First Men in the Moon* (1901). *Anticipations* produced the 'guardians' of the 'New Republic', which by 1905 had further mutated into the notorious Samurai of *A Modern Utopia*. These were a voluntary nobility resembling the 'Knights Templar', whose name recalled the 'swordsmen of Japan'. 'So far as the Samurai have a purpose in common in maintaining the state and the order and progress of the world', Wells wrote, 'so far, by discipline and denial, by their public work and effort, they worship God together.'[48]

By 1907 Harold Monro and Maurice Browne set up the Samurai Press and published *Proposals for a Voluntary Nobility* (Samurai Press 1907). Writing in fashionably Nietzschean terms the author argued that 'blind groping is no longer the characteristic of seekers for excellence and truth ... they have deliberately set themselves to evolve a higher type'.[49] Wells was invoked as a major influence – 'the clearest-sighted idealist in England'[50] – together with Shaw, Tolstoi, Nietzsche, the new Theologians, the Simple Life Settlements and the Vegetarian Leagues. 'Opposed to anything in the nature of class spirit', the Samurai must be 'unostentatiously apart, but not aloof',[51] a sentiment which denoted the somewhat ambiguous relationship of Wells and the Fabians to organised labour.

This identification of a disciplined, progressive élite fell on fruitful soil. The Fabian, Sidney Olivier, who for the Society was the very 'model imperial administrator'[52] – he had held posts in Ceylon and Jamaica – approached Wells in 1905, probably because they had friends in common – Shaw and Graham Wallas. Olivier expressed support for the Samurai idea: 'I recognise your trumpeting Angel of the Samurai as my desire for the League of Sane Men', he wrote, claiming an allegiance from 1897, and enclosing 'one of my testimonials to the claim of Samuraiship'.[53] By 1907 A. R. Orage's periodical the *New Age* reported in its first number a 'Public conference on Mr. H. G. Wells's "Samurai" '.[54]

Two months later Beatrice Webb reported that she had just entertained a group of Cambridge undergraduates; these were young Fabians down for the long vacation: Rupert Brooke, Clifford Allen and the future Labour cabinet minister Hugh Dalton. Were these young men the types of Wells's 'voluntary nobility'? 'They are', wrote Beatrice Webb, 'a remarkably good set of hardworking clean living youths – mostly clever and enthusiastic and who look upon us as the Patriarch of the Movement.'[55] And Wells's Samurai attracted favourable comment from the political right. John Buchan noticed the 'resemblance ... between the idea of the Samurai ... and the remarkable boy scout movement' and urged his publishers, Thomas Nelson, who had just published a cheap edition of Wells's *A Modern Utopia* in 1909, to associate 'the book with that movement', in view of the 'quarter of a million boy scouts who will presently be grown up to the book-reading age'.[56]

But there was a darker side to Wells's thinking about the implications of 'man-making'. Amongst the duties of the guardians of his 'New Republic' was the elimination of the worst consequences of urban degeneracy: the existence of 'this bulky irremovable excretion ... of vicious helpless and pauper masses', as he puts it in *Anticipations*, requires action.[57] An increasingly complex society disgorges its inefficient waste products. This is as inevitable in the social body, Wells says, 'as are the waste matters and disintegrating cells in the body of an active and healthy man'.[58] His analogy between the human and political body is not only highly traditional but manifestly unscientific – Wells here exchanges a Darwinian natural selection for a flawed Spencerian organicism. Since the existence of this wretched sink class of human beings is both 'integral' and 'inevitable', the national body must take steps to be rid of it.

Wells's customary scepticism about a liberal individualism which upholds respect for the inalienable liberty of the subject was propelling him to a position on the 'unfit' which was soon to be enunciated in 'negative' eugenics. The uproar over the 'Rapid Multiplication of the Unfit and the future of the lower races', he says, takes on a different aspect if we face facts which are 'known, if indelicate'. The 'undesirable' are 'quite willing to die out through such suppressions if the world would only encourage them a little'.[59] It is not then so surprising to find that Wells attended, in 1904, Francis Galton's address to the Sociological Society (founded in June 1903) in which Galton placed 'eugenics' squarely on the ideological agenda of Edwardian re-generation.

Why did conditions now appear more favourable to a eugenic assault on the 'residuum' than they were back in the eighties, when the problem of the residuum had been so productive of anxiety and moral panic? The explanation lies in a complex realignment of scientific positivism, culture and politics at the turn of the century. There were a number of factors at work: the demands of a more consciously imperialist ethos; the redefinition of the relationship between individual and state; the growing acceptability of a collectivist approach to social questions; the shifting perception of the validity of Lamarckian biology; the new prestige of social science.

In 1907 the Eugenic Education Society emerged from under the wing of the Sociological Society, with Galton its honorary president until his death in 1911. Its membership drew mainly on sociologists, psychologists, doctors and professional men with interests in political and social questions – Wells's 'highbrow from Highbury' in *The History of Mr Polly* (1911) is such a figure. Its membership included psychologists William Macdougall and the young Cyril Burt, Havelock Ellis and Neville Chamberlain. There was an accompanying spate of new journals, all of which carried articles on eugenics questions such as 'Race Progress and Democracy', 'Eugenic Ideals for Womanhood'. The *Lancet* ran articles on eugenics from 1911, and it was in that year that the academic credentials of eugenics became established with the foundation at University College London, of a Chair of Eugenics, held by Karl Pearson until 1933.[60] Wells's work, from 1901–5, anticipates the interest in 'negative' eugenics which was to become popular among many (if not all) Edwardian eugenists. In *Anticipations* he fuses several key contemporary anxieties:

The nation that produces in the near future the largest proportional development of educated and intelligent engineers and agriculturalists, of doctors, schoolmasters, professional soldiers, and intellectually active people of all sorts; the nation that most resolutely picks over, educates, sterilises, exports, or poisons its People of the Abyss ... the nation that by wise interventions, death duties and the like, contrives to expropriate and extinguish incompetent rich families while leaving individual ambitions free; the nation ... that turns the greatest proportion of its irresponsible adiposity into social muscle ... will certainly be the ascendant or dominant nation before the year 2,000.[61]

In the interests of national efficiency and future prosperity Wells is prepared to justify any means to achieve these ends. Those 'afflicted with indisputably transmissable diseases, with transmissable mental disorders ... exist only on sufferance, out of pity and patience, and on the understanding that they do not propagate'. 'I do not foresee any reason to suppose', he continues, 'that they will hesitate to kill when that sufferance is abused.'[62] In contrast to the ethically more circumspect sociologist L. T. Hobhouse, who did rise to the moral challenge which eugenics posed, Wells believed that the intolerable burden which certain groups imposed on the state justified the limitation of their freedom. But Hobhouse and other 'new liberals' did not believe that the interests of the individual and the State were identical. In any case, the causal relationship between personal and national efficiency had not been proved.

IV

The biologist August Weismann had radically shifted the grounds of debate with the publication in England from 1889 of his theory of the 'germ plasm'. It was the germ plasm which contained the building-bricks of heredity. Out of the mixture of parental germ plasms arose random congenital variations in the offspring: these were the new 'raw materials of evolutionary change'.[63] Weismann received a broadly favourable response from turn-of-the-century biologists. The pioneering work on genetics of Bateson, De Vries and others, leading to the rehabilitation of the experimental work of Gregor Mendel, was carried out in a new climate which Weismann had done much to create. One consequence of Weismann's success was to help undermine the belief in the efficacy of Lamarckianism, the essence of which was that the beneficial effects of environment could be acquired and transmitted from parent to child. And this posed a difficulty for liberal gradualists and social reformers: it was understandable that they should pin their faith to the ameliorating and improving effects of acquired characteristics.

But with the Lamarckian view increasingly challenged, optimists like the biologist G. A. Paley could argue that since the continuity of the germ plasm could be established irrespective of the life experience of the parents, all that was debilitating in the environment, all that told against the poor, might be discounted.[64] However, Weismann's theory was generally taken to support quite opposite conclusions: what use was there in attempting to reform social conditions if 'the force of heredity resided in a substance impermeable to environmental improvement and influence'?[65] 'There was now little room in the development of the individual', wrote Leonard Doncaster, an authority on heredity in 1910, 'for the effects of environment even on the intellect or mind ... still less is there room for the inheritance of mental acquirements made by the individual during his life'. It followed that 'the hopes held out for improving the race by education and by special care of the dull or feeble-minded are illusory'.

He continued: 'if man is almost entirely the product of unborn factors which are little affected by environment then improved conditions may only encourage the propagation of the degenerate and the race as a whole may go back rather than forward'.[66]

In such a climate of opinion the strategies of biometricians and demographers offered persuasive scientific justification for pessimism about the improvement of the race. Now the question of 'population' was clearly in view, with attendant anxieties about the 'falling birth-rate', about the 'multiplication of the unfit', and 'race-suicide'.

Karl Pearson had been among the first to draw attention to the threat which demographic trends posed, back in 1897. His central contention, that half of the next generation would be bred by 20%-25% of present married couples, was frequently taken up and magnified onto a great screen of concern for the future of the race. The declining birth-rate was, without doubt, a striking demographic fact. After generations of high rates of reproduction, averaging 34 births per 1,000 population in the nineteenth century, fertility was now dropping dramatically. By 1901 it stood at 28.5, by 1914 it was 24.0. The three-child Edwardian family was, on average, half the size of its Victorian counterpart.[67] For Havelock Ellis this was a far from disastrous trend. A falling birth-rate was proof of the effects of better education: a long overdue decline in infant mortality provided the evidence. 'Not the least service done by the fall in the birth-rate', he said, 'has been to teach us the worth of children'.[68]

But for Pearson the salient fact was that the lower orders and types of undesirables were 'outbreeding' the middle and upper classes. The statistical trends naturally confirmed his pessimism. Sidney Webb wrote in a frequently quoted Fabian tract in 1907 that, given Pearson's projections, 'this can hardly result in anything but national deterioration; or, as an alternative, in this country gradually falling to the Irish and the Jews'.[69] The year before, a general practitioner, R. R. Rentoul, produced a virulently eugenicist book – *Race Culture or Race Suicide?* The *Times*, also in 1906, carried two lengthy letters by Sidney Webb, captioned 'Physical Degeneracy or Race Suicide?', and the same month reported the 'Declining Birth-Rate in Lancashire'.[70] The first readers of E. M. Forster's *Howards End* (1910) would have recognised the topicality of one neatly observed minor episode in the novel. Leonard Bast passes the time of day with a neighbour as he returns to his South London flat:

'Evening, Mr Bast.'
'Evening, Mr Cunningham.'
'Very serious thing this decline of the birth-rate in Manchester.'
'I beg your pardon?'
'Very serious thing this decline of the birth-rate in Manchester' repeated Mr Cunningham, tapping the Sunday paper in which the calamity in question had just been announced to him.'
'Ah yes,' said Leonard, who was not going to let on that he had not bought a Sunday paper.
'If this kind of thing goes on the population of England will be stationary in 1960.'
'You don't say so.'
'I call it a very serious thing, eh?'
'Good evening Mr Cunningham.'
'Good evening Mr Bast'.[71]

The tedium and the dreariness of the journalese on this well-worn topic come through in Leonard's blank response. But we may also infer his unconscious unease, for the discourse of anxiety about the birth-rate has a sub-text – differential birth-rates by class. Leonard, we are told, 'stood at the extreme edge of gentility. He was not in the abyss, but he could see it.'[72] Leader writers and their readers (like Leonard's neighbour) knew that the right people, such as the Schlegels, in their tall thin house in Wickham Place (from which Leonard had just tramped) did not breed nearly as much as they should, and that the wrong people, down in the abyss, bred beyond all measure. In his marginal state, Leonard is neither implicated nor immune: while he is not 'in the abyss', he could quite easily fall into it. Yet quite against the grain of these eugenicist years, Forster emphatically ends his novel with a baby who is both a Schlegel and a Bast.

A diary entry for 1908 by a young working woman, Ruth Slater, records something of the transmission, at the level of the public lecture, of the ideology of race-regeneration: 'Met Eva in evening. Went first of four lectures on "Parenthood and Race Culture". Splendid! And to our ignorant, untrained minds, most illuminating. Think I am beginning to understand what is meant by Natural Selection.'[73] Wells himself satirises the undifferentiated appetite of the well-meaning re-generationists of the period in his novel *Ann Veronica* (1909). In a dig at *The New Age*, the narrator describes the eclecticism of a female columnist who writes 'a weekly column in New Ideas upon vegetarian cookery, vivisection, degeneration, the lacteal secretion, appendicitis, and the Higher Thought generally, and assisted in the management of a fruit shop in the Tottenham Court Road'.[74]

Two degenerate groups of particular interest to Edwardian race hygienists were the so-called 'feeble-minded', and the much-deplored 'vagrants' or 'tramps'. By the end of the nineteenth century the 'feeble-minded' had come to be seen as people who were 'sufficiently weak-minded to be incapable of receiving the benefits of sociali-sation in general, and education in particular', but who were not eligible for an asylum under the various lunacy laws. An extensive widening of the scope of such laws was one recommendation of the Royal Commission on the Feeble-Minded, which was appointed in 1904 and reported in 1908. It reaffirmed that defects were inherited and that measures taken to prevent 'mentally defective persons from becoming parents' would 'tend largely to diminish the number of such persons in the population'[75] – estimated at 105,000 in England and Wales. Yet its definition of the feeble-minded was elastic enough to include people who were, as Clive Ponting puts it, 'not by any stretch of the imagination suitable for mental institutions', the 'less-well educated, less intelligent or not socially well-adjusted'.[76]

For Dr Alfred Tredgold, a psychologist, adviser to the Commis-sion and leading member of the Eugenics Education Society, who produced an influential clinical text book *Mental Deficiency – (Amentia)*, 'the feeble-minded are not an isolated class, but they are merely one phase and manifestation of a deeply ingrained degener-acy. They are kith and kin of the epileptic, the insane and mentally unstable, the criminal, the chronic pauper and unemployable classes.'[77] The identification of feeble-mindedness with the life of the slums, as Nikolas Rose notes, remained an hereditarian argument and not an environmental one[78], for as Tredgold argued, the slum environment 'is not the cause, but the *result* of that heredity'.[79] Havelock Ellis added to the momentum of public debate when he devoted much space in two books – *The Problem of Race-Regeneration* (1911) and *The Task of Social Hygiene* (1912) – to this particular object of racial degeneracy (there were few topics on which he appeared more passionate and obsessive). 'After seventy years we find no convincing proof that the quality of our people is one whit better', he wrote.[80] The feeble-minded were 'an absolute dead-weight on the race ... an evil that is unmitigated'.[81] The 'bulk of them need to be isolated from the world in special institutions and colonies'.[82]

After a private member's bill had failed, and a second, government-sponsored bill had lapsed, a Mental Deficiency Bill was passed in the summer of 1913, attracting only three opponents.[83] By this act the 'feeble-minded' had finally been netted; their so-called predisposition to immorality and fecklessness and its hereditary transmission were now checked. The following year, as Tredgold's text book went into a second edition, the Elementary Education (Defective and Epileptic Children) Act came into force. In a toughening of the 1899 legislation which had empowered education authorities to set up special schools for the feeble-minded, or offer boarding-out arrangements,[84] the 1914 act required authorities to determine which children were 'defective' and to take steps to segregate them.

These debates were so much in the air that they could hardly have failed to have reached a writer who had had first-hand knowledge of difficult school children – D.H.Lawrence. We see this in *The Rainbow* (1915, composed from 1913) where the schoolboy Williams helps drive Ursula out of teaching. Lawrence invoked this, by now, highly visible and topical type of degeneracy (his modifiers perhaps glancing at the problematic of classification which had exercised the framers of the recent legislation)[85] to ground Ursula's feelings of anger and powerlessness:

He was a sort of defective, not bad enough to be so classed. He could read with fluency, and had plenty of cunning intelligence. But he could not keep still. And he had a kind of sickness very repulsive to a sensitive girl, something cunning and etiolated and degenerate. Once he had thrown an ink-well at her, in one of his mad rages.[86]

In the face of the incomprehensible and malign, a pathological discourse is to hand. And like Conrad's Donkin, Lawrence's Williams evades the efforts of diagnosis to net him.

A rather different figure who tried harder than most to net the feeble-minded, and who has some claim to be a paradigmatic figure of Edwardian social imperialism – if not degenerationism – was Winston Churchill (1874–1965). As President of the Board of Trade in Asquith's Liberal administration, he wrote to the Prime Minister after the appearance of the Royal Commission report on the feeble-minded in 1908:

The unnatural and increasingly rapid growth of the feeble-minded and insane classes, coupled as it is with a steady restriction among all the thrifty, energetic and superior stocks constitutes a national and a race danger which it is impossible to exaggerate. I feel that the source from which the stream of madness is fed should be cut off and sealed before another year has passed.[87]

G. R. Searle has shown that Churchill eagerly took steps to dam the 'stream' by circulating to his cabinet colleagues a 1909 paper by Tredgold, 'The Feeble-Minded – A Social Danger'[88], foreseeing 'national destruction' if the feeble-minded, breeding at twice the average rate, were not to usher in 'a preponderance of citizens lacking in the intellectual and physical vigour which is absolutely essential to progress'.[89] On his appointment as Home Secretary in February 1910, Churchill, now with supreme responsibility in this area, was determined to channel growing degenerationist concern away from a policy of segregation, as advocated by the Commission, towards forcible sterilisation. Clive Ponting shows from Home Office papers (originally closed for one hundred years but opened for public scrutiny in 1992) that Churchill obtained an American booklet 'The Sterilisation of the Degenerates' which described sterilisations of men and women conducted in a Reformatory in Indiana, and invited his officials to consider what was 'the best surgical operation'. 'It is cruel to shut up numbers of people in institutions for their whole lives', he wrote, 'if by a simple surgical operation they can be permitted to live freely in the world without causing much inconvenience to each other.'[90]

But neither Home Office officials, Asquith, nor Churchill's parliamentary under-secretary, Charles Masterman, were prepared to countenance open government support for such measures. There was some scepticism, too, about Churchill's belief in the hereditary transmission of degeneracy among the feeble-minded.[91] Churchill also had plans for 'forced labour camps' for 'mental defectives'. At their second offence, convicted criminals would be declared 'criminally weak-minded', and undergo a medical inspection which might lead to indefinite enforced detention.[92]

Churchill also identified a further category of the 'unfit': 'tramps and wastrels', for whom 'labour colonies' were the appropriate destination. The phenomenon of vagrancy had become an object of increasing concern, and some fascination, through the 1900s. As author of *The Condition of England* (1909) Charles Masterman had devoted ten pages to it.[93] The problem was analysed in studies such as W. H. Dawson's *The Vagrant Problem* (1911), reviewed by the prominent Fabian elder-statesman, E. R. Pease. Tramps, he believed, begot 'social wastrels' who invariably ended as a burden on the state – in prison or the workhouse. It is 'deplorable folly', he declared, to 'let this breeding of social pests go on year after year'.[94] For Ellis the common tramp formed 'a very degenerate class'. Along with inebriates, prostitutes and paupers, tramps were 'unfit to become parents of the coming generation'.[95]

Such anxiety is all the more paradoxical given the considerable cult of rambling, or 'wayfaring', in the English – invariably southern – countryside in the same period. In books like *The South Country* (1909) and *Afoot in England* (1909) Edward Thomas and W. H. Hudson made popular a new genre of 'heritage' travel book which aimed to conduct the reader around 'a rapidly disappearing England'.[96] Bart Kennedy and W. H. Davies entertained urban readers in a more demotic idiom with stories of the vagabond life along the 'open road'[97] – the title of a turn-of-the-century anthology of pastoral writing by E. V. Lucas (1899). In Kenneth Grahame's *The Wind in the Willows* (1908) Rat's pining for the peripatetic in 'Wayfarers All' expressed for a generation (which included Leonard Bast) a bachelor's longing for the romance of vicarious adventure, fed by the stories of George Borrow and Robert Louis Stevenson. The publisher, J. M. Dent, inaugurated a series of titles in an aptly chosen series, *The Wayfarer's Library*, in 1914, with compact volumes (including Clement Shorter's *Life of George Borrow*, Richard Jefferies' *The Open Air* and Hudson's *Afoot in England*) to accompany the traveller out of the city and the suburbs.

Here was the contradictory face of Edwardianism, by turns romantic and sternly utilitarian, devoted to fresh air and freedom, yet intent on limiting the freedom of those other habitués of the highways and byways, for whom there was no 'traveller's rest' at the end of the day. Along with the 'open road' went the closed mind: 'if we are to become a healthy race', wrote Havelock Ellis, the 'permanent segregation' of tramps must be 'deliberately undertaken'.[98] Tramps were deeply offensive, not just because of the perceived biological threat, but because they threatened to expose the integrity of this pervasive cultivation of civilised vagrancy for the urban myth that it was. It was Masterman who gave the game away in a revealing image: tramps were, he said, 'the underside of the world'.[99]

V

The official female equivalent of the 'coming man' was the sort of woman who wished, as Wells put it, to 'mother the future'.[100] Attitudes to motherhood, as we have seen in chapter seven, had been changing in the last decade of the nineteenth century. There had been an increasing exhortation to women of the middle class not to shirk motherhood when it had become apparent that the birth-rate was falling in middle-class families and when, as Anna Davin has noted, 'middle and upper-middle class women were pursuing new opportunities in education and employment'.[101] For Pearson 'child-bearing activity' was 'essentially part of her contribution to social needs' and 'ought to be acknowledged as such by the State'. Maternity should be 'citizen-making in the first place', not the 'accidental result of the private relation to an individual'.[102] Some revulsion from this utilitarian doctrine of the function of women was memorably enunciated by Stephen Dedalus in James Joyce's *Portrait of the Artist as a Young Man* (1916) where he scorns the hypothesis 'that every physical quality admired by men in women is in direct connection with the manifold functions of women for the propagation of the species'. It seems to him to lead to the dreary prospect of

a new gaudy lecture room where MacCann, with one hand on *The Origin of Species* and the other on The New Testament, tells you that you admired the great flanks of Venus because you felt that she would bear you burly offspring and admired her great breasts because you felt that she would give good milk to her children and yours.[103]

The rhetoric of eugenics and maternalism was designed to appeal to women in specifically class-determined ways. Working-class women bore the brunt of the increasingly interventionist machinery of child welfare, with its lessons on hygiene and domestic science. But amongst the middle class, money and time allowed the growth of a new self-conscious attitude towards children and childhood. *The Children's Encylopaedia*, edited by Arthur Mee, which had appeared from 1908, expresses an engagingly holistic vision of childhood. Addressing 'All Who Love Children All Over The World', Mee set out the aims of his encyclopaedia:

The first attempt that has ever been made to tell the whole sum of human knowledge so that a child may understand ... It conceives the bringing up of a child as the supreme task in which we can engage, but it has no sympathy with those who would set a child down at a desk almost before it can run. It believes that in its early years a child is its own teacher ...[104]

Reaching back over the immediate Victorian period to early Words-worth, Mee's recovery of the child's subjectivity expresses, in its practical idealism, a more admirable face of Edwardianism.

The editor of two of the continuous fourteen sections of the *Encylopaedia* was Dr Caleb William Saleeby, a key liberal-minded eugenicist (he deplored negative eugenic measures such as sterili-sation, urged by Rentoul, Wells, Shaw and Churchill). Saleeby was a symptomatic blend of progressive and reactionary. He raised 'motherhood' into a creed which assimilated child-centred edu-cation to a Darwinian vision of future struggle: 'the history of nations is determined not on the battlefield', he wrote in 1909 (the year the arms race took off), 'but in the nursery'. The 'battalions which give lasting victory are the battalions of babies'.[105]

Wells had naturally pronounced on this point. Wellsian mothers rear children for the nation in a 'household ... built and ordered after their own hearts':[106] it is a domesticated, efficient pastoral, with a clean, bright nursery, a resourceful nurse in attendance, the children exposed to fresh air and weighed regularly for progress. Responsible parenthood is habitually found only among mothers of this type and class, such as Mrs Morton in Gissing's *The Whirlpool*. Her robust maternalism would certainly have been applauded by Saleeby, who had declared with a memorable flourish in 1908 that 'there is no State womb, there are no State breasts, there is no real substitute for the beauty of individual motherhood'.[107]

But the anti-individualist Wells thought differently: if mothers were to fail in their duty then the penalties would be properly severe, for the children of the future must under no circumstances be sacrificed to the parents. The state had a duty to step in as the 'reserve guardian' of all children. Indeed, it is in the interests of the child as the repository of racial worth that Wells most urgently invokes the machinery of the early twentieth-century state. If chil-dren are unwanted or neglected, then the state will exact its penalty by charging the parent for maintaining the child. In extreme cases parents will be confined to 'celibate labour establishments' until they have worked off their debt to society: the parent is always the 'debtor to society on account of the child'.[108] Wells insists that 'reckless' parentage should be invested 'with a quite unprecedented gravity' which would 'enormously reduce the births of the least desirable sort'.[109] This was a theme which was reiterated in his promotion of the 'Endowment of Motherhood' programme, a centre-piece of Fabian thinking[110], 'the only possible way which will ensure the permanently developing civilized state', as the aspiring politican-hero puts it in his semi-autobiographical *The New Machiavelli* (1911). In a unabashed piece of Wellsian wish-fulfilment, the politician makes it the subject of an enthusiastically received speech at a triumphant by-election: 'the Endowment of Motherhood as a practical form of Eugenics got into English politics'.[111]

By the late 1900s there was little doubting the popularity of eugenics. Typical lectures given to the Eugenics Education Society included 'Eugenics and Womanhood', 'The New Woman and Race Progress', and 'Women and Eugenics'.[112] Yet what was the source of their appeal to free-thinking or socially radical women? Eugenics certainly possessed a radical and transforming potential. The Edwardians lived under the long shadow of Victorian prudery; a eugenic concern for race-regeneration offered an acceptable means of expressing unspoken anxieties about childbirth and contraception, sexual relations and hygiene. As Daniel Kevles suggests, eugenics drew strength from the social purity movements, going back to the 1870s, which stressed the need to make motherhood a more voluntary experience, and had led the way in attacking male sexual attitudes, exposing the 'double-standard', in the interests of purity, health and sexual liberation.[113] Eugenics held out a powerful attraction to Edwardian women, for whom virtues as well as vices were still inheritable commodities. These eugenic concerns, according to Penny Boulmelha, condensed an important shift from a preoccupation with 'personal tragedy' alone, to an anxiety over 'a generalised social threat': 'this sense of social mission, combined with the simplistic pre-genetic notion of transmission of characteristics (physical, psychological, moral, even economic, all jumbled together) on which eugenic theories were based, led many contemporary feminists to support the idea of state control of, or intervention in, fertility'.[114]

There was evidence too that eugenic ideas empowered Edwardian women to state more openly than before the necessity of curbing the curse of male promiscuity in the interests of social purity and racial health. Edwardian debates among social purity campaigners expressed a greater frankness about the perils and the extent of venereal infection. And extending the debate from marriage to the nation and the race, some women now held male sexual conduct responsible for racial decline and eventual race-suicide.[115] The evidence of the 'sexual rule of the human male' was only too evident for the feminist eugenicist Frances Swiney in her degenerationist catalogue of social ills: 'Vices, however, like curses, come back to roost. In his own enfeebled frame, in his diseased tissue, in his weak will, his gibbering idiocy, his raving insanity and hideous criminality, he reaps the fruits of a dishonoured motherhood, an outraged womanhood, an unnatural, abnormal stimulated childbirth and starved poison-fed infancy.'[116]

'Today I have been looking through Christabel Pankhurst's book The Hidden Scourge, but I cannot read it,' wrote Ruth Slater to her friend Eva Slawson in June 1914.[117] Christabel Pankhurst's *The Great Scourge and How To End It* (1913) was indeed a frank and uncompromising polemic. She insisted that the prevalence of venereal disease among men (up to 80% infected with gonorrhea, and a substantial percentage with syphilis) would lead eventually to racial disaster. Only an end to prostitution and the 'subjection of women', male continence and the franchise would bring amelioration. She ingeniously linked these subjects:

A very large number of married women are infected by their husbands with gonorrhea. The common result is sterility, which prevents the birth of any child, or may prevent the birth of more than one child. Race Suicide! ... the female ailments which are urged by some ignoble men as a reason against the enfranchisement of women are not due to weakness, but – to gonorrhea.[118]

But the dominant discourse of race-improvement, with its attendant anxiety about the differential birth-rate, continued to blunt the radical cutting-edge of these late Edwardian campaigns. Eugenic commentary seemed to reveal the tenacious hold of an ideology of hygienic exclusiveness, still grounded in narrow attitudes and mistaken assumptions. The underprivileged classes were invariably felt to be a principal source of racial pollution, even by progressive women. Campaigning for birth control, the American feminist and anarchist Emma Goldman claimed in 1916 that those who denied women access to such methods would 'legally encourage the increase of paupers, syphilitics, epileptics, dipsomaniacs. cripples, criminals, and degenerates'.[119]

After the first world war, the famous campaigner for birth control and 'radiant motherhood', Marie Stopes, squared up to the members of her own class who still turned a blind eye to their dysgenic practices and should know better. Ahead of her time on the birth-control question, her rhetoric on the topic of working-class ignorance of racial duties was decidedly old hat. In an article for the *Daily Mail* in 1919, 'How Mrs Jones Does Her Worst', she invited the reader to go down the 'mean streets' of any city, as if in the company of Arthur Morrison and Lord Rosebery back at the turn of the century. 'Are these puny-faced, gaunt, blotchy, ill-balanced, feeble, ungainly, withered children the young of an Imperial race?', she asked. 'Why has Mrs Jones had nine children, six of them dead, and one of them defective?'

Now is it for Mrs Jones to take the initiative? Isn't it for the leisured, the wise, to go to tell her and tell her what are the facts of life, the meaning of what she is doing, and what she ought to do? ... not many of the leisured and the learned have bothered to think out the meaning of what she is doing. If they realised it, surely an outcry of dismay would be raised, *for Mrs Jones is destroying the race!*[120]

Marie Stopes's tendentious, and, mercifully, unperformed play *The Race* was written in late 1914: it offers a stepping-stone from the world of Edwardian anxiety to the trauma of the first world war, the effects of which would displace and redraw these concerns for the 1920s. Rosemary Pexton, a solicitor's daughter, is expected by her parents to marry the local squire, but she is really in love with young Ernest Clive, about to leave for the front. In the opening scene she is shown reading Edward Carpenter's *Love's Coming of Age*. In this exchange the heroine gives voice both to Stopes' indebtedness to Carpenter's sex-mysticism and her own eugenic earnestness of purpose so ill-matched to the slaughter to come:

ROSEMARY: To think that it is *my* father who makes it impossible for us to bring *your* children to gladden the world ... (Triumphantly) ... why should we allow him to commit murder? The murder of the child which might be ours? Why should *my* father rob you of your fatherhood?
ERNEST: (Starting away from her as though overwhelmed by a new and vivid idea) Rosemary!
What do you mean? (He retreats a step and gazes at her)
ROSEMARY: (with a look of mystical devotion) My beloved, may God grant that you may live for ever in thy children's children. (She leans forward ... He goes towards her eagerly, but incredulously.)[121]

Ernest dies in battle and when Rosemary reveals that she is pregnant, her family tries to marry her off to Pexton's clerk. She refuses her parents' entreaties as she holds up the baby garment she is knitting:

PEXTON: (Turns on her furiously) Good God! Could any honourable man forsee that his daughter would be an abandoned woman?

ROSEMARY: ... the world would be a better place if there were more men like Ernest in it. Heredity *does* matter – and it seems to me of supreme importance that Ernest's child should be in the world. For the sake of our race all fine young men such as Ernest should have children – and others should *not* ...

MRS PEXTON: Hush, darling; you cannot argue against the truth that for an unmarried woman to have a child is wrong.

ROSEMARY: But, mother! Is it not *more* wrong that not only Ernest, but all the fine, clean, strong men like him who go out to be killed, should leave no sons to carry on the race; but that the cowardly and unhealthy ones who remain behind can all have wives and children? Think what it will mean to the race if the war is a *long* war – and *all* the best are killed![122]

CHAPTER 10

Masculinity, morbidity and medicine
'Howards End' and 'Mrs Dalloway'

One true cure for suffering, and that is action ... a healthy mind, like a healthy body, should lose the consciousness of self in the energy of action.

     (Henry Maudsley, Responsibility in Mental Disease (1874))[1]

The relation of the physician to his female patient is important. First, she must believe in his superior knowledge and skill, and that he possesses the clue to the puzzle of her symptoms.

     (J. A. Ormerod, 'Hysteria' in *A System of Medicine* (1898))[2]

[The Great War was] a vast crucible in which all our pre-conceived views concerning human nature have been tested.

     W. H. R. Rivers, 'Freud's Psychology of the Unconscious'(1917))[3]

I

At the end of the century, the idea of 'fitness', which encoded both the human and the imperial body, helped to perpetuate the organic relationship, embedded in political and psychiatric discourse, between the nation and the individual. The citizen was seen as a repository and carrier of a part of the disposable national energy. This imperial support system was even affirmed as divinely ordained by the public-school laureate Henry Newbolt in 'Clifton Chapel':

> My son, the oath is yours: the end
> Is His, Who built the world of strife, ...
> Henceforth the School and you are one,
> And what You are, the race shall be.[4]

Manly assertion was held to be the 'highest virtue to which a British schoolboy could aspire'.[5] The dualities of softness and hardness, introspection and participation, intellectual and physical, feminine and masculine offered ways of projecting sets of assumptions about what was and what was not acceptable, normal and natural.

The practice of sport offered, according to James Walvin, 'the comforting illusion of continuing effortless superiority and of the means of restoring the nation to good health'.[6] This is obviously right, but the appeal of sport ran deeper. The rhetoric by which physical activity was lauded seemed always to imply, and often explicitly invoked, the presence of the 'other'. At the turn of the century the preoccupation with the urban masses, and their ever increasing cultural ascendancy, found a discursive object: the young male spectator who sat passively on the sidelines. 'The position of the people', wrote Arnold White in 1901, 'consists of watching the hirelings of the football field' or (at one further remove) 'backing horses they have never seen.'[7] To watch the match, not to play in it – this was the way to national decadence. As the British working class filled the terraces at Preston and Highbury, so the voice of reaction solemnly invoked classical parallels to ancient empires laid low: formerly in Rome *panem et circenses*, now in Britain, as articles with titles like 'The Fall of the Roman Empire and Its Lesson For Us' made only too clear, soccer.[8]

As we have seen, young boys and adolescents, in whom the Empire had staked a large investment of racial capital, were the obvious targets for self-appointed guardians of 'healthy' attitudes. 'Of all faults', wrote physician William Bevan Lewis, 'introspection and subjectivity at this age should be avoided.'[9] Leading medical commentators, including Lewis and T. S. Clouston, believed there was a strong connection between these morbid, egoistic impulses and the horrors of 'masturbational insanity'. Dementia and delusional insanity might be the horrible issue.[10]

In the year that the critic Charles Whibley had excoriated Wilde's *Picture of Dorian Gray*, his editor, W. E. Henley, brought out *Lyra Heroica: A Book of Verse for Boys*. Its reception was instructive: the *Saturday Review* (7 November 1891) hoped that it would 'help to keep the blood of many English boys from the wretched and morbid stagnation of "modernity" '.[11] 'It would be hard ... to make a milksop of a lad nourished on these noble numbers', remarked the reviewer for the *Irish Daily Independent* (4 January 1892).[12] Such verses, which Henley said celebrated the 'glory of battle and adventure', were obviously of a piece with the countless yarns for boys available in the *Boy's Own Paper* and the novels of G. A. Henty,

Ballantyne and others, in which a pervasive notion of healthy manliness promoted imperialist ambition. A typical contributor to the *Boys Own Paper* in 1892 wrote that if England wanted to maintain its supremacy and reputation as a great nation 'our boys must be trained in those games which develop physical strength, endurance, skill and courage'.[13] For Henley, 'England My England', in a revealing image, was 'proud and hard'. And in his *National Observer* Henley was apt to publish poetry, such as Paul Cushing's 'For England's Sake', which in a social-Darwinian celebration of 'force', reasserted 'manliness' in the cause of a narrow patriotism:

> Give us war, O Lord,
> For England's sake ...
> Ere the tricks and arts of peace
> Make our manliness to cease,
> While our world-wide foes increase ...
> That amid the stress and strain
> And the discipline of pain
> We grow Englishmen again
> For England's sake.[14]

To entertain thoughts of peace in these invigorating days of imperial assertion was the merest effeminacy.

The maintenance of certain ideas about the organic relationship between the individual and the state, what was conducive to the 'health' of the nation and what militated against it, implied certain unquestioned assumptions about masculinity itself. But when these assumptions are scrutinised by two major novelists, E. M. Forster and Virginia Woolf, the sounds of late Victorian imperialism, psychiatric Darwinism and blind positivism are rendered discordant, troubling, sinister – and absurd. In their different ways both writers showed themselves to be contemptuously hostile to the discursive apparatus which, with such facile certainty, separated the healthy from the weak, the fit from the unfit, the normal from the tainted.

Forster's achievement is to give full play to the most socially and ideologically arrogant of these discourses at this period with a telling raid on the territory of masculinity with its coercive discourses of power, its command of social and economic space, its emotional hollowness and deep repressions: the fortress that Henry Wilcox inhabits in *Howards End* (1910). Forster can offer a new slant on the politics of masculinity. But it would take a further fifty years, and in the context of late twentieth-century feminism, for the debate to be taken forward. Even so, there is evidence of another *fin de siècle* reaction, of a recrudescence of traditional patterns of response with a revival of 'machismo', the cult of the body, the dogma of competitiveness, and the cult of the 'free market'. Forster's world of 'telegrams and anger', of 'the hurrying men who know so much and connect so little'[15] is, dismayingly, our world too.

In his 1928 essay on T. S. Eliot, Forster recalled a moment in 1917, when, convalescing with the decadents' manual, Huysman's *A Rebours*, he felt revived by a world

which lived for its sensations and ignored the will – the world of des Esseintes. Was it decadent? Yes, and thank God ... here was a human being who had time to feel and experiment with his own feelings ... the waves of edifying bilge rolled off me, the newspapers ebbed; Professor Cramb ... floated out into an oblivion which, thank God, has since become permanent.[16]

J. A. Cramb was an historian, the author of *Reflections on the Origins and Destiny of Imperial Britain* (1915) in which he had declared that war is 'the supreme act in the life of the State'. It is 'the motives which impel, the ideal which is pursued, that determines the greatness or insignificance of that act'. And it was the Boer War which was 'the first conspicuous expression of this ideal in the world of action – of heroic action, which now as always implies heroic suffering'.[17] By 1917 Forster had clearly taken his fill of 'edifying bilge'. If no longer pervasive by the late twenties it had been tediously reiterated in the public rhetoric of war at the turn of the century, the formative years of his youth.

II

The repertoire of the Edwardian male ethic of 'force' is convincingly explored in *Howards End*. The Wilcoxes are not mere types but are embodiments of a way of life which, as with Lawrence's Gerald Crich in *Women in Love* (1920), Forster sees as powerfully hegemonic in contemporary society. By explaining the Wilcoxes, Forster can explain a good deal about the state of English society. The imperial command of time and place – metonymically represented by a realist narrative structure, with the motor car its apogee of ideological power – is one index of this formation; and the narrative enacts with a sustained ironic intelligence the destructive 'force' of this social Darwinism.

This is of course assimilated to the explicit thematic centre of the novel: to explore the tension between the 'beast' and the 'monk'; between the way of living which denies the inner life and is brutal and ignorant about personal relationships, and the Schlegels' assertion of wholeness and the necessity for active connection between the two. The incident in chapter twenty-five, in which Charles runs over a cat while driving his father's car, is a particularly good example of the converging of these perspectives. Forster's command of the dominant ideological formation which governs sexual politics is impressive, and still underestimated.

Forster had much more to say about 'those business people' than Lawrence, for one, gave him credit for.[18] Like Lawrence, Forster explores and exposes the psychological springs of the incessant need for control – the fear and hollowness at the centre of the Edwardian male: 'We are all in a mist – I know', says Helen, but 'men like the Wilcoxes are deeper in the mist than any. Sane, sound Englishmen! Building up empires, levelling all the world into what they call common sense. But mention Death to them and they're offended, because Death's really imperial, and He cries out against them for ever' (236). '... pierce through him you'd find panic and emptiness in the middle' (232), she says. Elsewhere, 'outwardly he was cheerful, reliable and brave; but within, all had reverted to chaos' (187–8). It is fear of that chaos that prompts Henry Wilcox to smother the Schlegel curiosity in people, with their psychology and their desire to 'connect'. Whereas Margaret has 'chosen to see [life] whole, Mr Wilcox saw steadily. He never bothered over the mysterious or the private.' (165). To 'know what's going on beneath', for Wilcox, 'leads to morbidity, discontent and socialism' (151).

Henry Wilcox's fear of the morbid has a significant context. As John Stokes has convincingly shown, in the 1890s 'the single word "morbid" ... carried a burden of meaning greater than any other derogatory adjective'. The word was invoked, of course, to conjure the enemy within, that 'internal threat to the organism, whether it were society as a whole or the media through which society found expression'. Crucially, it 'linked the artistic minority with those other social outsiders whose insidious activities corrupted the whole – the lunatics, criminals and sexual deviants of scientific treatise'. Arthur Symons assimilated 'Decadence' to the cliché current in 1893 – 'that morbid subtlety of analysis, that morbid curiosity of form'.[19] On both sides of the divide the term was actively deployed.

12   'Athletics versus Aesthetics', *Illustrated London News*, 17 March 1883.

Harry Quilter was fairly typical of the anti-decadents. Beardsley's paintings, he thought, depicted 'manhood and womanhood ... mingled together ... in a monstrous sexless amalgam, miserable, morbid, dreary and unnatural'.[20]

Artists' addiction to the 'unnatural' was the sign of the artist's degenerate constitution which governed both his unmanly conduct and suspect sexual orientation. The whiff of homophobia is never far away. And as Stokes points out, 'morbid' had, in any case, become a 'euphemism for homosexuality':[21] 'I shall be obliged', says Clive Durham to Maurice, in Forster's novel of that name, 'if you will not mention my criminal morbidity to anyone.'[22] Later when Maurice informs him he is in love with the gamekeeper Alec Scudder, Clive, sounding the very different tones of medical orthodoxy, advises Maurice not to 'dally with morbid thoughts'. He continues: 'I do beg you to resist the return of this obsession. It'll leave you for good if you do. Occupation, fresh air, your friends ... '[23] In *Degeneration*, Max Nordau had employed the code when he insinuated the masturbatory habits of 'egomaniacs', decadents and aesthetes who 'fritter away their life in solitary, unprofitable, aesthetic debauch ... all that their organs, which are in full regression, are still good for is ennervating enjoyment'.[24]

'Morbid', as coded insult, returned as recently as 1988, during a debate about homosexuality and the law in the House of Commons. Like Leonardo da Vinci, said the Conservative MP Sir Nicholas Fairbairn, the singer Sir Peter Pears suffered from a 'morbid squint'. Homosexuality was a 'deep-seated psychopathological perversion'. But, Fairbairn added, this was 'not a reason to condemn him for all else that he does'.[25]

The countervailing values of healthy, 'natural', manly assertion were heard, at the turn of the nineteenth century, in a heightened rhetoric of social Darwinism which grounded competitiveness and assertiveness not just in an individual, but in an imperial and racial ethic. This assertion was bound up in a complex way with an increasing requirement to expunge the unnatural, morbid and degenerate influence from the imperial body. According to the physician, G. E. Morrison, who was also the *Times* correspondent in Peking, 'undersized men' were 'sexually vicious' since they played 'no healthy games'.[26]

For the degenerationist mentality, an increasingly complex and urban society seemed inevitably to encourage 'softness' and 'decadence'. In the nineties a movement of reaction, characterised by a language of toughness and hardness constructs its symbolic 'other', the introspective or aesthetically sensitive temperament possessed by morbid thinking, whose 'unfitness' made it 'fit' for modern decadence. Lombroso's work on 'genius' along with

Nordau's assimilation of a range of pathological and psychiatric writing, including Maudsley, had led to the association of the condition of morbidity with aestheticism and alleged unmanliness. Appropriately it was Wilde, ever alert to the nuanced traffic in such epithets, who re-appropriated the term, and took it back to the opposition on behalf of the traduced artist. The public, he said, were 'all morbid because the public can never find expression for anything'. Whereas 'the artist is never morbid. He expresses everything. He stands outside his subject, and through its medium produces incomparable and artistic effects. To call an artist morbid because he deals with morbidity as his subject-matter is as silly as if one called Shakespeare mad because he wrote *King Lear*.'[27]

'Be not solitary, be not idle', Robert Burton had counselled in *The Anatomy of Melancholy*; this was an idea taken up in late nineteenth-century psychiatry. Morbidity was associated with what made for a-social behaviour and the domination of obsessive ideas. The two came together in an intense suspicion of introspection, of men and women examining their own motives, of being preoccupied by their own thought processes. Late Victorian pathologists and doctors required that 'morbid introspection' and 'self-absorption', be policed by continual vigilance. For Maudsley, Hack Tuke, Clouston, Mercier, Hyslop and others, as Michael Clark puts it: 'Introspection and self-absorption, persistent abstention from ordinary social intercourse, and neglect of active pursuits all tended to weaken the will, undermine the 'natural' moral affections, and encourage idleness, eccentricity, and the growth of perverse or immoral tendencies.'[28] Self-absorption had long been associated with various states of hypochondriasis: day-dreaming and states of reverie posed a danger to the sanity and morals of the subject. Excessive attention to a single idea or thought could, it was believed, 'progressively ... increase its hold over the mind' resulting eventually in the 'subjugation of the reason and the will'.[29]

When the narrator remarks in *Howards End* that Henry Wilcox 'misliked the very word "interesting"', connoting it with wasted energy and even with morbidity' (180), he is drawing on the antithetical terms of a structure of ideas which was fundamental to degenerationist diagnosis. Morbidity is indeed a key term in this novel. Forster is generally alert to its meaning, relayed through psychiatric orthodoxy, as something akin to a disease, an infection of the personality, unhealthy and troubling. For Henry Wilcox it is an unquestionably pejorative ascription, and in his actions he demonstrates its antithesis. 'Morbidity', articulated in discourse, exists in a dialectical relationship with those qualities of assertive force which he and his sons show so prodigiously. So we negotiate the Wilcox world both by what it stands for, and by the Schlegels' negative critique in their adherence to those 'personal relations' which that world suppresses.

III

Howards End offers a striking and thoroughgoing exploration of the terms of this debate, editorialised through the Schlegel sisters, Margaret and Helen, both of whom reveal at different times what it is necessary to suppress. There is Helen's brief infatuation with Paul and the Wilcox family whose 'energy ... fascinated her'(37) before she sees it for what it is, a 'fraud'(40). And Margaret surrenders her true self to the alluring false totality of Henry precisely because of his invigorating energy: 'he was not a rebuke, but a stimulus, and banished morbidity'(165). She peppers her frequent defences of Henry with comments about his energy and the imperialism and economic assertion into which that energy has to run.

At this point, Forster, whose narrative voice frequently veers between the authorial and the 'free indirect' or 'represented' speech of Margaret (with some overlapping as well), remarks, in what is an unhappy concession, that 'at present, homage is due to [this type] from those who think themselves superior, and who possibly are' (165). And resisting the critique of her sister, he seems to endorse Margaret's over-simplistic defence of men of action: 'If Wilcoxes hadn't worked and died in England for thousands of years, you and I couldn't sit here without having our throats cut' (177). Even more insistently during this phase of the book, Margaret appears to lure the narrator to reproduce – even endorse – a pathological model of morbidity. This is the case when Margaret is trying to make up her mind about the cause of Helen's erratic behaviour during the eight months of her exile in Germany, following her abrupt departure from the hotel in Shropshire.

A sick-bed could recall Helen, but she was deaf to more human calls ... she would retire into her nebulous life behind some poste restante ... she scarcely existed ... she had no wants and no curiosity ... It was morbid, and, to her alarm, Margaret fancied she could trace the growth of morbidity back in Helen's life for nearly four years. The flight from Oniton; the unbalanced patronage of the Basts; the explosion of grief up on the downs – all connected with Paul, an insignificant boy whose lips had kissed hers for a fraction of time. Margaret and Mrs Wilcox had feared that they might kiss again. Foolishly: the real danger was reaction. Reaction against the Wilcoxes had eaten into her life until she was scarcely sane. At twenty-five she had an idée fixe. What hope was there for her as an old woman?

The more Margaret thought about it the more alarmed she became. For many months she had put the subject away, but it was too big to be slighted now. There was almost a taint of madness. Were all Helen's actions to be governed by a tiny mishap, such as may happen to any young man or woman? Can human nature be constructed on lines so insignificant? The blundering little encounter at Howards End was vital. It propagated itself where graver intercourse lay barren; it was stronger than sisterly intimacy, stronger than reason or books. In one of her moods Helen had confessed that she still 'enjoyed' it in a certain sense. Paul had faded, but the magic of his caress endured. And where there is enjoyment of the past there may also be reaction – propagation at both ends. (272–3)

Margaret offers us a diagnosis which appears to rationalise her sister's inexplicability; morbidity and its pathology offer her a ready discursive tool with which to settle her doubts about how to read her sister. By the end of the paragraph Helen is 'scarcely sane'. And Margaret expresses a teleology in a psychiatric observation which, melodramatically, foreshortens the terms of her sister's future life: 'At twenty-five she had an idée fixe. What hope was there for her as an old woman?' Margaret suggests the cause is the 'tiny mishap' over Paul Wilcox: 'the blundering little encounter at Howards End was vital. It propagated itself where graver intercourse lay barren' (272).

Margaret, with authorial endorsement, will shortly rally impressively to Helen, and precisely against this sort of stigmatising. Indeed, Margaret's eventual rejection of the medical model, with its attendant stratagems and specialists, will constitute a striking defense of female and human rights in the face of the discourse of appropriation, Foucault's 'hysterization' of the woman.[30] But Forster is in genuine doubt about Helen's status; he does not seem to have made his mind up about her.

Margaret 'fancied', 'had feared'; the represented speech of this important paragraph imperceptibly permits Margaret's point of view to become normative: 'There was almost a taint of madness. Were all Helen's abstractions to be governed by a tiny mishap ...

'(272). The authorial point of view and that of Margaret now merge, Forster needing, it seems, to join hands with Margaret to form a bridgehead against his own evident uncertainty. Now it is the vagaries of Helen's mind which are foregrounded rather than Margaret's evident fumblings. The authorial commentary veers vertiginously from open enquiry: 'were all Helen's actions to be governed by a tiny mishap ... ', to definite closure: 'the blundering little encounter at Howards End was vital'.

But is it? Do not the springs of Helen's subsequent wild desires run deeper than this would imply? Yet from what we are told, there would appear to be little room for doubt about the cause of Helen's distress. The pathological centrality of her suppressed desire receives authorial endorsement in formulaic, vague phrasing: 'Paul had faded, but the magic of his caress endured' (272). Then the author-commentator, confident in his omniscience, pulls back, to engage with the idea, latent in the text, of the extent of our ignorance of psychology and the limits of self-understanding: 'Well, it is odd and sad that our minds should be such seed-beds, and we without the power to choose the seed. But man is an odd, sad creature as yet, intent on pilfering the earth, and heedless of the growths within himself' (273). Unlike the Wilcoxes – 'deeper in the mist than any'(236) – the Schlegels have been more 'patient'. But Margaret has been more successful than Helen: she 'has succeeded', with 'some rudimentary control over her own growth. Whether Helen has succeeded one cannot say' (273).

This evasiveness suggests that the effort to fix Helen as an immature ingénue, without the self-understanding of her sister derives from authorial uncertainty. Forster would like to believe it, but he cannot since he has already allowed Helen to emerge as the only really effective critic of the social process for which the Wilcoxes are the apologists. Helen's analysis of the limited vision of the powerful is cogent and penetrating. Of Jackie, who has been discovered as Wilcox's mistress, she comments acidly that 'they end in two ways: either they sink till the lunatic asylums and the workhouses are full of them, and cause Mr Wilcox to write letters to the papers complaining of our national degeneracy, or else they entrap a boy into marriage before it is too late' (249). And after Wilcox has just been talking about the permanence of the Edwardian class system – the existence of rich and poor, the necessity of civilisation moving forward and the shoe pinching in places – she notes the way that supposed common sense is a cover for ideology: 'I don't like those men. They are scientific themselves, and talk of the survival of the fittest, and cut down the salaries of their clerks' (193). It is not merely that Helen's observation is extremely shrewd, but that she is so obviously in full command of what she is saying; she speaks with an authority which cannot be erased by insinuations of unreliability.

Helen's next letter to Margaret, which assumes that Aunt Juley is unwell, is for Margaret 'tiresome', since it now tempts her to lie to Helen that their aunt is still 'in danger', and so entice her back to England. Margaret's guilt at this thought now prompts in the narrator the idea of Helen's contagiousness, a morbidity which will in some way infect Margaret's moral sense: 'we cannot be in contact with those who are in a morbid state without ourselves deteriorating'(273). Presented as an unproblematic truth, it offers a serviceable medium for Margaret's shame, but it is, for all that, a glib and unperceptive concession to contemporary ideology. What, after all, is 'morbid' about Helen's letter?

It is far from clear whether these are the sentiments of the author, or of Margaret, or the endorsement of one by the other: the use of represented speech here may offer the author a cover, or it may serve to ironically point up a tissue of obvious clichés which the implied contemporary reader can be counted on to recognise. Forster's susceptibility to these clichés of contemporary degenerationism can hardly be overlooked. His sentimentality about the virtues of yeomen (for which Galton and other degenerationists had provided a pseudo-scientific rationale) is revealed in his remark that Leonard can 'still throw back to a nobler stock'. And in the case of Helen her radicalism is purchased at the price of her being seen as a neurasthenic, or worse, as carrying 'the taint of madness'.

IV

Yet what follows is a compelling sequence of dramatic realism which traces the actions taken to master Helen's contagious condition. The convenient lure of morbidity, with Margaret's collusion in the labelling of her sister, are part of the necessary education she has to undergo in the understanding of the burden of her sex.

Tibby, her brother, puts the suggestion to Margaret that Wilcox be consulted, and that there is something 'mental' about Helen's state of mind. From this point the narrative brilliantly brings into play a process of labelling and tracking down the now explicitly deviant woman, which culminates in the attempt of the 'pack' to ambush and capture her. Her 'madness' is seen to be discursively constructed and controlled by a strategy of power: of the 'imperial' formation, with its ethic of necessary 'force'. Energies which drive the nation forward are replicated in the personal and in the sexual. What is so memorably captured is the insidious ease with which the labelling process appropriates Helen and reduces her to the carrier of a disease. She is thus excluded from rational discourse as sick and mad. Margaret's uncertainty, ' "mad" is too terrible a word, but she is not well' (277), counts for little as 'Henry began to grow serious'. The assimilation of the narrator's voice into represented speech, as the paragraph gains momentum, captures our involvement in the unstoppable process of Henry's will to order, while allowing us a critical placing of the man. We have access to him as both subject and object:

Ill-health was to him something perfectly definite. Generally well himself, he could not realize that we sink to it by slow gradations. The sick had no rights; they were outside the pale; one could lie to them remorselessly. When his first wife was seized, he had promised to take her down into Hertfordshire, but meanwhile arranged with a nursing-home instead. Helen, too, was ill. And the plan that he sketched out for her capture, clever and well-meaning as it was, drew its ethics from the wolf-pack. (277)

Margaret senses that she has made a mistake, but 'retreat was impossible'(278). She sees that the more Helen is talked about the more she 'faded as he talked'. 'Her fair, flying hair and eager eyes counted for nothing, for she was ill, without rights, and any of her friends might hunt her. Sick at heart, Margaret joined in the chase' (279). The image of the capturing car running 'silently like a beast of prey', enforces the insight into the low instinct beneath the civilised strategies of force: to police the 'mad', you become less than human. The car is offered, with tactful insistence, as a symbol of male power and containment of women. Earlier, when Margaret throws herself from the car, there is a knee-jerk male stereotyping of the woman who has transgressed the usual boundaries: it is a piece of 'devilry', 'probably nerves in Miss Schlegel's case', 'that woman had a tongue' (214).

When Margaret realises that her own finer instincts have capitulated to the brutal show of force, she turns on Henry with near equal brutality. She defends her beloved sister with the directness of a woman recalled both to the allegiances of 'heart' and to the larger issues which divide them both from him:

The doctor, a very young man, began to ask questions about Helen. Was she normal? Was there anything congenital or hereditary? Had anything occurred that was likely to alienate her from her family?

'Nothing', answered Margaret, wondering what would have happened if she had added: 'Though she did resent my husband's immorality.'

'She always was highly strung,' pursued Henry, leaning back in the car as it shot past the church. 'A tendency to spiritualism and those things, though nothing serious. Musical, literary, artistic, but I should say normal – a very charming girl.'

Margaret's anger and terror increased every moment. How dare these men label her sister! What horrors lay ahead! What impertinences that shelter under the name of science! The pack was turning on Helen, to deny her human rights, and it seemed to Margaret that all Schlegels were threatened with her. Were they normal? What a question to ask! And it is always those who know nothing about human nature, who are bored by psychology and shocked by physiology, who ask it. However piteous her sister's state, she knew that she must be on her side. They would be mad together if the world chose to consider them so. (282)

And it is Mansbridge the doctor who now comes into view provoking Margaret's outburst, which Forster makes explicitly representative of a wider assault on male systems: 'Stop that at least, she said piteously; the doctor had turned back, and was questioning the driver of Helen's cab. A new feeling came over her: she was fighting for women against men' (283). Mansbridge is identified as doctor and man; his expertise at the service of social and sexual power. He is one of the 'pack', moving efficiently at the bidding of its leader who commands the material and ideological space. This alliance of medical science and plutocratic power has denied Helen her rights. Against their systems of containment and enforcement, Margaret asserts the Forsterian belief in the radical cutting edge of feeling: 'Affection ... surely you see. I like Helen very much, you not so much. Mr Mansbridge doesn't know her. That's all. And affection, when reciprocated, gives rights. Put that down in your notebook, Mr Mansbridge. It's a useful formula' (285).

It was indeed 'useful' in 1910, in the light of physician J. A. Ormerod's advocacy of Weir Mitchell's injunction in *A System of Medicine* (which went into a second edition in that year) that some hysterical patients should be 'urged and scolded, teased, bribed and decoyed along to the road to health'.[31] In Margaret's sardonic and robust rejoinder, we hear Forster's exposure of the late Victorian craze for systems which never did do justice to the complexity of human relationships. What is striking is that his representation of the menace of the diagnostician is felt as a function of a dominant ideological formation – an hegemony of interest. The exercise of power draws on the different elements: masculinity, the objectification of women by men, the fear of the imagination and of the life within, the assertion of the authority of the 'expert'. Forster's text enables us to experience the connections.

v

The psychiatric Darwinists were ill-prepared to pay attention to psychotherapeutic techniques and were, in any case, reluctant to give up the authority to which for so many years they had laid claim. They saw a therapy based on the cultivation of 'self-absorption' as an encouragement to 'morbid introspection' or 'unnatural egoism', so compounding the neurosis.[32] As Michael Clark suggests, for the psychiatric Darwinists 'the association of morbid introspection, exaggerated self-consciousness, and "unnatural egoism" with mental disorder was ... fundamental, even causal, rather than merely symptomatic or accidental'.[33] Henry Maudsley had argued that 'what such patients need to learn is, not the indulgence but a forgetfulness of their feelings, not the observation but the renunciation of self, not introspection but useful action'.[34] And by and large this held good as unquestioned orthodoxy up to the first world war.

The concepts of masculinity which informed orthodox medical practice were firmly entrenched at the outset of the war. And in so far as dominant cultural norms of masculine self-sufficiency, of 'force' and strength, pervaded the medical and psychiatric professions, the crisis for pathology was a crisis of the attribution of masculinity itself – a 'trial of the Victorian masculine ideal'.[35]

By the end of the war there were seismic shifts in these assumptions. Established psychiatry was in trouble, as was the prevailing theory of hereditary degeneration which underpinned it. It was the treatment of shell-shocked patients which exposed the contradictions and extreme limitations of a pathology grounded in a materialist view of behavioural abnormalities. This experience helped to undermine for good the credibility of the degenerationist diagnosis which had held sway in Britain since the 1870s.

Young men in their prime were slaughtered in hundreds of thousands. But thousands more were visibly breaking down under the stress of shell-shock. Early on in the war the conventional response to shell-shock was to regard its effects as symptoms of the old enemy, hereditary degeneration. But as Martin Stone has tellingly noted, the cruel and simple facts of war were that it was not the products of the abyss – the working-class degenerate or 'feeble-minded' – but the flower of England, 'young men of respectable and proven character [who] were reduced to mental wrecks after a few months in the trenches'.[36] As Stone argues, the 'ideological tables had been turned':

when the eminent psychiatrist Sir Robert Armstrong Jones launched a predictable attack on G. Elliot Smith and T. H. Pears's book on shellshock in *Nature* (1917), criticizing them for their 'environmentalist' tendencies and claiming that tainted heredity lay behind the pathology of shellshock, Smith and Pears were able to reply that this was 'a slur on the noblest of our race'.[37]

The neuroses and nervous debility brought on by shell-shock were visible in many soldiers on active service. And it brought about a transformation both in the diagnoses made by doctors working with such patients and in attitudes to manliness and to how men should behave. Early on in the war victims of shell-shock were often seen as 'shirkers', their behavioural abnormalities a cover for malingering. The usual medical response was to look for physical damage to the nervous system – to the cerebral tissues or the spinal pathways. If no such damage was found, then the charge was malingering.

But it became increasingly evident that symptoms of shell-shock were experienced by soldiers who had not been directly exposed to bombardment. After the war it was revealed that only a small number of shell-shock victims had suffered organic damage to the central nervous system.[38] The experience of treating shell-shock convinced many army doctors that new psychological techniques had much to offer. By the end of the war medical officers were being given short courses on the techniques of 'abreactive psychotherapy', which included dream analysis. In fact, as Cyril Burt noted, the symptoms of shell-shock proved 'quickly curable by psycho-therapeutic means'.[39]

The well-known case of the poet Siegfried Sassoon demonstrated the success of the new therapies and the irrelevance of the old. As a second-lieutenant, committed to Craiglockhart Military Hospital near Edinburgh in 1917, he was fortunate to experience the advanced therapeutic treatment of W. H. R. Rivers, a key figure in the transmission of Freudian psychology in Britain. While Rivers did not accept the sexual theories of Freud, he upheld as crucial the concept of repression, to explain 'the process by which moments of terror or disgust were suppressed and converted into physical symptoms'.[40] It is 'a wonderful turn of fate', wrote Rivers in 1917, that 'just as Freud's theory of the unconscious and the method of psychoanalysis founded upon it should be so hotly discussed, there should have occurred events which have produced on an enormous scale just those conditions of paralysis and contracture, phobia and obsession, which the theory was especially designed to explain'.[41]

But at the 1920 annual meeting of the Medico-Psychological Association of Great Britain, the psychiatrist W. H. B. Stoddart reported a Professor as having expressed, at Cambridge, with regard to psychoanalysis, 'his thankfulness that it did not fall to his lot to seek pearls in that sty', although he 'did not take the trouble to learn anything about it'.[42] The Professor was Clifford Allbutt. At the same meeting the robustly die-hard Sir Robert Armstrong-Jones declared in the teeth of the evidence (including papers he had listened to) that 'Freudism' was 'dead in England today'. Freudism, he said, might be 'applicable to life on the Austrian and German frontiers, but not to virile, sport-loving, open-air people like the British'.[43]

Crystallised in this hilarious remark is a pervasive ideology, with its cocktail of familiar phobias, the potency of which was only now being realised. It was certainly no accident that female novelists, such as Woolf and Rebecca West were best equipped to hasten the breakdown of the authority of this pre-war way of thinking, and to confront the crisis of masculinity which the 1914–18 war had precipitated. But as Woolf at least knew, Forster had been there before. In his distinctive exploration of the 'condition of England', he had identified the power of the ethic of male 'force', and had more than hinted at the medical and psychiatric orthodoxy which sustained it.

VI

Virginia Woolf's experience of this orthodoxy was direct and traumatic. In *Mrs Dalloway* (1925), as recent criticism has shown,[44] she produced a fictional transmutation of the victimisation that she herself experienced over a period of nearly twenty years, at the hands of a medical establishment which was ignorant of the nature of her mental condition. By the time she came to write *Mrs Dalloway* in 1923, she was ready to objectify her personal suffering. But she understood, as few of her contemporaries could have done, the symptomatic nature of her experience and the ideological foundations of the psychiatric medicine which had shaped it. The experience of mental breakdown had become a political question through the lived experience of her powerlessness before the discourses of medical appropriation. Its politics were part-determinant of her condition, a cause and an effect of her prolonged suffering.

Mrs Dalloway contains an objectification of this interpenetration of the conceptual with the personal, the representative with the unique. In her assault on the discursive practice of psychiatric medicine, the novel delivers a direct attack on myths which she had lived with through her adult life and which, even in the 1920s, refused to die. Woolf delivered the final obsequies and the killer punch. No novelist before her had exposed this value system as clear-sightedly and rigorously; none, significantly, after her. In this respect *Mrs Dalloway* is both the first and the last fiction to deconstruct the fictions of degeneration.

Of the clutch of doctors who attended Virginia Woolf during her periodic breakdowns, or to whom she or her husband Leonard Woolf turned for advice, the public activities and writings of two of them, T. B. Hyslop and George Savage, amply represent the degenerationism that she would expose. Hyslop, we recall from chapter six, was a practising artist, as well as a doctor and a leading eugenicist critic of art and literature; a figure quite out of sympathy with the cultural and aesthetic allegiances of Woolf and of Bloomsbury.

Take the two Post-Impressionist exhibitions which Hyslop so openly reviled. Bloomsbury, as we have have seen, responded to them with enormous enthusiasm. For Woolf, the idea of artistic innovation had acquired a profoundly symbolic force; it offered a means to self-definition and freedom. Some years before, she had reacted against portraits of her parents, painted by the respected academician, G. F. Watts, which had found their way to their home in Gordon Square, London. At a 1903 retrospective of Watts's work, both Virginia and her sister Vanessa turned against this establishment painter. According to Quentin Bell, Virginia's nephew, 'Watts belonged to the dark Victorian past ... the new generation wanted air, simplicity and light'.[45] And 1910 was to be a year in which, it was hoped, the darkness would be banished for good.

Hyslop's views on women certainly belonged to that 'Victorian past'; they were those of an orthodox Spencerian, a believer in the conservation of energy principle applied to women's 'nature', and her 'natural' role – motherhood. 'The more our women aspire to exercising their nervous and mental functions', he said, 'so they become not only less virile, but also less capable of generating healthy stock.' Moreover, this question 'has very direct bearings upon the increase of our nervous instability. In fact, the higher women strive to hold the torch of intellect the dimmer the rays of light for the vision of their progeny.'[46]

Woolf's first doctor, George Savage, was, we have seen, a leading specialist in the treatment of the mentally ill. Savage attended Virginia Woolf during two serious breakdowns in 1895 and in 1904. Like Hyslop, Maudsley, Clouston and others, he had pronounced ideas about the predisposing factors in female neurosis, and, like them, opposed female education in the interest of preserving the balance of women's faculties. He shared the fashionable anxiety, common to this generation of mental specialists, of the deleterious effect of prolonged mental effort for women 'cramming' for examinations, which would result in a 'disorder of her functions'. If a girl, he said, 'is allowed to educate herself at home, the danger of solitary work may be seen in conceit developing into insanity'.[47]

According to Leonard Woolf, Savage 'had not the slightest idea of the nature or cause of Virginia's mental state'.[48] This is undeniable, and yet given the state of knowledge available to Edwardian psychiatry it was not so surprising. Savage himself was no more nor less culpable than his contemporaries in this respect. Janet Oppenheim emphasises 'the reluctance of leading British psychiatrists in these years to confront psychological pain directly'. Preferring to address its physical symptoms, they 'treated the possible mental causes of depressive illness primarily by trying to rally the patient's will.'[49] In the manuscript of *Mrs Dalloway* Woolf writes sarcastically about this treatment, here meted out by the general practioner, Dr Holmes: 'Milk is the great standby, with raw eggs beaten up in it taken every hour, oftener if possible.'[50] This was the still fashionable Weir Mitchell 'rest cure', prescribed for patients suffering nervous dis-

orders; their treatment consisted of 'isolation, immobility, pro-
hibition of all intellectual activity' and – cramming of a different
kind – overfeeding.[51]

In her depiction of the general practioner Holmes and the nerve-
specialist Bradshaw, who attend the shell-shock victim Septimus
Smith, Woolf vividly conveys their grey, conformist and unambi-
tious view of human nature and the establishment hegemony of
which they are a part. And in this respect the novel exhibits a strong
affinity with *Howards End*: the offensive figure of degenerate masculinity, the mentally damaged soldier, has been anticipated in Helen,
the assertive, 'unwomanly' neurasthenic.

For the doctors the mentally disturbed man presents a spectacle of
unpardonable deviancy which requires a counter-assertion of order,
a redrawing of the boundaries of normality by which that behaviour
can be fixed as transgressive. 'Once you fall, Septimus repeated to
himself, human nature is on you. Holmes and Bradshaw are on
you. They scour the desert. They fly screaming into the wilderness.
The rack and the thumbscrew are applied. Human nature is
remorseless.'[52]

Earlier Septimus has felt that coercion as bestial: 'the repulsive
brute with the blood-red nostrils. Holmes was on him' (101). One
thread of this coercive display is the reassertion of conventional
gender expectations. Like Forster's Helen Schlegel, Septimus is the
target of a violent reassertion of what is discursively rationalised as
commonsense. In these images of assault by the monstrous, we sense
in their displacement the critique. Holmes's method of dealing with
Septimus's anguish is an all too predictable recipe of the banishing
of morbidity through diverting entertainment and 'healthy' action,
expressed in the culture of 'middle-class English masculine conduct'.[53]

There was nothing whatever the matter, said Dr. Holmes. Oh, what a
relief. What a kind man! what a good man! thought Rezia. When he felt
like that he went off to the music hall, said Dr. Holmes. He took a day off
with his wife and played golf ... (99)

Dr Holmes came again. Large, fresh-coloured, handsome, flicking his
boots, looking in the glass, he brushed it all aside – headaches, sleeplessness,
fears, dreams, nerve symptoms and nothing more, he said. If Dr Holmes
found himself even half a pound below eleven stone six, he asked his wife for
another plate of porridge at breakfast (Rezia would learn to cook porridge). But, he continued, health is largely a matter in our own control.

Throw yourself into outside interests; take up some hobby. He opened Shakespeare – *Anthony and Cleopatra*; pushed Shakespeare aside. Some hobby, said Dr Holmes, for did he not owe his own excellent health ... (100)

The hunt is up. The social police of society are after their quarry, armed with their manuals on human nature.

Holmes's menace is intensified by the very comic certainty with which he proffers advice. It is an effect developed in Woolf's devastating anatomy of the nerve-specialist Sir William Bradshaw to whom Holmes refers Septimus. Underpinning Bradshaw's appeals to 'proportion' is an impenetrable stratum of banality:

To his patients he gave three-quarters of an hour; and if in this exacting science which has to do with what after all, we know nothing about – the nervous system, the human brain – a doctor loses his sense of proportion, as a doctor he fails. Health we must have; and health is proportion; so that when a man comes into your room and says he is Christ (a common delusion), and has a message as they mostly have, and threatens, as they often do, to kill himself, you invoke proportion; order rest in bed; rest in solitude; silence and rest; rest without friends, without books, without messages: six months' rest; until a man who went in weighing seven stone six comes out weighing twelve.

Proportion, divine proportion, Sir Williams's goddess, was acquired by Sir William walking hospitals, catching salmon, begetting one son in Harley Street by Lady Bradshaw ... Worshipping proportion, Sir William not only prospered himself but made England prosper, secluded her lunatics, forbade childbirth, penalised despair, made it impossible for the unfit to propagate their views until they, too, shared his sense of proportion – his, if they were men, Lady Bradshaw's if they were women (she embroidered, knitted, spent four nights out of seven at home with her son), so that not only did his colleagues respect him, his subordinates fear him, but the friends and relations of his patients felt for him the keenest gratitude for insisting that these prophetic Christs and Christesses, who prophesied the end of the world, or the advent of God, should drink milk in bed, as Sir William ordered; Sir William with his thirty years' experience of these kinds of cases, and his infallible instinct, this is madness, this sense; in fact his sense of proportion. (108–9)

In this pillar of the medical establishment, Woolf condenses her profound understanding of the sources of authority he exerts. Here is a degenerationist who in his persona and in the nature of the advice he propounds is exposed as fraudulent. On one level, his espousal of 'proportion' is no more than homespun philosophy masquerading as profundity – 'understanding of the human soul'; he never talks

about madness but readily represses it – 'covers it with treatment
and rest'. But on another, his 'proportion' expresses what Forster
had Margaret Schlegel register as truly disproportionate: 'the
impertinences that shelter under the name of science'. For Bradshaw
wields a formidable Foucauldian 'coercive discourse of power'
which Lyndall Gordon rightly identifies behind 'the cant of duty
and family ... connecting Harley Street with Westminster' – the
hegemony which Septimus has 'fought for years in the trenches to
preserve'.[54] But it is, I think, clear that Woolf also had in mind the
frame of reference of Edwardian race-regeneration with its concern
for the health and fitness of the nation, its distrust of the life of the
imagination, its obsession with the 'other' of mental and physical
unfitness, its strategies of intervention, containment and separation:
it is against this hegemony that Septimus is vainly struggling.

Bradshaw's 'proportion', we discover, is a surface of emergence of
a eugenic discourse, targeted at those troublesome elements of the
nation whose reproductive and cultural power must be halted or
terminated: Bradshaw 'secluded ... [England's] ... lunatics,
forbade childbirth, penalised despair, made it impossible for the
unfit to propagate their views, until they, too, shared his sense of
proportion'. What Bradshaw calls 'proportion', of course, is a
measure of 'normality' against which Woolf has herself been
defined, from girlhood onwards; the personal experience lends the
demolition of the doctors a brilliant viciousness. Theirs is not an
authoritative but an arbitrary notion, 'arrived at by the consent of
generations of practical men'[55], nurtured by the prestige of early
twentieth-century medical science.

Like Conrad, Woolf is alive to the mystique which accrues around
the purveyors of science as she satirises the basis and substance of
Bradshaw's professional eminence. A little earlier he is described as a
'ghostly helper', the 'priest of science', conveying his person in a
ghostly 'low, powerful grey' motor car (103). The Conradian note of
banality is fully sounded in this passage, in the innocence and
conceit which comically keeps him so ignorant: 'proportion, divine
proportion, Sir William's goddess, was acquired by Sir William,
walking hospitals, catching salmon, begetting one son in Harley
Street by Lady Bradshaw'. Unlike the breeding of the degenerate
unfit, the generation of a Bradshaw is a desirable and significant
event, but 'proportion' dictates there is only 'one son' to inherit the
title – 'Sir William' is ironically repeated, to deflating effect.

Inscribed within the medicine of Holmes and Bradshaw is the complex of late nineteenth and early twentieth-century myths which in Woolf's imaginative vision of the early 1920s is still potent and insidious. The psychiatry which pronounces on normality, outlaws the morbid and disposes of the introspective and effeminate, produces its symbolic victim, Septimus Smith. When he takes his life, it is, for the doctors, a confirming sign of his failure to measure up – the act of an unmanly shirker. Doctor Holmes's reaction – 'the coward' (164) – signals that for the unmanned and mentally deranged shell-shock victim there is no hiding-place – in war or in peace – from the expression of these myths. For Woolf, the medical profession, which victimises Septimus, is the most damaging expression of that patriarchal structure of authority which degeneration has both shored up, and discursively perpetuated.

CHAPTER 11

The way out is the way back: the anti-modernists

I

The returning soldier is a key symbolic figure in the post-1918 English novel. Pre-eminently he was weighed down with intolerable tensions, as he crossed the border between military and civilian life. Behind him was the unmanning trauma of trench warfare, suffered with his fellow males. Ahead was the social and familial role expected of a man. As he moved from the 'heroism' of war to his unheroic reinstatement into a changing civilian order, he carried with him stories which could not be told, experience which was literally unspeakable, and which, being repressed, found irrational displacement in a land fit for 'no-man'.

But novelists took up the significance of the returned soldier in different ways. Five years elapsed before Virginia Woolf had been able to exploit the uncomprehending treatment of the shell-shocked victim. Rebecca West's response was more immediate. In her fine novel of 1918, *The Return of the Soldier*, an upper middle-class officer has shell-shock which creates in him a profound amnesia. It has blocked out not only all memory of trench warfare, but all memory of his previous fifteen years, including his conventional marriage to a brittle and superficial wife. He regresses to a happy time in late adolescence when indifferent to class barriers, he had fallen in love with a working-class girl. Baldry's rejection of his immediate past is the vehicle for West's devastating critique of narrow type-casting by class and gender, and for her celebration of individual worth in the face of the emotional poverty of privilege.

By contrast, in the widely read post-war fiction of the prolific and high-selling novelist, Warwick Deeping (1877–1950), the returning soldier is the medium for the entrenchment of those old prejudices and sources of authority which West's novel had exposed as inadequate. In the fiction of Woolf and West, the way out was the way in: for the popular male writers of the 1920s it was, defiantly, the way back.

In Deeping's *The Secret Sanctuary* (1923), John Stretton resumes civilian life, needing to heal the scar of a momentary loss of self-control where he had attacked another soldier in the trenches. A sympathetic alienist diagnoses his condition – in terms which range from old-style organicism to more up-to-date psychology – as the giving way of the 'membrane', under pressure, permitting 'a sort of leak in the brain' through which rush 'our most primitive and savage impulses'.[1] Though Deeping makes it clear that this is no Freudian ('he saw more in Stretton than a lonely man obsessed by his own sex'), the doctor believes in the curative value of the 'healthy promptings' of instinct, of allowing for the expression of the patient's 'intuition' (22). It is a cure which can only be brought out by a retreat to a simpler, healthier environment, from the 'whole machine-made show' (33) and from 'modern people who rush about and who can't sit still' (38). Stretton, with the doctor's help, persuades his conventional father to buy him 'a bit of rather wild land which he can farm' (39), in spite of the opposition of his brother for whom Stretton is an embarassment. And once he sets to work he finds the life doing him good; he is aware of the world 'as motion, a flowing, an expanding; even the hills seemed to breathe. Never had he realized how blind was the life of the streets' (105). He is earning his right to his platitudinous faith in the 'country as against the town, for the peasant idea as against the mechanical'(99).

But this peace of mind is threatened by the intrusion of modern female energy. Isobel Copredy is lively and shockingly direct: her colouring 'blazed at you vividly from cheeks and lips' (63). Addressing men with 'a brilliant and provoking hardness' (65), she upsets and entices Stretton: 'he disliked this young woman ... because a part of him was afraid'. Deeping releases an erotic energy so as to bring it to heel, transmuting Isobel's attraction into a wilful, anti-social recklessness. She tracks Stretton relentlessly, her barbarism putting at risk the gains of his healthy cult of the primitive. Her assertiveness represents a degenerate sexuality, dangerous, disturbing and transgressive.[2] There is eventually a sexualised wrestling match during which 'the young blood in both of them began to flame' (151). Stretton 'sees something more than rage come into her eyes'. It is her atavism: 'he felt her strong young teeth in his shoulder' (151). Her teeth elsewhere are compared to the 'white teeth of her dog' – she is also a 'wild witch' (150).

The call to 'violence and to sexual congress' – the 'call of the wild', in fact – is resolved by an answering atavism, not of erotic display, but, predictably, of a resurfacing in Stretton of the homicidal impulse which he had hoped to have buried. But its reappearance denotes more than the latent neurosis of the shell-shocked ex-soldier: this is a sign both of the corrupting influence of the deviant woman and the degenerate forces of modernity (with its unsettling of fixed gender roles) whose type Isobel is. The threat is also to his masculinity: those teeth figure her devouring and castrating sexuality. For the implied reader, Stretton's attack on her is a legitimate reassertion of manhood.[3]

Physically cowed by the grip round the throat, Isobel's defeat needs to be finally taken in hand by the better woman, Jess Viner, who resists being browbeaten by Isobel's effort to discredit Stretton as a man of violence: 'You don't seem to realize that something else happened' (260), she reminds Stretton. Isobel is a synecdoche for the chaotic breakdown and confusion of conduct in the post-war world. Indeed, the leitmotif of anti-modernity is made explicit. Stretton's younger brother sees in Isobel's glance 'the effect the war had had upon certain women' (81). Stretton is aware of 'her modernity'. 'She had the flat, breastless figure and the rather stooping carriage and narrow hips of the particularly modern type' (91). She is 'fast', with a sports car which she pounds into the ground.

Predictably, in this programmatic fiction, the wholesome farmer's daughter, Jess, who can give Stretton solace, companionship and sympathetic hospitality, is idealised as the madonna to Isobel's whore: 'she smiled easily, but not too easily' (176), speaking low and soft, without any of the silliness that spoils so many country voices' (176). Her face has a 'healthy cream-like pallor': she radiates, of course, a 'tranquility' which has 'depths and character'. She has a 'wholesome firmness of flesh and spirit' (199), and, above all, the 'happy vitality which heals' (199). The Viner's farm offers a further sanctuary from the rapacious attentions of Isobel and her sexual challenge: 'the peace of the place cooled his thoughts and effaced the glow of Isobel Copredy's provocative colouring. It was a house that accepted you, put you in a comfortable chair, and soothed you with simple sounds such as the crackling of the wood fire or the humming of the bees in the honeysuckle' (126–7). Bee-keeping and undemanding husbandry will support the eventual marriage between her and Stretton. Viners are stout, dependable rural stock.

A late product of the *fin de siècle*, Deeping maintained the fantasy of the angel in the house alongside that of the woman as vampire. He positions women as, in the end, ultimately responsible – both for the recovery of the war victim to psychic health and his deterioration into atavistic violence: 'He had the sensitive and clean man's instinct for things which were good and which were not good, and he knew that their goodness depended on the woman' (150). One of the last scenes has Jess, as ministering angel at Stretton's bedside, nursing him out of influenza, unafraid of Isobel's threat, and able to patronise her: 'I feel I ought to feel sorry for you' (324).

Deeping rationalises the distress of a middle class that is fast losing its servants and is having to face up to the new post-war world of industrial tension and assertive, organised labour. Gardeners, shepherds, farmers 'cannot go on strike against Nature'. Their instinctual knowledge that 'life moves whether we wish it or not' is contrasted with what the mechanic 'with a little cheap information stuffed into his noddle takes so long to learn' (163). Stretton's 'simple-life' cliché that 'the only life worth living is the life of growing things', prompts the normative Mrs Viner to berate 'those poor fools in the factories' who don't understand and are creatures of low greed: 'most of them have got nothing but stomachs. What's all the socialism but appealing to a man's stomach?' (213). Working people, in this text, are either possessed by dangerous ideas, or, as creatures of appetite, haven't an idea in their heads. Anti-socialist rhetoric, as we shall see, is one colourful thread of the skein of discursive assault on the modernity of the world of the 1920s. Running through Deeping's fiction is a recurrent animus against socialism as both symptom and cause of the parlous condition of the world.

Socialism is also contrary to the brutal, true facts of human nature, for it interferes with the struggle for survival which obsesses this late social Darwinist, tunnel-visioned fabulist. Deeping's fiction is acutely attuned to the conservative frame of mind. The readers, who in their hundreds of thousands read his novels, sought reassurance, stability, above all, continuity with values which appeared to have dominated in the period before 1914, expressed in an ideology of romantic essentialism. In the aftermath of world war, his popular fiction is the literary equivalent of the old-style turn-of-the-century medicine he was originally trained for. With a canny mixture of sentiment and knowingness he administers to a readership which is worried about poverty and social deprivation, the power of organised labour, the democratisation of culture, the shifting in manners and gender roles – even the new psychoanalysis. His work is constructed to bring out and magnify the threats to the well-being and integrity of the male subject, and to offer, via the romance of self-reliance and emotional trial, bulwarks against the menace of those threats which seek to wash it overboard.

Chief amongst those threats are the mass of the working class. The whiff of the abyss is unmistakable in the sentimental *Sorrell and Son* (1925), Deeping's best-known book and one of the best-selling novels of the 1920s and beyond. Here middle-class snobbery and the romance of self-reliance join hands to contest the forces of modernity. Captain Sorrell's bravery in war earned him the Military Cross, but now England has no use for him (Deeping skilfully exploits the obsessive resentments and rancour of post-war society). Down on his luck, divorced but with a young son, he is reduced to taking a job as an under-porter and bootboy in a hotel. The seductive romance of the book is his rise from porter to manager, and his son's preservation, through Sorrell's sacrifices, from the taint of common life, as through private tuition and Cambridge he emerges as a gentleman and doctor. These privileging qualities set father and son against the debased influences of modern life.

Snobbery and disgust are the response of Sorrell and the fastidious son Kit to the physical presence of working-class boys. Passing through a London street, the son is 'conscious of himself as of something other than those Lavender Street children. He did not want to be touched by them.'[4] The prospect of a 'Council School' for his boy fills the father with 'resentment', while the son's feelings are conveyed through the author-narrator's heavy-handed assertion of middle-class decency: 'it had meant contact with common children, and Kit was not a common child. He had all the fastidious nauseas of a boy who has learnt to wash and to use a handkerchief, and not to yell "cheat" at everybody in the heat of the game' (4).

London's 'unclean' come again into focus in the out-patients' ward of the teaching hospital, where, years later, Kit is a medical student. He sees for himself the

blotched bodies, the sores, the rottennesses, the stigmata stamped there by poor festering souls. He saw young men and young girls filthy with venereal disease, and the blurred and shiny faces and angry eyes of the drunkards. Often it seemed to him that Fate herded these people like cattle into the white-tiled galleries and the out-patient rooms, poor stupid cattle sinned against, ignorantly sinning. It was the problem of the ignorant, of the unfit, of the people with uncontrolled lusts and greeds, of ugly lives and ugly souls and bodies growing out of them, of children who who should never have been born. "What a mess!" was Kit's feelings about it. (246)

The shock of dealing with the blemishes of a girl with venereal disease prompts Kit to voice his concern about the 'question of stopping it'. The mix of environmental and inherited suffering, fecklessness and irresponsibility is identified by Sorrell's senior consultant (who would like to see that 'half the babies are not born') with 'the Socialist cabbage patch'. But, he goes on, 'we are not – all – cabbages Sorrell. The world wants cleaning and replanting ... I would halve the population, and try to see that the half that remained had a better chance'. (247)

This is a world predicated on the principle of struggle and greed (it is essentially a social-Darwinian world) armed with a repertoire of automatic reflexes to individuals to defuse their threat: this is achieved by converting them instantly into types of the 'other'. (In a knee-jerk response Sorrell refers to the boots of the commercial travellers he is forced to clean as 'swine's trotters'(31)). Deeping unironically makes this typologising explicit. Faced with a disagreeable chauffeur, Sorrell's son translates his medical experience into the necessary resourcefulness of the watchful man of the world:

Kit had given the chauffeur a smile, and one quick, discriminating glance. He had learnt to place men and women with a shrewdness shorn of sentimental illusions. He had observed and handled and smelt them for years in the out-patient departments of St. Martha's. He had seen them cringe and swagger and pretend, and try to hide what it was madness to hide; and he had learnt to tell false faces from true ones, and to know almost by instinct when someone was lying. He had his gallery of 'types', and the fellow at the wheel in front of him was a rodent, a nasty, acute little man of the Nosey Parker genus, very self-pleased, with one of those long, intrusive noses, a patch of radled red on each cheek bone, and bright, insolent, treacherous little eyes. (302)

The poor chauffeur has no discernible function in the novel other than to display Kit's diagnosis: the racial insinuation carries the suggestion of inherited degeneracy[5] (the chauffeur actually has a daughter who is a 'pale and strumous child with a bulging forehead and weak blue eyes' (304)). His very lack of narrative function serves to position him as an object of observation itself; it can only be as a demonstration of Kit's sure way with the disreputable. What is reinforced is the unquestionable authority of a common-sense angle of vision of the expert who is also a man of the world, whose social seeing is instant diagnosis – 'types'. Away from the cesspool of the out-patients ward which is, increasingly, post-war England, one can find respite from the degenerate. But it is as well to be on your guard, Deeping seems to say, lest one should hove into sight, as inevitably, will happen. With the appropriate typology to hand, fire this discursive apparatus with precision. Take your word of command from the doctor.

II

The romantic essentialism in Deeping is an important constituent of the anti-modernist reaction which determinedly sought an exit from the messy post-war present. In 1924 Stanley Baldwin, Conservative politican and future prime minister, accepted an invitation to speak to the Royal Society of St George. He did not disappoint his audience. 'To me, England is the country, and the country is England', he addressed with charming circularity this charmed circle.[6] In his conflation of the 'native' with 'nature' delivered as a deeply held sentiment of attachment, Baldwin expressed a desire to look beyond the catastrophe of war, to revitalise the myth of a simpler, nobler England. For Baldwin, the complexity of modernity expressed itself in the inexorable encroachment of urbanism into the countryside. Again, the way out led to the way back: England's salvation lay in resurrecting its agricultural base and so recovering the nation's identity: the nation might know itself again through the deployment of these myths of continuity.

In a collection of essays, *After-War Problems* (1917), compiled by W. H. Dawson while the long battles of the war were still being fought, a hankering for a return to a 'natural' way of life based on a rural economy was unmistakable. The figure of the 'countryman' takes centre stage. He is admired for his innate qualities, recently displayed in wartime: 'We have realized how important the countryman is as a soldier, a better soldier than his town brother.'[7] This leitmotif of urban degenerationism, which had reached a crescendo at the time of the Boer War, is sounded once again. A back-to-the-land policy is put forward, enshrining a vision of new village life in which 'England will be provided with a virile and happy rural population, able to enjoy its happiness in peacetime and to defend it in the terrible hour of war'.[8] The countryman resurfaces as the dependable mainstay of the nation whose best characteristics he is believed to embody. His healthy virility is effortlessly translated, in instrumental terms, into an eugenically desirable quality of racial worth: 'Help the countryman to raise a large and healthy family, and England will be safe.'[9] And the familiar dysgenic, racial consequences of urbanism are now counterpoised with the health-giving properties of the rural way of life: 'Why should you concentrate such masses in towns, with the evils of factory life impairing the health of the future of the race? . . . Attach the people to the country, breed a stronger race – the soil is more patriotic than the street.'[10]

The myopia of this proposition is staggering – particularly given that the most severely dysgenic and racially disruptive battles were being fought as this essay was presumably being written for publication: it surely attests to the extraordinary resilience of that elision between the poetry and the prose in the establishment character – that curious synthesis of romanticism and utilitarianism which characterises so much concerned commentary on the condition of England from the 1880s onwards. The two impulses coalesce in rehabilitated ideas of 'race' and 'stock'. In the 1920s, neither carried the connotation which they have now in the multi-racial 1990s, yet for some, even now, these symbolic, deeply held beliefs still touch, without irony, conservative political discourse; Enoch Powell has been an exemplary case.[11]

The sense of the city and the city-dweller as a blight on civilisation was a key tenet for the degenerationist frame of mind in the interwar period. Here was a figure symbolically constructed not just in discussions of racial decline, but in writing hostile to new forms of mass media for predominantly urban consumption and to their perceived effect on the imagination and the sensibility of the urban population. Not surprisingly it was cinema, as a fast-emergent form of mass entertainment in the twenties, which claimed attention: 'Is it not better to enjoy a sunset than to attend the cinema?', mused a contributor to *After-War Problems*.[12]

In his well-known essay 'Marie Lloyd' (1923), T. S. Eliot argued that with the decay of music-hall the working class would be reduced to the moral bankruptcy of the English middle class.

Spicing his comments with unmistakable eugenic distaste, Eliot found in the cinema an emblem of degenerate vitality: '[with] the encroachment of the cheap and rapid-breeding cinema, the lower classes will tend to drop into the same state of protoplasm as the bourgeoisie'.[13] John Buchan warned in 1932, with the advent of the 'talkies', that the vulgarity of cinema 'may be a real danger, if it results in a general degradation of the public taste and a communal softening of the brain'.[14] The deleterious effects of cinema on juvenile behaviour was not proven by the report of a commission on the subject in 1917,[15] but throughout the late twenties and thirties public doubts about the effect on the culture elicited degenerationist sentiments. The authors of *The Devil's Camera* (1932) had no doubts about the cinema's potential to generate harm:

> The cinema is still revealed as ... a dread menace to civilization. Unless it is cleared up within this generation it will undermine every existing agency for decency and public order ... the basest passions are exhibited in their morbid brutality to a degree that would have been unthinkable a year ago ... Our very civilisation is at stake ... the cinema as at present debased, is the Hun of the modern world.[16]

The 'basest passions' were felt to be on display in another symptom of cultural degeneration – jazz. 'Sensual, noisy and incredibly stupid' was the verdict of the conductor, Sir Hamilton Harty, in 1929.[17] Jazz was 'reversionary' music: associated with sexual promiscuity, the triumph of lower over higher instincts, a rebellion of the lower, inferior races against the superior white races of Europe. The black jazz artist Josephine Baker condensed in her person all such attributed characteristics.

Commentary on the development of popular culture frequently invoked the perils of standardisation of taste, or of the passivity of the viewer or listener which new media both induced and required.[18] It was, perhaps, difficult for older commentators to adjust to the apparent passivity induced by the wireless. For men like E. V. Lucas and Sidney Webb wireless listening was a form of addiction. Webb compared it to 'dram drinking',[19] and a hostile critic in 1923 compared the activity of listening to radio to an epidemic 'that you sicken for, catch and then spend an inordinate amount of money getting rid of'.[20]

When the wireless was welcomed, it was the urban working class who could be invoked as its principal beneficiaries. In 1924 the Christian commentator Harold Begbie, described by *Radio Times* as an 'informed writer of the day on questions affecting the welfare of the poor', praised the power of 'broadcasting' to penetrate the unconscious mental life of city-dwellers as 'the good fairy of the slums', the 'genius of Romance'. The 'younger people of East London', he said, 'must surely be moved by these things in those deeps of character which are partly conscious, partly unconscious, and help to determine human destiny'.[21] Perhaps the wireless could send the signal of philanthropy, to activate moral and psychic health for those in most need.

This well-meaning concern discursively constructed the working-class – as writing on 'darkest London' had done from the 1880s – as unknowable and impenetrable, and so fit objects of the commentator-explorer's transcendent knowledge and insight. The wireless was assimilated to this way of seeing, and seen as a potent new medium for it:

Never before in all the black history of slumland has such a light shone upon the darkness of human ignorance and domestic wretchedness ... Imagine what it must mean to East London when the Queen's Hall Orchestra floods its foul courts and alleys with the majestic strains of the Fifth symphony, or when the pain and longing of Chopin come breaking against the souls of men and women whose only knowledge of music hitherto has been got from the rattle of a street-piano outside a public house.[22]

Many a late-Victorian commentator on the working poor would have found the tenor and figures of this rhetoric perfectly congenial. Forster, too, would have understood. In *Howards End* the 'most sublime noise' of the 'Fifth Symphony' of Beethoven satisfies 'all sorts and conditions' of men.[23]

III

If you scratch a Russian you come to a Tartar, if
you scratch a human being you come to an animal;
only in some cases you scratch more, in others less.
(John Sinjohn *pseud.* [John Galsworthy], *Jocelyn* (1898)).[24]

'Scratch a Russian and you will find a Tartar underneath' is a familiar saying ... It is the same with all the higher peoples of the earth. Civilization is only a skin. The great core of human nature is barbaric.
(J.Howard Moore, *Savage Survivals: The Story of the Race Told in Simple Language* (1932))[25]

For that most prestigious of anti-modernists, W. R. Inge, Dean of St Pauls, post-war England was surrendering to an 'epidemic of irrationalism'. It was a vision which owed much to the degenerationist tropes deployed by Nordau in the early nineties into the 1920s with other 'survivals' for whom *Degeneration* had been a formative influence:

This epidemic of irrationalism has given us pragmatism in philosophy, magic and superstition in religion, antinomianism in morals, post-impressionism in art, and Bolshevism in politics ... they all come from the father of lies ... They all begin by saying 'The true is what I choose to believe, and if I choose ... persistently enough I can make it so'.[26]

As Professor of Divinity at Cambridge, he had been a vocal pre-war eugenicist on the 'negative' wing of the movement. He had urged 'any legislation' which, in Anna Davin's words, 'might reduce the slum dwellers' desire to breed'. His fears about the burden of degeneration were expressed to one of the most active branches of the Eugenics Education Society at Cambridge University in May 1911 in a restatement of views expressed in the inaugural number of the *Eugenics Review*, two years earlier: 'I cannot say I am hopeful in the near future. I am afraid that the urban proletariat may cripple our civilisation as it destroyed that of ancient Rome. These degenerates, who have no qualities that confer survival value, will probably live as long as they can by "robbing hen roosts" ... and will then disappear'.[27]

These tropes of degenerationism express an attitude of disappointment with the times which would, in the significant cultural criticism of Leavis and *Scrutiny*, find other than strictly degenerationist outlets.[28] In an essay, 'Spoonfeeding' (1924), Inge finds in the unwillingness of housewives to make home-made bread and jam, in the extinction of the habit of walking and riding, in health insurance for workers and in the decline in the art of drawing and engraving, proof positive of an age gone soft. His crisis metaphors are drawn from popular Darwinism – society's 'power of grappling with difficulties ... will soon be lost if we no longer need it'[29].

It was the Russian revolution of 1917, and its perceived threat to a European civilisation demoralised by war, which roused in Inge the old fear of reversion. The onset of revolution confirmed the essential primitivism of the Russian people, easy prey to the subversive attentions of the 'sub-man': 'It is no accident', he said, 'that Russia, largely inhabited by thinly veneered tartars, an uncivilisable race, has been the scene of the supreme triumph of the sub-man'.[30] The 'subman' embraces more than the proletarian worker. He is 'spawned by all classes' and is powerful enough to undermine the 'highly organised state'. European civilisation – in a neat natural-istic conflation – is being 'poisoned by its own waste products, by the rotten human material that we protect and foster so carefully'.

For the degenerationist, the Russian revolution was symptomatic of a chaotic and disorderly society which world war had rendered tubercular and sick. Revolution had produced 'morbid excitement among all enemies of the social order'; war had 'given all authority a shake and ... increased the hope of the enemies of society'.[31] Inge's post-war Europe is promising breeding ground for political sub-versives.

Inge's medicalising discourse has the effect of transforming the political menace of communism into a disease. The bolshevik and his communist sympathisers in Europe are the latest recruits to that benighted degenerate army of untouchables and rejects. In post-war conditions numerous degenerates who might have been eliminated under ruder social conditions are now encouraged to live and multiply – 'imbecile, neurotic and half insane ... psychopaths with some morbid strain in their character'.[32] Here are ranks of semi-invalided revolutionaries, brooding, in their wheelchairs, on schemes for the overthrow of the state: 'All these cherish a sullen or maniacal hatred against the social order which gives them so much scope. A blind lust for destruction takes hold of them. To this class is naturally added the people of the abyss, criminals, hooligans, loafers, wastrels, who are always ready to emerge from their lair if they think their time has come'.[33] This standing army of the dis-affected is prepared to follow a new breed of 'able leaders' – 'renegades from the ranks of civilization', 'brilliant men with a fatal moral and mental twist, really insane but with a frightful method in their madness'.[34]

Of such a type was Rousseau, and now Lenin, the latest specimen of 'tainted genius' who might 'exert a dreadful power for evil ... Max Nordau has made a detailed study of this type.'[35] Are Inge's 'renegades' the inevitable Spencerian waste product of the evolu-tionary process, or are they a political threat in a class-based social order? Inge's terms habitually waver between the biological and the political, allowing him to deliver his polemical aim of tangling these separate threads into a garment of seamless common sense.

Post-war England offered, for the traditionalist, a settlement in which nothing was settled. Four and a half years of armed conflict had transformed pre-war attitudes to authority which, in the new perspective, looked immutable. The perennial complaint of the traditionalist faced by the new, the old confronted by the young, seemed intensified in an age which had so recently been denied those prized virtues of continuity and stability. It was as if the present had to take the rap for no longer being Edwardian. In his introduction to a collection of poems of 1923, *The Rural Scene*, Bernard Gilbert lamented that for 'thinking Englishmen' the immediate post-war period has been a wretched time 'because it has become evident that nobody knows where they are ... this confusion extends to religion, politics, patriotism, manners and sex, and has attacked the deeper roots of conduct until now unquestioned'.[36]

The same year, Baldwin voiced his concern to the House of Commons that the war had unleashed forces which pre-war Europe believed had been within its control. Using a key metaphor of precariousness he argued that the experience of war had shown 'how thin is the crust of civilisation on which this generation is walking'. And he called for 'people of all nations' to join hands to 'save what we have', since 'we had all of us slipped down in our views of what constituted civilisation'.[37] War had intensified not only change but the perception of the rate of change. To the traditionalist, the present seemed doubly unstable: firstly, because the certainties of the pre-war past now seemed to belong firmly on the other side of a gulf separating the post-war present from the pre-war past; secondly, because the present was fearfully hospitable to the 'other', which now seemed to gorge itself on a demoralised present. This paranoia, generated by modernist and political challenges of this period, displayed all the tautology and circularity of degenerationist polemic: the hated 'new' was pathologised both into a symptom of the sick society and a source and cause of its sickness.

Degeneration thrived stubbornly in the shrill tones of paranoic hostility which spoke of the pain of loss. But war had exposed and mocked their conventional rhetoric as outworn and irrelevant. No longer could the 'other' be so innocently diagnosed in the 'funny eyes' of Galsworthy's recidivist clerk.[38] The 'other' was increasingly everyone – and so ceased to exist as 'other': the war had been the responsibility of all. In time, the assertion of personal responsibility in the face of collective tragedy would constitute a denial and a partial exorcism of the tenacious hold of degenerationist symptomology. But for the present it maintained its grip through best-selling fantasies of world-wide conspiracy, such as those produced by the prolific John Buchan.

IV

In one of his best novels *The Three Hostages* (1924), it is appropriately a doctor who theorises at length about the times. At the outset, Dr Greenslade is taken up with the state of contemporary detective fiction which seems no longer to 'take account of the infernal complexity of life'.[39] The voicing of opinions by the professional *raisonneur* is a means by which Buchan can write up a diagnosis of the condition of England. For Greenslade, the war has left in its wake large tracts of irrationality: 'Have you ever realized, Dick, the amount of stark craziness that the War has left the world?' As a 'pathologist', he is 'fairly staggered':

I hardly meet a soul who hasn't got some slight kink in his brain as a consequence of the last seven years. With some people it's rather a pleasant kink – they're less settled in their grooves, and they see the comic side of things quicker, and are readier for adventure. But with some its *pukka* madness, and that means crime. (12)

Hannay observes that 'the poor old War is getting blamed for a good deal that I was taught in my childhood was due to original sin', but Greenslade insists that the war has had a decisive impact:

The meaning of civilisation was that we had got it battened down under the hatches, whereas now it's getting its head up ... It's a dislocation of the mechanism of human reasoning, a general loosening of screws ... You can't any longer take the clear psychology of most civilized human beings for granted. Something is welling up from primeval deeps to muddy it. (14)

And one of the effects of this 'loosening' (the same phrase is picked up in Buchan's *The Dancing Floor* (1926)) is the breaking down of barriers 'between the conscious and the subconscious'. The 'result is confusion, and if the fluids are of a certain character, explosions'.[40] Buchan's use of the authoritative doctor figure endows a certain credence (which a more direct authorial voice would not) to the existence of abysses of the unknown and uncharted. And so the doctor gradually wears away Richard Hannay's scepticism on the subject – the unpleasant facts of the 'loosening of screws', revealed

by the narrative, will naturally assist his case. Buchan co-opts the
expert to turn rational and scientific analysis to degenerationist ends.

In spite of the perfunctory presentation of the idea of the
unconscious at the beginning of the novel, the 'loosening of the
screws' has enabled the unconscious to wander at large through
post-war England as criminal madness. The plot appropriately turns
on the criminal potential of the manipulation of the unconscious
through hypnosis. The post-war malaise expresses itself in plots
which assume the existence of nameless world-wide conspiracies
against civilisation.

Weimar Germany also found its master-criminal in 'a man of
apparently enormous and comprehensive powers', a currency-
smuggler called Dr Mabuse. In Norbert Jacques's novel of that name
(translated into English in 1923 – the film version from the German
original was directed by Fritz Lang in 1922) the state-attorney
wonders whether he possesses the 'strength to fight the age, for his
opponent was more than a cheat, a criminal – he was the whole spirit
of the age, a spirit torn through the catastrophe of the war from the
hellish depths where it was created, to fall upon the world and the
homes of men'.[41]

Much of Buchan's post-war fiction is precisely plotted to show how
the masters of international conspiracy and crime are confronted by
the defenders of the forces of civilisation, and the British political
establishment – represented by his characters Hannay, Leithen and
Melfort. In *The Three Hostages* Hannay's very reluctance to come out
of retirement gives MacGillivray, a senior policeman, the opportunity of impressing upon him the urgency of his assignment.
Post-war Europe is seething with wrongdoing as never before,
according to MacGillivray:

A large part of the world had gone mad, and that involved the growth of
inexplicable and unpredictable crime. All the old sanctities had become
weakened ... The moral imbecile ... had been more or less a spent force
before the War; now he was a terribly common product, and throve in
batches and battalions ... a hideous, untameable breed has been engen-
dered, You find it among the young Bolshevik Jews, of the wild gentry of the
wilder Communist sects and very notably among the sullen murderous
hobbledehoys in Ireland. (23)

The degenerate army is on the move. It is the story, told before, of an
unspecified criminal source, a civilisation at risk, its degenerate
product easy meat for 'a few clever men who are not degenerates or

anything of that sort, but only evil'. Notwithstanding the disclaimer, these 'clever men' are themselves variants of the 'higher degenerate' criminal geniuses of the 1890s. The master-criminal of *The Three Hostages*, Dominic Medina, possessed the roundest head Hannay had ever seen, 'except in a Kaffir'(51). 'What did a head like that portend? ... I had heard somewhere that it meant madness – at any rate degeneracy'(107).

Buchan's forty-year writing career was launched back in the late 1890s. What that career confirms, repeatedly, is that while his best work is written during and after the first world war, he remains essentially a turn-of-the-century writer. Allowing for minor shifts of emphasis, for up-dating in manners, speech and historical placing, his fiction offers few modifications in the range and type of characters he deploys, or in their preoccupations and plots. His work records a sustained effort to write *against* the dynamics of change, including contemporary literary experiment. The modernist artistic obligation to make it new does not trouble Buchan.

His anti-modernism finds its voice in tactics of reversion. What survives into the 1920s is a mutation of a familiar figure from the *fin de siècle*, civilised man in combat with barbarism, with its ever-present reversionary threat. The Calvinistic struggle in Stevenson between good and evil is transformed by Buchan, from the outset of his writing career, into a secular, even politicised, war between civilisation and barbarism through tropes of 'precariousness'. In his early story 'Fountainblue' (1901), the central figure Maitland, finds the space between 'the warm room and the savage outdoors' to be no more than 'a line, a thread, a sheet of glass'.[42] In *The Power-house* (1913), the hero, Leithen, is the target of the Nietzschian broodings of a figure called Lumley who proposes a 'power-house' of brains to save civilisation from impending anarchy: 'You think that a wall as solid as the earth separates civilisation from barbarism. I tell you the division is a thread, a sheet of glass. A touch here, a push there, and you bring back the reign of Saturn.'[43]

In Buchan's fiction, contrasting worlds collide, and the odds of the outcome are usually uncertain: the comfortable milieus of club and country-house are barely separate from the primitive wastes of Scotland and the Celtic or northern fringe (with its anarchists and radical workers). The Buchan hero is invariably placed at a precarious intersection of these worlds – fraught and insecure, his project a paradoxical one. While the protagonist may crave a measure of undiluted adventure (barbarism), he can only achieve this outlet, legitimately, in defense of the very civilised way of life which stifles him. The Hannays, Leithens and Melforts are, in varying degrees, at odds with the introspective, intellectual tendencies which Buchan identifies disparagingly with the modernist frame of mind – over-complex, neurotic, indulgently subjective, and obsessed with modern art and Freud.

At the start of these narratives the adventurer-hero is frequently at a loose end – he is alternately preoccupied and restless. But the prospect of doing battle with the enemy enables these feelings to be channeled and externalised, their unsettling potential defused. The hero's initial detachment from the project gives his eventual com-mitment to it an authenticity which a cruder knee-jerk response to the call of the wild would not. In the early novel *The Half-Hearted* (1900) Lewis Haystoun's desultory attitude to action is interestingly a response to his feelings of personal inadequacy. Yet rather than explore the psychological implications of the call to action, Buchan is content to allow imperialistic, fighting rhetoric to talk down the 'decadence' of the introspective temperament:

There are two sorts of people who will never do any good on this planet. One is the class which makes formulae and shallow little ideals its gods and has no glimpse of human needs and the plain issues of life – the other is the egotist whose eye is always filled with his own figure, who investigates his own motives, and hesitates and finicks; till Death knocks him on the head.[44]

At the opening of *John Macnab* (1925), the established politician-adventurer Leithen is suffering from a prolonged bout of exhaustion. His medical advisor urges action as antidote: 'You've grown too competent. You need to be made to struggle for your life again – your life or your reputation.'[45] Given this revivified social Darwin-ism it is no surprise to learn that peacetime England offers a poor prospect to the adventurer, that is, unless the battle can be rejoined on new territory and the enemy similarly recast. And in *A Prince of the Captivity* (1933), it is the experience of fighting which has disci-plined Adam Melfort for the bigger mission of marshalling the talents of three men of 'genius' for the regeneration of Europe. Melfort was 'in the war, but not *of* it ... For him it was only a spell of training for something much bigger.' The war has left men in a state of nervous inactivity – 'Too tired to rest – must have some other kind of excitement – running round like sick dogs till the real crash comes.'[46]

The Russian revolution and the spectre of bolshevik infiltration into European centres of power send a Russian exile to the ideological barricades in *Huntingtower* (1922):

You good people in England think that they are well-meaning dreamers who are forced into violence by the persecution of Western Europe. But you are wrong. Some honest fools there are among them, but the power – the true power – lies with madmen and degenerates, and they have for allies the special devil that dwells in each country.[47]

The ideological and political threat is pathologised, translated into a fear of an epidemic of crime. What Lenin's Russia has released into Europe and England is felt as an epidemic sickness:

Russia is mortally sick ... all evil is unchained, and the criminals have no one to check them ... After a war evil passions are loosed, and since Russia is broken, in her they can make their headquarters ... It is not Bolshevism, the theory, you need fear, for that is a weak and dying thing. It is crime which today finds its seat ... not only [in] Russia. It has no fatherland. It is as old as human nature and wide as the earth.[48]

Pathological and biological metaphor vividly establishes the Russian threat as merely the most recent and most virulent strain of a trans-historical degenerate condition, endemic in Europe before 1917 and perpetually in the body politic. By fixing criminality as the semi-permanent condition of Europe, he accommodates a generalised sense of insecurity and paranoia, and allows other tendencies in European culture to be framed, along with political revolution, as the source of the contamination spreading into England, London and the heart of Empire. The idea of revolutionary Russia as a harbinger of criminal lawlessness is perpetuated in 'Sapper''s thriller of 1926, *The Final Count* in which Russia is ruled by a 'clique of homicidal despots'.[49]

And stalking its margins is a familiar figure – the genius criminal. There is Marker, in *The Half-Hearted*, a smooth, apparently civilised, manipulator of anti-English sentiment on the Indian frontier, 'a man of uncanny powers, an intelligence beyond others, the iron will of the true adventurer' (315). In *Mr Standfast* (1918) Hannay is pitted against Moxon Ivery who is masterminding a German conspiracy. In spite of his impeccable establishment credentials, 'enough alibis to choke a boa-constrictor',[50] 'he's as cruel as a snake and deep as hell. But by God, he's got a brain below his hat'.[51] Buchan's agents of anarchy, are, on the surface, pillars of the establishment, integrated and plausible: the contemporary fanatic, according to a character in *The Three Hostages*, derives his strength precisely from his quality of 'balance': 'you cannot say that there is any one thing abnormal about him, for he is all abnormal. He is as balanced as you or me ... within his insane postulates he is brilliantly sane. Take Lenin for instance. That's the kind of fanatic I'm afraid of.'(61)

The fanatical man of genius is singled out by Adam Melfort, in *A Prince of the Captivity*, as a type who exemplies the Darwinian struggle for conquest. As Melfort's friend Stannix puts it 'I have seen in the body two anti-types – Warren Creevey and Adam Melfort ... the one all grossness and genius, the other with his "flesh refined to flame" '. For Melfort, Creevey is: 'something formidable ... perverse and dangerous ... a perilous force against which the world must be protected'.[52] The arch-enemy, higher-degenerate is there too in 'Sapper's fiction. Bulldog Drummond's enemy, Carl Peterson, possesses 'a stupendous brain, unshakeable nerve, and unlimited ambition'. But a 'kink' in that brain has 'turned him into an utterly unscrupulous criminal'.[53]

The villain of the thriller of the 1920s is thus a mutation of the criminal degenerate postulated by Magnan and Lombroso, fifty years before. In the fictions of Buchan, 'Sapper' and Deeping, those whose talents might have been harnessed for the rejuvenation of the post-war world have simply, and conveniently, 'gone wrong'. With such anachronistic, if still vaguely menacing epithets, the anti-modernist fabulists continued to parade their degenerationist credentials from the *fin de siècle*, as the challenges of the moment were translated into the myths of evasion. Their typologies were still able to ignite the old fears and fantasies, even as the boundaries of the pre-war European culture in which they were nurtured, were collapsing around them.

CHAPTER 12

Postscripts

1 'BACKWARD EDDIES'

In the 1920s British doctors, educationalists, politicians and journalists could not shake off the old concern with the racial consequences of the differential birth-rate in degenerate spaces of the nation – the slums, and, less predictably, the rural backwaters, or at the geographical margins of the country. In the slums it was said that 'a large proportion ... consists of ... "morons" – that is, of mental defectives ... lacking not only in intelligence but also in self-control, which is the basis of morality, and they reproduce recklessly'.[1] A report on mental deficiency in 1929 from the Board of Education suggested that its incidence was twice that of 1908. The *Daily Telegraph* commented in terms which might have been heard thirty years before: 'the general complacent belief in the inevitability of steady progress is subject occasionally to rude shocks, when we are reminded that there may be strongly marked backward eddies in the main stream ... mental deficiency is much greater in the rural districts ... not surprising when one remembers to what extent the best rural stock has been drained away'.[2] Sir Richard Gregory, the editor of *Nature* 1914–39 (as well as of *School World* and the *Journal of Education*) had been calling repeatedly for compulsory, not just voluntary, sterilisation.[3] The Board of Education came under heavy pressure to adopt sterilisation measures. Lord Riddell, a newpaper proprietor and friend of Churchill, argued that sterilisation would reduce promiscuity among mental defectives, and so would limit their 'multiplication' – a 'most serious national menace'. Lunacy and mental deficiency were 'festering sores'.[4] After concerted lobbying by the Eugenic Society a sterilisation bill was introduced into Parliament in July 1931, but was voted out.

At the height of the Depression in Britain, in 1936, a prominent eugenicist, E. W. MacBride, diverted attention from mass un-employment to a racial factor among the 'dock labourers and miners' – an 'Iberian element ... from Wales and Ireland' who 'figure prominently in the over-production of children'.[5] Such degenerationist sentiments and rhetoric were also levelled at slum-dwellers of the East End, when, as evacuees at the beginning of the second world war, they crossed the boundary into visibility: many of them were verminous and suffered from ringworm and scabies. Disease was the sign of their unfitness, which was encoded in the accusation of feckless and irresponsible behaviour. Fears of crime and the infectious condition of children channelled old fears of the 'unwashed', whilst contagion and infection reinforced the sense of their 'otherness', as a separate race marked out by unacceptable values and conduct. Evacuees incurred the sometimes open hostility of local communities and national commentators: 'brushing their teeth and saying their prayers were exercises of which they knew nothing', wrote the *Times Educational Supplement* censoriously in Sept-ember 1939.[6] In the same month the historian R. C. K. Ensor described some mothers of evacuated children as 'the lowest grade of slum women – slatternly malodorous tatterdemalions trailing chil-dren to match'.[7]

These reflex attitudes, voiced with what now must seem astonishing insouciance, still relied on an unthinking application of biological models of 'fitness' derived from a value-laden social Darwinism. It fell at last to the biological scientists and socialists Lancelot Hogben, J. B. S. Haldane and others to unpack the socio-biological inheritance which had upheld such notions for the best part of sixty years. Hogben and Haldane believed that eugenicists were attempting to force political decisions that went far beyond the current state of knowledge about human heredity. In 1937 Haldane condemned German racial measures on scientific grounds, and he was also critical of the persistent misappropriation of the terms 'fitness' and 'unfitness' by the British eugenics movement, which was actively seeking sterilisation of mental defectives and people of low intelligence ('words to which I object very strongly when used as eugenists often use them ... When we use the word fit, we must ask "fit for what?" And that brings us up against the whole question of social ideals').

Haldane was clear about the double standards of the eugenists, derived from their own class position. Cases of lunacy or gross idiocy 'are probably reported in all social classes', he said, but 'mild mental defect' is 'much less frequently certified among the rich than the poor ... A well-to-do family can afford to keep a "backward boy" or "a girl who was no good at school." A poor family cannot'. 'Sterilization of all certified defectives', he argued, 'would thus in our society be a class measure.'[8] And in the course of a survey of genetics, Haldane observed in 1936 that eugenics was 'largely a product of the class struggle based on the desire of the governing class to prove their innate superiority'.[9]

Haldane was also aware of the 'psychology' of those who demanded sterilisation, taking into account 'one's emotional reaction to mental defectives'. While people usually regarded them with 'horror', 'personally', he said, 'I must confess a certain liking for them ... '[10] And in a fascinating, if perfunctory discussion – prompted, no doubt, by his reading of Freud – he suggested another 'unconscious motive': 'internal contradictions in the human soul are unconsciously projected as hatred, and ... in a society where this must be normally repressed it is readily directed at objects discredited for some reason'.[11]

There was a singular appropriateness in Haldane's skilful assimilation of psychoanalytical concepts in his deconstruction of degenerationist attitudes to mental defectives. For the theory and practice of psychoanalysis, as we have seen, had been decisive in undermining the credibility of degenerationism. By 1938 Haldane would have known that the 'unfit' were being compulsorily sterilised in Nazi Germany (and even in certain American states). Within a few years sterilisation would be superceded by extermination, in occupied Europe.

It will be clear from the argument of this book that there is a line of descent from the academic debates about degeneration in Britain, Europe and America from the 1880s, through to the holocaust of the 1940s. There had, after all, been a well-canvassed 'final solution' to the problems of society's waste-products in the idea, circulating in the glib talk within eugenicist circles since the turn of the century, of the 'lethal chamber'. Arnold White in 1901 had urged a vast programme of assisted emigration for the bulk of the 'residuum', as a solution. But more grotesque fantasies were indulged, if only, as White put it, 'by flippant people of lazy mind [who] talk lightly of the "lethal chamber" '.[12] Every university or hospital laboratory had such a device for the disposal of unwanted animals.[13]

Aldous Huxley had his finger on the pulse of this dehumanising appeal to a last resort. In *Crome Yellow* (1921) the determinedly rationalist Scogan has no room in his blueprint of a 'Rational State' for the poet and would-be hero Denis Burlap: 'You're too independent and too suggestible to belong to the larger Herd; you have none of the characteristics required in the Man of Faith ... no, I can see no place for you; only the lethal chamber'.[14] In the view of Spandrell the nihilist in *Point Counter Point* (1928), the same destination should await another type of the unfit, an ageing arthritic.[15] The 'lethal chamber', maintained in the punitive rhetoric of the despairing middle-classes for two generations, was eventually to retreat from utterance as its figurativeness was overtaken by its dreadful referent.

II FROM 'CULTURAL BACKWATER' TO MAIN STREAM.

> We Irish, born into that ancient sect
> But thrown upon this modern tide
> And by its formless, spawning, fury wrecked ...
>
> (W. B. Yeats, ' The Statues')[16]

For mid-nineteeth century observers the city poor, the inhabitants of the slums, living amongst filth, became, in the discourse of reportage, filth and excrement themselves – 'a vast heap of social refuse ... the great living mixen'.[17] But by the 1880s, with the hereditarian consciousness well established, the people in the mass were represented less as waste-matter (though that concept of the 'residuum' persisted) than as a persistently degenerate 'abysmal' fecundity; intensely active, and out of control, as fascinating and disgusting as a jar of writhing maggots. The 'refuse' which had been thought of as a source of a 'miasma' was now biologised into a breeding mass, horribly fertile. Post-Darwinian science had changed the metaphorical agenda. The labouring classes *breed*, their offspring are a 'rank evilly-fostered growth'.[18]

One consequence of the socio-biological inheritance, persisting as we have seen into the 1930s, was a dire continuity in the life of these tropes of disgust and disapproval, when what was believed to be the dysgenic was in question. Dean Inge's 'sub-man', after the first world war, is 'spawned from all classes'.[19] In Huxley's *Antic Hay* (1923), Gumbril listens to an earnest anti-semite talking of people who breed 'like maggots, sir, like maggots ... hideous red cities pullulating with Jews'.[20] Huxley skilfully satirises both the idiom of degenerationism and the credulous Gumbril drawn into compliance with it. But there is no irony in the diary entry of the Labour cabinet minister, Hugh Dalton, who in 1950 talked of 'pullulating, poverty-stricken, diseased nigger communities'.[21]

While it was predictable that Inge should reiterate the familiar language of disgust at the masses, it is more significant that the reach of these ideas should extend to poets like Yeats and Eliot. Yeats's 'modern tide' had a 'spawning fury', Eliot's Jew was 'spawned in some estaminet of Antwerp',[22], the verb suggesting precisely that threatening degenerative coupling of the fertile and the low. For Eliot, the new art for the people, the cinema, is not only 'cheap', but 'rapid-breeding'.[23] Yeats, particularly in the late thirties, infused into his aristocratic mythology of social hierarchy a profound distaste for 'base-born products of base-beds'. He repeated, without any sense of banality, old eugenic fears of the differential birth-rate: 'the danger is that ... European civilisation, like those older civilisations that saw the triumph of their gangrel stocks, will accept decay'. And again in 'A Bronze Head' (1939) we find 'gangling stocks grown great, great stocks run/dry'.[24] Eliot's degenerationism is more neurotic and contradictory: his work shows both the familiar anxiety over sterility, and a disgust at procreative fecundity. The poet contemplates a 'waste' land where the loveless, neurasthenic ménage is contrasted with the sickly fertility of cockney Lil of the lower-classes – 'She's had five already, and nearly died of young George.'[25] Eliot both wills and suppresses her fertility – 'its them pills I took, to bring it off'.[26]

It hardly needs to be said that many of the racist and degenerationist utterances of modernist writers like Yeats and Eliot, Lawrence and Woolf, are repellent, even unforgiveable. This aspect of early twentieth-century writing has been thoroughly aired in John Carey's *The Intellectuals and the Masses* (1992). His charge can be summed up in his indictment: 'the principle around which modernist literature and culture fashioned themselves was the exclusion of the masses, the defeat of their power, the removal of their literacy, the denial of their humanity'.[27] When faced by Yeats, Eliot, Pound and Lewis, there is clearly some truth in Carey's not wholly new argument (it is the ground of John Harrison's treatment of this particular aspect of modernism in his book *The Reactionaries*, published in 1967).[28]

From Carey's perspective the twentieth-century intellectual, a category, in Carey's view, synonymous with modernist novelists and poets, looked out at the masses with fear and contempt. But from the vantage point I have been using, modernist novelists, poets and painters were themselves the objects of hostility, stereotyped as deviant and dangerous, and subjected to the persistent insinuation of a powerful generalised anti-modernism, which, as I have shown in the previous chapter, seeped through the nineties into the post-first world war reaction: the best-selling novels of Deeping, 'Sapper', Buchan and others offer ample witness to this frame of mind.

Lying behind this widespread attribution of deviancy and degeneracy to modern culture is the long shadow cast by the institutionalised authority of positivistic science and medicine. I suggest that an underestimated consequence was a damaging long-term effect on the popular idea of serious art, of the artist and of artistic and intellectual innovation. Indeed the appeal of scientific, medical and psychological teaching was to render 'art' profoundly suspect since art was itself deemed to be a source of instability and disorientation in the modern world. In the 'exclusion of the masses', from the experience of art and literature, the influence of such teaching was, I think, a more potent agency than has been generally recognised.

For, as Roy Porter reminds us, we need to weigh more fully the formidable 'medico-psychiatric imperialism' which strove 'to appropriate for itself the domains of the critic, aesthetician, and man of letters'. Porter continues: 'the labelling of the innovative artist as insane, or at least neurotic, also served the wider purpose of discrediting the voice of the writer and furthering medicine's normalizing mission in an increasingly conservative social climate'.[29] While Porter's immediate context here is the 1890s, there was, as I have shown, a powerful afterglow of these ideas in popular culture right through the inter-war period, despite the fact that the respectability of degeneration theory in medical circles had ebbed away by the 1920s.

In the aftermath of Nordau's *Degeneration*, William James was one of those who kept his head when, in a telling phrase, he recorded feeling 'menaced and negated in the springs of [his] innermost life' by the positivist critic Taine, with his 'proclamations of the intellect bent on showing the existential condition of absolutely everything' ('vice and virtue are products like vitriol or sugar'). 'Such cold-blooded assimilations' threatened, James believed, 'our soul's vital secrets.' Having quoted from medical pathologists such as Moreau de Tours, Lombroso and Nisbet (author of *The Insanity of Genius*), James then turns on these 'medical materialists'. In no other field, he protests, does it occur to anyone 'to try to refute opinions by showing up their author's neurotic constitution'.[30]

James's sensitive critique attests to the existence of a body of independent and responsive thinkers at the turn of the century, who resisted the totalising claims of this late phase of 'triumphant positivism'[31] and the tyranny of the norm. Another such figure at the time was Edward Garnett (Conrad's and later Lawrence's editor) who, in speaking out against *Degeneration*, remarked 'how perfectly it represents the attitude of all modern commercialised societies towards art'. *Degeneration*, he claimed, was 'strictly speaking, a *reductio ad absurdum* of the utilitarian theory in the life of the middle classes. All the ignorance, prejudice, limitations of the average man in matters aesthetic were deified there, and set up before his delighted eyes as scientific truths.'[32]

Aldous Huxley was moved to make virtually the same point a generation later in 1929, when he dismissed 'Nordauites' ('who take a peculiar pleasure in asserting that all great men have been diseased or lunatic') as suffering from Podsnappery: 'they see everything *sub specie Podsnapitatis*'.[33] Though separated by thirty years, both Huxley and Garnett had identified a reason for the success of the Nordau effect: a distrust of originality and innovation – a fear of the new.

That presumptive expression of *schadenfreude* – at how 'great men' are 'diseased' – which Huxley noted, had been abundantly displayed following the fall of Oscar Wilde in 1895 – the consequences of which, within English society and culture, were to be felt for a long time. *Punch* had expressed this resentful reaction with unmistakable ebullience. A 'Philistine Paean' rang out: 'I know I'm relieved from one horrible bore, – / *I need not admire what I hate any more.*'[34] The integrity of critics of this period like James was the more admirable, and, in retrospect, the more necessary.

The argument of John Carey's book seems to me to be made quite seriously defective by his failure to refer not only to Nordau, *Degeneration* and this whole medico-pathological tradition, but also to the deeply entrenched fear of art which these specialists legitimised, in Europe and America, for well over half a century. Medico-psychia-

13　'Hitler at the "Degenerate Art" [*Entartete Kunst*] Exhibition', Munich 1937.

tric orthodoxy entailed, as we have seen, the subordination of the personal and the private to the dictates of 'normality' and 'health', defined by the higher authority of social positivism. It was in the name of this orthodoxy 'for the benefit of the greatest number' that, in 1912, T. B. Hyslop had expressed his fervent support for the legislation, currently being debated, to incarcerate the 'feeble-minded'. The slow progress of this legislation he attributed to the 'soft-hearted and misguided opponents of such vital "prophylactic" measures'. It is worth recalling the key phrase in Hyslop's dismissal of the soft-hearted – their 'fetish-worship of the liberty of the subject'.[35]

The Mental Deficiency Act, as we have seen, was passed in 1913. As with subsequent legislation in America and Europe through the twenties and thirties, here was a victory for the medical-political establishment over the faint-hearts. The erosion and invasion of the 'liberty of the subject' was, in the doctors' eyes, a reasonable price to pay to halt the prolific breeding of undesirable citizens.

But to the tens of thousands of the 'feeble-minded', newly discovered by the late Victorian and Edwardian doctors, there would be matched, but horrifically over-matched, the millions liquidated by state terrorism. As far as writers, musicians, painters, sculptors were concerned, the seeds of the state terrorism against them under Fascist and Communist regimes in the twentieth century can be seen to be predicated in the final pages of Nordau's *Degeneration*. Looking forward to the twentieth century, Nordau proposed that 'society' was 'the natural organic form of humanity in which alone it can . . . develop itself to higher destinies'. Such 'destinies' could only be reached if society 'unconditionally' defended itself against its 'enemies', the 'ego-maniacs and filthy pseudo-realists', the 'anti-social vermin' which it must 'mercilessly crush'.[36] In this perspective the ill-tempered outbursts against the masses of a Woolf or a Lawrence, reprehensible as they may have been, seem relatively unimportant.

So it comes as a surprise to find John Carey arguing that German Fascism was distinguished by its reverence for the artist and the 'divine spark' of artistic genius. In Carey's topsy-turvy world Nazi book-burning vandals are the defenders of high art.[37] Yet Hitler and his kind propagated their bogus populist ethic of Aryan nobility, seeing to the destruction of the work of 'deviants' such as Thomas Mann, Freud, Proust and Picasso. It was precisely in the name of the 'masses' whom Carey claims to have been so hugely patronised and condescended to by modernist writers, that Hitler's exhibition of Degenerate Art (*Entartete Kunst*) was held in Munich in 1937. Here was the ultimate consequence of that tendency which both William James and Garnett had detected: the 'deification' of the 'ignorance, prejudice, limitations of the average man in matters aesthetic'. In fact such a reservoir of fear of 'intellectuals', artists and modernists was essential for the Nazi project to succeed. The modernist artist was the enemy necessary to the régime.

In 1936 a purge had been made of modern paintings held by galleries across Germany: among them contemporary German expressionist paintings by Nolde, Beckmann, Kirchner and others, and works by Cézanne, Gauguin, Van Gogh and Matisse – specimens of whose work had aroused so much hostility in London back in 1910–13.[38] As the German critic Ernst Bloch noted at the time, the 'degenerate' paintings in the exhibition which followed, *Entartete Kunst*, 'were seen by four times as many people as the true-to-type ones.'[39] The pictures were displayed interspersed with inciting graffiti and labels: 'insanity at any price', 'German peasants looked at in the Yiddish manner', 'the negro becomes the racial ideal of degenerate art'.[40]

A 'Great Exhibition of German Art 1937' also opened in Munich, only the day before, held in the neo-classical Haus der Deutschen Kunst. In this exhibition all the orthodox Nazi national and racial virtues were celebrated. From the perspective of this demonstration of healthy art, Hitler cast the degenerate artist as 'other' – the kind, he said, who

see the present population of our nation only as rotten cretins; who, on principle, see meadows blue, skies green, clouds sulphur yellow ... in the name of the German people, I want to forbid these pitiful misfortunates who quite obviously suffer from an eye disease, to try vehemently to foist these products of their misinterpretation upon the age we live in, or even wish to present them as 'Art'.

'This House', he added, was not 'built for the works of this kind of incompetent or art criminal ... With the opening of this exhibition the end of German art foolishness and the end of its destruction of its culture will have begun. From now on we will wage an unrelenting war of purification against the last elements of putrefaction in our culture.' And he assured his audience that the cultural support-structure for modernist work would be torn down: the 'cliques of babblers, dilettantes and art crooks which lend support to each other and are therefore able to survive, will be eliminated and abolished'.[41] As a Zionist, Nordau, had he lived, would not have approved of Hitler. Even so, such sentiments could have come straight out of *Degeneration*. For as Bloch observed, these rantings of Hitler had 'often existed before in the gazettes of cultural backwaters'.

Writing from within the Third Reich itself, Bloch added, with heroic irony, that 'people have learnt to take the ridiculous seriously'.[42] Out of the 'backwaters', ideas of degeneration now flooded, grotesquely and terribly, into the mainstream of world history.

Notes

INTRODUCTION

1 Doris Lessing, *The Fifth Child* (London: Grafton Books, 1988), p. 156.
2 Peter Gay, *The Bourgeois Experience* Vol. 2 (New York and Oxford: Oxford University Press, 1986), p. 348.
3 Michel Foucault, *The Archaeology of Knowledge* (trans. A. M. Sheridan-Smith, London: Tavistock Publications, 1972) (first published as *L'Archéologie du savoir* (1969)), see, in particular, Part 2, chs. 1–7; *The History of Sexuality* Vol. 1 (trans. R. Hurley, 1978; Harmondsworth: Penguin, 1981) (first published as *La Volonté de savoir* (1976)), see, in particular, Part 2 ch. 1, Part 4 ch. 2.
4 Frank Kermode, *The Sense of an Ending* (New York: Oxford University Press, 1967), p. 39.
5 R. P. Blackmur, *Henry Adams* (revised edn San Diego: Harcourt Brace Jovanovich, 1980), pp. 275–6.
6 Gillian Beer, *Arguing with the Past: Essays in Narrative from Woolf to Sidney* (London: Routledge, 1989), pp. 4–5.
7 Gillian Beer, review of Redmond O'Hanlon, *Joseph Conrad and Charles Darwin* (1984), *Sunday Times* (27 May 1984), p. 43.
8 Cited by Beer, *Arguing with the Past*, p. 5.
9 John Goode, 'E.P.Thompson and the Significance of Literature', in Harvey J. Kaye and Keith McClelland (eds.) *E.P.Thompson: Critical Perspectives* (Cambridge: Polity Press, 1990), 183–203 (p. 190).
10 George Gissing, *Demos* (1886; repr. Brighton: Harvester, 1974), p. 350.
11 Daniel Pick, *Faces of Degeneration; A European Disorder c. 1848 – c. 1918* (Cambridge University Press, 1989), pp. 85–7.
12 Paul Weindling, *Health, Race and German politics between National Unification and Nazism, 1870–1945* (Cambridge University Press, 1989), pp. 87–9; see also Maurice Larkin, *Man and Society in Nineteenth-Century Realism: Determinism and Literature* (London: Macmillan, 1977), p. 186.
13 See Lyn Pykett, *The 'Improper' Feminine: The Women's Sensation Novel and the New Woman Writing* (London: Routledge, 1992).
14 Peter Brooks, *The Melodramatic Imagination* (New Haven & London: Yale University Press, 1976), p. 42, p. 8.

15 Joseph Conrad, *The Nigger of the "Narcissus"* (1897; repr. Harmondsworth: Penguin, 1963), p. 20.
16 D. H. Lawrence, *Women in Love* (repr. Harmondsworth, Penguin, 1986), pp. 279–80.
17 Michael Bell, *Primitivism* (London: Methuen, 1972), pp. 38–9.
18 See Frank Kermode, 'D.H.Lawrence and the Apocalyptic Types', in *Modern Essays* (London: Fontana, 1971); David Trotter, 'Modernism and Empire: Reading *The Waste Land*', *Critical Quarterly* 28 (1986): 143–53.
19 See Roger Ebbatson, *The Evolutionary Self: Hardy, Forster, Lawrence* (Brighton: Harvester, 1982).
20 John Goode, 'D.H.Lawrence', in Bernard Bergonzi (ed.) *The Twentieth Century* (London: Sphere Books, 1970), pp. 106–49.
21 David Trotter, *The English Novel in History 1895–1920* (London: Routledge, 1993), pp. 124–7. This important book came to my notice too late for me to give it the attention it deserves. I am grateful to David Trotter for making available extracts from his book before publication.
22 See Tony Bennett, Introduction to T. Bennett (ed.) *Popular Fiction: Technology, Ideology, Production, Reading* (London: Routledge, 1990), pp. 3–7.
23 See Pick, *Faces of Degeneration*, p. 237.
24 Henry J. Walton (ed.) *Dictionary of Psychiatry* (Oxford: Blackwell Scientific, 1985).
25 See Richard Hofstadter, *Social Darwinism in American Thought* (1944; revised edn. New York: Braziller, 1965); Milton P. Foster, 'The Reception of Max Nordau's *Degeneration* in England and America', Ph.D. dissertation, University of Michigan, 1954; Milton Gold, 'The Early Psychiatrists on Degeneracy and Genius', in *Psychoanalysis and the Psychoanalytic Review* 47 (1960–1): 37–55.
26 Richard D. Walter, 'What Became of the Degenerate?: A Brief History of a Concept', *Journal of the History of Medicine* 11 (1956): 422–9.
27 For full details of these and other studies mentioned subsequently in this chapter, see Bibliography.

I DE-GENERATION

1 This is the sub-title of J. Edward Chamberlain and Sander L. Gilman's collection of essays *Degeneration: The Dark Side of Progress* (New York: Columbia University Press, 1985).
2 Cited by Erwin A. Ackerknecht, *A Short History of Psychiatry* (New York: 1959), p. 48.
3 Ackernecht, *A Short History of Psychiatry*, p. 49.
4 *Ibid.*, p. 50.
5 Greta Jones, *Social Darwinism and English Thought* (Brighton: Harvester Press, 1980), p. 78.

6 *Ibid.*, p. 79.

7 Max Nordau, *Degeneration* (1895; Popular Edition, London: William Heinemann, 1913), p. 21; see Adrian Poole, *Gissing in Context* (London: Macmillan, 1975), p. 21.

✗ 8 John Stokes, *In The Nineties* (Hemel Hempstead: Harvester-Wheatsheaf, 1989), p. 12.

✗ 9 Elaine Showalter, *Sexual Anarchy: Gender and Culture at the Fin de Siècle* (London: Bloomsbury, 1991), p. 4.

10 Bram Dijkstra, *Idols of Perversity: Fantasies of Feminine Evil in Fin de Siècle Culture* (Oxford University Press, 1986).

11 Arthur Conan Doyle, *The Parasite* (London: A. Constable, 1894), p. 62, p. 50, p. 60, p. 59; see Anne Cranny-Francis, 'Arthur Conan Doyle's *The Parasite*: The Case of the Anguished Author', in Clive Bloom *et al.* (eds.) *Nineteenth-Century Suspense from Poe to Doyle* (London: Macmillan, 1988), pp. 93–106.

12 George Gissing, *In The Year of Jubilee* (1894; repr. Brighton: Harvester Press, 1976), p. 253.

13 Robert A. Nye, *Crime, Madness and Politics in Modern France: The Medical Concept of National Decline* (Princeton University Press, 1984), pp. 47–8.

14 Robert A. Nye, 'Sociology and Degeneration: The Irony of Progress', in Chamberlain and Gilman (eds.) *Degeneration*, 49–71 (pp. 59–60).

15 Charles Mercier, 'Vice, Crime and Insanity', in T. C. Allbutt and H. D. Rolleston (eds.) *A System of Medicine* (9 vols., 1898; 2nd edn London: Macmillan, 1910), VIII 842–74 (p. 851).

16 Nye, *Crime, Madness and Politics*, pp. 47–8.

17 Renato Poggioli, *The Theory of the Avant-Garde* (Cambridge, Mass.: Harvard University Press, 1968), p. 166.

18 Frank Kermode, *Continuities* (New York: Random House, 1968), p. 63.

19 Jones, *Social Darwinism and English Thought*, pp. 4–6.

20 Nancy Stepan, 'Biology and Degeneration: Races and Proper Places', in Chamberlain and Gilman (eds.) *Degeneration*, 97–120 (p. 98).

21 Cited by Loren C. Eiseley, *Darwin's Century: Evolution and the Men Who Discovered It* (London: Victor Gollanz, 1959), p. 39.

22 Cited by Gay Weber, 'Industrialisation and Degeneration: The Contribution of Ethnological Theory to Early Nineteenth-Century Social Medicine', *Bulletin of Society for the Social History of Medicine*, 19 (December 1976): 7–9.

23 Cited by Stepan, 'Biology and Degeneration', p. 98.

24 Cited by James Walvin, 'Symbols of Moral Superiority: Slavery, Sport and the Changing World Order', in J. A. Mangan and J. Walvin (eds.) *Manliness and Morality: Middle-Class Masculinity in Britain and America 1800–1940* (Manchester University Press, 1987): 242–60.

25 T. H. Huxley, 'Emancipation – Black and White' (1865), in *Collected Essays* (9 vols. London: Macmillan, 1893–1908), III, 67.

26 See Arthur de Gobineau, *Essay on the Inequality of the Human Races*

(1853–5), in Michael D. Biddiss (ed.) *Gobineau: Selected Political Writings* (London: Cape, 1970).

27 Reginald Horsman, 'The Origins of Anglo-Saxonism in Great Britain before 1850', *Journal of the History of Ideas* 37 (July-September 1976): 387–410 (pp. 405–6).

28 Cited by Walvin, 'Symbols of Moral Superiority', p. 252.

29 Stepan, 'Biology and Degeneration', p. 98.

30 Jack London, *The People of the Abyss* (London: Thomas Nelson & Sons, 1903), p. 363, p. 325.

31 Gareth Stedman Jones, *Outcast London* (1971; revised edn Harmondsworth: Penguin, 1984), p. 336.

32 Jean Izoulet, *La Cité moderne et la métaphysique de la sociologie* (2 vols. Paris: Felix Alcan, 1894), I, 64–6.

33 See D. L. LeMahieu, *A Culture for Democracy: Mass Communication and the Cultivated Mind in Britain between the Wars* (Oxford: Clarendon Press, 1988), p. 108.

34 Daniel Pick, *Faces of Degeneration: A European Disorder c. 1848 – c.1918* (Cambridge University Press, 1989), p. 92, and generally, pp. 88–92.

35 See D. A. Miller '*Cage aux folles*: Sensation and Gender in Wilkie Collins's *The Woman in White*', in Catherine Gallagher and Thomas Laqueur (eds.) *The Making of the Modern Body: Sexuality and Society in the Nineteenth Century* (Berkeley: University of California Press, 1987), 107–36 (p. 135); see also Jeffrey Weeks, *Sex, Politics and Society* (Harlow: Longman, 1981), p. 104, p. 144, pp. 140–1.

36 Cyril Connolly, *Enemies of Promise* (1938; repr. Harmondsworth: Penguin, 1961), p. 182. How the figure of Wilde enabled the 'unspeakable' to be spoken of, down to the 1940s, is described by Ed Cohen, *Talk on the Wilde Side: Toward a Genealogy of a Discourse on Male Sexualities* (New York: Routledge, 1993), pp. 100–1.

37 See Joan Busfield, *Managing Madness: Changing Ideas and Practice* (London: Hutchinson, 1986), pp. 256–87; David Ingleby, 'Mental Health and Social Order', in Stanley Cohen and Andrew Scull (eds.) *Social Control and the State* (Oxford: Robertson, 1983), 141–90 (pp. 160–1) and Andrew Scull, *The Most Solitary of Afflictions: Madness and Society in Britain 1700–1900* (New Haven and London: Yale University Press, 1993), pp. 365–70.

38 See Steve Humphries, *A Secret World of Sex: Forbidden Fruit : The British Experience 1900–1950* (1988; repr. London: Sigwick and Jackson, 1991), pp. 63–5.

39 See Robert L. Dugdale, *The Jukes: A Study in Crime, Pauperism, Disease and Heredity* (1877; 4th edn 1910). A measure of the anxiety attached to familial degeneracy in France was the invention of the 'neuropathic family' by French psychiatrist Charles Féré. This was 1884 – the 'heyday of hereditarianism in French psychiatry' (Ian R. Dowbiggin, *Inheriting Madness: Professionalization and Psychiatric Knowledge in Nine-*

teenth-Century France (Berkeley: University of California Press, 1991), pp. 121–2).

40 See Robert Procter, *Racial Hygiene: Medicine under the Nazis* (Cambridge, Mass.: Harvard University Press, 1988), p. 99.

41 Discussions appeared in, among other studies, Havelock Ellis, *The Criminal* (1890), J. B. Haycraft, *Darwinism and Race Progress* (1895), Havelock Ellis, *The Task of Social Hygiene* (1912), Clarence Darrow, *Crime: Its Cause and Treatment* (1922); see Germaine Greer, *Sex and Destiny: The Politics of Human Fertility* (London: Picador, 1984), p. 262.

42 See Proctor, *Racial Hygiene*, pp. 97–9; see also Eric T. Carlson, 'Medicine and Degeneration', in Chamberlain and Gilman (eds.), *Degeneration*, 121–44 (pp. 132–3).

43 Henry Maudsley, *The Pathology of Mind: A Study of its Distempers, Deformities and Disorders* (London: Macmillan, 1895), p. 536.

44 *Otello*, Act Two Scene Two; see *Otello* (Milan: G. Ricordi & C. , 1887). My thanks to Stella Swain for her assistance with the translation.

45 W. H. Mallock, *Is Life Worth Living?* (2nd edn London: Chatto and Windus, 1879), xxii.

46 Francis Galton, *Natural Inheritance* (1889), p. 6, cited by Reba N. Sofer, 'The Revolution in English Social Thought 1880–1914', *American Historical Review* 75 (1970): 1555.

47 Francis Galton, *Inquiries into the Human Faculty and its Development* (London: Macmillan, 1883), p. 304. See on this point and Galton's 'legacy' Richard A. Soloway, *Demography and Degeneration: Eugenics and the Declining Birth-Rate in Twentieth-Century Britain* (Chapel Hill and London: University of North Carolina Press, 1990), p. 31, pp. 18–27.

48 Havelock Ellis, *The New Spirit* (1890; 4th edn Constable and Co., 1926) p. 8, p. 7.

49 *Ibid.*, pp. 5–6.

50 See Tom Gibbons, *Rooms in the Darwin Hotel* (Nedlands: University of Western Australia Press, 1973), pp. 36–7.

51 See Hubert Bland, 'Concerning Heredity', in *With the Eyes of a Man* (London: T. Werner Laurie, 1905), pp. 177–92. The socialist and journalist Robert Blatchford is another scientific populariser: see his 'The Ancestral Struggle within Us', or 'How Heredity and Environment Work', in *Not Guilty: A Defence of the Bottom Dog* (London: Clarion Press, 1906).

52 Henry Maudsley, 'Materialism and its Lessons', *Fortnightly Review* n. s. 26 (1879), 244–60 (pp. 258–9), see G. C. Lindop, 'A Study of the Influence of Contemporary Psychological Theory on the Fiction of Thomas Hardy, George Gissing and the Early Novels of George Moore', B. Litt. dissertation, University of Oxford, 1974, p. 15.

53 Maudsley, *The Pathology of Mind*, p. 43. See on this point Elaine Showalter, *The Female Malady* (London: Virago, 1987), p. 114.

54 See Lindop, 'A Study of the Influence of Contemporary Psychological Theory', p. 15.

55 Francis Galton, 'Eugenics, its Definitions, Scope and Aims' read before the Sociological Society, 16 May 1904, in *Sociological Papers*, Vol. 1 (1904), p. 45. See, on this point, Soloway, *Demography and Degeneration*, p. 23.

56 Charles Darwin to Hooker, 25 January 1862, cited by Jones, *Social Darwinism and English Thought*, p. 36. On opposition to primogeniture and inherited privilege, in a eugenic context, see Soloway, *Demography and Degeneration*, p. 74. The way in which degeneration theory was used by psychiatrists in France to bolster their prestige and maintain their professional hegemony is described in Dowbiggin, *Inheriting Madness*, p. 143. p. 170, p. 211.

57 G. R. Searle, 'Eugenics and Social Class', in Charles Webster (ed.) *Biology, Medicine and Society 1840–1940* (Cambridge University Press, 1981), 217–42 (p. 218).

58 Galton, *Inquiries*, p. 23.

59 See Arnold White, *Efficiency and Empire* (London: Methuen, 1901), pp. 296–7; Pick, *Faces of Degeneration*, p. 27.

60 Edward Carpenter, 'The Enchanted Thicket: An Appeal to the "Well To Do" ', in *England's Ideal* (London: George Allen & Unwin, 1887), 166–77 (p. 167).

61 Henry James to Charles Eliot Norton, cited by Leon Edel, *Henry James; A Life* (2 vols. Harmondsworth: Penguin, 1977), $I, 779–80.

62 Cited by Jones, *Social Darwinism*, p. 99.

63 Galton, *Inquiries*, p. 318.

64 G. H. Lewes, 26 April 1847; cited by T. H. Pickett, 'George Henry Lewes's Letters to K. A. Varnhagen Von Ense', *Modern Language Review* 80 (3) (July 1985): 529.

65 See Raymond Williams, *The Country and the City* (1973; repr. London: Hogarth Press, 1985).

66 John Donne, 'First Anniversarie', line 209, in Marius Bewley (ed.) *The Selected Poetry of Donne* (New York: New American Library, 1966), p. 211.

67 Anon., 'Made in Germany', *New Review* 81 (February 1896): 113–27 (p. 127). See Peter Mathias, *The First Industrial Nation: An Economic History of Britain 1700–1914* (London: Methuen, 1969), p. 416.

68 See Raymond F. Betts, 'The Allusion to Rome in British Imperialist Thought of the Late Nineteenth and Early Twentieth Centuries', *Victorian Studies* 15 (2) (December 1971): 149–59; Patrick Brantlinger, *Bread and Circuses: Theories of Mass Culture and Decay* (Ithaca: Cornell University Press, 1983), pp. 140–4.

69 Anon., 'Sex-Mania', *Reynolds Newspaper*, 21 April 1895: 1.

70 W. R. Inge, 'Some Moral Aspects of Eugenics', *Eugenics Review* 1 (1909): 30, cited by Anna Davin, 'Imperialism and Motherhood', *History Workshop Journal* 5 (Spring 1978): 20.

71 H. B. Gray, *The Public Schools and the Empire* (London: Williams & Norgate, 1913), pp. 11–12; see Michael Howard, 'Empire, Race

and War in pre-1914 Britain', in H. Lloyd-Jones *et al.* (eds.) *History and Imagination* (London: Duckworth, 1981), 340–53 (p. 345).

72 'The Remoralization of Public Life', *Times* (21 October 1974): 3. The controversy ignited by this speech is discussed by Soloway, *Demography and Degeneration*, pp. 359–60.

2 BIOLOGICAL POETICS

1 Edwin Ray Lankester, Professor of Zoology, University College London 1874–91; Linacre Professor of Comparative Anatomy, Oxford 1891–8; Director of Natural History, British Museum 1898–1907.

2 E. R. Lankester, *Degeneration: A Chapter in Darwinism* (London: Macmillan, 1880), p. 33. The book was based on a paper to the British Association, Sheffield, August 1879; see R. K. R. Thornton, *The Decadent Dilemma* (London: Edward Arnold, 1983), pp. 10–11; Tom Gibbons, *Rooms in the Darwin Hotel* (Nedlands: University of Western Australia Press, 1973), p. 34.

3 Lankester, *Degeneration*, p. 33.

4 *Ibid.*, p. 33.

5 *Ibid.*, p. 60.

6 H. G. Wells, 'Zoological Retrogression', *Gentleman's Magazine* 271 (September 1891): 246–53 (p. 246). See my 'Fitness and the Fin de Siècle' in John Stokes (ed.) *Fin de Siècle/Fin du Globe: Fears and Fantasies of the Late Nineteenth Century* (London: Macmillan, 1992), 37–51 (p. 40). Lankester and Wells shared a common admiration for T. H. Huxley, and became good friends and allies. Lankester supported Wells when he was ostracised after the publication of *Ann Veronica* (1909). Wells included an essay of Lankester's, 'The Making of New Knowledge', in his volume of essays *Socialism and the Great State* (1912), and consulted him about *The Outline of History* in 1918; see Lewis S. Feuer, 'The Letters of Edwin Ray Lankester to Karl Marx: The Last Stage in Marx's Intellectual Revolution', *Journal of the History of Ideas* 40 (4) (Oct.-Dec. 1979): 640–1.

7 Wells, 'Zoological Retrogression', p. 252.

8 *Ibid.*, p. 253.

9 H. G. Wells, 'On Extinction', *Chambers's Journal* 10 (30 September 1893): 623–4 (p. 624).

10 *Ibid.*, p. 624.

11 *Ibid.*, p. 624.

12 H. G. Wells, 'The Rate of Change in Species', *Saturday Review* 78 (15 December 1894): 655–6, repr. in R. M. Philmus and D. Y. Hughes (eds.) *H.G.Wells: Early Writings in Science and Science Fiction* (Berkeley: University of California Press, 1975), pp. 128–31 (p. 131).

13 H. G. Wells, 'The Extinction of Man', *Pall Mall Gazette* (23 September 1894); repr. in H. G. Wells, *Certain Personal Matters: A Collection of*

Material, Mainly Autobiographical (London: Lawrence and Bullen, 1898), pp. 172–9 (p. 172).

14 'Darwin' in *Encylopaedia of the Social Sciences* (1931), cited by Robert M. Young, 'Evolutionary Biology and Ideology: Then and Now', *Science Studies* 1 (1971): 203.

15 Gillian Beer, *Darwin's Plots* (1983; repr. London: Ark, 1985), p. 51.

16 Darwin, *The Origin of Species by Means of Natural Selection or the Preservation of Favoured Races in the Struggle for Life* (1859; Harmondsworth: Penguin, 1968), p. 459.

17 Robert M. Young 'Malthus and the Evolutionists: The Common Context of Biological and Social Theory', *Past and Present* 43 (May 1969): 130.

18 Frederich Engels to P. Y. Lavrou, 12–17 November 1875, in S. W. Ryazanskaya (ed.) *Marx Engels Selected Correspondence* (1955; 3rd rev. edn Moscow: Lawrence & Wishart, 1975), p. 284.

19 Darwin, *The Origin of Species*, p. 129.

20 Robert Bannister, *Social Darwinism: Science and Myth in Anglo-American Social Thought* (Philadelphia: Temple University Press, 1980), p. 4; see also Raymond Williams, 'Social Darwinism' in *Problems of Materialism and Culture* (London: Verso, 1980), 86–107.

21 Francis Galton, *Inquiries into the Human Faculty and its Development* (London: Macmillan, 1883), p. 318.

22 Olive Pratt Rayner [Grant Allen], *The Type-Writer Girl* (London: C. Arthur Pearson, 1897), p. 28; see Jane Lewis, *Women in England 1870–1950* (Brighton: Harvester-Wheatsheaf, 1980), p. 82.

23 Somerset Maugham, *A Writer's Notebook* (1949; repr. Harmondsworth: Penguin, 1967), p. 66.

24 Karl Pearson, *National Life from the Standpoint of Science*, cited by Bernard Semmel, *Imperialism and Social Reform: English Social-Imperial Thought 1895–1914* (London: Allen and Unwin, 1960), p. 41.

25 Benjamin Kidd, *Social Evolution* (2nd edn, 1896), p. 39, cited by Michael Howard, 'Empire, Race and War in Pre-1914 Britain', in H. Lloyd-Jones *et al.* (eds.), *History and Imagination* (London: Duckworth, 1981), 340–54 (p. 347).

26 W. E. Henley, 'Song of the Sword' in *London Voluntaries* (1892; 3rd edn London: David Nutt, 1912), p. 34; see Jerome Buckley, *W. E. Henley: A Study in The Counter-Decadence of the Nineties* (Princeton University Press, 1945), p. 138.

27 Henley, 'Song of the Sword', p. 34.

28 William Booth, *In Darkest England and the Way Out* (London: Salvation Army, 1890), p. 15; see Elaine Showalter, *Sexual Anarchy: Gender and Culture at the Fin de Siècle* (London: Bloomsbury, 1991), pp. 5–6.

29 Anthony Wohl, *Endangered Lives: Public Health in Victorian Britain* (London: J. M. Dent, 1983), pp. 212–13.

30 Edward Carpenter, *Towards Democracy* (Complete Edition in Four

Parts, 1905; London: George Allen and Unwin, 5th edn, 1931), pp. 266–7, p. 462, p. 244.

31 H. G. Wells, 'The Time Machine', in *H.G.Wells Selected Short Stories* (Harmondsworth: Penguin, 1958), 7–83 (p. 51, p. 43, p. 45).

32 Carpenter, *Towards Democracy*, pp. 266–7.

33 George Gissing, *The Nether World* (1889; repr. Brighton: Harvester Press, 1974), p. 9.

34 Pierre Coustillas (ed.) *London and the Life of Literature: The Diary of George Gissing* (Hassocks: Harvester Press, 1978), p. 24 (entries for 15, 18 and 19 March 1888).

35 Thomas Hardy, *The Woodlanders* (1888; repr. London: Macmillan, 1975), p. 83. Subsequent quotations are included in the text.

36 See David Lodge, Introduction to *The Woodlanders* (London: Macmillan, 1975), p. 22.

37 See Thomas Hardy, 'The "1867" Notebook', in Lennart Bjork (ed.) *The Literary Notebooks of Thomas Hardy* (2 vols. London: Macmillan, 1985), II, 474–5 (entries 193–201).

38 E. M. Forster, *Howards End* (Harmondsworth: Penguin, 1975), p. 122.

39 'National Muscle' (Science Jottings), *Illustrated London News* (22 June 1889), p. 798.

40 Arnold White, *Efficiency and Empire* (London: Methuen, 1901), p. 96.

41 Francis Galton, *Inquiries into the Human Faculty*, pp. 23–4.

42 See Francis Galton, 'The Relative Supplies from Town and Country Families to the Population of Future Generations', *Journal of the Statistical Society*, 36 (1873): 19–26, and reiterated in *Inquiries*, p. 20. See Richard Soloway's discussion of this evidence in *Demography and Degeneration: Eugenics and the Declining Birthrate in Twentieth-Century Britain* (Chapel Hill and London: University of North Carolina Press, 1990), pp. 39–40.

43 Francis Galton, 'Our National Physique: Prospects for the British Race: Are We Degenerating?', *Daily Chronicle*, 29 July 1903, cited by D. W. Forrest, *Francis Galton: The Life and Work of a Victorian Genius* (London: Paul Elek, 1974), p. 255.

44 James Crichton-Browne, Foreword to James Cantlie, *Physical Efficiency: A Review of the Deleterious Effects of Town Life upon the Population of Britain* (1906), xx; see also Soloway, *Demography and Degeneration*, p. 43.

45 Cantlie, *Physical Efficiency* p. 62.

46 James Cantlie, *Degeneration amongst Londoners* (London: Field and Tuer, 1885), pp. 32–3.

47 J. P. Williams-Freeman, *On the Effect of Town Life on the General Health, with Especial Reference to London* (London: W. H. Allen, 1890), p. 4. First published in *The Sanitary Record* n. s. 11 (August-November 1889), 49–52; 101–4; 215–17.

48 *Ibid.*, p. 5.

49 E. M. Forster, *Howards End*, p. 314.
50 Williams-Freeman, *On the Effect of Town Life*, p. 25.
51 *Ibid.*, pp. 34–5.
52 *Ibid.*, p. 35.
53 Gareth Stedman Jones, *Outcast London* (1971, rev. edn Harmondsworth: Penguin, 1984), p. 150.
54 David Feldman, 'The Importance of Being English: Jewish Immigration and the Decay of Liberal England', in David Feldman and Gareth Stedman Jones (eds.) *Metropolis; London Histories and Representations since 1800* (London: Routledge & Kegan Paul, 1989), 56–84 (p. 59).
55 Earl of Dunraven (Windham T. W. Quin), 'The Invasion of Destitute Aliens', *Nineteenth Century*, 31 (June 1892): 985–1000, (p. 988), see Bernard Gainier, *The Alien Invasion: A Study of Jewish Immigration* (London: Heinemann, 1972), p. 111.
56 See Thomas Boyle, *Black Swine in the Sewers of Hampstead* (London: Hodder and Stoughton, 1990), p. 204; Geoffrey Pearson, *The Deviant Imagination* (London: Macmillan, 1977), p. 162.
57 W. H. Wilkins, *The Alien Invasion* (in Social Questions of Today (1891 etc.)) (London: Methuen, 1892), pp. 57–8, cited by Gainier, *The Alien Invasion*, p. 127.
58 E. Phillips Oppenheim, *The Secret* (London: Ward Lock & Co., 1907), p. 311; see Donald A. T. Stafford, 'The Birth of the British Spy Novel', *Victorian Studies* 24 (1981): 498–9. As Daniel Pick notes, novels by Le Queux, Max Pemberton and others, which played on fears of invasion and racial miscegenation, turned on a 'shared problematic' of a 'ceaselessly threatened but essential island of Englishness' (Pick, *War Machine: The Rationalisation of Slaughter in the Modern Age* (New Haven and London: Yale University Press, 1993), p. 320.
59 H. Rider Haggard, *Rural England* (1902), cited by Merryn Williams, *Thomas Hardy and Rural England* (London: Macmillan, 1972), p. 27.
60 C. W. Sorensen, 'Back to the Land ("Why Don't We Feed Ourselves?")', *Contemporary Review* 81 (January 1902): 68.
61 W. T. Stead, *Royal Commission on the War in South Africa compiled from the Blue Books for the Information of the Public* (1903), para. 5476.
62 J. B. Haycraft, *Darwinism and Race Progress* (London: Swan Sonnenschein & Co.,1895), p. 152.

3 DEGENERATE SPACES: THE URBAN CRISIS OF THE 1880S AND
THE MAYOR OF CASTERBRIDGE

1 See A. Susan Williams, *The Rich Man and the Diseased Poor* (London: Macmillan, 1987), ch. 3.
2 *Ibid.*, p. 95.

3 *Ibid.*, p. 94.
4 [Andrew Mearns], *The Bitter Cry of Outcast London* (London: James Clarke & Co., 1883), pp. 5–6.
5 George Gissing, *The Unclassed* (rev. edn London: Lawrence and Bullen, 1895, repr. Brighton: Harvester Press, 1976), p. 278.
6 Samuel Smith, 'The Industrial Training of Destitute Children', *Contemporary Review* 47, (January 1885): 111, cited by G. Stedman Jones, *Outcast London* (1971, rev. edn Harmondsworth: Penguin, 1984), p. 309.
7 Anthony Wohl, *Endangered Lives: Public Health in Victorian Britain* (London: J. M. Dent, 1983), p. 91.
8 Peter Stallybrass and Allon White, *The Poetics and Politics of Transgression* (London: Methuen, 1986), p. 145. Judith Walkowitz also draws on this work in her discussion of the representation of the topography of the Victorian city, see *City of Dreadful Delight; Narratives of Sexual Danger in Late Victorian London* (London: Bloomsbury, 1992), pp. 19–20.
9 See also Geoffrey Pearson on the importance of 'the image of the sewer in nineteenth-century thinking', Pearson, *The Deviant Imagination* (1975; repr. London: Macmillan, 1977), p. 161.
10 Elizabeth Wilson, *The Sphinx in the City: Urban Life, the Control of Disorder and Women* (London: Virago, 1991), p. 37, and generally, pp. 34–9.
11 See Williams, *The Rich Man and The Diseased Poor*, pp. 9–27, 92–3.
12 Nikolas Rose, *The Psychological Complex* (London: Routledge, 1985), p. 51.
13 *Ibid.*, p. 51.
14 Nikolas Rose, 'The Psychological Complex: Mental Measurement and Social Administration', *Ideology and Consciousness* no. 5 (Spring 1979): 5–68 (p. 25). I am indebted to this innovative article.
15 Charles Booth, *Life and Labour of the People in London* (17 vols. London: Macmillan, 1902–3) Ist series I, 157.
16 *Ibid.*, I, 176.
17 *Ibid.*, I, 176.
18 *Ibid.*, I, 38.
19 *Ibid.*, I, 38.
20 *Ibid.*, I, 38. This is an example of what Judith Walkowitz identifies as Booth's infusion of 'drama and moral significance' into an ostensibly dispassionate statistical study; see Walkowitz, *City of Dreadful Delight*, p. 34, and generally on Booth, pp. 30–38.
21 Booth, *Life and Labour* Vol. 3. *Poverty* ch.2 (Influx of Population (E. London)) by H. Llewellyn Smith, p. 82.
22 *Ibid.*, p. 110. See also on this point Walkowitz, *City of Dreadful Delight*, p. 35.

23 George Gissing, *The Unclassed* (rev. edn 1895; repr. Brighton: Harvester Press, 1976), p. 66.

24 Gissing, *The Unclassed* (3 vols. London: Chapman and Hall, 1884), $i, 183.

25 Raymond Williams, *The Country and the City* (1973; repr. London: The Hogarth Press, 1985), p. 221; see generally, ch. 19 'Cities of Darkness and of Light'.

26 Anthony Wohl, *The Eternal Slum*, (London: Edward Arnold, 1977), p. 203.

27 *Ibid.*, p. 206.

28 T. H. S. Escott, 'The Future of the Radical Party', *Fortnightly Review*, n. s. 34 (July 1883): 1–11 (p. 1).

29 Thomas Hardy to John Morley, 25 June 1883, in R. L. Purdy and M. Millgate (eds.) *Collected Letters of Thomas Hardy* (Oxford: Clarendon Press, 1978), I, 118–19.

30 See Michael Millgate, *Thomas Hardy: A Biography* (Oxford University Press, 1982), p. 236.

31 Thomas Hardy, 'The Dorsetshire Labourer', in *Longman's Magazine*, 2 (July 1883): 252–69; repr. in Harold Orel (ed.) *Thomas Hardy's Personal Writings* (London: Macmillan, 1967), 169–89 (pp. 181–2).

32 *Ibid.*, p. 171.

33 *Ibid.*, p. 181.

34 See Roger Bromley's important reading of the novel 'The Boundaries of Hegemony: Thomas Hardy and *The Mayor of Casterbridge*', in Francis Barker *et al.* (eds.) *Literature, Society and the Sociology of Literature* (Colchester: University of Essex, 1977), pp. 30–40 (especially pp. 34–5).

35 Thomas Hardy, *The Mayor of Casterbridge* (3 vols. 1886; repr. London: Macmillan, 1974), p. 248. Subsequent references are incorporated in the text.

36 See John Goode, *Thomas Hardy: The Offensive Truth* (Oxford: Basil Blackwell, 1988), p. 91.

37 There is an echo here of John Morley's essay 'Of the Possible Utility of Error', in *On Compromise* (1886), where he considers the view that 'the history of mankind is a huge *pis aller* just as our present society is; a prodigious wasteful experiment'. *On Compromise* (Thinker's Library: London: Watts and Co., 1933), p. 46.

38 Henry Mayhew, *London, Labour and the London Poor*, III, 429, cited by Williams, *The Rich Man and The Diseased Poor*, p. 92.

39 See Ian Gregor's note to his edition of Hardy, *The Mayor of Casterbridge* (London: Macmillan, 1974), p. 368.

40 Erving Goffman, *Asylums* (1961; repr. Harmondsworth: Penguin, 1968), p. 209.

41 Raphael Samuel, 'Comers and Goers', in H. J. Dyos and Michael Wolff (eds.) *The Victorian City; Images and Realities* (2 vols. London: Routledge, 1973), I, 123–60 (p. 126).

42 *Ibid.*, p. 126.
43 See Renton Nicholas, *Autobiography* (1860), pp. 262–3, cited by Gareth Stedman Jones, 'Working Class Culture and Working Class Politics in London 1870–1900: Notes on the Remaking of a Working Class', *Journal of Social History*, 7 (4) (1974): 470; see also J. J. Tobias, *Crime and Industrial Society in the Nineteenth Century* (London: Batsford, 1967), pp. 24–7, pp. 131–5, pp. 176–7.
44 Samuel, 'Comers and Goers', p. 126.
45 See Tobias, *Crime and Industrial Society*, p. 232. The multitude of seasonal fairs were also frequented by the migratory and the deviant – from Ben Jonson's *Bartholomew Fair* to Hardy's seasonal fair at Weyhill and to Howard Brenton's *Epsom Downs*.
46 See H. J. Dyos and D. A. Reeder, 'Slums and Suburbs', in *The Victorian City*, I, 362–3.
47 Booth, *Life and Labour*, I, 174.
48 *Ibid.*, I, 174.
49 Lucas Malet [Mary Kingsley], *Colonel Enderby's Wife* (3 vols. London: Kegan Paul Trench, 1885), II, 299–300. The symbolic passage of the female philanthropist through the slum appears in an earlier novel, but without degenerationist overtones. The heroine of Rhoda Broughton's *Not Wisely, but Too Well* (3 vols., 1867; repr. London: Cassell, 1967), Kate Chester, who nurses a 'mortal fear of men of the lower orders' (178), carries 'a philanthropic basket on her arm' (162), and enters 'a narrow bricked passage ... down into the region of back slums and alleys, where the sun has far too good taste to show its grand kingly face' (104).
50 Frederich Engels, *The Condition of the Working-Class in England* (1844; repr. Oxford: Basil Blackwell, 1958), cited by Stephen Marcus, 'Reading the Illegible', in *The Victorian City*, I, 257–76 (p. 267).
51 Wohl, *Endangered Lives*, p. 238.
52 George Gissing, *Demos* (3 vols. 1886; repr. Brighton: Harvester Press, 1972), p. 25.
53 *Ibid.*, p. 26.
54 George Gissing, *A Life's Morning* (3 vols. 1888; repr. London: Home and Van Thal, 1947), p. 85.
55 George Sanger, *Seventy Years a Showman* (1910; repr. London: J. M. Dent, 1927), p. 76.
56 Victor Hugo, *Les Misérables* (1862; repr.. Harmondsworth: Penguin, 1980), II, 371, cited by p. Stallybrass and A. White, *The Politics and Poetics of Transgression*, pp. 141–2.
57 *Ibid.*, p. 141.
58 Thomas Hardy, *Facts from Newspapers, Histories, Biographies and other chronicles – mainly local* (abbreviated to 'Facts Notebook'), p. 117; see William Greenslade, 'Thomas Hardy's "Facts" Notebook: A Further Source for *The Mayor of Casterbridge*', *Thomas Hardy Journal* 2 (January 1986): 33–5.

59 Merryn Williams, *Thomas Hardy and Rural England* (London: Macmillan, 1972), p. 201, and generally, pp. 201–5.

60 Laurence Lerner, *Thomas Hardy's 'The Mayor of Casterbridge': Tragedy or Social Vision?* (London: Chatto and Windus, 1975), pp. 31–2.

61 Douglas Gray has also noticed the element of satiric performance in this act of charivari in 'Rough Music: Some Early Invectives and Flytings', in Claude Rawson (ed.) *English Satire and the Satiric Tradition* (Oxford: Basil Blackwell, 1984): 21–43 (pp. 24–5)

62 See E.P.Thompson, ' "Rough Music": Le Charivari anglais', *Annales*, 27 (2) (Mars-Avril 1972): 285–312. An extended version of this article appears in *Customs in Common* (London: Merlin Press, 1991), pp. 467–538.

63 Designed to determine the effective distribution of charity, it was a distinction employed by individuals like Octavia Hill and the Charity Organisation Society – satirised by Gissing in the figure of the philanthropist, Miss Lant, in *The Nether World* (1889).

64 See also Nooral Hasan, *Thomas Hardy; The Sociological Imagination* (London: Macmillan, 1982), pp. 70–1.

4 REVERSIONARY TACTICS

1 Joseph Conrad, *Heart of Darkness* (1899; repr. Harmondsworth: Penguin, 1983) p. 69.

2 D. H. Lawrence, 'The Novel and the Feelings' (1923), in Edward E. McDonald (ed.) *Phoenix: The Posthumous Papers of D. H. Lawrence* (London: Heinemann, 1936), 755–60 (pp. 757–8). I owe this reference to Anthony Kearney.

3 William Morris, *Letters* p. 236, cited by E. P. Thompson, *William Morris: Romantic to Revolutionary* (1955; rev. edn London: Merlin Press, 1977), p. 805.

4 Thompson, *William Morris*, p. 805.

5 Edward Carpenter, *Civilisation: Its Cause and Cure* (London: Swan Sonnenschein, 1889), p. 29.

6 Carl Gustav Jung, 'Archaic Man' (1931) in Herbert Read *et al.* (eds.) *The Collected Works of C. G. Jung* (20 vols. London: Routledge & Kegan Paul, 1953–79) x, 51.

7 Daniel Hack Tuke, 'Case of Moral Insanity or Congenital Moral Defect with Commentary', *Journal of Mental Science* 31 (1885–6): 365, cited by Havelock Ellis, *The Criminal* (3rd edn London: Walter Scott, 1901), pp. 253–4.

8 Charles Darwin, *The Variation of Animals and Plants under Domestication* (2 vols. London: John Murray, 1868), ii, 28.

9 Charles Darwin, *The Descent of Man and Selection in Relation to Sex* (2 vols. 1871; repr. 1 vol. London: John Murray, 1901), p. 54.

10 *Ibid.*, p. 64.

11 *Ibid.*, p. 63.
12 Arthur Conan Doyle, 'The Adventure of the Empty House' (1903), in *Sherlock Holmes: The Complete Short Stories* (London: John Murray, 1961), pp. 580–1.
13 See Peter L. Bowler, *Evolution: the History of an Idea* (Berkeley: University of California Press, 1984), p. 190.
14 Henry Maudsley, *Body and Mind, An Inquiry into their Connection and Mutual Influence, specially in reference to Mental Disorders* (2nd edn London: Macmillan, 1873), p. 52. See Vieda Skultans (ed.) *English Madness: Ideas on Insanity 1580–1890* (London: Routledge, 1975), pp. 248–9.
15 Havelock Ellis, *The Criminal* (1890), cited by Stephen Jay Gould, *Ontogeny and Phylogeny* (Cambridge, Mass.: Harvard University Press, 1977), p. 124.
16 Maudsley, *Body and Mind*, p. 135.
17 Havelock Ellis, *Man and Woman* (1894; 4th edn London: Walter Scott, 1904), p. 63, cited in Gould, *Ontogeny and Phylogeny*, p. 117.
18 Gillian Beer, *Darwin's Plots* (1983; repr. London: Ark, 1985), p. 62.
19 Gillian Beer, *Arguing with the Past: Essays in Narrative from Woolf to Sidney* (London: Routledge, 1989), p. 163.
20 Sander L. Gilman, *Difference and Pathology* (Ithaca and London: Cornell University Press, 1985), p. 20.
21 See Karl Miller, *Doubles: Studies in Literary History* (Oxford University Press, 1985), particularly chs. 11 and 12.
22 Peter Brooker and Peter Widdowson, 'A Literature for England', in Robert Colls and Philip Dodd (eds.) *Englishness: Politics and Culture 1880–1920* (London: Croom Helm, 1986), p. 142.
23 Henry Maudsley, *The Pathology of Mind* (London: Macmillan, 1895), p. 48.
24 Terence Cave, *Recognitions: A Study in Poetics* (Oxford: Clarendon Press, 1988), p. 2.
25 *Ibid.*, p. 1.
26 Brooker and Widdowson, 'A Literature for England', p. 142.
27 Not a cave dweller, as Brooker and Widdowson have it, *ibid.* p. 142.
28 Gould, *Ontogeny and Phylogeny*, p. 121.
29 William Hale White, *Mark Rutherford's Deliverance* (1885), cited by Patrick Brantlinger, *Rule of Darkness: British Literature and Imperialism 1830–1914* (Ithaca, NY: Cornell University Press, 1988), p. 230.
30 *Pall Mall Gazette*, 8 September 1888, see Deborah Cameron and Elizabeth Frazer, *The Lust to Kill* (Oxford: Polity Press, 1987), p. 126.
31 Rod Edmonds, 'The Conservatism of Gissing's Early Novels', *Literature and History* 7 (Spring 1978), 48–69 (p. 47).
32 George Gissing, *The Nether World* (1889; repr. Brighton: Harvester Press, 1974), p. 8. Subsequent references are included in the text.
33 Darwin, *The Variation of Animals and Plants*, II, 51.

34 Beer, *Darwin's Plots*, p. 139.
35 Gill Davies, 'Foreign Bodies: Images of the London Working-Class at the End of the Nineteenth Century', *Literature and History* 14 (1) (Spring 1988): 76.
36 George Gissing, *The Unclassed* (3 vols. London: Chapman and Hall, 1884), I, 183.
37 Elaine Showalter, *The Female Malady: Women, Madness and English Culture, 1830–1980* (London: Virago, 1985), p. 105.
38 Gissing, *The Unclassed* (1884 edn) I, 180.
39 See Peter Keating, *The Haunted Study: A Social History of the English Novel 1875–1914* (London: Secker and Warburg), p. 319.
40 Adrian Poole, *Gissing in Context* (London: Macmillan Press, 1975), p. 70.
41 Friedrich Engels, Preface to Karl Marx, *Capital* (1886; rpt. Harmondsworth: Penguin, 1976), p. 113. (Engels is writing on 5 November.)
42 Walter Bagehot, *Physics and Politics* (London: H. S. King, 1872), p. 154.
43 W. H. Mallock, *The Old Order Changes* (3 vols. London: R. Bentley & Son, 1886), I, 112–13, cited by John Lucas, 'Conservatism and Revolution in the 1880s', in John Lucas (ed.), *Literature and Politics in the Nineteenth Century* (London: Methuen, 1971), 173–219 (p. 203).
44 Edmonds, 'The Conservatism of Gissing's Early Novels', pp. 56–7.
45 George Gissing, *Demos, A Story of British Socialism* (1886; repr. Brighton: Harvester Press, 1972), p. 38. Subsequent references are included in the text.
46 Mary Cowling, *The Artist as Anthropologist: The Representation of Type and Character in Victorian Art* (Cambridge University Press, 1989), p. 78.
47 Edmonds, 'The Conservatism of Gissing's Early Novels', p. 57.
48 Lucas, 'Conservatism and Revolution in the 1880s', p. 199.
49 Robert Louis Stevenson, *The Strange Case of Dr Jekyll and Mr Hyde* (Harmondsworth: Penguin, 1979), p. 82.
50 *Ibid.*, p. 80.
51 *Ibid.*, p. 61.
52 David Punter, *The Literature of Terror* (London: Longman, 1980), pp. 240–5.
53 Cameron and Frazer, *The Lust to Kill*, p. 126, and generally, pp. 125–8. The play, by T. Russell Sullivan, starred the actor Richard Mansfield whose startling physical and mental transformations convinced some members of the audience that he was the true 'Ripper'. For the social and ideological meaning of the 'Ripper' murders and their narrative pleasures, see Judith Walkowitz's *City of Dreadful Delight: Narratives of Sexual Danger in Late Victorian London* (London: Virago, 1992), ch. 7.
54 *Pall Mall Gazette*, 8 September 1888, p. 1, cited in Cameron and Frazer, *The Lust to Kill*, p. 126.
55 Conrad, *Heart of Darkness*, p. 70.

56 See Donald Rumbelow, *The Complete Jack the Ripper* (1975; rev. edn, Harmondsworth: Penguin, 1988), pp. 116–17.

57 *Pall Mall Gazette*, 8 September 1888, p. 8, cited by Cameron and Frazer, *The Lust to Kill*, p. 126.

58 Wilfred Trotter, *Instincts of the Herd in Peace and War* (London: Ernest Benn, 1916), p. 179.

59 Valentine Williams, *The Man with the Clubfoot* (London: Herbert Jenkins, 1918), p. 135; see John Atkins, *The British Spy Novel: Styles in Treachery* (London: John Calder, 1984), pp. 51–7.

60 Williams, *The Man with the Clubfoot*, pp. 135–6.

5 CRIMINAL DEGENERACY: ADVENTURES WITH LOMBROSO

1 Jaroslav Hasek, *The Good Soldier Svejk* (trans. C. Parrott) (Harmondsworth: Penguin, 1974), p. 20.

2 Edgar Wallace, *Terror Keep* (London: Hodder and Stoughton, 1927), p. 127.

3 Les Daniels, *Fear: A History of Horror in the Mass Media* (London: Granada, 1977), p. 121.

4 R. Austin Freeman, *A Savant's Vendetta* (London: C. Arthur Pearson, 1920), p. 105. Subsequent references are included in the text. For a brief discussion of Freeman's work see D. W. Smithers, *This Idle Trade: On Doctors Who Were Writers* (Tunbridge Wells: Dragonfly Press, 1989), pp. 207–15.

5 Geoffrey Pearson, *The Deviant Imagination* (London: Macmillan, 1975), p. 151.

6 *Ibid.*, p. 151.

7 Alexander Morison, *Outline of Lectures on Mental Diseases* (Edinburgh: 1824), p. 125, cited by Jenny Bourne Taylor, *In the Secret Theatre of Home: Wilkie Collins, Sensation Narrative, and Nineteenth-Century Psychology* (London: Routledge, 1988), p. 104, fn. 270; see also Janet Brown, 'Darwin and Madness' in W. F. Bynum, Roy Porter and Michael Shepherd (eds.) *The Anatomy of Madness: Essays in the History of Psychiatry* (London: Tavistock, 1985–8), I, 150–165 (pp. 154–5).

8 Taylor, *In the Secret Theatre of Home*, p. 49.

✗ 9 Mary Cowling, *The Artist as Anthropologist: The Representation of Type and Character in Victorian Art* (Cambridge University Press, 1989), p. 9.

10 See Vieda Skultans, *Madness and Morals: Ideas on Insanity in the Nineteenth Century* (London: Routledge & Kegan Paul, 1975), p. 6. There is a helpful discussion of the principles and practices of moral management in Skultans, pp. 9–20. For the role of John Conolly, see Andrew Scull, *Social Order/Mental Disorder* (London: Routledge, 1989), pp. 162–212.

11 Cesare Lombroso, Introduction to Gina Lombroso-Ferrero, *Criminal*

Man According to the Classification of Cesare Lombroso (New York and London: G. P. Putnam's & Sons, 1911), xiv-xv; see Stephen Jay Gould, *The Mismeasure of Man* (1981; repr. Harmondsworth: Penguin, 1984), p. 124, and, generally, pp. 122–42.

12 B. A. Morel, *Traite des dégénérescences physiques, intellectuelles et morales de l'éspèce humaine et des causes qui produisent ces variétés maladives* (Paris: J. B. Baillière, 1857), p. 5.

13 Cesare Lombroso, *L'Homme criminel* (Paris, 1895), 1, 222, cited by Maurice Parmelee, Introduction to *Crime: Its Causes and Remedies* (Boston: Little, Brown & Co., 1911), xviii.

14 Sander L. Gilman, *Difference and Pathology* (Ithaca, NY: Cornell University Press, 1985), p. 21.

15 Michel Foucault, *The Archaeology of Knowledge* (London: Tavistock Publications, 1972), p. 44.

16 Cesare Lombroso, *The Man of Genius* (London: Walter Scott, 1891), pp. 5–6.

17 *Ibid.*, p. 9.

18 See Allon White, *The Uses of Obscurity: The Fiction of Early Modernism* (London: Routledge, 1981), pp. 46–7.

19 Robert A. Nye. *Crime, Madness and Politics in Modern France: The Medical Concept of National Decline* (Princeton University Press, 1984), p. 104.

20 Charles Mercier, 'Vice, Crime and Insanity' in T. Clifford Allbutt and H. D. Rolleston (eds.) *A System of Medicine* (9 vols., 1898; 2nd edn London: Macmillan, 1910) VIII, 842–74 (p. 851).

21 Nye, *Crime, Madness and Politics*, p. 102.

22 John Galsworthy, *Justice* (1910, repr. in *The Plays of John Galsworthy* (London: Duckworth, 1929), pp. 234–5, 243, 252, 256–7. I owe this reference to John Stokes.

23 As Home Secretary February 1910 – October 1911, Winston Churchill responded by initiating a programme of reform 'which included a reduction of the period of mandatory solitary confinement'; see Ian Clarke, *Edwardian Drama: A Critical Study* (London: Faber, 1989), p. 68, and generally, pp. 64–8; see also J. A. V. Chapple, *Documentary and Imaginative Literature 1880–1920* (London: Blandford Press, 1970), p. 136.

24 Havelock Ellis, *The Criminal* (London: Walter Scott & Co., 1890), p. 206.

25 *Ibid.*, pp. 206–7.

26 Havelock Ellis, *The Criminal* (London: Walter Scott & Co., 1901), p. 253.

27 *Ibid.*, xv-xvi.

28 *Ibid.*, xvi.

29 Havelock Ellis to J. A. Symonds 1 July 1892, cited in Phyllis Grosskurth, *Havelock Ellis* (London: Allen Lane, 1980), p. 116. As Grosskurth says, 'all through *The Criminal* [Ellis] ... goes out of his way

to take Lombroso to task for his indiscriminate procedures in collecting data, but Lombroso is quoted more often than any other authority, so it is probably fair to say that Lombroso was the main inspiration for the book' (Grosskurth, p. 116).

30 *Ibid.*, p. 116.

31 Ellis, *The Criminal* (1890), p. 187.

32 Ellis had already dismissed the attribution of degeneration to artists in his 1896 essay (written in the wake of Nordau's *Degeneration*), 'The Colour Sense in Literature', *Contemporary Review* (May 1896): 714–29.

33 Havelock Ellis, *From Rousseau to Proust* (1935; repr. London: Constable & Co., 1936), p. 268.

34 See Gilman, *Difference and Pathology*, pp. 95–8.

35 Sander L. Gilman, *Seeing the Insane* (New York: John Wiley, 1982), p. 164, Elaine Showalter, *The Female Malady: Women, Madness and English Culture 1830–1980* (London: Virago, 1987), p. 86.

36 *Ibid.*, p. 179; see also Browne, 'Darwin and Madness' in Bynum *et al.* (eds.) *The Anatomy of Madness*, 1, 151–65 (pp. 153–4). The best discussion to date of Crichton-Browne's paradigmatic place in late nineteenth century psychiatry is in Janet Oppenheim, *'Shattered Nerves' Doctors, Patients, and Depression in Victorian England* (New York and Oxford: Oxford University Press, 1991), pp. 54–78.

37 Gilman, *Difference and Pathology*, pp. 98–9.

38 Cited by Showalter, *The Female Malady*, p. 97.

39 *Cassell's Saturday Journal* 14 (26 February 1896), p. 461.

40 *Ibid.*, 25 December 1895, p. 281.

41 Arthur Conan Doyle, *The Hound of the Baskervilles* (1902; repr. Harmondsworth: Penguin, 1981), p. 10. Subsequent references are included in the text.

42 Arthur Conan Doyle, *A Study in Scarlet* (Harmondsworth: Penguin, 1982), p. 13.

43 Arthur Conan Doyle, 'The Blue Carbuncle', in *Sherlock Holmes; The Complete Short Stories* (London: John Murray, 1928), p. 154. Subsequent references are to *Complete Short Stories*.

44 Arthur Conan Doyle, 'The Final Problem', in *ibid.*, p. 541. Subsequent references are included in the text.

45 Henry Maudsley, *The Pathology of Mind: A Study of its Distempers, Deformities, and Disorders* (London: Macmillan, 1895), p. 536, cited by Showalter, *The Female Malady*, p. 107.

46 Max Nordau, *Degeneration* (1895; trans. from the 2nd edn of *Entartung* (1893) [1892]; Popular Edition, London: William Heinemann, 1898), p. 23.

47 Doyle, *A Study in Scarlet*, p. 17.

48 Doyle, 'The Bruce-Partington Plans', *Complete Short Stories*, p. 1000.

49 John Buchan, *The Half-Hearted* (London: Isbister and Co., 1900), p. 269.

50 Catherine Belsey, *Critical Practice* (London: Methuen, 1980), p. 111.
51 *Ibid.*, p. 117.
52 Doyle, 'The Norwood Builder', in *Complete Short Stories*, p. 583.
53 See Ian Watt, *Conrad in the Nineteenth Century* (London: Chatto and Windus, 1980), pp. 152–3, and Cedric Watts, *A Preface to Conrad* (London: Longman, 1982), p. 68.
54 See Norman Sherry, *Conrad's Western World* (Cambridge University Press, 1971), pp. 274–5; C. T. Watts, 'Nordau and Kurtz: A Footnote to *Heart of Darkness*', *Notes and Queries*, 219 (June 1974): 226–7; C. T. Watts, *Conrad's 'Heart of Darkness': a Critical and Contextual Discussion* (Milan: Mursia International 1977), p. 19; Martin Ray, 'Conrad, Nordau and Other Degenerates: The Psychology of *The Secret Agent*', *Conradiana*, 15–16 (1983–4): 125–40. Ray (p. 125) cites evidence of a later disenchantment, from *Chance* (1914), where the character Fyne gets hold of 'the theory of poetical genius being allied to madness' from an 'idiotic book everybody was reading a few years ago'.
55 See Harold V. Marrot, *The Lives and Letters of John Galsworthy* (London: Heinemann, 1935), pp. 230–1, cited by Alec Fréchet, *John Galsworthy: A Reassessment* (London: Macmillan, 1982), p. 133, p. 214.
56 Joseph Conrad, *The Nigger of the 'Narcissus'* (Harmondsworth: Penguin, 1963), p. 95. Subsequent references are included in the text.
57 Jeremy Hawthorn, 'The Incoherences of *The Nigger of the 'Narcissus'*', *Conradiana* 11 (2) (November 1986): 107–8.
58 Conrad to Spiridion Kliszczewski, 19 December 1885, in Frederick R. Karl and Laurence Davies (eds.) *Collected Letters of Joseph Conrad* (Cambridge University Press, 1983), I, 15–17 (p. 17).
59 Hawthorn, 'The Incoherences of *The Nigger of the 'Narcissus'*', p. 108.
60 Conrad to Kliszczewski, in *Collected Letters* I, 16.
61 Joseph Conrad, *Heart of Darkness* (Harmondsworth: Penguin, 1985), pp. 37–8. Subsequent references are included in the text.
62 Tony Tanner, Introduction to *Victory* (Oxford University Press, 1986), xiii.
63 Nordau, *Degeneration*, Book 111, *passim*.
64 Michael Levenson, *A Genealogy of Modernism* (Cambridge University Press, 1984), p. 19.
65 *Ibid.*, pp. 19–20.
66 *Ibid.*, p. 34.
67 See Watts, 'Nordau and Kurtz: A Footnote to *Heart of Darkness*', 226–7.
68 Nordau, *Degeneration*, p. 23.
69 Chris Baldick, *In Frankenstein's Shadow: Myth, Monstrosity and Nineteenth-Century Writing* (Oxford: Clarendon Press, 1987), p. 166.
70 Joseph Conrad, *The Secret Agent: A Simple Tale* (1907; repr. Harmondsworth: Penguin, 1986), p. 76. Subsequent references are included in the text.

71 See Cedric Watts, *A Preface to Conrad*, p. 95. Martin Ray has shown from a close reading of passages from *Degeneration* how Conrad used Nordau in a double way: to offer a perspective from which he could maintain his ironic detachment from his characters, and also as a psychological source (particularly in Nordau's exhaustive anatomy of various forms of ego-mania) for his characters. Ray is also interesting on the origin in *Degeneration* of Stevie's 'degenerate' characteristics: including his 'mad art', emotionalism and altruism; all have their origins, according to Nordau, in particular degenerate types. While this helps to 'place' Stevie (as all the characters in the novel are placed) as a psychological 'type', who is morally incorrupt and incorruptible, Ray does not develop the full ironic significance of the fact that it is the degenerate Ossipon who is responsible for the designation of degeneracy in Stevie. This alone seems to subvert the authority implied in this diagnosis of Stevie, whose manifest humanity offers a medium through which we register the absurdity and injustice of the degenerationist's claims. (See Ray, 'Conrad, Nordau and Other Degenerates', 127–33.)

6 MAX NORDAU AND THE *DEGENERATION* EFFECT

1 For Nordau's transition to an uneasy Zionism see P. M. Baldwin, 'Liberalism, Nationalism, and Degeneration: The Case of Max Nordau', *Central European History* 13 (June 1980): 99–120.
2 Amongst them, H. G. Wells, *The Time Machine*; Grant Allen, *The Woman Who Did*; Thomas Hardy, *Jude the Obscure*.
3 Allon White, *The Uses of Obscurity* (London: Routledge, 1981), p. 45.
4 Max Nordau, *Degeneration* (1895; trans. from the 2nd edn of *Entartung* (1893) [1892]; Popular Edition, London: William Heinemann, 1898), p. 285. Subsequent references are included in the text.
5 White, *The Uses of Obscurity*, p. 49.
6 Milton P. Foster, 'The Reception of Max Nordau's *Degeneration* in England and America' (unpublished Ph.D. dissertation, University of Michigan, 1954), p. 10.
7 *Ibid.*, p. 55; see also R. K. R. Thornton, *The Decadent Dilemma* (London: Edward Arnold, 1983), p. 66.
8 Hugh E. M. Stutfield, 'Tommyrotics', *Blackwood's Edinburgh Magazine*, 157 (June 1895): 835.
9 Wilde's first petition to the Home Secretary, dated 2 July 1896. MS P. R. O. H 04J/24514 AJ 6887. See H. Montgomery Hyde, *Oscar Wilde: The Aftermath* (New York: Farrar, Straus, 1963), pp. 70–1.
10 See John Stokes, *In the Nineties* (Hemel Hempstead: Harvester-Wheatsheaf, 1989), p. 108; see also Thornton, *The Decadent Dilemma*, pp. 63–4.
11 See Tom Gibbons, *Rooms in the Darwin Hotel* (Nedlands: University of Western Australia Press, 1973), p. 34; White, *The Uses of Obscurity*, p. 44 and p. 168 (note 47).

12 J. F. Nisbet, *The Insanity of Genius and the General Inequality of Human Faculty Physiologically Considered* (London: Ward and Downey, 1891) xv. See George Becker, *The Mad Genius Controversy* (Beverly Hills: Sage Publications, 1978), pp. 38–9, pp. 43–4. pp. 93–102; see also Gibbons, *Rooms in the Darwin Hotel*, p. 34; J. E. Chamberlin, 'Images: Turnings and Transformations', in J. E. Chamberlin and Sander L. Gilman (eds.) *Degeneration: the Dark Side of Progress* (New York: Columbia University Press, 1985), pp. 261–85 (p. 280).

13 Anton Chekhov to Suvorin, 27 March 1894, cited by John Tulloch, *Chekhov: A Structuralist Study* (London: Macmillan, 1980), p. 127. I owe this reference to John Reid.

14 Eliot read Nordau at Harvard in the years 1909–14. See Lyndall Gordon, *Eliot's Early Years* (1977; Oxford University Press, 1978), p. 140.

15 Foster, 'The Reception of Max Nordau's *Degeneration*', pp. 54–5.

16 *Ibid.*, pp. 61–3.

17 G. B. Shaw, 'The Sanity of Art' (1907), repr. in Michael Holroyd (ed.) *G.B.Shaw: Major Critical Essays* (Harmondsworth: Penguin, 1986), pp. 309–60 (p. 341).

18 *Ibid.*, p. 352.

19 B. A. Crackenthorpe, 'Sex and Modern Literature', *Nineteenth Century* 37 (April 1895): 607–16 (p. 611 and note). See a similar jibe from another contemporary reviewer, Janet Hogarth, cited by Stokes, *In the Nineties*, p. 13.

20 Bram Stoker, *Dracula* (1897; repr. Oxford University Press, 1983), p. 342; see Baldwin, 'Liberalism, Nationalism and Degeneration', 99; Stephen Jay Gould, *The Mismeasure of Man* (1981; repr. Harmondsworth: Penguin, 1984), p. 123.

21 H. G. Wells, 'The Plattner Story', in *New Review* 14 (April 1896): 349–66 (p. 351), repr. in *The Short Stories of H. G. Wells* (London: Ernest Benn, 1927), pp. 325–45 (p. 327); see also Bernard Bergonzi, *The Early H. G. Wells* (Manchester University Press, 1961), pp. 93–4.

22 H. G. Wells, *The Wonderful Visit* (London: J. M. Dent, 1895), p. 58.

23 *Ibid.*, p. 205.

24 H. G. Wells, *The Food of the Gods* (1904), in *The Works of H. G. Wells* (London: Odhams Press, 1926–7), p. 422.

25 Havelock Ellis, *From Rousseau to Proust* (London: Constable & Co., 1936), p. 276.

26 Gibbons, *Rooms in the Darwin Hotel*, p. 76.

27 Havelock Ellis, 'The Colour Sense in Literature', *Contemporary Review* 69 (May 1896): 714–29.

28 William James, *The Varieties of Religious Experience: A Study in Human Nature* (1902; repr. London: Fontana, 1960), p. 38.

29 William James, 'Degeneration and Genius', *Psychological Review* 2 (May 1895): 287–94 (p. 289), cited by Foster, 'The Reception of Max Nordau's Degeneration', p. 97.

30 F. C. S. Schiller, 'Regeneration: A Reply to Max Nordau', *Philosophical Review* 5 (July 1896): 436–7, cited by Foster, pp. 103–4.

31 *Ibid.*, p. 104.

32 Daniel Pick. *Faces of Degeneration: A European Disorder c. 1848 – c.1918* (Cambridge University Press, 1989), p. 8.

33 Havelock Ellis, *The Criminal* (3rd rev. edn London: Walter Scott, 1901), xvi.

34 Wilfred Trotter, *Instincts of the Herd in Peace and War* (London: Ernest Benn, 1916), p. 64.

35 Josef Breuer and Sigmund Freud, *Studies in Hysteria 1893–95* (repr. Harmondsworth: Penguin, 1973), pp. 146–7.

36 *Ibid.*, p. 380.

37 Sigmund Freud, *Introductory Lectures on Psychoanalysis* (repr. Harmondsworth: Penguin, 1973), pp. 299–300; see Larry Stewart, 'Freud before Oedipus: Race and Heredity in the Origin of Psychoanalysis', *Journal of the History of Biology* 9 (1976): 215–26; Sander L. Gilman, 'Sexology, Psychoanalysis, and Degeneration: From a Theory of Race to a Race to Theory', in Chamberlain and Gilman (eds.) *Degeneration: The Dark Side of Progress*, 72–96 (particularly pp. 80–4); Jean-Marc Dupeu, 'Freud and Degeneracy: A Turning-Point', *Diogenes* 97 (1977): 43–64, and for Freud's indebtedness to late nineteenth-century biological thought, Frank J. Sulloway, *Freud, Biologist of the Mind* (London: Burnett Books, 1979).

38 See Milton Gold, 'The Continuing "Degeneration" Controversy', *Bucknell Review*, 10 (2): 87–101 (p. 90).

39 *Ibid.*, pp. 91–2; see also Neil Kessel, 'Genius and Mental Disorder: A History of Ideas Concerning their Conjunction', in Penelope Murray (ed.) *Genius: The History of an Idea* (Oxford: Basil Blackwell, 1989), 196–212 (pp. 206–7).

40 Virginia Woolf, 'Mr Bennett and Mrs Brown', in *The Captain's Death Bed And Other Essays* (London: Hogarth Press, 1950), 90–111 (p. 91).

41 See Samuel Hynes, *The Edwardian Turn of Mind* (1968; repr. London: Pimlico, 1991), pp. 325–6., and, generally, his important discussion in chapter nine.

42 Sir William Blake Richmond, 'Post-Impressionists', *Morning Post*, 16 November 1910, cited by J. B. Bullen (ed.) *The Post-Impressionists in England* (London: Routledge, 1988), p. 116.

43. S. K. Tillyard, *The Impact of Modernism 1900–1920: Early Modernism and the Arts and Crafts Movement in Edwardian England* (London: Routledge, 1988), p. 92.

44 Roger Fry, 'The Grafton Gallery – 1', *Nation*, 19 November 1910, 331, cited by Bullen (ed.) *The Post-Impressionists in England*, p. 121.

45 Desmond MacCarthy, 'The Post-Impressionists', Introduction to the catalogue of the exhibition 'Manet and the Post-Impressionists', Grafton Galleries, 8 November 1910 – 14 January 1911, cited by Tillyard, *The Impact of Modernism*, p. 106, p. 88.

46 See Frances Spalding, *Vanessa Bell* (London: Weidenfeld & Nicholson, 1983), p. 92.
47 See Tillyard, *The Impact of Modernism*, p. 115.
48 Robert Ross, 'The Post-Impressionists at the Grafton: The Twilight of the Idols', *Morning Post*, 7 November 1910, see Hynes, *The Edwardian Turn of Mind*, p. 330; Tillyard, *The Impact of Modernism*, p. 119. As Samuel Hynes notes, Ross, aesthete and associate of Wilde in the nineties, was on the face of it an unlikely opponent of Post-Impressionism. (Hynes, *The Edwardian Turn of Mind*, p. 330.) Ross had exhibited Beardsley in 1904, and Orpen and Augustus John at the Carfax Gallery, London (of which he was a director), but he could not make the leap to Cézanne and Matisse who, he believed, had 'said good-bye to form, anatomy, to harmony, and to artistic probity'; see 'The Present and Future for English Art' (a lecture of 1910), cited by Maureen Borland, *Wilde's Devoted Friend; A Life of Robert Ross 1869–1918* (Oxford: Lennard Publishing, 1990), p. 301 (I owe this reference to John Stokes); Hynes p. 330.
49 Ross, 'The Post-Impressionists at the Grafton', cited by Tillyard, *The Impact of Modernism*, p. 119.
50 Cited by Tillyard, *The Impact of Modernism*, p. 119.
51 *Ibid.*, p. 121.
52 *Ibid.*, p. 121.
53 *Ibid.*, p. 106.
54 My grandfather, a Bristol Church of England Primary School headmaster, apparently made such an observation in the mid-1930s.
55 Ebenezer Wake Cook, *Anarchism in Art and Chaos in Criticism* (1904), p. 47, cited by Kate Flint (ed.) *Impressionists in England: The Critical Reception* (London: Routledge, 1984), p. 15.
56 Ebenezer Wake Cook, *Retrogression in Art* (1924), p. 26, cited by Tillyard, *The Impact of Modernism*, p. 107.
57 Ross, 'The Post-Impressionists at the Grafton', p. 3; *ibid.*, p. 120.
58 *Ibid.*, p. 118.
59 *Ibid.*, p. 115.
60 *Ibid.*, p. 106.
61 Virginia Woolf, *Roger Fry* (1940; repr. London: Hogarth Press, 1990), p. 156.
62 T. B. Hyslop, 'Post-Illusionism and Art in the Insane', *Nineteenth Century and After*, 69 (1911): 271, cited by Stephen Trombley, *'All That Summer she was Mad': Virginia Woolf and her Doctors* (London: Junction Books, 1981), p. 227.
63 Ruth Bernard Yeazell, 'Doctors' Orders', *London Review of Books* 4 (3) (1982): 18.
64 T. B. Hyslop, 'The Mental Deficiency Bill, 1912', *Journal of Mental Science*, 58 (October 1912): 555, cited by Trombley, *'All That Summer'*, p. 223.
65 T. B. Hyslop, 'Degeneration: The Medico-Psychological Aspects of

Modern Art, Music, Literature, Science and Religion', *Trans. Med, Soc. of London* 4 (1918): 275–6, cited by Trombley, *'All That Summer'*, p. 234.

66 Pierre Nordon, *Conan Doyle* (London: John Murray, 1966), p. 338, cited by Howard Brotz, 'Sherlock Holmes as Conservative Thinker', *Salisbury Review* 8 (1) (September 1989): 51.

7 WOMEN AND THE DISEASE OF CIVILISATION
GEORGE GISSING'S *THE WHIRLPOOL*

1 Herbert Spencer, *Education* (London: Williams and Norgate, 1861), p. 187. George Gissing read Spencer on 13 December 1895. He began 'Benedict's Household', later *The Whirlpool*, towards the end of April 1896, see Pierre Coustillas (ed.) *London and the Life of Literature: The Diary of George Gissing* (Hassocks: Harvester Press, 1978), p. 396, p. 409.

2 Herbert Spencer, *The Principles of Ethics* (2 vols. London: Williams and Norgate, 1892–3), I, 533, cited by Lorna Duffin, 'Prisoners of Progress: Women and Evolution,' in Sara Delamont and Lorna Duffin (eds.) *The Nineteenth-Century Woman: Her Cultural and Physical World* (London: Croom Helm, 1978), 57–91 (p. 62).

3 Henry Maudsley, 'Sex in Mind and Education', *Fortnightly Review* 15 (1874): 467, cited by Patricia Hollis (ed.) *Women in Public: The Women's Movement 1850–1900* (London: Allen and Unwin, 1979), pp. 24–6; Paul Atkinson, 'Fitness, Feminism and Schooling', in Delamont and Duffin (eds.) *The Nineteenth-Century Woman*, 92–133 (p. 101); Elaine Showalter, *The Female Malady: Women, Madness and English Culture 1830–1980* (London: Virago, 1987), p. 125; Anne Digby, 'Women's Biological Straitjacket', in Susan Mendus and Jane Rendall (eds.) *Sexuality and Subordination: Interdisciplinary Studies of Gender in the Nineteenth Century* (London: Routledge, 1989), pp. 192–220.

4 Eric T. Carlson, 'The Nerve Weakness of the Nineteenth Century', *International Journal of Psychiatry*, 9 (1970–1): 51; Charles Rosenberg, 'The Place of George M. Beard in Nineteenth Century Psychiatry', *Bulletin of the History of Medicine* 36 (May-June 1962): 249.

5 Carlson, 'The Nerve Weakness of the Nineteenth Century': 51.

6 *Ibid.*, 51.

7 *Ibid.*, 52.

8 While Beard was the first to coin the term, it was used extensively by the reforming physician Silas Weir Mitchell to describe nerve weakness in both women and men. See John C. Chatel and Roger Peele, 'The Concept of Neurasthenia', *International Journal of Psychiatry* 9 (1970–1): 37; George Mora, 'Antecedents to Neurosis', *International Journal of Psychiatry* 9 (1970–71):58; Showalter, *The Female Malady*, p. 135. On this topic essential reading is Janet Oppenheim, *'Shattered Nerves'*:

Doctors, Patients and Depression in Victorian England (New York and Oxford: Oxford University Press, 1991), especially ch. 3, 'Nerve Force and Neurasthenia'.

9 Herbert Spencer's influence was more pronounced in America than in Britain, although it was not inconsiderable there (as the work of Walter Bagehot the political theorist, W. S. Jevons the economist and J. Hughlings Jackson the neurologist testify). Paul F. Boller believes that 'for middle class Americans, Spencer was the greatest thinker of his age', *American Thought in Transition: The Impact of Evolutionary Naturalism 1863–1900* (Chicago: Rand McNally, 1970), p. 48. The Spencerian law of evolution relied heavily on the concept of 'force' – working through the evolution and dissolution of a constant amount of energy, measured by matter and subject to the laws of motion. What was expended by way of progress in one area was compensated for in another. All structures were subject to this law of progessive development, as expressed in *First Principles* (London: Williams and Norgate, 1861; 4th edn 1880): 'Evolution is an integration of matter and concomitant dissipation of motion; during which the matter passes from an indefinite, incoherent homogeneity to a definite, coherent heterogeneity; and during which the retained motion undergoes a parallel transformation' (p. 376). Spencer's influence can be traced to a variety of important American figures. Weir Mitchell introduced 'force' into an analysis of the nervous system; Spencer's evolutionary naturalism was incorporated into 'social Darwinism' as exemplified in the work of W. G. Sumner, L. H. Morgan and L. F. Ward and in the political ideology of Theodore Roosevelt. See, generally, J. D. Y. Peel, *Herbert Spencer: The Evolution of a Sociologist* (London: Heinemann, 1971); Boller, ch. 3.

10 Rosenberg, 'The Place of George M. Beard in Nineteenth Century Psychiatry': 247.

11 Spencer, *Principles of Ethics*, I, 534.

12 Michel Foucault, *The History of Sexuality* Vol. I (Harmondsworth: Penguin, 1981), p. 104, p. 110.

13 See John Goode, *George Gissing: Ideology and Fiction* (London: Vision Press, 1978), p. 184.

14 What Lionel Johnson wrote of *One of Our Conquerors* could equally be applied to both *In the Year of Jubilee* and *The Whirlpool*: 'It is not too much to say that the "world", or "society", or "the public", or "the nation", seems to rank among the *dramatis personae*,' *Academy*, 39 (13 June 1891): 555, cited by Allon White, *The Uses of Obscurity* (London: Routledge and Kegan Paul, 1981), p. 35. Gissing read Meredith's novel on 6 November 1892, see Coustillas, *The Diary of George Gissing*, p. 288.

15 Gissing to Clara Collet (undated). Cited by David Grylls, *The Paradox of Gissing* (London: Allen and Unwin, 1986), p. 188.

16 Gissing probably developed this topic out of Spencer's strictures on 'over-education' in *Education*, pp. 182–4.

17 David Grylls observes that Gissing took (undated) notes from a *Nineteenth Century* article of 1887 by the biologist George Romanes: 'Useful Differences between Men and Women', which adopted a standard post-Darwinian position on women's inferiority to men – notably their mental capacity; see Grylls, *The Paradox of Gissing*, p. 161.

18 Gissing read *Degeneration* in March 1895, a month after its publication in England; see Coustillas, *The Diary of George Gissing*, p. 365.

19 Gissing to Henry Hick, 16 January 1896, in Pierre Coustillas (ed.) *Henry Hick's Recollections of George Gissing Together with Gissing's Letters to Hick* (London: Enitharmon Press, 1973), p. 25.

20 Ian Fletcher, Introduction to *British Poetry and Prose: 1870–1905* (Oxford University Press, 1987), xvii.

21 Max Nordau, *Degeneration* (1895; trans. from the 2nd edn of *Entartung* (1893) [1892]; Popular Edition, London: William Heinemann, 1898), p. 42.

22 The implications of the whirlpool image are lucidly described by Rachel Bowlby in a review of a new edition of *The Whirlpool*, see *The Gissing Newsletter* 21 (2) (1985): 23.

✗ 23 T. Clifford Allbutt, 'Nervous Diseases and Modern Life', *Contemporary Review* 67 (1895): 214.

24 H. G. Wells, 'The Novels of Mr. George Gissing', *Contemporary Review* 72 (1897): 192–201.

25 See Royal A. Gettmann (ed.) *George Gissing and H. G. Wells: A Record of their Friendship and Correspondence* (London: Rupert Hart-Davis, 1961), pp. 47–8.

26 George Gissing, *The Whirlpool* (Hassocks: Harvester Press, 1977), p. 419. Subsequent references are included in the text.

27 Patrick Parrinder, Introduction to George Gissing, *The Whirlpool* (Hassocks: Harvester Press, 1977), xv.

28 A condition described by Elaine Showalter as 'the insoluble conflict' between women's desire to 'act as individuals and the internalized obligations to submit to the needs of the family and to conform to the model of self-sacrificing "womanly" behaviour', Showalter, *The Female Malady*, p. 144.

29 *Ibid.*, p. 160.

30 Carroll Smith-Rosenberg, 'The Hysterical Woman: Sex Roles and Role Conflict in Nineteenth Century America', *Social Research* 37 (1972): 671. See Lorna Duffin, 'The Conspicuous Consumptive: Woman as an Invalid', in Delamont and Duffin (eds.) *The Nineteenth-Century Woman*: 26–56 (p. 51).

31 Greenough White, 'A Novelist of the Hour', *Sewanee Review* 6 (July 1898): 360–70 (p. 367).

32 *Ibid.*, 367.

33 *Ibid.*, 367.

34 Henrik Ibsen, *A Doll's House* (1888; trans. Michael Meyer, London: Methuen, 1980), p. 49.

35 See Coustillas, (ed.), *The Diary of George Gissing*, p. 385 (entry for 29 August 1895).

36 C. Lombroso and G. Ferrero, *The Female Offender* (London: T. Fisher Unwin, 1895), p. 187.

37 For a discussion of how the 'new woman' was perceived as a threat to 'traditional gender boundaries' in the nineties, see Lyn Pykett, *The 'Improper' Feminine: The Women's Sensation Novel and the New Woman Writing* (London: Routledge, 1992), ch. 14. For the representation of the 'new woman' in fiction, see, among other studies, Gail Cunningham, *The New Woman and the Victorian Novel* (London: Macmillan, 1978); Penny Boumehla, *Thomas Hardy and Women* (Brighton: Harvester Press, 1982), ch. 4; Ann Ardis, *New Women New Novels: Feminism and Early Modernism* (New Brunswick: Rutgers University Press, 1990); Pykett, pp. 137–97.

38 Grant Allen, 'The New Hedonism', *Fortnightly Review* 55 (1894): 392.

39 George Gissing, *In the Year of Jubilee* (1894; repr. Hassocks: Harvester Press, 1976), p. 429.

40 Grant Allen, *The Woman Who Did* (London: John Lane, 1895), p. 145.

41 [William Barry], 'The Strike of a Sex', *Quarterly Review* 179 (1894): 317.

42 See Anna Davin's seminal essay, 'Imperialism and Motherhood', *History Workshop Journal* no.5 (1978), 9–65; see also Jane Lewis, *The Politics of Motherhood* (London: Croom Helm, 1980), p. 224, and Jane Lewis, *Women in England 1870–1950* (Brighton: Wheatsheaf Press, 1980), p. 32; Ardis, *New Women New Novels*, pp. 91–8.

43 Karl Pearson, 'Woman and Labour', *Fortnightly Review* 55 (1894): 569–70.

44 Marie Corelli, 'Mother-Love', *Windsor Magazine* 11 (1899–1900): 99; see Gillian Kersley, *Darling Madame* (London: Virago, 1983), p. 79.

45 Spencer, *Education*, pp. 142–3.

46 Discussions of this topic include: Cunningham, *The New Woman and the Victorian Novel*, ch. 4; Patricia Stubbs, *Women and Fiction: Feminism and the Novel 1880–1920* (Brighton: Harvester, 1979); and, most fully, Grylls, *The Paradox of Gissing*, ch. 5.

47 A.M., review of *The Whirlpool*, *Bookman* (May 1897): 38–9. See Pierre Coustillas (ed.) *Gissing: The Critical Heritage* (London: Routledge, 1972), p. 280.

48 Goode, *George Gissing: Ideology and Fiction*, p. 188.

49 Elaine Showalter, 'Syphilis, Sexuality and the Fiction of the Fin de Siècle', in R. B. Yeazell (ed.) *Sex, Politics and Science in the Nineteenth Century Novel* (Baltimore and London: Johns Hopkins University Press, 1986), 88–115 (p. 110).

8 THE LURE OF PEDIGREE AND THE MENACES OF HEREDITY
IN *TESS OF THE D'URBERVILLES* AND *JUDE THE OBSCURE*

1 See F. E. Hardy, *The Life of Thomas Hardy 1840–1928* (1962, repr. London and Basingstoke: Macmillan, 1975), pp. 214–15; see also, Roger Ebbatson, *The Evolutionary Self* (Brighton: Harvester, 1982), p. 25.

2 Thomas Hardy, *Tess of the D'Urbervilles* (3 vols. London: Osgood, McIlvaine and Co., 1891; repr. London: Macmillan, 1975), pp. 364–5. Subsequent references are included in the text.

3 Thomas Hardy, *A Laodicean* (3 vols. 1881; repr. London: Macmillan, 1975), p. 204.

4 P. Fancourt Hodgson, *How to Trace your own Pedigree, or, a Guide to Family Descent* (London: Pickering and Chatto, 1889), pp. 5–6. The pursuit of ancestry, according to the writer, must be 'either to prove a right to estates, unclaimed money or a title of honour; or ... to trace the varying changes and chequered fortunes and, perchance, to bring to light the heroic acts and sacrifices, of our own ancestors'. 'One of the most striking developments of modern democracy', wrote James Dallas, curator of the Albert Memorial Museum, in the same year, 'is the wide-spread ambition amongst ordinary folks to ascertain pedigrees' (J.Dallas, 'On Pedigrees', *Cassell's Family Magazine* (Cassell & Co. 1889): 299).

5 Francis Galton, 'Medical Family Registers', *Fortnightly Review* 34 (July 1883): 245.

6 Michel Foucault, *The History of Sexuality* Vol.1 (Harmondsworth: Penguin Books, 1981), pp. 124–5; see also Janet Oppenheim, *'Shattered Nerves': Doctors, Patients and Depression in Victorian England* (Oxford University Press, 1991), p. 277.

7 Thomas Hardy, *The Woodlanders* (3 vols. 1887; repr. London: Macmillan, 1981), p. 182, p. 91.

8 Juliet Grindle, 'A Critical Edition of *Tess of the D'Urbervilles*', (unpublished D. Phil. dissertation, University of Oxford, 1974), xxii.

9 Ian Gregor, *The Great Web: The Form of Hardy's Major Fiction* (London: Faber, 1974), p. 195.

10 T. H. Huxley, 'The Struggle For Existence: A Programme', *Nineteenth Century* 23 (February 1888): 165.

11 T. H. Huxley, 'On the Natural Inequality of Man', *Nineteenth Century* 27 (January 1890): 20.

12 John Goode, 'Woman and the Literary Text', in J. Mitchell and A. Oakley (eds.) *The Rights and Wrongs of Women* (Harmondsworth: Penguin, 1976), 217–55 (p. 255).

13 Roger Robinson has come to a similar conclusion about this passage in an essay which converges with my own discussion at several points. See R. Robinson, 'Hardy and Darwin', in Norman Page (ed.) *Thomas*

Hardy: The Writer and his Background (London: Bell and Hyman, 1980), 128–49 (p. 140) and generally, 137–43.

14 See Peter Morton, *The Vital Science: Biology and the Literary Imagination* (London: George Allen & Unwin, 1984), p. 207.

15 Morton, *The Vital Science*, p. 198; see also Peter A. Dale, 'Thomas Hardy and the Best Consummation Possible', in John Christie and Sally Shuttleworth (eds.) *Nature Transfigured; Science and Literature 1700– 1900* (Manchester University Press, 1989), 201–21 (p. 207). Weismann's first lectures on heredity were delivered in 1883, and his essays on heredity began to appear from that date in English translation. The publication of his *Essays upon Heredity and Kindred Biological Problems* from 1889 provided a stimulus for wide-ranging debate between the neo-Darwinists and the adherents to the Lamarckian belief in the inheritance of acquired characteristics. It was the *Contemporary Review* which played host to the competing views: between August 1889 and October 1894 it ran three articles by George Romanes and five from an elderly Herbert Spencer. A. R. Wallace contributed two further articles in the *Fortnightly Review* (in 1893). Greta Jones points out that Weismann's work on heredity had been debated at the British Association in 1887 (*Social Darwinism and English Thought* (Brighton and New Jersey: Harvester Press, 1980), p. 84). And it was in that year the anthropologist Edward Westermarck recalled that: ' "the inheritance of acquired characters" had [from 1887 onwards] suffered a severe check from Weismann, whose denial of ... such characters had an ardent champion in Ray Lankester' (who was well known to Hardy). 'It was through him ... that I first became acquainted with the new doctrine, which impressed me greatly, as the earlier inheritance theory seemed to be without any confirmation in proven facts' (Edward Westermarck, *Memories of My Life* (London: Allen & Unwin, 1929), pp. 77–8).

16 Morton, *The Vital Science*, p. 206.

17 This comparison is also noted by David Skilton in his edition of *Tess of the D'Urbervilles* (Harmondsworth: Penguin, 1978), p. 528.

18 See Gillian Beer, *Darwin's Plots* (1983; repr. London: Ark, 1985), p. 257.

19 J. T. Laird, *The Shaping of 'Tess of the D'Urbervilles'* (Oxford University Press, 1975), p. 31.

20 *Ibid.*, pp. 15–16.

21 *Ibid.*, p. 14.

22 British Library, Additional MS 38182, 'Tess of the D'Urbervilles', fol. 1; Laird, *The Shaping of 'Tess'*, p. 143.

23 *Ibid.*, pp. 43–4.

24 BL Add MS 'Tess', fol. 2; Laird, *The Shaping of 'Tess'*, p. 44.

25 BL Add MS 'Tess', fol. 323.

26 Thomas Hardy, *Tess of the D'Urbervilles* (London: Osgood, McIlvaine and Co., 5th edn 1892), II, 254.

27 Hardy, *Tess of the D'Urbervilles* (1891 edn), III, 140–1. In the 1912 Wessex edition, 'mailed' is revised to 'armed'.

28 Laird, *The Shaping of 'Tess'*, pp. 16–17.

29 Mary Jacobus, 'Tess's Purity', *Essays in Criticism* 26 (1976): 323.

30 Interview with Raymond Blaythwayt in *Black and White* (27 August 1892), p. 238, cited by F. R. Southerington, *Hardy's Vision of Man* (London: Chatto, 1969), p. 132.

31 Foucault, *The History of Sexuality*, p. 118.

32 May Sinclair, *Audrey Craven* (1897), p. 12, cited by Wallace Martin, *The 'New Age' Under Orage* (Manchester University Press, 1967), p. 83.

33 D. G. Ritchie, *Darwinism and Politics* (London: Swan Sonnenschein, 1889; 2nd edn with additions, 1891), p. 42.

34 Henry Maudsley, *Body and Mind* (London: Macmillan, 1873), pp. 75–6, cited in V. Skultans (ed.) *Madness and Morals: Ideas on Insanity in the Nineteenth Century* (London: Routledge, 1975), pp. 206–7.

35 Henry Maudsley, *The Pathology of Mind* (London: Macmillan, 1879), p. 88.

36 *Encylopaedia Britannica* 9th edn (1887), p. 687. For the cultural manifestation of syphilis in a context of gender politics at the *fin de siècle*, see Elaine Showalter, *Sexual Anarchy: Gender and Culture at the Fin de Siècle* (London: Bloomsbury, 1991), pp. 193–200. For the extent to which the belief in inheritable syphilis maintained its grip as widespread myth, see Claude Quétel, *History of Syphilis* (Cambridge: Polity Press, 1990), pp. 166–70.

37 *Encyclopaedia Britannica* 11th edn (1911), p. 985. Writing in 1948, the authors of a popular but expert work on genetics asserted that there is a 'widespread superstition ... that congenital diseases are synonymous with hereditary diseases. There is no such thing as hereditary syphilis or tuberculosis.' See Henry Kalmus and Lettice M. Crump, *Genetics* (Harmondsworth: Penguin, 1948), p. 159.

38 Henry Maudsley, *The Pathology of Mind: A Study of its Distempers, Deformities and Disorders* (London: Macmillan, 1895), p. 467.

39 Pat Jalland, *Women, Marriage and Politics* (Oxford University Press, 1988), p. 85. Bertrand Russell recalls in his *Autobiography* the 'thick atmosphere of sighs, tears, groans and morbid horror' which accompanied his family's discussion of his choice of marriage partner; there was alleged insanity in both families. Russell and his wife decided not to have children on 'medical grounds' (cited by Skultans, p. 22). Marie Stopes was another figure obsessed with the eugenic health of the prospective marriage partner, and who, as late as 1947, attempted to terrorise her son into abandoning his fiancée. To marry her, she said, would be a crime against 'his *Country* ... his family ... *his children*'; see Ruth Hall, *Marie Stopes* (1977; London: Virago, 1978), pp. 301–2, and generally, pp. 300–4.

40 Val Warner, Introduction to *Charlotte Mew; Collected Poems and Prose* (London: Virago, 1982), xiv-xv.
41 Jalland, *Women, Marriage and Politics*, p. 87.
42 See Jane Marcus, 'Virginia Woolf And Her Violin: Mothering, Madness and Music', in E. K. Ginsberg and L. M. Gottlieb (eds.) *Virginia Woolf; Centennial Essays* (Troy, NY: Whitston, 1983), pp. 27–49 (p. 30, pp. 47–8).
43 Virginia Woolf to Ethel Smyth, 27 February 1930, *ibid.*, p. 48.
44 Henrik Ibsen, *A Doll's House*, trans. Michael Meyer (London: Methuen, 1980), pp. 54–5.
45 Elaine Showalter, *A Literature of Their Own: British Women Novelists from Bronte to Lessing* (London: Virago, 1978), p. 205; see also David Trotter, *The English Novel in History 1895–1920* (London: Routledge, 1993), pp. 117–21.
46 Hardy first met Sarah Grand six months after the publication of *The Heavenly Twins*, in June 1893; see Hardy to Florence Henniker 7 June 1893, in Richard L. Purdy and Michael Millgate (eds.) *The Collected Letters of Thomas Hardy* (Oxford: Clarendon Press, 1980), II, 18. The previous month he had copied into his literary notebook an extract from *The Heavenly Twins* which he found congenial in the light of his intentions for Jude and Sue in the novel he was preparing to start later that summer: 'We are long past the time when there was only one incident of interest in a woman's life, & that was its love affair … It is stupid to narrow it [life] down to the indulgence of one particular set of emotions … to swamp every faculty by the constant cultivation of the animal instincts' (Lennart Bjork (ed.), *The Literary Notes of Thomas Hardy* II, 57 (item 1913). For Hardy and Grand see also, F. B. Pinion, '*Jude the Obscure*: Origins in Life and Literature', in Norman Page (ed.) *Thomas Hardy Annual* No. 4 (London: Macmillan, 1986), pp. 148–64.
47 Henry A. Allbutt, *The Wife's Handbook* (1886), cited by Jalland, *Women, Marriage and Politics*, p. 85.
48 Sarah Grand, *The Heavenly Twins* (3 vols. 1893; repr. London: William Heinemann, 1894), p. 79. Subsequent references are included in the text.
49 Elaine Showalter, 'Syphilis, Sexuality and the Fiction of the Fin de Siècle', in R. B. Yeazell (ed.) *Sex, Politics, and Science in the Nineteenth Century Novel* (Baltimore and London: Johns Hopkins University Press, 1986), pp. 88–115 (p. 88).
50 *Ibid.*, p. 108.
51 Emma Frances Brooke, *A Superfluous Woman* (London: William Heinemann, 1894), p. 257. Subsequent references are included in the text.
52 Maudsley, *The Pathology of Mind* (1895 edn) p. 48.
53 Oscar Wilde, 'The Critic as Artist' in *Intentions* (1891), see Isobel

Murray (ed.) *Oscar Wilde* (Oxford University Press, 1989), 241–97 (p. 276); also cited in Morton, *The Vital Science* , p. 149.

54 George Gissing's *The Whirlpool* (1897) satirised the authority which these popular studies seemed to have commanded. Recovering from the after effects of her baby's death – 'during its mother's absence at a garden-party' – Mary Abbott exhibits 'wider interests' by reading about the influence of heredity in Théodule Ribot's 'intensely interesting' *L'Hérédité psychologique* (1873). (See Gissing, *The Whirlpool* (Brighton: Harvester Press, 1977), p. 28.) This was a popular and influential Spencerian work, from which Gissing himself took careful notes. (See J. Korg (ed.) *George Gissing's Common Place Book* (New York: New York Public Library, 1962), pp. 59–62.)

55 Showalter, 'Syphilis, Sexuality, and the Fiction of the Fin de Siècle', p. 106.

56 S. A. K. Strahan, *Marriage and Disease: A Study of Heredity and the More Important Family Degenerations* (London: Kegan Paul, 1892). Strahan was also the author of *Suicide and Insanity*, published in 1893, a year which seemed to measure the high-water mark of the 'suicide craze'. Other key texts were Henry Morselli's *Suicide: An Essay on Comparative Moral Statistics* (1879), translated into English in 1881, and W. Wynn Westcott's *Suicide. Its History, Literature, Jurisprudence, Causation and Prevention* (1885); see John Stokes, *In The Nineties* (Hemel Hempstead: Harvester, 1989), pp. 121–3, and generally, ch.5.

57 Strahan, *Marriage and Disease*, p. 4.

58 *Ibid.*, p. 98.

59 *Ibid.*, p. 117.

60 Ibid., p. 102.

61 F. E. Hardy, *The Life of Thomas Hardy*, p. 254.

62 T. Clifford Allbutt, 'Nervous Diseases and Modern Life', *Contemporary Review*, 67 (February 1895): 230.

63 *Ibid.*, p. 230.

64 See Josef Breuer and Sigmund Freud, *Studies on Hysteria* (1893–95) (reprinted Harmondsworth: Penguin Freud Library, 1974) III, 165 (the case of Frau Emmy Von N.).

65 F. E. Hardy, *The Life of Thomas Hardy*, p. 259. It is possible that this topic may have been prompted by an article in that month's *New Review* on the subject; see Ludwig Buchner, 'The Brain of Women', 9 (August 1893), 166–76, but Crichton-Browne had freely addressed the subject in the 1880s and nineties, as had other medical figures like Clouston, Allbutt and Savage, see Oppenheim, *'Shattered Nerves'*, pp. 195–6.

66 Lewis S. Feuer, 'The Friendship of Edwin Ray Lankester and Karl Marx: The Last Episode in Marx's Intellectual Evolution', *Journal of the History of Ideas*, 60 (October–December 1979): 633–48.

67 Spencer had been a member of the Savile since 1883, and Romanes

since 1879. Lankester had joined in 1869, Maudsley 1871, Rolleston 1888 and Allbutt 1891. In 1891 Hardy was elected to the Athenaeum where he joined Romanes, who was elected the same year, Galton (1855), Spencer (1868), Allbutt (1880) and Lankester (1889); see *The Savile Club 1868–1923* (privately printed for the Committee of the Club) (1923), pp. 99–186, and *The Athenaeum; Rules and List of Members* (1891), p. 64, p. 74, p. 94.

68 See Elaine Showalter, *The Female Malady: Women, Madness and English Culture 1830–1980* (London: Virago, 1987), p. 131.

69 H. D. Rolleston, 'Alcoholism' in T. C. Allbutt and H. D. Rolleston (eds.) *A System of Medicine* (9 vols. London: Macmillan & Co., 1905–11), II, 850–1. See Virginia Berridge, 'Concepts of Narcotic Addiction in Britain, 1820–1926', *Annals of Science* 36 (1979): 78.

70 'The Tree of Knowledge', *New Review* 10 (June 1894): 675–90 (p. 681); see Patricia Ingham, 'The Evolution of *Jude the Obscure*', *Review of English Studies* n. s. 27 (1976): 160. Among the other contributors were the novelists Walter Besant, Hall Caine and Israel Zangwill.

71 'The Tree of Knowledge', p. 681.

72 *Ibid.*, p. 682.

73 *Ibid.*, p. 681. Hardy almost certainly would have known of the guide by Henry Allbutt (1846–1904), a cousin of Hardy's acquaintance, T. Clifford Allbutt. His controversial *The Wife's Handbook* was designed to 'diffuse among the general populace hygienic knowledge' (i.e. contraceptive techniques). It was denounced as of 'a decidedly immoral tendency' by the General Medical Council. Allbutt was taken off the *Medical Register* in 1887. The book went on to sell 390,000 copies over the next twenty years. See Peter Fryer, *The Birth Controllers* (London: Corgi Books, 1967), pp. 188–91; Lesley A. Hall, *Hidden Anxieties: Male Sexuality 1900–1950* (Cambridge: Polity Press, 1991), p. 19.

74 Beer, *Darwin's Plots* ch. 8, especially pp. 256–8.

75 Penny Boumelha, *Thomas Hardy and Women* (Brighton: Harvester, 1982), p. 140.

76 Thomas Hardy, *Jude the Obscure* (1895; rpt. London: Macmillan, 1975), p. 38. Subsequent references are included in the text.

77 John Goode, 'The Decadent Writer as Producer', in Ian Fletcher (ed.) *Decadence and the 1890s* (London: Edward Arnold, 1979): 109–29 (p. 123).

78 Edmund Gosse, 'Mr Hardy's New Novel', *Cosmopolis*, 1 (January–March 1896): 67. It is surely not the case, as Ann Thwaite claims, that Gosse 'saw to the heart of Hardy's intention with Sue'. See Ann Thwaite, *Edmund Gosse; A Literary Landscape* (London: Secker, 1984), p. 386.

79 R. Y. Tyrell, 'Jude the Obscure', *Fortnightly Review*, n. s. 59 (June 1896): 857–64, cited in R. G. Cox (ed.) *Thomas Hardy: The Critical Heritage*, (London: Routledge, 1970), p. 295.

80 Gosse, 'Mr Hardy's New Novel': 65.
81 Tyrell, cited in Cox (ed.), *Hardy: The Critical Heritage*, p. 295.
82 Havelock Ellis, 'Concerning Jude the Obscure', *Savoy Magazine* 6 (October 1896): 35–49, in Cox (ed.) *Hardy: The Critical Heritage*, 300–15 (p. 311).
83 Gosse, 'Mr Hardy's New Novel': 65.
84 George Savage, *Insanity and Allied Neuroses* (Philadelphia: Henry C. Lea, 1884), p. 37, cited by Marcus, 'Mothering, Madness and Music', p. 34 and Showalter, 'Syphilis, Sexuality and the Fiction of the *Fin de Siècle*', p. 107.
85 See Showalter, 'Syphilis, Sexuality and the *Fin de Siècle*', p. 97. Showalter draws attention to Egerton's story 'The Spell of the White Elf' in which a woman desires to 'have a child ... without a husband or the disgrace', *Keynotes and Discords* (London: Virago, 1983), p. 80 (Showalter p. 97). Hardy copied lengthy extracts from *Keynotes* in January 1894, a month after its publication by the Bodley Head; see Bjork (ed.) *The Literary Notes of Thomas Hardy* II, 60–1 (items 1918–21). A copy (extant) of *Keynotes*, with Hardy's marginal annotations, including a passage transcribed into one of his Literary Notebooks, was exchanged between Hardy and Florence Henniker; see Michael Millgate, *Thomas Hardy; A Biography* (1982; Oxford University Press, 1985), p. 356.

9 RACE-REGENERATION

1 Havelock Ellis in *The New Age* (11 April 1908), cited by C. W. Saleeby, *Parenthood and Race Culture: An Outline of Eugenics* (London: Cassell & Co., 1909), p. 132.
2 Harley Granville-Barker, *The Voysey Inheritance* (1905), Act II in Dennis Kennedy (ed.) *Plays by Harley Granville-Barker* (Cambridge University Press, 1987), p. 98.
3 W. T. Stead, 'How the Other Half Lives' (review of B. S. Rowntree, *Poverty: A Study of Town Life* (1901)), *Review of Reviews* 24 (December 1901): 642–5 (p. 642).
4 Lord Rosebery's Address delivered as Lord Rector to the students of Glasgow University, 16 November 1900, in Lord Rosebery, *Miscellanies: Literary and Historical* edited by John Buchan (2 vols. London: Hodder & Stoughton, 1921), II, 250–1.
5 The statistics of 'unfitness' were first given contemporary currency by Arnold White, in *The Weekly Sun* (28 July 1900), and *Efficiency and Empire* (London: Methuen, 1901), pp. 102–3. He was followed by General Frederick Maurice ['Miles'], 'Where to Get Men?', *Contemporary Review* 82 (January 1902): 78–86, and George F. Shee, 'The Deterioration in the National Physique', *Nineteenth Century and After* 53 (May 1903): 797–805. This historical moment has been discussed by, among others, Samuel Hynes, *The Edwardian Turn of Mind* (1968; repr. London: Pimlico, 1991), p. 21; G. R. Searle, *The Quest for National*

Efficiency: A Study in British Politics and Political Thought 1899–1914 (1971; repr. London: The Ashfield Press, 1990), pp. 61–2; Richard Soloway, 'Counting the Degenerates: The Statistics of Race Deterioration in Edwardian England', *Journal of Contemporary History* 17 (1982): 139–64 (p. 140); Anthony Wohl, *Endangered Lives* (London: J. M. Dent, 1983), pp. 332–3; Nikolas Rose, *The Psychological Complex* (London: Routledge & Kegan Paul, 1985), p. 78; Deborah Dwork, *War is Good for Babies And Other Young Children: A History of the Infant and Child Welfare Movement in England 1898–1918* (London: Tavistock Publications, 1987), pp. 12–17.

 6 See Raymond Betts, 'The Allusion to Rome in British Imperialist Thought of the Late Nineteenth and Early Twentieth Centuries', *Victorian Studies* 15 (2) (December 1971): 149–59.

 7 See Searle, *The Quest For National Efficiency*, pp. 35–46.

 8 David Feldman, 'The Importance of Being English: Jewish Immigration and the Decay of Liberal England' in David Feldman and Gareth Stedman Jones (eds.) *Metropolis: London Histories and Representations since 1800* (London: Routledge and Kegan Paul, 1989), 56–84 (pp. 72–3).

 9 See Searle, *The Quest for National Efficiency*, pp. 111–15.

10 Bernard Semmel, *Imperialism and Social Reform: English Social-Imperial Thought 1895–1914* (London: Allen & Unwin, 1960), pp. 67–70.

11 Sidney Webb, 'Lord Rosebery's Escape From Houndsditch', *Nineteenth Century and After* 50 (September 1901): 386; see Semmel, *Imperialism and Social Reform*, p. 73.

12 Webb, 'Lord Rosebery's Escape From Houndsditch': 386, cited by Semmel, p. 74. For 'efficiency' see Jonathan Rose, *The Edwardian Temperament 1895–1919* (Athens, Ohio: Ohio University Press, 1986), ch. 4.

13 Lord Rosebery, *Liberal League Publication* no. 37, cited by Semmel, *Imperialism and Social Reform*, p. 63.

14 Semmel, *Imperialism and Social Reform*, p. 63.

15 Cited by Michael Freeden, *The New Liberalism: An Ideology of Social Reform* (Oxford: Clarendon Press, 1978), p. 183.

16 Norman Mackenzie (ed.) *The Letters of Sidney and Beatrice Webb* (3 vols. (Cambridge University Press, 1978), II, 169–70; see also Semmel, *Imperialism and Social Reform*, pp. 75–6.

17 See Semmel, *Imperialism and Social Reform*, p. 76; Searle, *The Quest for National Efficiency*, pp. 150–2.

18 Rose, *The Psychological Complex*, p. 77

19 Sir Thomas Lauder Brunton was Consulting Physician to St Bartholomew's Hospital, Chief Medical officer for the City of London Cadet Brigade, Vice-Chairman of the Executive Council of the National League for Physical Improvement and a member of the Council of Boy Scouts.

20 There is a useful discussion of such rhetoric in John Springhall,

'Building Character in the British Boy: The Attempt to Extend Christian Manliness to Working-Class Adolescents 1880–1914', in J. A. Mangan and J. Walvin (eds.) *Manliness and Morality: Middle-Class Masculinity in Britain and America 1800–1940* (Manchester University Press, 1987), 52–74 (p. 65).

21 See Hynes, *The Edwardian Turn of Mind*, p. 21.

22 Brunton, letter to *The Times*, 'War Games For Children', 7 January 1902, repr. in *Collected Papers on Physical and Military Training* (1915) (unpaginated).

23 J. B. Atkins, 'National "Physical Education". A Proposed League', *The Manchester Guardian*, 23 July 1903, p. 12; see Brunton, *Collected Papers*.

24 Verbatim report of speeches delivered on 28 June 1905 at the Mansion House, in Brunton, *Collected Papers*.

25 Pelham Warner, *How We Recovered the Ashes* (London: Chapman & Hall, 1905), p. 13. For the role of cricket in the elaboration of the imperial myth, from 1890–1914, see John Simons, 'The Golden Age of Cricket' in Gary Day (ed.) *Readings of Popular Culture: Trivial Pursuits?* (London: Macmillan, 1990), pp. 151–63.

26 Rudyard Kipling, 'The Army of a Dream' (1904), in *Traffics and Discoveries* (1904; repr. Harmondsworth: Penguin, 1987), p. 211.

27 Rose, *The Edwardian Temperament*, p. 135.

28 *Ibid.*, p. 135.

29 See Jean Donnison, *Midwives and Medical Men: A History of Inter-Professional Rivalries and Women's Rights* (London: Heinemann, 1977), p.167. For the impact of these ideas on infant and child welfare see Dwork, *War is Good For Babies*, particularly chaps. 1 and 2.

30 William Odell, *The Physique of the British Nation* (Torquay: 'Directory' Office, 1903), p. 21.

31 Springhall, 'Building Character in the British Boy', p. 56.

32 *Report of the Inter-Departmental Committee on Physical Deterioration*, p. 1904: Vol. XXXii, Vol. 1. Cd. 2175 Report and Appendix, Vol. 2. Cd. 2210 List of Witnesses, Minutes of Evidence, Vol. 3. Cd. 2186 Appendix and General Index.

33 *Ibid.*, 1, 46.

34 *Ibid.*, 2, 97.

35 *Ibid.*, 1, 38–9.

36 *Ibid.*, 1, 85–6.

37 *Ibid.*, 1, 88.

38 *Ibid.*, 1, 86–7.

39 *Ibid.*, 1, 87.

40 See Richard Soloway, 'Counting the Degenerates: The Statistics of Race Deterioration in Edwardian England', *Journal of Contemporary History* 17 (1982): 151; Dwork, *War is Good for Babies*, pp. 171–4, pp. 179–80.

41 H. G. Wells, 'The Land Ironclads', *Strand Magazine*, 26 (December 1903): 751–64; repr. in *The Complete Short Stories of H. G. Wells* (London: Ernest Benn, 1927): 131–57 (p. 134). Subsequent references are included in the text.

42 The idea of the 'coming man' had considerable currency in the years after the Boer War, propelled by the Nietzschean *ubermentsch* and the collectivism of the new Liberalism and the Fabians. Gissing initially chose it as the title of his 1899 novel *Our Friend the Charlatan*. W. T. Stead published a series in his *Review of Reviews*, later collected as *Coming Men on Coming Questions* (1905). It addressed problems which it was thought an anticipated Liberal government would need to tackle, and was written by men whose political prospects seemed bright – Haldane, Churchill, Keir Hardie and Ramsay Macdonald among them. A characteristic 'coming man' was T. J. McNamara (a Liberal MP appropriately for the rising suburb of North Camberwell) who was eulogised by Stead as 'typical of the new generation. A self-made man, promoted from the ranks for sheer merit, and destined to go far' (*Coming Men* p. 43). The type was satirised by Shaw as the polytechnic-educated chauffeur Straker in *Man and Superman* (1903), first performed in 1905.

43 H. G. Wells, *Anticipations of the Reaction of Mechanical and Scientific Progress upon Human Life and Thought* (London: Chapman & Hall, 1901 [1902]), p. 97.

44 *Ibid.*, p. 183.

45 *Ibid.*, p. 183.

46 Sidney Webb to H. G. Wells, 8 December 1901, in Mackenzie (ed.), *Letters*, II, 144.

47 Webb to Wells, ibid., II, 144.

48 H. G. Wells, *A Modern Utopia* (London: Chapman & Hall, 1905), p. 446, p. 458.

49 *Proposals For a Voluntary Nobility* (Samurai Press, 1907), p. 7.

50 *Ibid.*, p. 9.

51 *Ibid.*, p. 19.

52 Cited in Rose, *The Edwardian Temperament* p. 131

53 Sidney Olivier to Wells, 29 May 1905, in M. Olivier (ed.) *Letters and Selected Writings of Sidney Olivier* (London: Allen & Unwin, 1948), p. 127.

54 *New Age* I (2 May 1907): 9–11.

55 Beatrice Webb to M. Playne, 21 August 1907 in Mackenzie *Letters* (ed.), II, 272. Ironically Beatrice and Sidney were now locked in battle for the hearts, and especially the minds, of groups of young Fabians. Wells was attracting huge audiences among the young, to the unmistakable irritation of the Webbs. See Mackenzie, *Letters*, II, 262–3.

56 John Buchan to George Brown, 19 July 1909, Edinburgh University

Special Collections, Gen. 1728, B/1/348, cited by Kate Macdonald, 'Wells's Correspondence with John Buchan', *The Wellsian* no. 13 (Summer 1990): 44. On Baden-Powell and the Boy Scout movement see Martin Green, *Dreams of Adventure: Deeds of Empire* (London: Routledge & Kegan Paul, 1980), p. 211.

57 Wells, *Anticipations*, p. 81.

58 *Ibid.*, p. 81.

59 *Ibid.*, p. 305.

60 See Daniel J. Kevles, *In the Name of Eugenics; Genetics and the Uses of Heredity* (1985; Harmondsworth: Penguin, 1986), p. 38. Ronald Fisher, who succeeded Pearson, held the chair from 1933 until 1943. L. S. Penrose subsequently held it from 1945 until 1963, when its title was changed to 'Human Genetics'.

61 Wells, *Anticipations*, p. 212.

62 *Ibid.*, pp. 299–300.

63 J. R. Moore, *The Post-Darwinian Controversies: A Study of the Protestant Struggle to Come to Terms with Darwin in Great Britain and America, 1870–1900* (Cambridge University Press, 1979), p. 182.

64 See Freeden, *The New Liberalism*, pp. 88–9.

65 Kevles, *In the Name of Eugenics*, p. 70.

66 Leonard Doncaster, *Heredity in the Light of Recent Research* (The Cambridge Manuals of Science and Literature) (Cambridge University Press, 1910–30; 1910), pp. 49–50, pp. 119–20.

67 Soloway, 'Counting the Degenerates': 153; see also Soloway, *Demography and Degeneration: Eugenics and the Declining Birth-Rate in Twentieth-Century Britain* (Chapel Hill and London: University of North Carolina Press, 1990), pp. 10–17.

68 Havelock Ellis, *The Problem of Race-Regeneration: New Tracts for the Times* (London: Cassell & Co., 1911), p. 54.

69 Sidney Webb, 'The Decline in the Birthrate', Fabian Tract 131 (London: The Fabian Society, 1907), 1–20 (p. 17); cited by Semmel, *Imperialism and Social Reform*, pp. 50–1.

70 See E. M. Forster, *Howards End*, ed. Oliver Stallybrass (Harmondsworth: Penguin, 1975), p. 347.

71 *Ibid.*, pp. 59–60.

72 *Ibid.*, p. 58.

73 Ruth Slater, diary entry for 23 November 1908, in Tierl Thompson (ed.) *Dear Girl: The Diaries and Letters of Two Working Women 1897–1917* (London: Women's Press, 1987), p. 134.

74 H. G. Wells, *Ann Veronica* (1909; repr. London: Virago, 1980), p. 111.

75 Rose, *The Psychological Complex*, p. 99.

76 Clive Ponting, 'Churchill's Plan for Race-Purity', *Guardian* (20–21 June 1992): 23.

77 Alfred Tredgold, 'The Feeble-Minded', *Contemporary Review* 97 (1910): 721.

78 See Rose, *The Psychological Complex*, p. 107.
79 Alfred Tredgold, *Mental Deficiency – (Amentia)* (1908; 2nd edn London: Bailliere, Tyndall & Cox, 1914), p. 38, cited by Rose, pp. 107–8.
80 Ellis, *The Problem of Race-Regeneration*, p. 30.
81 *Ibid.*, p. 45.
82 *Ibid.*, p. 66.
83 Kathleen Jones, *A History of the Mental Health Services* (London: Routledge, 1972), pp. 200–2.
84 Jones, *A History of the Mental Health Services*, p. 186.
85 The 1913 legislation had been held up in committee because of the difficulty of defining 'mental defective', 'idiot', 'imbecile' and 'feeble-minded'; see Jones, p. 202.
86 D. H. Lawrence, *The Rainbow* (1915; repr. Harmondsworth: Penguin, 1981), p. 446.
87 Churchill to Asquith, cited by Ponting, 'Churchill's Plan For Race-Purity': 23.
88 See G. R. Searle, *Eugenics and Politics in Britain 1900–1914* (Leyden: Noordhof, 1976), pp. 107–9.
89 Ponting, 'Churchill's Plan for Race-Purity': 23.
90 *Ibid.*, p. 23. Old habits died hard. In 1955, in the last months of his political career, Churchill, together with Lord Salisbury, worried in cabinet about immigrants from the Commonwealth and the implications for the future of Britain's 'racial stock'; see David Walker, 'Tories "planned to restrict immigration of blacks" ', *Times* (2 January 1986): 1.
91 Ponting, 'Churchill's Plan for Race Purity': 23.
92 *Ibid.*, 23. It is somewhat ironic that Churchill, the arch-enemy of a régime committed to the liquidation of the 'unfit', should, thirty years earlier, have urged the need for policies of compulsory sterilisation in his capacity as a minister.
93 See C. F. G. Masterman, *The Condition of England* (1909; 7th edn London: Methuen & Co., 1912), pp. 150–60.
94 E. R. Pease, *Fabian News* (January 1911), p. 18, cited by G. R. Searle, 'Eugenics and Social Class', in Charles Webster (ed.) *Biology, Medicine and Society 1840–1940* (Cambridge University Press, 1981), 217–42 (p. 230).
95 Ellis, *The Problem of Race-Regeneration*, p. 43.
96 Anthea Trodd, *A Reader's Guide to Edwardian Literature* (Hemel Hempstead: Harvester Wheatsheaf, 1991), p. 41.
97 See Masterman, *The Condition of England*, pp. 151–5.
98 Ellis, *The Problem of Race-Regeneration*, p. 12.
99 Masterman, *The Condition of England*, p. 151.
100 Wells, *Anticipations*, p. 49.
101 Anna Davin, 'Imperialism and Motherhood', *History Workshop Journal* no. 5 (1978): 14.

102 Karl Pearson, 'Woman and Labour', *Fortnightly Review* no. 329 (May 1894): 569–70, 575.
103 James Joyce, *Portrait of the Artist as a Young Man* (1916; repr. London: Granada, 1977), p. 189.
104 Arthur Mee, Preface to *The Children's Encyclopaedia* (8 vols. London: The Educational Book Co. Ltd., 1910–11), I, 3.
105 C. W. Saleeby, *Parenthood and Race Culture: An Outline of Eugenics* (London: Cassell & Co., 1909), p. 285.
106 Wells, *Anticipations*, p. 49.
107 C. W. Saleeby, 'The Human Mother', *Infant Mortality Conference 1908*, cited by Anna Davin, 'Imperialism and Motherhood': 63.
108 Wells, *Mankind in the Making* (London: Chapman & Hall, 1903), pp. 99–100.
109 *Ibid.*, p. 101.
110 See H. G. Wells, 'The Endowment of Motherhood', in *An Englishman Looks at the World* (London: Cassell & Co., 1914), pp. 229–34.
111 See H. G. Wells, *The New Machiavelli* (1911; repr. Harmondsworth: Penguin, 1946), pp. 325–6, and see pp. 299–300.
112 See Kevles, *In the Name of Eugenics*, p. 317.
113 *Ibid.*, p. 65; see also Frank Mort, *Dangerous Sexualities: Medico-moral Politics in England Since 1830* (London: Routledge, 1987), p. 181. Lucy Bland has a good discussion of the origins of these concerns and their voicing by middle-class feminists in 'Marriage Laid Bare: Middle-Class Women and Marital Sex 1880s-1914', in Jane Lewis (ed.) *Labour and Love: Women's Experience of Home and Family 1850–1940*. (Oxford: Basil Blackwell, 1986), 123–46 (pp. 124–6).
114 Penny Boumelha, *Thomas Hardy and Women* (London: Macmillan, 1982), p. 21.
115 See Mort, *Dangerous Sexualities*, pp. 181–2.
116 *Ibid.*, p. 183.
117 See Thompson (ed.) *Dear Girl*, p. 226.
118 Christabel Pankhurst, *The Great Scourge and How To End It* (London: E. Pankhurst, 1913), p. 17.
119 Cited by Kevles, *In the Name of Eugenics*, p. 90.
120 Marie Stopes, 'How Mrs Jones Does Her Worst', *Daily Mail* (13 June 1919): 4, cited by Ruth Hall, *Marie Stopes* (London: Virago, 1977), p. 173; see also Lesley A. Hall, *Hidden Anxieties: Male Sexuality 1900–1950* (Cambridge: Polity Press, 1991); Soloway, *Demography and Degeneration*, pp. 178–81.
121 Marie Stopes, 'The Race', in *'Gold in the Wood' and 'The Race': Two New Plays of Life* (London: A. C. Fifield, 1918), pp. 46–8.
122 *Ibid.*, p. 70.

10 MASCULINITY, MORBIDITY AND MEDICINE: *HOWARDS END*
AND *MRS DALLOWAY*

1 Henry Maudsley, *Responsibility in Mental Disease* (1874), p. 228, cited by Michael J. Clark, ' "Morbid Introspection", Unsoundness of Mind, and British Psychological Medicine c1830 – c1900', in W. F. Bynum, Roy Porter and Michael Shepherd (eds.) *The Anatomy of Madness: Essays in the History of Psychiatry* (3 vols. London: Tavistock Publications, 1985–88), III, 71–101 (p. 91).

2 J. A. Ormerod, 'Hysteria', in T. C. Allbutt and H. D. Rolleston (eds.) *A System of Medicine* (9 vols. 1898; 2nd edn London: Macmillan, 1910), VIII, 720), cited by Michael J. Clark, 'The Rejection of Psychological Approaches to Mental Disorder in Late Nineteenth-Century British Psychiatry', in Andrew Scull (ed.) *Madhouses, Mad-Doctors and Madmen: The Social History of Psychiatry in the Victorian Era* (London: Athlone Press, 1981), 271–312 (p. 297).

3 W. H. R. Rivers, cited by Elaine Showalter, *The Female Malady* (London: Virago, 1987), p. 189.

4 Henry Newbolt, 'Clifton Chapel', in *The Island Race* (London: Elkin Mathews, 1898), p. 76.

5 See John Springhall, 'Building Character in the British Boy: The Attempt to Extend Christian Manliness to Working-Class Adolescents, 1880–1914', in J. A. Mangan and James Walvin (eds.) *Manliness and Morality: Middle-Class Masculinity in Britain and America 1800–1940* (Manchester University Press, 1987), 52–74 (p. 65). There is a good discussion of this topic by Joseph Bristow, *Empire Boys: Adventures in a Man's World* (London: HarperCollins, 1991), ch. 2.

6 James Walvin, 'Symbols of Moral Superiority: Slavery, Sport and The Changing World Order', in *Manliness and Morality*: 242–60 (p. 258).

7 Arnold White, *Efficiency and Empire* (London: Methuen, 1901), pp. 101–2.

8 Thomas Hodgkin, 'The Fall of the Roman Empire and Its Lesson For Us', *Contemporary Review* 73 (January 1898): 51–70, cited by Geoffrey Pearson, *Hooligan: A History of Respectable Fears* (London: Macmillan, 1983), pp. 70–1.

9 William Bevan Lewis, *A Text-book of Mental Diseases* (2nd edn, London: C. Griffin & Co., 1899), cited by Clark, ' "Morbid Introspection" ' in Bynum, Porter and Shepherd, III, 86.

10 Clark, ' "Morbid Introspection" ', III, 87–9; see also Alison Hennegan, 'Personalities and Principles: Aspects of Literature and Life in *Fin de Siècle* England', in Mikulas Teich and Roy Porter (eds.) *Fin de Siècle and Its Legacy* (Cambridge University Press, 1990), 170–215 (p. 202); Janet Oppenheim, *'Shattered Nerves': Doctors, Patients and Depression in Victorian England* (New York and Oxford: Oxford University Press,

1991), pp. 159–63; Ed Cohen, *Talk on the Wilde Side: Towards a Genealogy of a Discourse on Male Sexualities* (New York: Routledge, 1993), ch. 2.

11 Anon., 'Three Poetry Books', *Saturday Review* 72 (7 November 1891): 537.

12 Anon., 'Our Reviewer's Table', *Irish Daily Independent* (4 January 1892): 7.

13 John Springhall, 'Building Character in the British Boy', in *Manliness and Morality*, p. 67. The romantic imperialism of the *Boy's Own Paper* is discussed by Bristow, *Empire Boys*, pp. 38–48.

14 Paul Cushing, 'For England's Sake', *National Observer* (16 April 1892), cited by Thomas Hardy, in Lennart Bjork (ed.) *The Literary Notebooks of Thomas Hardy* (2 vols. London: Macmillan, 1985), II (item 2141), pp. 114–15: an entry of about 1901.

15 E. M. Forster, *Howards End* (1910; Harmondsworth: Penguin, 1975), p. 321. Subsequent references are incorporated in the text.

16 E. M. Forster, 'T.S.Eliot' in *Abinger Harvest* (1936; repr. Harmondsworth: Penguin, 1967), p. 102. (This essay was first published in 1928.)

17 J. A. Cramb, cited by Michael Howard, 'Empire, Race and War in Pre-1914 Britain', in H. Lloyd-Jones *et al.* (eds.) *History and Imagination* (London: Duckworth, 1981), 340–55 (p. 350).

18 D. H. Lawrence to E. M. Forster (20 September 1922), in Warren Roberts, James T. Boulton and Elizabeth Mansfield (eds.), *The Letters of D. H. Lawrence* IV (1921–1924) (Cambridge University Press, 1987), p. 301.

19 John Stokes, *In the Nineties* (Hemel Hempstead: Harvester-Wheatsheaf, 1989), pp. 26–7.

20 Cited by Richard Davenport-Hines, *Sex, Death and Punishment* (London: Collins, 1990), pp. 126–7. The campaign against decadence seemed to reach a climax during 1894 and up to the verdict against Wilde in May 1895, to judge by the satiric offensive mounted by *Punch*. See R. K. R. Thornton, *The Decadent Dilemma* (London: Edward Arnold, 1983), p. 43, pp. 57–8.

21 Stokes, *In the Nineties*, p. 26.

22 E. M. Forster, *Maurice* (1971; repr. Harmondsworth: Penguin, 1972), p. 57.

23 *Ibid.*, p. 212.

24 Max Nordau, *Degeneration* (1895; trans. from the 2nd edn of *Entartung* (1893) [1892]; Popular Edition, London: William Heinemann, 1898), p. 540. Taking its cue from Nordau, one review of *Degeneration* (in the *Weekly Sun*) published shortly after Wilde was sentenced, insisted on an elision between manliness and health in order to expose the 'bestialities which raise their brazen and brutal heads in the literature of our time': it positioned the appalled reader as 'honest, pure and manly'. See Cohen, *Talk on the Wilde Side*, pp. 15–19, 254–5 (fn. 5).

25 Parliamentary Debates *Hansard* 9 March 1988, p. 372, p. 382, p. 384.

26 See Davenport-Hines, *Sex, Death and Punishment*, p. 140.

27 Oscar Wilde, 'The Soul of Man Under Socialism', in *De Profundis and Other Writings* (Harmondsworth: Penguin, 1973): 19–53 (p. 38); see also Stokes, *In the Nineties*, pp. 27–8.

28 M. J. Clark, ' "Morbid Introspection" ', in Bynum *et al.* (eds.) III, 72.

29 *Ibid.*, III, 80.

30 Michel Foucault, *The History of Sexuality* Vol. I (Harmondsworth: Penguin, 1981), p. 104.

31 J. A. Ormerod, 'Hysteria', in *A System of Medicine*, VIII, 721.

32 Clark, ' "Morbid Introspection" ', in Bynum *et al.* (eds.), III, 91.

33 *Ibid.*, III, 75.

34 Henry Maudsley, *Body and Mind* (London: Macmillan, 1873), pp. 84–5, cited by Clark, in Bynum *et al*, III, 91.

35 Showalter, *The Female Malady*, p. 171.

36 Martin Stone, 'Shellshock and the Psychologists', in Bynum *et al.* II, 242–71 (p. 245). A good general account of the phenomenon of the shell-shocked soldier is in Samuel Hynes, *A War Imagined: The First World War in English Culture* (1990; repr. London: Pimlico, 1992), ch. 8: 'Dottyville', pp. 171–88.

37 Stone, p. 252.

38 *Ibid.*, p. 252.

39 *Ibid.*, p. 245.

40 Showalter, *The Female Malady*, p. 189.

41 W. H. R. Rivers, 'Freud's Theory of the Unconscious', *The Lancet* 16 June 1917, in *Instinct and the Unconscious*, p. 166, cited by Showalter, p. 189. The crisis in British psychiatric medicine, and the response by the psychiatric establishment to Freudian psychology, is charted by Oppenheim, in *'Shattered Nerves'*, pp. 304–8.

42 W. H. B. Stoddart, quoted in report of *Annual Meeting, Medico-Psychological Association of Great Britain*, *Lancet* 199, Part Two (1920): 402–5.

43 Sir Robert Armstrong-Jones, quoted in report of *Annual Meeting, Medico-Psychological Association of Great Britain*: 402–5, cited by Stone, in Bynum *et al.*, II, 247. His comments form part of the reported 'Discussion' of papers, given at the meeting, on Freud's psychology, and on homosexuality, sadism and masochism. This was no doubt strong meat for Armstrong-Jones, who probably felt that he had taken quite enough!

44 See Lyndall Gordon, *Virginia Woolf: A Writer's Life* (London: Virago, 1978); Roger Poole, *The Unknown Virginia Woolf* (1978; 3rd rev. edn Atlantic Highlands NJ: Humanities Press, International, 1990); Stephen Trombley, *'All That Summer She Was Mad'; Virginia Woolf and Her Doctors* (London: Junction Books, 1981); Showalter, *The Female Malady*.

45 Quentin Bell, *Virginia Woolf: A Biography* (2 vols. London: Triad/ Granada, 1976), 1, 95.

46 T. B. Hyslop, 'A Discussion on Occupation and Environment as Causative Factors of Insanity', *British Medical Journal* (14 October 1905): 942.

47 George Savage, *Insanity and Allied Neuroses* (Philadelphia: Henry C. Lea's Son & Co, 1884), p. 24., cited by Jane Marcus, 'Virginia Woolf And Her Violin: Mothering, Madness and Music', in E. K. Ginsberg and L. M. Gottlieb (eds.) *Virginia Woolf: Centennial Essays* (Troy, NY: Whitston, 1983), 27–49 (p. 34).

48 Leonard Woolf, *Beginning Again* (London: Hogarth Press, 1965), p. 160, cited by Martine Stemerick, 'Virginia Woolf and Julia Stephen: The Distaff Side of History', in Ginsberg and Gottlieb (eds.), 51–80 (p. 63).

49 Oppenheim, *'Shattered Nerves'*, p. 310.

50 Gordon, *Virginia Woolf*, pp. 63–4.

51 Elaine Showalter, *A Literature of Their Own* (London: Virago, 1978), p. 274; see also Oppenheim, *'Shattered Nerves'*, p. 213.

52 Virginia Woolf, *Mrs Dalloway* (1925; repr. Harmondsworth: Penguin, 1992), p. 107. Subsequent references are incorporated in the text.

53 Elaine Showalter, Introduction to *Mrs Dalloway* (1925; repr. Harmondsworth: Penguin, 1992), xlii.

54 Gordon, *Virginia Woolf*, p. 66.

55 *Ibid.*, p. 64.

11 THE WAY OUT IS THE WAY BACK: THE ANTI-MODERNISTS

1 Warwick Deeping, *The Secret Sanctuary* (London: Cassell & Co., 1923), p. 21. All subsequent references are included in the text. After Trinity College, Cambridge (George) Warwick Deeping trained as a doctor at the Middlesex Hospital. He practised for a year then turned to full-time writing. He wrote over seventy novels, nineteen of them before 1914.

2 The representation by male writers of female erotic release at this period is discussed by Sandra M. Gilbert and Susan Gubar in *No Man's Land; The Place of the Woman Writer in the Twentieth Century*. Vol. 2 *Sexchanges* (New Haven & London: Yale University Press, 1989), pp. 290–2.

3 For the controversies aroused by cases of acts of violence by 'shell-shocked veterans' in the 1920s, see Eric T. Deane, 'War and Psychiatry: Examining the Diffusion Theory in the Light of the Insanity Defence in post-World War 1 Britain', *History of Psychiatry* 4 (1) (March 1993): 61–82. I owe this reference to Michael Neve.

4 Warwick Deeping, *Sorrell and Son* (London: Cassell & Co., 1925), p. 4. Subsequent references are included in the text. The disenchantment of the returned soldier as a theme in popular literature is discussed by

Samuel Hynes in *A War Imagined: The First World War and English Culture* (1990; repr. London: Pimlico, 1992), pp. 348–52.

5 There are degenerate and anti-semitic overtones in the description of the villain, Blaber, in another of Deeping's novels of the period, *Suvla John* (London: Cassell & Co., 1924).

6 Stanley Baldwin, 'On England and the West' (1924), in *On England and Other Addresses* (London: p. Allan & Co., 1926), p. 6. See Martin Wiener, *English Culture and the Decline of the Industrial Spirit* (Cambridge University Press, 1981), pp. 100–2; Alun Howkins, 'The Discovery of Rural England', in Robert Colls and Philip Dodd (eds.) *Englishness: Politics and Culture 1880–1920* (London: Croom Helm, 1986), 62–88 (p. 82).

7 W. H. Dawson (ed.) *After-War Problems* (London: George Allen & Unwin, 1917), p. 220.

8 *Ibid.*, p. 232.

9 *Ibid.*, p. 232.

10 *Ibid.*, pp. 116–17.

11 The journal of the Royal Society of St George, *The English Race*, was founded in 1894. Its opening number expressed the fear that 'the English stock is getting deficient in that healthy and legitimate egotism which is necessary to self-preservation ... the Englishman must assert his indefeasable birthright'. Cited by Tom Nairn, 'Enoch Powell: the New Right', *New Left Review*, no. 61 (May-June 1970): 5.

12 Sir Joseph Compton-Rickett, 'Organisation of the National Resources' in Dawson (ed.) *After-War Problems*, p. 116.

13 T. S. Eliot, 'Marie Lloyd' in Frank Kermode (ed.) *T.S.Eliot; Selected Prose* (London: Faber, 1975), 172–4 (p. 174). Originally an obituary notice in *The Dial* (December 1922), Kermode reprints the revised version published in *Criterion* (January 1923): 192–5.

14 *House of Commons Debates* Vol. 266 (1932), 741–2, cited by Jeffrey Richards, *The Age of the Dream Palace: Cinema and Society 1930–1939* (London: Routledge, 1984), p. 54.

15 Richards, *The Age of the Dream Palace*, p. 71.

16 R. G. Burnett and E. D. Martell, *The Devil's Camera; Menace of a Film-Ridden World* (London: Epworth Press, 1932), pp. 11–12, cited by Richards, p. 55.

17 Sir Hamilton Harty, 'Accursed Jazz: An English View', *Literary Digest* (2 October 1929), cited by D. L. LeMahieu, *A Culture For Democracy* (Oxford: Clarendon Press, 1988), p. 116, and generally, pp. 113–17.

18 These themes were also sounded insistently through the inter-war period by the critics of suburban ribbon development such as H. J. Massingham and Clough Williams-Ellis in *Britain and the Beast* (London: Dent, 1937); of Americanisation by C. E. M. Joad in *The Babbitt Warren* (1926) and *The Horrors of the Countryside* (1931) (see LeMahieu, p. 119.); of the standardisation which accompanied mass-

production by J. B. Priestley (see Wiener, *English Culture*, pp. 123–4), or of mass culture by F. R. Leavis.

19 Susan Briggs, *Those Radio Times* (London: Weidenfeld & Nicholson, 1981), p. 55.

20 *Ibid.*, p. 55.

21 Harold Begbie, 'A Good Fairy in Mean Streets', *Radio Times* (September 1924), cited by Briggs, *Those Radio Times*, p. 55.

22 Begbie in Briggs, *Those Radio Times*, p. 55.

23 E. M. Forster, *Howards End* (1910; repr. Harmondsworth: Penguin, 1975), p. 44. The proponents of cinema and radio demonstrated the same capacity to speak on behalf of the mass audience as did those hostile to these new media. Sir John Reith put the official BBC point of view at its inception: 'It is occasionally indicated to us that we are apparently setting out to give the public what we think they need – and not what they want – but few know what they want and very few what they need.' (Cited in Mark Pegg, *Broadcasting and Society 1918–1939* (London: Croom Helm, 1983), p. 95.)

24 John Sinjohn *pseud.* [John Galsworthy], *Jocelyn* (London: Duckworth and Co., 1898), p. 24.

25 J. Howard Moore, *Savage Survivals: The Story of the Race Told in Simple Language* (Thinkers's Library: London: Watts & Co., 1933).

26. W. R. Inge, 'Psychotherapy (i)', in *Lay Thoughts of a Dean* (New York & London: G. P. Putnam's Sons, 1926), p. 232.

27 See W. R. Inge 'Some Moral Aspects of Eugenics', *Eugenics Review* 1, (1909): 30, cited by Anna Davin, 'Imperialism and Motherhood', *History Workshop* 5, (Spring 1978): 59; Pauline M. H. Mazumdar, *Eugenics, Human Genetics and Human Failings: The Eugenics Society, its Sources and its Critics in Britain* (London: Routledge, 1992), pp. 97–8.

28 'The prospects of culture', wrote Leavis in 1930, 'are very dark. There is the less room for hope in that a standardised civilisation is rapidly enveloping the whole world' (*Mass Civilization and Minority Culture* (Cambridge: Gordon Fraser, 1930), p. 30); see also the influential textbook on advertising and popular culture, *Culture and Environment* (1933) by Denys Thompson, a disciple and collaborator of Leavis.

29 W. R. Inge, 'Spoonfeeding', in Inge, *Lay Thoughts of a Dean*, p. 221.

30 Inge, 'Revolutions', in *ibid.*, p. 159.

31 W. R. Inge, 'Democracy', in Inge, *England* (London: Ernest Benn, 1926), p. 264.

32 *Ibid.*, p. 266.

33 *Ibid.*, p. 266. See Hynes, *A War Imagined*, pp. 354–60.

34 Inge, *England*, pp. 266–7.

35 *Ibid.*, p. 267.

36 Bernard Gilbert, Introduction to *The Rural Scene: Poems to Gilbert K. Chesterton* (Vol. IV of the 'Old England Series'), (London: William Collins, 1923), p. 20.

37 Stanley Baldwin, 'Disarmament', in *On England*, pp. 229–30.
38 John Galsworthy, *Justice* (1910; repr. in *The Plays of John Galsworthy* (London: Duckworth, 1929), pp. 234–5, p. 243, p. 252.
39 John Buchan, *The Three Hostages* (1924; repr. Harmondsworth: Penguin, 1953), p. 12. Subsequent references are included in the text.
40 John Buchan, *The Dancing Floor* (London: Hodder & Stoughton, 1926), p. 69.
41 See Norbert Jacques, *Dr Mabuse Master of Mystery; A Novel* (trans. Lilian A. Clare, London: George Allen & Unwin, 1923), p. 131; p. 90.
42 John Buchan, 'Fountainblue' in David Daniell (ed.) *The Best Short Stories of John Buchan* (London: Panther, 1984), p. 235. It first appeared in *Blackwood's* (August 1901), subsequently included in *The Watcher by the Threshold* (1902); see Janet Adam Smith, *John Buchan* (London: Rupert Hart-Davis, 1965), p. 103.
43 John Buchan, *The Power-House* (1913; repr. London: Dent, 1984), p. 35; see Smith, *John Buchan*, p. 253.
44 John Buchan, *The Half-Hearted* (London: Isbister and Co., 1900), p. 203.
45 John Buchan, *John Macnab* (London: Hodder & Stoughton, 1925), p. 12.
46 John Buchan, *A Prince of the Captivity* (London: Nelson, 1933), p. 101.
47 John Buchan, *Huntingtower* (London: Hodder and Stoughton, 1922), pp. 101–12.
48 *Ibid.*, pp. 212–13.
49 'Sapper', *pseud.* [H.C.McNeile] *The Final Count* (1926; repr. London: Dent, 1985), p. 153.
50 John Buchan, *Mr Standfast* (London: Nelson, 1923), p. 57.
51 *Ibid.*, p. 56.
52 Buchan, *A Prince of the Captivity*, p. 154, p. 379.
53 'Sapper', *The Final Count*, p. 2.

12 POSTSCRIPTS

1 E. W. MacBride, 'Social Biology and Birth-Control', *Nature* 113 (31 May 1924): 774, cited by Gary Werskey, *The Visible College* (London: Allen Lane, 1978), p. 32.
2 *Daily Telegraph* 20 April 1929, cited by R. A. Lowe, 'Eugenicists, Doctors and the Quest for National Efficiency: An Educational Crusade 1900–1939', *History of Education* 8 (4) 1979: 302. Heard again in the inter-war period were rekindled anxieties about 'race-suicide', the 'menace' of the 'falling birth-rate' and 'depopulation', see Richard Soloway, *Demography and Degeneration: Eugenics and the Falling Birth-Rate in Twentieth-Century Britain* (Chapel Hill and London: University of N. Carolina Press, 1990), pp. 226–32, pp. 240–46.
3 See Werskey, *The Visible College*, p. 30.

4 Lowe, 'Eugenicists, Doctors and the Quest for National Efficiency', p. 303.
5 E. W. MacBride, 'Cultivation of the Unfit', *Nature* 137 (11 January 1936): 45, cited by Werskey, pp. 32–3.
6 Travis L. Crosby, *The Impact of Civilian Evacuation in the Second World War* (London: Croom Helm, 1986), p. 33, p. 5.
7 R. C. K. Ensor, 'The Great Evacuation', *Spectator* 163 (8 September 1939): 349.
8 J. B. S. Haldane, *Heredity and Politics* (London: George Allen & Unwin), p. 7, p. 90, p. 91, p. 98.
9 J. B. S. Haldane, 'Forty Years of Genetics', in Joseph Needham and Walter Pagel (eds.), *Background to Modern Science* (Cambridge University Press, 1938), 223–43 (p. 230).
10 Haldane, *Heredity and Politics*, p. 94.
11 *Ibid.*, pp. 92–3.
12 Arnold White, *Efficiency and Empire* (London: Methuen, 1901), p. 117.
13 In an analysis of the origins and development of a twentieth-century 'war machine', Daniel Pick shows how the industrial technology of the animal slaughterhouse served as a practice and metaphor for the modern state, with its 'capacity to monopolise the means of violence' and to 'routinise' 'mass-murder', see Pick, *War Machine: The Rationalisation of Slaughter in the Modern Age* (New Haven and London: Yale University Press, 1993), 178–88 (pp. 186–7). I owe this reference to Michael Neve.
14 Aldous Huxley, *Crome Yellow* (1921; repr. London: Chatto & Windus, 1928), p. 247.
15 Aldous Huxley, *Point Counter Point* (1928; repr. London: Grafton Books, 1978), p. 161.
16 W. B. Yeats, 'The Statues' (1939), in Timothy Webb (ed.) *W.B.Yeats: Selected Poetry* (Harmondsworth: Penguin, 1991), p. 215.
17 Henry Mayhew, *London, Labour and the London Poor* (1851) III, 429, cited by A. Susan Williams, *The Rich Man and the Diseased Poor* (London: Macmillan, 1987), p. 92.
18 George Gissing, *The Nether World* (1889; repr. Brighton: Harvester Press, 1974).
19 W. R. Inge, 'Democracy', in Inge, *England* (London: Ernest Benn, 1926), p. 264.
20 Aldous Huxley, *Antic Hay* (1923; repr. Harmondsworth: Penguin, 1948), p. 192.
21 A diary entry for 1950, cited by David Cairns and Shaun Richards, 'No Brave Causes? The Alienated Intellectual and the End of Empire', *Literature and History* 14 (2) (Autumn 1988): 199.
22 T. S. Eliot, 'Gerontion' (1919), in *Collected Poems 1909–1962* (London: Faber & Faber, 1963), p. 39.
23 T. S. Eliot, 'Marie Lloyd' (1922), in Frank Kermode (ed.), *T.S.Eliot: Selected Prose*, (London: Faber & Faber, 1975), 172–4 (p. 174).

24 W. B. Yeats, 'Tomorrow's Revolution' in *Explorations* (1962), p. 423, cited by Cairns Craig, *Yeats, Eliot, Pound and the Politics of Poetry* (University of Pittsburgh Press, 1982), p. 5; W. B. Yeats, 'Under Ben Bulben' (1939), in Webb (ed.), *W.B.Yeats: Selected Poetry*, p. 211; Yeats, 'A Bronze Head' (1939), *ibid.*, p. 218.

25 T. S. Eliot, 'The Waste Land', in *Collected Poems*, pp. 66–9.

26 Juan Leon, '"Meeting Mr Eugenides": T. S. Eliot and Eugenic Anxiety', *Yeats-Eliot Review* 9 (4) (1988): 173; for Eliot's involvement with eugenics see Leon, *passim*, and David Trotter, 'Modernism and Empire: Reading *The Waste Land*', *Critical Quarterly* 28 (1986): 143–53 (pp. 150–2).

27 John Carey, *The Intellectuals and the Masses: Pride and Prejudice among the Literary Intelligentsia 1880–1939* (London: Faber and Faber, 1992), p. 21.

28 A good account of the inference of 'social decay' from 'mass culture' is in Patrick Brantlinger's *Bread and Circuses: Theories of Mass Culture as Social Decay* (Ithaca: Cornell University Press, 1983).

29 Roy Porter, Review of Penelope Murray (ed.) *Genius: the History of an Idea* (1989), in *Social History of Medicine* 4 (April 1991): 141.

30 William James, *The Varieties of Religious Experience: A Study in Human Nature* (1902; repr. London: Collins, 1960), p. 32, p. 39.

31 Renato Poggioli, *The Theory of the Avant-Garde* (Cambridge, Mass.: Harvard University Press, 1968), p. 165.

32 Edward Garnett, 'Nordau Reconsidered', *Academy* 56, 21 January 1899: 96–7 (p. 96).

33 Aldous Huxley, 'Pascal', in *Do What You Will* (1929; London: Chatto & Windus, 1931), 227–310 (p. 265).

34 'A Philistine Paean', *Punch* (11 May 1895), cited by R. K. R. Thornton, *The Decadent Dilemma* (London: Edward Arnold, 1983), pp. 68–9. See Alison Hennegan, 'Personalities and Principles: Aspects of Literature and Life in *Fin de Siècle* England', in Mikulas Teich and Roy Porter (eds.) *Fin de Siècle and its Legacy* (Cambridge University Press, 1990), 170–215 (p. 208).

35 T. B. Hyslop, 'The Mental Deficiency Bill, 1912', *Journal of Mental Science*, 58 (October 1912): 555, cited by Trombley, '*All That Summer she was Mad': Virginia Woolf and Her Doctors* (London: Junction Books, 1981), p. 223.

36 Max Nordau, *Degeneration* (1895; trans. from the 2nd edn. of *Entartung* (1893) [1892]; Popular Edition, London: William Heinemann, 1898), p. 557.

37 Carey, *The Intellectuals and the Masses*, p. 199.

38 Richard Grunberger, *A Social History of the Third Reich* (1971; repr. Harmondsworth: Penguin, 1974), 534–5, and generally, ch. 28.

39 Ernst Bloch, 'Expressionism Seen Now' (1937) in *Heritage of Our Times* (Cambridge: Polity Press, 1991), pp. 234–40 (p. 234).

40 See Grunberger, *A Social History*, p. 536; Matthew Collings, 'Resistance Heroes of Art', *Guardian* (20 May 1992): 58.
41 Adolf Hitler, cited in Herschel B. Chipp, *Theories of Modern Art; A Source Book by Artists and Critics* (Berkeley: University of California Press, 1968), pp. 474–83 (pp. 480–2); see also, Neil Ascherson, 'The Fuhrer's Freak Show', *Independent on Sunday* (1 March 1992): 12–13.
42 Ernst Bloch, 'Jugglers' Fair Between the Gallows' (1937), in *Heritage of Our Times*, pp. 75–80 (p. 75).

Bibliography

PRIMARY SOURCES TO 1940

UNPUBLISHED ITEMS

Carpenter, Edward. Letter to Kate Salt, 7 March 1896. Sheffield City Library, *Edward Carpenter Collection* MS 354/41.

Hardy, Thomas. *Facts from Newspapers, Histories Biographies and other chronicles – mainly local* (abbreviated to 'Facts Notebook'). Dorset County Library, Dorchester. Thomas Hardy MSS.

Hardy, Thomas. *Tess of the D'Urbervilles*. British Library. Additional MS 38182.

Wilde, Oscar. Petition to Home Secretary, 2 July 1896. Public Record Office, Kew, MS H O4J/24514 AJ 6887.

PUBLISHED ITEMS

A.M. Review of *The Whirlpool*. *Bookman* (May 1897): 38–9.

Allbutt, Henry A. *The Wife's Handbook* (1886).

Allbutt, T. Clifford. 'Nervous Diseases and Modern Life', *Contemporary Review*, 67 (1895): 210–31.

Allbutt, T. Clifford and Rolleston, H. D. (eds.). *A System of Medicine*. 9 vols., 1898; (2nd edn London: Macmillan, 1910).

Allen, Grant. 'The New Hedonism', *Fortnightly Review*, 55 (1894): 377–92. *The Woman Who Did* (London: John Lane, 1895).

Anon. 'National Muscle' [Science Jottings], *Illustrated London News* (22 June 1889): 798.

Anon. 'Three Poetry Books', *Saturday Review*, 72 (7 November 1891): 536–7.

Anon. 'Our Reviewer's Table', *Irish Daily Independent* (4 January 1892): 7.

Anon. 'Sex-Mania', *Reynolds Newspaper* (21 April 1895): 1.

Anon. *Cassell's Saturday Journal* 14 (25 December 1895): 281.

Anon. *Cassell's Saturday Journal* 14 (26 February 1896): 461.

Anon. 'Made in Germany', *New Review* 81 (February 1896): 113–27.

Athenaeum, The. *Rules and List of Members*. (1891).

315

Atkins, J. B. 'National Physical Education. A Proposed League', *Manchester Guardian* (23 July 1903): 12.

Bagehot, Walter. *Physics and Politics* (London: H. S. King, 1872).

Baldwin, Stanley. *On England and Other Addresses* (London: P. Allan & Co., 1926).

[Barry, William.] 'The Strike of a Sex', *Quarterly Review* 179 (1894): 289–318.

Begbie, Harold. 'A Christian Fairy in the Streets', *Radio Times* (September 1924)

Bland, Hubert. *With the Eyes of a Man* (London: T. Werner Laurie, 1905).

Blatchford, Robert. *Not Guilty: A Defence of the Bottom Dog* (London: Clarion Press, 1906).

Booth, Charles. *Life and Labour of the People in London* (17 vols., London: Macmillan, 1902–3).

Booth, William. *In Darkest England and the Way Out* (London: Salvation Army, 1890).

Breuer, Josef and Freud, Sigmund. *Studies on Hysteria* (1893–5; repr. Harmondsworth: Penguin, 1974).

[Brooke, Emma Frances.] *A Superfluous Woman* (London: William Heinemann, 1894).

Broughton, Rhoda. *Not Wisely, but Too Well* (3 vols. London: 1867; repr. London: Cassell, 1967).

Brunton, Lauder. *Collected Papers on Physical and Military Training* (1915) (privately printed).

Buchan, John. *The Half-Hearted* (London: Isbister and Co., 1900).
  The Power-House (1913; repr. London: Dent, 1984).
  Huntingtower (London: Hodder and Stoughton, 1922).
  Mr Standfast (London: Nelson, 1923).
  The Three Hostages (1924; repr. Harmondsworth: Penguin, 1953).
  John Macnab (London: Hodder & Stoughton, 1925).
  The Dancing Floor (London: Hodder and Stoughton, 1926).
  A Prince of the Captivity (London: Nelson, 1935).

Buchan, John (ed.). Lord Rosebery, *Miscellanies: Literary and Historical* (2 vols. London: Hodder and Stoughton, 1921).

Buchner, Ludwig. 'The Brain of Women', *New Review* 9 (August 1893): 166–76.

Burnett, R. G. and Martell, E. G. *The Devil's Camera; Menace of a Film-Ridden World* (London: Epworth Press, 1932).

Cantlie, James. *Degeneration amongst Londoners* (London: Field and Tuer, 1885).
  Physical Efficiency: A Review of the Deleterious Effects of Town Life upon the Population of Britain with suggestions *for their arrest* (London & NY: G. P. Putnam's Sons, 1906).

Carpenter, Edward. *England's Ideal* (London: George Allen & Unwin, 1887).

Civilisation: Its Cause and cure (London: Swan Sonneschein, 1889).

Towards Democracy (complete edition in Four Parts, 1905; London: George Allen and Unwin, 5th edn, 1931).

Connolly, Cyril. *Enemies of Promise* (1938; Harmondsworth: Penguin, 1961).

Conrad, Joseph. *The Nigger of the 'Narcissus'* (1897; repr. Harmondsworth: Penguin, 1963).

Heart of Darkness (1899; repr. Harmondsworth: Penguin, 1985).

The Secret Agent: A Simple Tale. (1907; repr. Harmondsworth: Penguin, 1986).

Victory (1915; repr. Oxford University Press, 1986).

Corelli, Marie. 'Mother-Love', *Windsor Magazine* 11 (1899–1900): 99.

Crackenthorpe, B. A. 'Sex and Modern Literature', *Nineteenth Century* (April 1895): 607–16.

Cramb, J. A. *The Origins and Destiny of Imperial Britain* (London: John Murray, 1915).

Crichton-Browne, James. Foreword to James Cantlie, *Physical Efficiency: A Review of the Deleterious Effects of Town Life upon the Population of Britain.* (London & New York, G. P. Putnam's Sons, 1906).

Cushing, Paul. 'For England's Sake', *National Observer* (16 April 1892).

Dallas, James. 'On Pedigrees', *Cassells's Family Magazine* (London: Cassell & Co., 1889): 299–300.

Darrow, Clarence S. *Crime: Its Cause and Treatment* (London: George G.Harrap & Co., 1922).

Darwin, Charles. *On the Origin of Species by Means of Natural Selection, or the Preservation of Favoured Races in the Struggle for Life* (1859; Harmondsworth: Penguin, 1968).

The Variation of Animals and Plants under Domestication (2 vols. London: John Murray, 1868).

The Descent of Man and Selection in Relation to Sex (2 vols. 1871; repr. 1 vol. 1871; London: John Murray, 1901).

Dawson, W. H. (ed.). *After-War Problems* (London: George Allen & Unwin, 1917).

Deeping, Warwick. *The Secret Sanctuary* (London: Cassell & Co., 1923).

Suvla John (London: Cassell Co., 1924).

Sorrell and Son (London: Cassell & Co., 1925).

Doncaster, Leonard. *Heredity in the Light of Recent Research* (The Cambridge Manuals of Science and Literature) (Cambridge University Press, 1910–30; 1910).

Doyle, Arthur Conan. *A Study in Scarlet* (1887; repr. Harmondsworth: Penguin, 1982).

The Parasite (London: A. Constable, 1894).

The Hound of the Baskervilles (1902; repr. Harmondsworth: Penguin, 1981).

Sherlock Holmes: The Complete Short Stories (London: John Murray, 1961).

Dugdale, Richard L. *'The Jukes': A Study in Crime, Pauperism, Disease and Heredity* (1877; 5th edn, G. P. Putnam's Sons, 1877).

Dunraven, Earl of (Windham T. W. Quin). 'The Invasion of Destitute Aliens' *Nineteenth Century* 31 (June 1892): 985–1000.

Egerton, George. [*pseud* Mary Chavelita Dunne]. *Keynotes and Discords* (1894; repr. London: Virago, 1983).

Ellis, Havelock. *The Criminal* (London: Walter Scott & Co., 1890).

The New Spirit (1890; 4th edn London: Constable & Co., 1926).

'The Colour Sense in Literature', *Contemporary Review* 69 (May 1896): 714–29.

'Concerning *Jude the Obscure*', *Savoy Magazine* 6 (October 1896: 35–49.

The Criminal (London: Walter Scott & Co., 1901).

The Problem of Race-Regeneration: New Tracts for the Times (London: Constable & Co., 1911).

The Task of Social Hygiene (1912; 2nd edn London: Constable & Co., 1927).

From Rousseau to Proust (1935; repr. London: Constable & Co., 1936).

Encylopaedia Britannica (9th edn 24 vols. 1887; Edinburgh: A & C Black, 1875–9).

(11th edn 29 vols. 1911; Cambridge University Press., 1910–11).

Engels, Friedrich. Preface to Karl Marx, *Capital* (3rd edn 1883; rpt. Harmondsworth: Penguin, 1976).

The Condition of the Working-Class in England (1844; repr. Oxford: Basil Blackwell, 1958).

English Race, The. Journal of the Royal Society of St George Vol. 1 (1894).

Ensor, R. C. K. 'The Great Evacuation', *Spectator* 163 (8 September 1939): 349–50.

Forster, E. M. *Howards End* (1910; repr. Harmondsworth: Penguin, 1975).

Abinger Harvest (1936; repr. Harmondsworth: Penguin, 1967).

Maurice (1971; repr. Harmondsworth: Penguin, 1972).

Freeman, R. Austin. *A Savant's Vendetta* (London: C. Arthur Pearson, 1920).

Freud, Sigmund. *Introductory Lectures on Psychoanalysis* (1915–17; repr. Harmondsworth: Penguin, 1973).

Galsworthy, John. *Justice* (1910; repr. in *The Plays of John Galsworthy* (London: Duckworth, 1929).

Galton, Francis. *Hereditory Genius* (1869; 2nd edn London: Macmillan, 1892).

'The Relative Supplies from Town and Country Families to the population of Future Generations', *Journal of the Statistical Society* 36 (1873): 19–26.

Inquiries into the Human Faculty and its Development (London: Macmillan, 1883).

'Medical Family Registers', *Fortnightly Review* 34 (July 1883): 244–50.

Letter to the *Daily Chronicle*, 29 July 1903.

Garnett, Edward. 'Nordau Reconsidered', *The Academy* 56 (21 January 1899): 96–7.

Gilbert, Bernard. *The Rural Scene* (Vol 4. of 'Old England Series') (London: William Collins, 1923).

Gissing, George. *The Unclassed* (3 vols. London: Chapman and Hall, 1884). *Demos* (1886; repr. Brighton: Harvester Press, 1972).
A Life's Morning (1888; repr. London: Home and Van Thal, 1947).
The Nether World (1889; repr. Brighton: Harvester Press, 1974).
In the Year of Jubilee (1894; repr. Brighton: Harvester Press, 1976).
The Unclassed (revised edn London: Lawrence and Bullen, 1895; repr. Brighton: Harvester, 1976).
The Whirlpool (1897; repr. Hassocks: Harvester Press, 1977).

Gosse, Edmund. 'Mr Hardy's New Novel', *Cosmopolis* 1 (January-March 1896): 60–9.

Grand, Sarah. *The Heavenly Twins* (1893; repr. London: William Heinemann, (1894).

Gray, H. B. *The Public Schools and the Empire* (London: Williams & Norgate, 1913).

Haggard, H. Rider. *Rural England. Being an Account of Agricultural and Social Researches Carried Out in the Years 1901 and 1902*, 2 vols. (London: Longmans & Co., 1902).

Haldane, J. B. S. *Heredity and Politics* (London: George Allen & Unwin, 1938).

Hardy, Thomas. *A Laodicean* (3 vols. 1881; repr. London: Macmillan, 1975).
'The Dorsetshire Labourer', *Longman's Magazine* 2 (July 1883): 252–69.
The Mayor of Casterbridge (2 vols., 1886; repr. London: Macmillan, 1974).
The Woodlanders (3 vols., 1887; repr. London: Macmillan, 1975).
Tess of the D'Urbervilles (3 vols., London: Osgood, McIlvaine and Co., 1891; repr. London: Macmillan, 1975).
Tess of the D'Urbervilles (London: Osgood, McIlvaine and Co., 5th edn 1892).
Jude the Obscure (1895; repr. London: Macmillan, 1975).
Winter Words, in Various Moods and Metres (London: Macmillan, 1928).

Harty, Sir Hamilton. 'Accursed Jazz: An English View', *Literary Digest* 2 (October 1929).

Hasek, Jaroslav. *The Good Soldier Svejk* (trans. C. Parrott) (Harmondsworth: Penguin, 1974).

Haycraft, J. B. *Darwinism and Race Progress* (London: Swan Sonnenschein & Co., 1895).

Henley, W. E. *London Voluntaries* (1892; 3rd edn London: David Nutt, 1912).

Hodgkin, Thomas. 'The Fall of the Roman Empire and its Lesson for Us', *Contemporary Review* 73 (January 1898): 51–70.

Hodgson, P. Fancourt. *How to Trace your own Pedigree, or, a Guide to Family Descent*. (London: Pickering and Chatto, 1889).

Hugo, Victor. *Les Misérables* (1862; Harmondsworth: Penguin, 1980).

Huxley, Aldous. *Crome Yellow* (1922; repr. London: Chatto & Windus, 1928).

Antic Hay (1923; repr. Harmondsworth, 1948).

Point Counter Point (1928; repr. London: Grafton Books, 1978).

Do What You Will (1929; repr. London: Chatto & Windus, 1931).

Huxley, T. H. 'The Struggle For Existence: A Programme', *Nineteenth Century* 23 (February 1888): 161–80.

'On the Natural Inequality of Man', *Nineteenth Century* 27 (January 1890): 1–23.

Collected Essays, 9 vols. (London: Macmillan, 1893–1908).

Hyslop, T. B. 'A Discussion on Occupation and Environment as Causative Factors of Insanity', *British Medical Journal* (14 October 1905): 941–5.

'Post-Illusionism and Art in the Insane', *Nineteenth Century and After* 69 (1911): 270–81.

'The Mental Deficiency Bill, 1912', *Journal of Mental Science* 58 (October 1912): 548–97.

'Degeneration: The Medico-Psychological Aspects of Modern Art, Music, Literature, Science and Religion', *Trans. Med. Soc. of London* 4 (1918): 271–95.

Ibsen, Henrik. *A Doll's House* (1888; trans. M. Meyer, London: Methuen, 1980).

Inge, W. R. 'Some Moral Aspects of Eugenics', *Eugenics Review* 1 (1909): 26–36.

England (London: Ernest Benn, 1926).

Lay Thoughts of a Dean (New York & London: G. P. Putnam's Sons, 1926).

Izoulet, Jean. *La Cité moderne et la métaphysique de la sociologie*, 2 vols. (Paris: Felix Alcan, 1894).

Jackson, Holbrook. *The Eighteen Nineties* (1913; repr. Harmondsworth: Penguin, 1939).

Jacques, Norbert. *Dr Mabuse Master of Mystery: A Novel* (trans. Lillian A.Clare) (London: George Allen & Unwin, 1923).

James, Henry. *The Princess Casamassima* (1886; Harmondsworth: Penguin, 1977).

James, William. 'Degeneration and Genius', *Psychological Review* 2 (May 1895): 287–94.

The Varieties of Religious Experience: A Study in Human Nature (1902; repr. London: Collins (Fontana Library), 1960).

Johnson, Lionel. *The Academy* 39 (13 June 1891): 555–6.

Joyce, James. *Portrait of the Artist as a Young Man* (1916, repr. London: Granada, 1977).

Jung, Carl, Gustav. *The Collected Works of C. G. Jung*, 20 vols. (London: Routledge & Kegan Paul, 1953–1979).

Kidd, Benjamin. *Social Evolution* (1894; 2nd edn London: Macmillan, 1896).

Kipling, Rudyard. *Traffics and Discoveries* (1904; repr. Harmondsworth: Penguin, 1987).

Lankester, E. R. *Degeneration: A Chapter in Darwinism* (London: Macmillan, 1880).

Lawrence, D. H. *The Rainbow* (1915; repr. Harmondsworth: Penguin, 1981).

'The Novel and The Feelings' (1923) in E. D. McDonald (ed.) *Phoenix The Posthumous Papers of D. H. Lawrence* (London: Heinemann, 1936).

Leavis, F. R. *Mass Civilization and Minority Culture* (Minority Pamphlet No. 1) (Cambridge: Gordon Fraser, 1930).

Lewis, William Bevan. *A Text-book of Mental Diseases* (2nd edn, London: C. Griffin & Co., 1899).

Lombroso, Cesare. *The Man of Genius* (1888; London: Walter Scott, 1891).

L'Homme criminel (2nd edn., Paris, 1895).

Introduction to Gina Lombroso-Ferrero, *Criminal Man According to the Classification of Cesare Lombroso* (New York and London: G. P. Putnam's Sons, 1911).

Lombroso, Cesare and Ferrero, G. *The Female Offender* (1893; London: T. Fisher Unwin, 1895).

London, Jack. *The People of the Abyss* (London: Thomas Nelson & Sons, 1903).

MacBride, E. W. 'Social Biology and Birth Control', *Nature* 113 (31 May 1924): 735–5.

'Cultivation of the Unfit', *Nature* 137 (11 January 1936): 44–5.

McDonald, Edward D. (ed.). *Phoenix: The Posthumous Papers of D. H. Lawrence* (London: Heinemann, 1936).

'Malet, Lucas' [Mary Kingsley]. *Colonel Enderby's Wife* (3 vols. London: Kegan Paul Trench, 1885).

Mallock, W. H. *Is Life Worth Living?* (2nd edn London: Chatto and Windus, 1879).

The Old Order Changes. A Novel (3 vols. London: R. Bentley & Son, 1886).

Masterman, C. F. G. *The Condition of England* (1909; 7th edn London: Methuen & Co., 1912).

Maudsley, Henry. *Body and Mind. An Inquiry into their Connection and Mutual Influence, specially in reference to Mental Disorders* (2nd edn London: Macmillan, 1873).

Responsibility in Mental Disease (2nd edn London: Kegan Paul, 1874).

'Sex in Mind and Education', *Fortnightly Review* 15 (1874) 466–83.

'Materialism and its Lessons For Us', *Fortnightly Review* 26 (1879: 26 (1879): 244–60.

The Pathology of Mind (London: Macmillan, 1879).

The Pathology of Mind: A Study of its Distempers, Deformities and Disorders (London: Macmillan, 1895).

Maurice, General Frederick ['Miles']. 'Where to Get Men?', *Contemporary Review* 82 (January 1902): 78–86.

Mayhew, Henry. *London Labour and the London Poor* (London: 1851).

[Mearns, Andrew]. *The Bitter Cry of Outcast London* (London: James Clarke & Co., 1883).

Medico-Psychological Association of Great Britain. Report of Annual Meeting (1920), *Lancet* 199 Part Two (1920): 402–5.

Mee, Arthur. Preface to *The Children's Encyclopaedia*, 8 vols. (London: The Educational Book Co. Ltd., 1910–11).

Morel, Bénédict, August. *Traité des dégénérescences physiques, intellectuelles et morales de l'éspèce humaine et des causes qui produisent ces variétés maladives.* (Paris: J. B. Baillière, 1857).

Morison, Alexander. *Outline of Lectures on Mental Diseases* (Edinburgh: 1824).

Morley, John. *On Compromise* (1886; Thinker's Library, London: Watts and Co., 1933).

Needham, Joseph and Pagel, Walter (eds.). *Background to Modern Science* (Cambridge University Press, 1938).

Newbolt, Henry. *The Island Race* (London: Elkin Mathews, 1898).

Nisbet, J. F. *The Insanity of Genius and the General Inequality of Human Faculty Physiologically Considered* (London: Ward and Downey, 1891).

Nordau, Max. *Degeneration* (1895; trans. from the 2nd edn of *Entartung* (1893) [1892]; Popular Edition, London: William Heinemann, 1898).

Odell, William. *The Physique of the British Nation* (Torquay: 'Directory' Office, 1903).

Oppenheim, E. Phillips. *The Secret* (London: Ward Lock & Co., 1907).

Pankhurst, Christabel. *The Great Scourge and How To End It* (London: E.Pankhurst, 1913).

Parmelee, Maurice. Introduction to *Crime: Its Causes and Remedies* (Boston: Little, Brown & Co., 1911).

Pearson, Karl. 'Woman and Labour', *Fortnightly Review* 55 (May 1894): 561–77.

National Life from the Standpoint of Science. An Address Delivered at Newcastle November 19 1900 (London: A. & C. Black, 1901).

Physical Deterioration, Report of the Inter-Departmental Committee on, 1904: Vol. XXXII, Vol. 1 Cd. 2175 Report and Appendix, Vol. 2 Cd. 2210 List of Witnesses, Minutes of Evidence, Vol. 3 Cd. 2186 Appendix and General Index.

Poulton, Edward B. *et al.* (eds.). *August Weismann; Essays upon Heredity and Kindred Biological Problems*, 2 vols. (Oxford: Clarendon Press, 1891–2).

Proposals For a Voluntary Nobility (Samurai Press, 1907).

Rayner, Olive Pratt [*pseud.* Grant Allen]. *The Type-Writer Girl* (London: C.Arthur Pearson, 1897).

Ritchie, David G. *Darwinism and Politics* (London: Swan Sonnenschein, 1889; 2nd edn with additions 1891).

Rivers, W. H. R. *Instinct and the Unconscious* (Cambridge University Press, 1920).

Rosebery, Lord. *Miscellanies: Literary and Historical* (2 vols., London: Hodder & Stoughton, 1921).

Sanger, George. *Seventy Years a Showman* (1910; repr. London: J. M. Dent, 1927).

Saleeby, C. W. *Parenthood and Race Culture: An Outline of Eugenics* (London: Cassell & Co., 1909).

Sapper [*pseud.* H. C. McNeile]. *The Final Count* (1926; repr. London: Dent, 1985).

Savage, George. *Insanity and Allied Neuroses Practical and Clinical* (Philadelphia: Henry C. Lea, 1884).

Savile Club 1868–1923, The. Privately printed (1923).

Schiller, F. C. S. 'Regeneration: A Reply to Max Nordau', *Philosophical Review* 5 (July 1896): 436–7.

Shaw, G. B.. 'The Sanity of Art' (1907), repr. in Michael Holroyd (ed.) *G.B. Shaw: Major Critical Essays* (Harmondsworth: Penguin, 1986): 309–60.

Shee, George F. 'The Deterioration in the National Physique', *Nineteenth Century and After* 53 (May 1903): 797–805.

Sinjohn, John [*pseud.* John Galsworthy]. *Jocelyn* (London: Duckworth & Co., 1898).

Smith, Samuel. 'The Industrial Training of Destitute Children', *Contemporary Review* 47 (January 1885): 107–119.

Sociological Papers 1, (1904).

Sorensen, C. W. 'Back to the Land ("Why Don't We Feed Ourselves?")', *Contemporary Review* 81 (January 1902): 61–8.

Spencer, Herbert. *Education* (London: Williams and Norgate, 1861).

First Principles (London: Williams and Norgate, 1861; 4th edn, 1880).

The Principles of Ethics (2 vols., London: Williams and Norgate, 1892–3).

Stead, W. T. 'How the Other Half Lives', *Review of Reviews* 24 (December 1901): 642–5.

Royal Commission on the War in South Africa compiled from the Blue Books for the Information of the Public (1903).

Coming Men on Coming Questions (London: 'Review of Reviews' Office, 1905).

Stevenson, Robert Louis. *The Strange Case of Dr Jekyll and Mr Hyde* (1885; (Harmondsworth: Penguin, 1979).

Stoker, Bram. *Dracula* (1897; repr. Oxford University Press, 1983).

Stopes, Marie. *'Gold in the Wood' and 'The Race': Two New Plays of Life* (London: A. C. Fifield, 1918).

'How Mrs Jones Does Her Worst', *Daily Mail* 13 June 1919.

Strahan, S. A. K. *Marriage and Disease: A Study of Heredity and the More Important Family Degenerations* (London: Kegan Paul, 1892).

Stutfield, Hugh. 'Tommyrotics', *Blackwood's Edinburgh Magazine* 157 (June 1895): 833–45.

Thompson, Denys. *Culture and Environment* (London: Chatto & Windus, 1933).

Tredgold, Alfred. 'The Feeble-Minded', *Contemporary Review* 97 (1910): 717–27.

Mental Deficiency – (Amentia) (1908; 2nd edn London: Bailliere, Tyndall & Cox, 1914).

'Tree of Knowledge', The. *New Review* 10 (June 1894): 675–90.

Trotter, Wilfrid. *Instincts of the Herd in Peace and War* (London: Ernest Benn, 1916).

Tuke, Daniel Hack. 'Case of Moral Insanity or Congenital Moral Defect with Commentary', *Journal of Mental Science* 31 (1885–6): 360–6.

Warner, Pelham. *How We Recovered the Ashes* (London: Chapman & Hall, 1905).

Webb, Sidney. 'Lord Rosebery's Escape from Houndsditch', *Nineteenth Century and After* 50 (September 1901): 366–86.

'The Decline in the Birthrate', Fabian Tract 131 (London: Fabian Society, 1907).

Wells, H. G. 'Zoological Retrogression', *Gentleman's Magazine* 271 (September 1891): 246–53.

'On Extinction', *Chamber's Journal* 10 (30 September 1893): 623–4.

The Wonderful Visit (London: J. M. Dent, 1895).

Certain Personal Matters (London: Lawrence and Bullen, 1898).

The War of the Worlds (1898; repr. London: Pan, 1975).

Anticipations of the Reactions of Mechanical and Scientific Progress upon Human Life and Thought (London: Chapman & Hall, 1901 [1902].

The Food of the Gods (1904) in *The Works of H. G. Wells* (London: Odhams Press, 1926–7).

Mankind in the Making (London: Chapman & Hall, 1903).

A Modern Utopia (London: Chapman & Hall, 1905).

Ann Veronica (1909; repr. London: Virago, 1980).

The New Machiavelli (1911; repr. Harmondsworth: Penguin, 1946).

An Englishman Looks at The World (London: Cassell & Co., 1914).

The Complete Short Stories of H. G. Wells (London: Ernest Benn, 1927).

H.G.Wells; Selected Short Stories (Harmondsworth: Penguin, 1958).

Westermarck, Edward. *Memories of My Life* (London: Allen & Unwin, 1929).

White, Arnold. *Efficiency and Empire* (London: Methuen, 1901).

White, Greenough. 'A Novelist of the Hour', *Sewanee Review.* 6 (July 1898): 360–70.

Wilde, Oscar. *De Profundis and Other Writings* (Harmondsworth: Penguin, 1973).

Wilkins, W. H. *The Alien Invasion* (in Social Questions of Today (1891 etc.) (London: Methuen, 1892.

Williams, Valentine. *The Man with the Clubfoot* (London: Herbert Jenkins, 1918).

Williams-Freeman, J.P. *On the Effect of Town Life on the General Health, with Especial Reference to London* (London: W. H. Allen, 1890).

Woolf, Leonard. *Beginning Again* (London: Hogarth Press, 1963).
Woolf, Virginia. *Mrs Dalloway* (1925; repr. Harmondsworth: Penguin, 1992).
    Roger Fry (1940; repr. London: Hogarth Press, 1990).
    The Captain's Death Bed and Other Essays (London: Hogarth Press, 1950).
Zola, Emile. *Germinal* (1885; repr. Harmondsworth: Penguin, 1954).

PRIMARY SOURCES FROM 1940

UNPUBLISHED ITEMS

Foster, Milton P. 'The Reception of Max Nordau's *Degeneration* in England and America'. Ph.D. dissertation, University of Michigan, 1954.
Grindle, Juliet. 'A Critical Edition of *Tess of the D'Urbervilles*', D.Phil. dissertation, University of Oxford, 1974.
Hoskin, A. J. 'Racialism and Popular Consciousness: Popular Fiction 1870– 1920', M.A. dissertation, University of Birmingham, 1973.
Lindop, G. C. 'A Study of the Influence of Contemporary Psychological Theory on the Fiction of Thomas Hardy, George Gissing and the Early Novels of George Moore', B. Litt. dissertation, University of Oxford, 1974.
Sippell, E. W. 'Degeneration and Virtue in American Literature and Culture 1871–1915', Ph.D dissertation, Brown University, 1975.
Wood, Martin R. 'Darwinism and Pessimism in Late Victorian Thought and Literature', Ph.D. dissertation, University of Nottingham, 1975.

PUBLISHED ITEMS

Ackerknecht, E. A. *A Short History of Psychiatry* (New York: Hafner Publishing Co., 1959).
Adam Smith, Janet. *John Buchan* (London: Rupert Hart-Davis, 1965).
Ardis, Ann. *New Women, New Novels; Feminism and Early Modernism* (New Brunswick: Rutgers University Press, 1990).
Ascherson, Neil. 'The Fuhrer's Freak Show', *Independent on Sunday*, 1 March 1992.
Atkins, John. *The British Spy Novel: Styles of Treachery* (London: John Calder, 1984).
Baldick, Chris. *In Frankenstein's Shadow: Myth, Monstrosity and Nineteenth-Century Writing* (Oxford: Clarendon Press, 1987).
Baldwin, P. M. 'Liberalism, Nationalism, and Degeneration: The Case of Max Nordau', *Central European History* 13 (June 1980): 99–120.
Bannister, Robert. *Social Darwinism: Science and Myth in Anglo-American Social Thought* (Philadelphia: Temple University Press, 1980).
Barker, Francis *et al.* (eds.) *Literature, Society and the Sociology of Literature* (Colchester: University of Essex, 1977).

Becker, George. *The Mad Genius Controversy* (Beverly Hills: Sage Publications, 1978).

Beer, Gillian. *Darwin's Plots* (1983; repr. London: Ark Paperbacks, 1985).
  Review of Redmond O'Hanlon, *Joseph Conrad and Charles Darwin* (1984) *Sunday Times* (27 May 1984): 43.
  Arguing with the Past: Essays in Narrative from Woolf to Sidney (London: Routledge, 1989).

Bell, Michael. *Primitivism* (London: Methuen, 1972).

Bell, Quentin. *Virginia Woolf: A Biography* (2 vols., London: Triad/ Granada, 1976).

Bennett, Tony. *Popular Fiction: Technology, Ideology, Production, Reading* (London: Routledge, 1990).

Bergonzi, Bernard. *The Early H. G. Wells* (Manchester University Press, 1961).

Bergonzi, Bernard (ed.). *The Twentieth Century* (Vol. 7 of *The Sphere History of Literature in the English Language*) (London: Sphere Books, 1970).

Berridge, Virginia, 'Concepts of Narcotic Addiction in Britain, 1820–1926', *Annals of Science* 36 (1979): 67–85.

Betts, Raymond. 'The Allusion to Rome in British Imperialist Thought of the Late Nineteenth and Early Twentieth Centuries', *Victorian Studies* 15 (2) (December 1971): 149–59.

Bewley, Marius (ed.). *The Selected Poetry of Donne* (New York: New American Library, 1966).

Biddiss, Michael D. (ed.). *Gobineau: Selected Political Writings* (London: Cape, 1970).

Bjork, Lennart (ed.). *The Literary Notebooks of Thomas Hardy* (2 vols., London: Macmillan, 1985).

Blackmur, R. P. *Henry Adams* (revised edn San Diego: Harcourt Brace Jovanovich, 1980).

Bloch, Ernst. *Heritage of Our Times* (Cambridge: Polity Press, 1991)

Boller, Paul, F. *American Thought in Transition: The Impact of Evolutionary Naturalism 1863–1900* (Chicago: Rand McNally, 1970).

Borland, Maureen. *Wilde's Devoted Friend: A Life of Robert Ross 1869–1918* (Oxford: Lennard Publishers, 1990).

Boumehla, Penny. *Thomas Hardy and Women* (Brighton: Harvester, 1982).

Bowlby, Rachel. Review of G. Gissing, *The Whirlpool*, *Gissing Newsletter* 21 (2) (1985): 22–9.

Bowler, Peter L. *Evolution: the History of an Idea* (Berkeley: University of California Press, 1984).

Boyle, Thomas. *Black Swine in the Sewers of Hampstead* (London: Hodder and Stoughton, 1990).

Brantlinger, Patrick. *Bread and Circuses: Theories of Mass Culture as Social Decay* (Ithaca, New York: Cornell University Press, 1983).
  Rule of Darkness: British Literature and Imperialism 1830–1914 (Ithaca, New York: Cornell University Press, 1988).

Briggs, Susan. *Those Radio Times* (London: Weidenfeld & Nicholson, 1981).

Brooks, Peter. *The Melodramatic Imagination* (New Haven & London: Yale University Press, 1976).

Brotz, Howard. 'Sherlock Holmes as Conservative Thinker', *Salisbury Review* 8 (1) (September 1989): 44–51.

Buckley, Jerome. *W.E.Henley: A Study in the Counter-Decadence of the Nineties* (Princeton University Press, 1945).

Bullen, J. B. (ed.). *Post-Impressionists in England* (London: Routledge, 1988).

Busfield, Joan. *Managing Madness: Changing Ideas and Practice* (London: Hutchinson, 1986).

Bynum, W. F. , Roy Porter and Michael Shepherd (eds.). *The Anatomy of Madness: Essays in the History of Psychiatry* (3 vols., London: Tavistock Publications, 1985–88).

Cairns, David and Shaun Richards. 'No Good Brave Causes? The Alienated Intellectual and the End of Empire', *Literature and History* 14 (2) (Autumn 1988): 194–206.

Cameron, Deborah and Elizabeth Frazer. *The Lust to Kill: A Feminist Investigation of Sexual Murder* (Oxford: Polity Press, 1987).

Carey, John. *The Intellectuals and the Masses: Pride and Prejudice among the Literary Intelligentsia 1880–1939* (London: Faber & Faber, 1992).

Carlson, Eric T. 'The Nerve Weakness of the Nineteenth Century', *International Journal of Psychiatry* 9 (1970–1): 50–6.

Carter, A. E. *The Idea of Decadence in French Literature 1830–1900* (University of Toronto Press, 1958).

Cave, Terence. *Recognitions: A Study in Poetics* (Oxford: Clarendon Press, 1988).

Chamberlin, J. E. and Sander L. Gilman (eds.). *Degeneration: the Dark Side of Progress* (New York: Columbia University Press, 1985).

Chapple, J. A. V. *Documentary and Imaginative Literature 1880–1920* (London: Blandford Press, 1970).

Science and Literature in the Nineteenth-Century (London: Macmillan, 1986).

Chatel, John C. and Roger Peele, 'The Concept of Neurasthenia', *International Journal of Psychiatry* 9 (1970–1971): 36–49.

Chipp, Herschel B. *Theories of Modern Art: A Source Book by Artists and Critics* (Berkeley: University of California Press, 1968).

Christie, John and Sally Shuttleworth (eds.). *Nature Transfigured; Science and Literature 1700–1900* (Manchester University Press, 1989).

Clarke, Ian. *Edwardian Drama: A Critical Study* (London: Faber, 1989).

Cohen, Ed. *Talk on the Wilde Side: Towards a Genealogy of a Discourse on Male Sexualities* (New York and London: Routledge, 1993).

Cohen, Stanley and Andrew Scull (eds.). *Social Control and the State* (Oxford: Robertson, 1983).

Collings, Matthew. 'Resistance Heroes of Art', *Guardian* (20 May 1992): 38.

Colls, Robert and Philip Dodd (eds.). *Englishness: Politics and Culture 1880–1920* (London: Croom Helm, 1986).

Coustillas, Pierre (ed.). *Collected Articles on George Gissing* (London: Cass, 1968).
 Gissing: The Critical Heritage (London: Routledge, 1972).
 Henry Hick's Recollections of George Gissing Together with Gissing's Letters to Hick (London: Enitharmon Press, 1973).
 London and the Life of Literature: The Diary of George Gissing (Hassocks: Harvester Press, 1978).
Cowling, Mary. *The Artist as Anthropologist: The Representation of Type and Character in Victorian Art* (Cambridge University Press, 1989).
Cox, R. G. (ed.). *Thomas Hardy: The Critical Heritage* (London: Routledge, 1970).
Craig, Cairns. *Yeats, Eliot, Pound and the Politics of Poetry* (Pittsburgh University Press, 1982).
Crosby, Travis L. *The Impact of Civilian Evacuation in the Second World War* (London: Croom Helm, 1986).
Cunningham, Gail. *The New Woman and the Victorian Novel* (London: Macmillan, 1978).
Daniell, David (ed.). *The Best Short Stories of John Buchan* (London: Panther, 1984).
Daniels, Les. *Fear: A History of Horror in the Mass Media* (London: Granada, 1977).
Davenport-Hines, Richard. *Sex, Death and Punishment* (London: Collins, 1990).
Davin, Anna. 'Imperialism and Motherhood', *History Workshop Journal* no. 5 (1978), 9–65.
Day, Gary (ed.) *Readings of Popular Culture: Trivial Pursuits?* (London: Macmillan, 1990).
Dean, Eric T. Jr. 'War and Psychiatry: Examining the Diffusion Theory in the Light of the Insanity Defence in Post-World War 1 Britain', *History of Psychiatry* 4 (1) (March 1993): 61–82.
Delamont, Sarah and Lorna Duffin (eds.). *The Nineteenth-Century Woman: Her Cultural and Physical World* (London: Croom Helm, 1978).
Dijkstra, Bram. *Idols of Perversity: Fantasies of Feminine Evil in Fin de Siècle Culture* (Oxford University Press, 1986).
Donnison, Jean. *Midwives and Medical Men: A History of Inter-Professional Rivalries and Women's Rights* (London: Heinemann, 1977).
Dowbiggin, Ian R. *Inheriting Madness: Professionalization and Psychiatric Knowledge in Nineteenth-Century France* (Berkeley: University of California Press, 1991).
Dupeu, Jean-Marc. 'Freud and Degeneracy: A Turning-Point', *Diogenes* 97 (1977): 43–64.
Dwork, Deborah. *War is Good for Babies and Other Young Children: A History of the Infant and Child Welfare Movement in England 1898–1918* (London: Tavistock Publications, 1987).
Dyos, H. J. and Michael Wolff (eds.). *The Victorian City: Images and Realities* (2 vols., London: Routledge, 1973).

Ebbatson, Roger. *The Evolutionary Self: Hardy, Forster, Lawrence* (Brighton: Harvester, 1982).

Edel, Leon. *Henry James: A Life* (2 vols., Harmondsworth: Penguin, 1977).

Edmonds, Rod. 'The Conservatism of Gissing's Early Novels', *Literature and History* 7 (Spring 1978): 48–69.

Eiseley, Loren C. *Darwin's Century: Evolution and the Men Who Discovered It* (London: Victor Gollanz, 1959).

Eliot, T. S. *Collected Poems 1909–1962* (London: Faber & Faber, 1963).

Feldman, David and Gareth Stedman Jones (eds.). *Metropolis; London Histories and Representations Since 1800* (London: Routledge and Kegan Paul, 1989).

Feuer, Lewis S. 'The Letters of Edwin Ray Lankester to Karl Marx: The Last Stage in Marx's Intellectual Revolution', *Journal of the History of Ideas* 40 (4) (October–December 1979): 633–48.

Fletcher, Ian (ed.). *Decadence and the 1890s* (London: Edward Arnold, 1979).

Introduction to *British Poetry and Prose: 1870–1905* (Oxford University Press, 1987).

Flint, Kate (ed.). *Impressionists in England: The Critical Reception* (London: Routledge, 1984).

Forrest, D. W. *Francis Galton: The Life and Work of a Victorian Genius* (London: Elek, 1974).

Foucault, Michel. *L'Archéologie du savoir* (1969) trans. as *The Archaeology of Knowledge* (London: Tavistock Publications, 1972).

La Volonté de savoir (1976) trans. as *The History of Sexuality* Vol. 1 (1978; Harmondsworth: Penguin, 1981).

Frechet, Alec. *John Galsworthy: A Reassessment* (London: Macmillan, 1982).

Freeden, Michael. *The New Liberalism: An Ideology of Social Reform* (Oxford: Clarendon Press, 1978).

Fryer, Peter. *The Birth Controllers* (London: Corgi Books, 1967).

Gainier, Bernard. *The Alien Invasion: A Study of Jewish Immigration* (London: Heinemann, 1972).

Gallagher, Catherine and Thomas Laqueur (eds.). *The Making of the Modern Body: Sexuality and Society in the Nineteenth Century* (Berkeley: University of California Press, 1987).

Gay, Peter. *The Bourgeois Experience* Vol. 2 (New York and Oxford: Oxford University Press, 1986).

Gettmann, Royal A. (ed.). *George Gissing and H. G. Wells: A Record of Their Friendship and Correspondence* (London: Rupert Hart-Davis, 1961).

Gibbons, Tom. *Rooms in the Darwin Hotel* (Nedlands: University of Western Australia Press, 1973).

Gilbert, Sandra M. and Susan Gubar. *No Man's Land: The Place of the Woman Writer in the Twentieth Century: Vol. 2 Sexchanges* (New Haven and London: Yale University Press, 1989).

Gilman, Sander L. *Seeing the Insane* (New York: John Wiley, 1982).

Difference and Pathology (Ithaca and London: Cornell University Press, 1985).

Sexuality: An Illustrated History (New York: John Wiley, 1990).

Ginsberg Elaine K. and Laura M. Gottlieb (eds.). *Virginia Woolf: Centennial Essays* (Troy, NY: Whitston, 1983).

Goffman, Erving. *Asylums* (1961; repr. Harmondsworth: Penguin, 1968).

Gold, Milton. 'The Early Psychiatrists on Degeneracy and Genius', *Psychoanalysis and the Psychoanalytic Review* 47 (1960–1): 37–55.

'The Continuing "Degeneration" Controversy', *Bucknell Review* 10 (2) (1961–2): 87–101.

Goode, John. *George Gissing: Ideology and Fiction* (London: Vision Press, 1978).

Thomas Hardy: The Offensive Truth (Oxford: Basil Blackwell, 1988).

Gordon, Lyndall. *Eliot's Early Years* (1977; Oxford University Press, 1978).

Virginia Woolf: A Writer's Life (Oxford University Press, 1986).

Gould, Stephen Jay. *Ontogeny and Phylogeny* (Cambridge, Mass.: Harvard University Press, 1977)

The Mismeasure of Man (1981; repr. Harmondsworth: Penguin, 1984).

Greenslade, William. 'Thomas Hardy's "Facts" Notebook: A Further Source for *The Mayor of Casterbridge*', *Thomas Hardy Journal* 2 (January 1986): 33–5.

Greer, Germaine. *Sex and Destiny: The Politics of Human Fertility* (London: Picador, 1984).

Gregor, Ian. *The Great Web: The Form of Hardy's Major Fiction* (London: Faber, 1974).

Introduction to Thomas Hardy, *The Mayor of Casterbridge* (London: Macmillan, 1974).

Grosskurth, Phyllis. *Havelock Ellis* (London: Allen Lane, 1980).

Grunberger, Richard. *A Social History of the Third Reich* (1971; repr. Harmondsworth: Penguin, 1974).

Grylls, David. *The Paradox of Gissing* (London: Allen and Unwin, 1986).

Hall, Leslie A. *Hidden Anxieties: Male Sexuality 1900–1950* (Cambridge: Polity Press, 1991).

Hall, Ruth. *Marie Stopes* (1977; London: Virago, 1978).

Hardy, Florence, Emily. *The Life of Thomas Hardy 1840–1928* (1933; repr. I vol. London: Macmillan, 1975).

Hasan, Narool. *Thomas Hardy; The Sociological Imagination* (London: Macmillan, 1982).

Hawthorn, Jeremy. 'The Incoherences of *The Nigger of the "Narcissus"'*, *Conradian* 11 (2) (November 1986): 98–115.

Henken, Leo. *Darwinism and the English Novel 1860–1910* (New York: Russell and Russell, 1940).

Hofstadter, Richard. *Social Darwinism in American Thought* (1944; revised edn New York: Braziller, 1965).

Hollis, Patricia (ed.). *Women in Public: The Women's Movement 1850–1900* (London: Allen and Unwin, 1979).

Holroyd, Michael (ed.). *G.B.Shaw: Major Critical Essays* (Harmondsworth: Penguin, 1986).

Horsman, Reginald. 'The Origins of Anglo-Saxonism in Great Britain Before 1850', *Journal of the History of Ideas* 37 (July-September 1976): 387– 410.

Humphries, Steve. *A Secret World of Sex* (1988; repr. London: Sidgwick and Jackson, 1991).

Hyde, H. Montgomery. *Oscar Wilde: The Aftermath* (New York: Farrar-Straus, 1963).

Hynes, Samuel. *The Edwardian Turn of Mind* (1968; repr. London: Pimlico, 1991).

A War Imagined: The First World War and English Culture (1990; repr. London: Pimlico, 1992).

Ingham, Patricia. 'The Evolution of *Jude the Obscure*', *Review of English Studies* n. s. 27 (1976): 156–69.

Thomas Hardy (Hemel Hempstead: Harvester-Wheatsheaf, 1989).

Jacobus, Mary. 'Tess's Purity', *Essays in Criticism* 26 (1976): 318–38.

Jacobus, Mary (ed.). *Women Writing and Writing about Women* (London: Croom Helm, 1979).

Jalland, Pat. *Women, Marriage and Politics* (Oxford University Press, 1978).

Jones, Gareth Stedman, *Outcast London* (1971, rev. edn Harmondsworth: Penguin, 1984).

'Working-Class Culture and Working-Class Politics in London, 1870–1900: Notes on the Re-Making of a Working-Class', *Journal of Social History* 7 (4) (1974): 460–509.

Jones, Greta. *Social Darwinism and English Thought* (Brighton and New Jersey: Harvester Press, 1980).

Jones, Kathleen. *A History of the Mental Health Services* (London: Routledge, 1972).

Kalmus, Henry and Lettice M. Crump. *Genetics* (Harmondsworth: Penguin, 1948).

Karl, Frederick A. and Laurence Davies (eds.). *Collected Letters of Joseph Conrad* (Cambridge University Press, 1983).

Kaye, Harvey and Keith McClelland (eds.). *E.P.Thompson: Critical Perspectives* (Cambridge: Polity Press, 1990).

Keating, Peter. *The Haunted Study* (London: Secker & Warburg, 1989).

Kennedy, Dennis (ed.). *Plays by Harley Granville-Barker* (Cambridge University Press, 1987).

Kermode, Frank. *The Sense of an Ending* (New York: Oxford University Press. 1967).

Continuities (New York: Random House, 1968).

Modern Essays (London: Fontana, 1971).

Kermode, Frank (ed.). *T. S. Eliot: Selected Prose* (London: Faber, 1975).

Kershner, R. B. 'Degeneration the Explanatory Nightmare', *Georgia Review* 40 (1986): 416–44 .

Kersley, Gillian. *Darling Madame* (London: Virago, 1983).

Kevles, Daniel, J. *In the Name of Eugenics: Genetics and the Uses of Heredity* (1985; Harmondsworth: Penguin, 1986).

Korg, Jacob (ed.). *George Gissing's Common Place Book* (New York: New York Public Library, 1962).

Laird, J. T. *The Shaping of 'Tess of the D'Urbervilles'* (Oxford University Press, 1975).

Langan, Mary and Bill Schwarz (eds.). *Crises in the British State: 1880–1930* (London: Hutchinson in Association with the Centre for Contemporary Cultural Studies, University of Birmingham, 1985).

Larkin, Maurice. *Man and Society in Nineteenth-Century Realism: Determinism and Literature* (London: Macmillan, 1977).

LeMahieu, D. L. *A Culture for Democracy: Mass Communication and the Cultivated Mind in Britain between the Wars* (Oxford: Clarendon Press, 1988).

Lerner, Laurence. *Thomas Hardy's 'Mayor of Casterbridge': Tragedy or Social History?* (London: Chatto and Windus, 1975).

Leon, Juan. ' "Meeting Mr Eugenides": T. S. Eliot and Eugenic Anxiety', *Yeats-Eliot Review* 9 (4) (1988): 169–77.

Lessing, Doris. *The Fifth Child* (London: Grafton Books, 1988).

Levenson, Michael. *A Genealogy of Modernism* (Cambridge University Press, 1984).

Lewis, Jane. *The Politics of Motherhood: Child and Maternal Welfare in England 1900–1939* (London: Croom Helm, 1980).

Women in England 1870–1950 (Brighton: Wheatsheaf Press, 1980).

Lewis, Jane (ed.). *Labour and Love: Women's Experience of Home and Family 1850–1940* (Oxford: Basil Blackwell, 1986).

Lloyd-Jones, H. *et al.* (eds.). *History and Imagination* (London: Duckworth, 1981).

Lowe, R. A. 'Eugenicists, Doctors and the Quest for National Efficiency: An Educational Crusade 1900–1939', *History of Education*. 8 (4) (1979): 293–306.

Lucas, John (ed.). *Literature and Politics in the Nineteenth Century* (London: Methuen, 1971).

Macdonald, Kate. 'Wells's Correspondence with John Buchan', *The Wellsian* no. 13 (Summer 1990): 43–7.

Mackenzie, Norman (ed.). *The Letters of Sidney and Beatrice Webb*, 3 vols. (Cambridge University Press, 1978).

Mangan, J. A. and James Walvin (eds.). *Manliness and Morality: Middle-Class Masculinity in Britain and America 1800–1940* (Manchester University Press, 1987).

Martin, Wallace. *The 'New Age' Under Orage* (Manchester University Press, 1967).

Mathias, Peter. *The First Industrial Nation: An Economic History of Britain 1700–1914* (London: Methuen, 1969).

Maugham, Somerset. *A Writer's Notebook* (1949; repr. Harmondsworth: Penguin, 1967).

Mazumdar, Pauline M. H. *Eugenics, Human Genetics and Human Failings: The Eugenics Society, its Sources and its Critics in Britain* (London: Routledge, 1992).

Mendus, Susan, and Jane Rendall (eds.). *Sexuality and Subordination: Interdisciplinary Studies of Gender in the Nineteenth Century* (London: Routledge, 1989).

Miller, Karl. *Doubles: Studies in Literary History* (Oxford University Press, 1985).

Millgate, Michael. *Thomas Hardy; A Biography* (1982; repr. Oxford University Press, 1985).

Mitchell, Juliet and Ann Oakley (eds.). *The Rights and Wrongs of Women* (Harmondsworth: Penguin, 1976).

Moore, J.R. *The Post-Darwinian Controversies: The Struggle to Come to Terms with Darwin in Great Britain and America, 1870–1900* (Cambridge University Press, 1979).

Mora, George. 'Antecedents to Neurosis', *International Journal of Psychiatry*, 9 (1970–1): 57–60.

Mort, Frank. *Dangerous Sexualities: Medico-moral Politics in England since 1830* (London: Routledge, 1987).

Morton, Peter. *The Vital Science: Biology and the Literary Imagination 1860–1900* (London: George Allen & Unwin, 1984).

Murray, Isobel (ed.). *Oscar Wilde* (The Oxford Authors) (Oxford University Press, 1989).

Murray, Penelope (ed). *Genius: The History of an Idea* (Oxford: Blackwell, 1989).

Nairn, Tom. 'Enoch Powell: the New Right', *New Left Review* no. 61 (May-June 1970): 3–27.

Nordon, Pierre. *Conan Doyle* (London: John Murray, 1966).

Nye, Robert A. *Crime, Madness and Politics in Modern France: The Medical Concept of National Decline* (Princeton University Press, 1984).

Olivier, Mary (ed.). *Letters and Selected Writings of Sidney Olivier* (London: Allen & Unwin, 1948).

Oppenheim, Janet. *'Shattered Nerves': Doctors, Patients, and Depression in Victorian England* (New York and Oxford: Oxford University Press, 1991).

Orel, Harold (ed.). *Thomas Hardy's Personal Writings* (London: Macmillan, 1967).

Page, Norman (ed.). *Thomas Hardy: The Writer and his Background* (London: Bell and Hyman, 1980).

Thomas Hardy Annual No. 4 (London: Macmillan, 1986).

Parliamentary Debates. *Hansard* 9 March 1988, 327, 382, 384.

Parrinder, Patrick. Introduction to George Gissing, *The Whirlpool* (Hassocks: Harvester Press, 1977).

Pearson, Geoffrey. *The Deviant Imagination* (London: Macmillan, [1975], 1977).
  Hooligan: A History of Respectable Fears (London: Macmillan, 1983).

Peel, J. D. Y. *Herbert Spencer: The Evolution of a Sociologist* (London: Heinemann, 1971).

Pegg, Mark. *Broadcasting and Society 1918–1939* (London: Croom Helm, 1983).

Philmus, R. M. and D. Y. Hughes (eds.). *H.G.Wells; Early Writings in Science and Science Fiction* (Berkeley: University of California Press, 1975).

Pick, Daniel. *Faces of Degeneration: A European Disorder c.1848 – c.1918* (Cambridge University Press, 1989).
  War Machine: The Rationalisation of Slaughter in the Modern Age (New Haven and London: Yale University Press, 1993).

Pickett, T. H. 'George Henry Lewes to K. A. Varnhagen von Ense', *Modern Language Review* 80 (3) July 1985: 513–32.

Poggioli, Renato. *The Theory of the Avant-Garde* (Cambridge, Mass.: Harvard University Press, 1968).

Ponting, Clive. 'Churchill's Plan For Race-Purity', *Guardian*, (20–1 June 1992): 23.

Poole, Adrian. *Gissing in Context* (London: Macmillan, 1975).

Poole, Roger. *The Unknown Virginia Woolf* (1978; 3rd edn Atlantic Highlands NJ: Humanities Press International, Inc., 1990).

Porter, Roy. (Review of P. Murray (ed.) *Genius: The History of an Idea* (1989)] *Social History of Medicine* 4 (April 1991): 141–2.

Procter, Robert. *Racial Hygiene: Medicine under the Nazis* (Cambridge, Mass.: Harvard University Press, 1988).

Punter, David. *The Literature of Terror* (London: Longman, 1980).

Purdy, Richard L. and Michael Millgate (eds.) *The Collected Letters of Thomas Hardy* (7 vols., Oxford: Clarendon Press, 1978–88).

Pykett, Lyn. *The 'Improper' Feminine: The Women's Novel and the New Woman Writing* (London: Routledge, 1992).

Quétel, Claude. *History of Syphilis* (Cambridge: Polity Press, 1990).

Rawson, Claude (ed.). *English Satire and the Satiric Tradition* (Oxford: Basil Blackwell, 1984).

Ray, Martin. 'Conrad, Nordau and Other Degenerates: The Psychology of *The Secret Agent*', *Conradiana* 15–16 (1983–4): 125–40.

Richards, Jeffrey. *The Age of the Dream Palace: Cinema and Society 1930–1939* (London: Routledge, 1984).

Roberts, Warren, James T. Boulton and Elizabeth Mansfield (eds.). *The Letters of D. H. Lawrence*, Vol. 4. (Cambridge University Press, 1984).

Rose, Jonathan. *The Edwardian Temperament 1895–1919* (Athens, Ohio: Ohio University Press, 1986).

Rose, Nikolas. 'The Psychological Complex: Mental Measurement and Social Administration', *Ideology and Consciousness* no. 5 (Spring 1979): 5–68.

The Psychological Complex (London: Routledge and Kegan Paul, 1985).

Rosenberg, Charles. 'The Place of George M. Beard in Nineteenth Century Psychiatry', *Bulletin of the History of Medicine* 36 (May-June 1962): 245–59.

Rumbelow, Donald. *The Complete Jack the Ripper* (1975; rev. edn, Harmondsworth: Penguin, 1988).

Ryazanskaya, S. W. (ed.). *Marx Engels: Selected Correspondence* (1955; 3rd rev. edn Moscow: Progress Publishers, 1975).

Scull, Andrew (ed.). *Madhouses, Mad-Doctors and Madmen: The Social History of Psychiatry in the Victorian Era* (London: Athlone Press, 1981).

Social Disorder/Mental Disorder (London: Routledge, 1989).

The Most Solitary of Afflictions: Madness and Society in Britain, 1700–1900 (New Haven and London, 1993).

Searle, G. R. *The Quest for National Efficiency: A Study in British Politics and Political Thought 1899–1914* (1971; repr. London: The Ashfield Press, 1990).

Eugenics and Politics in Britain 1900–1914 (Leyden: Noordhoff, 1976).

Semmel, Bernard. *Imperialism and Social Reform: English Social-Imperial Thought 1895–1914* (London: Allen & Unwin, 1960).

Sherry, Norman. *Conrad's Western World* (Cambridge University Press, 1971).

Showalter, Elaine. *A Literature of Their Own: British Women Novelists from Bronte to Lessing* (1977; repr. London: Virago, 1978).

The Female Malady: Women, Madness and English Culture 1830–1980 (London: Virago, 1987).

Sexual Anarchy: Gender and Culture at the Fin de Siècle (London: Bloomsbury, 1991).

Introduction to Virginia Woolf, *Mrs Dalloway* (Harmondsworth: Penguin, 1992).

Skilton, David. Introduction to Thomas Hardy, *Tess of the D'Urbervilles* (Harmondsworth: Penguin, 1978).

Skultans, Vieda. *Madness and Morals: Ideas on Insanity in the Nineteeth Century* (London: Routledge & Kegan Paul, 1975).

Smith-Rosenberg, Carroll. 'The Hysterical Woman: Sex Roles and Role Conflict in Nineteenth Century America', *Social Research* 39 (4) (1972): 652–78.

Smithers, D. W. *This Idle Trade: On Doctors Who Were Writers* (Tunbridge Wells: Dragonfly Press, 1989).

Sofer, Reba. 'The Revolution in English Social Thought 1880–1914', *American Historical Review* 75 (1970): 1938–64.

Soloway, Richard. 'Counting the Degenerates: The Statistics of Race Deterioration in Edwardian England', *Journal of Contemporary History* 17 (1982): 137–64.

Demography and Degeneration: Eugenics and the Declining Birthrate in Twentieth-Century Britain (Chapel Hill and London: University of N. Carolina Press, 1990).

Southerington, F. R. *Hardy's Vision of Man* (London: Chatto, 1969).

Spalding, Frances. *Vanessa Bell* (London: Weidenfeld and Nicholson, 1983).

Stafford, Donald. A. T. 'The Birth of the British Spy Novel', *Victorian Studies* 24 (1981): 489–509.

Stallybrass, Oliver (ed.). E.M.Forster, *Howards End* (Harmondsworth: Penguin, 1975).

Stallybrass, Peter and Allon White. *The Poetics and Politics of Transgression* (London: Methuen, 1986).

Stewart, Larry. 'Freud before Oedipus: Race and Heredity in the Origin of Psychoanalysis', *Journal of the History of Biology* 9 (1976): 215–26.

Stokes, John. *In The Nineties* (Hemel Hempstead: Harvester-Wheatsheaf, (1989).

Stokes, John (ed.). *Fin de Siècle/Fin du Globe: Fears and Fantasies of the Late Nineteenth Century* (London: Macmillan, 1992).

Street, Brian V. *The Savage in Literature: Representations of 'Primitive' Society in English Fiction 1858–1920* (London: Routledge & Kegan Paul, 1975).

Stubbs, Patricia. *Women and Fiction: Feminism and the Novel 1880–1920* (Brighton: Harvester Press, 1979).

Sulloway, Frank J. *Freud Biologist of the Mind* (London: Burnett Books & Andre Deutsch, 1979).

Taylor, Jenny Bourne. *In the Secret Theatre of Home: Wilkie Collins, Sensation Narrative, and Nineteenth-Century Psychology* (London: Routledge, 1988).

Teich, Mikulas and Roy Porter (eds.). *Fin de Siècle and its Legacy* (Cambridge University Press, 1990).

Thompson, E. P. *William Morris: Romantic to Revolutionary* (1955; rev. edn London: Merlin Press, 1977).

' "Rough Music": Le Charivari anglais', *Annales* 27 (2) (Mars-Avril 1972): 285–312.

Customs in Common (London: Merlin Press, 1991).

Thompson, Tierl (ed.). *Dear Girl: The Diaries and Letters of Two Working Women 1897–1917* (London: Women's Press, 1987).

Thornton, R. K. R. *The Decadent Dilemma* (London: Edward Arnold, 1983).

Thwaite, Ann. *Edmund Gosse: A Literary Landscape* (London: Secker, 1984).

Tillyard, S. K. *The Impact of Modernism 1900–1920: Early Modernism and the Arts and Crafts Movement in Edwardian England* (London: Routledge, 1988).

Times, The. 'The Remoralisation of Public Life', 21 October 1974: 3.

Tobias, J. J. *Crime and Industrial Society in the Nineteenth Century* (London: Batsford, 1967).

Trodd, Anthea. *A Reader's Guide to Edwardian Literature* (Hemel Hempstead: Harvester Wheatsheaf, 1991).

Trombley, Stephen. *'All That Summer She Was Mad': Virginia Woolf and Her Doctors* (London: Junction Books, 1981).

Trotter, David. 'Reading *The Waste Land*', *Critical Quarterly* 28 (1986): 143–53.

The English Novel in History 1895–1920 (London: Routledge, 1993).

Tulloch, John. *Chekhov: A Structuralist Study* (London: Macmillan, 1980).

Walker, David. 'Tories "Planned To Restrict Immigration of Blacks" ', *The Times*, 2 January 1986.

Walkowitz, Judith R. *City of Dreadful Delight: Narratives of Sexual Danger in Late-Victorian London* (London: Virago, 1992).

Walter, Richard D. 'What Became of the Degenerate?: A Brief History of a Concept', *Journal of the History of Medicine* 11 (1956): 422–9.

Walton, Henry J. *Dictionary of Psychiatry* (Oxford: Blackwell Scientific, 1985).

Warner, Val (ed.). *Charlotte Mew: Collected Poems and Prose* (London: Virago, 1982).

Watt, Ian. *Conrad in the Nineteenth Century* (London: Chatto and Windus, 1980).

Watts, C. T. 'Nordau and Kurtz: A Footnote to *Heart of Darkness*', *Notes and Queries* 219 (June 1974): 226–7.

Conrad's 'Heart of Darkness': A Critical and Contextual Discussion (Milan: Mursia International, 1977).

Watts, Cedric, *A Preface to Conrad* (London: Longman, 1982).

Webb, Timothy (ed.). *W.B. Yeats: Selected Poetry* (Harmondsworth: Penguin, 1991).

Weber, Gay. 'Industrialisation and Degeneration: The Contribution of Ethnological Theory to Early Nineteenth-Century Social Medicine', *Bulletin of the Society for the Social History of Medicine* 19 (December 1976): 7–9.

Webster, Charles (ed.). *Biology, Medicine and Society 1840–1940* (Cambridge University Press, 1981).

Weeks, Jeffrey. *Sex, Politics and Society* (Harlow: Longman, 1981).

Weindling, Paul. *Health, Race and German Politics between National Unification and Nazism, 1870–1945* (Cambridge University Press, 1989).

Werskey, Gary. *The Visible College* (London: Allen Lane, 1978).

Wiener, Martin. *English Culture and the Decline of the Industrial Spirit* (Cambridge University Press, 1981).

Williams, A. Susan. *The Rich Man and the Diseased Poor* (London: Macmillan, 1987).

Williams, Merryn. *Thomas Hardy and Rural England* (London: Macmillan, 1972).

Williams, Raymond. *The Country and the City* (1973; repr. London: Hogarth Press, 1985).

Problems of Materialism and Culture (London: Verso, 1980).

Wilson, Elizabeth. *The Sphinx in the City: Urban Life, the Control of Disorder and Women* (London: Virago, 1991).

Wohl, Anthony. *The Eternal Slum: Housing and Social Policy in Victorian London* (London: Edward Arnold, 1977).

  Endangered Lives: Public Health in Victorian Britain (London: J. M. Dent, 1983).

Woolf, Leonard. *Beginning Again: An Autobiography of the Years 1911 to 1918* (London: Hogarth Press, 1964).

Yeazell, Ruth Bernard. 'Doctors' Orders', *London Review of Books* 4 (3) (1982): 18–19.

Yeazell, Ruth Bernard (ed.). *Sex, Politics and Science in the Nineteenth Century Novel* (Baltimore and London: Johns Hopkins University Press, 1986).

Young, Robert M. 'Malthus and the Evolutionists: The Common Context of Biological and Social Theory', *Past and Present* 43 (May 1969): 109–45.

  'Evolutionary Biology and Ideology: Then and Now', *Science Studies* 1 (1971): 177–206.

SECONDARY SOURCES TO 1940

Adams, Brooks. *The Law of Civilisation and Decay: An Essay on History* (London: Swan Sonneschein & Co., 1895).

Adams, Henry. *The Education of Henry Adams: An Autobiography* (Boston: Houghton Mifflin Co., 1918).

Anglo Saxon Guide to the 1900 Paris Exposition (London: Boot & Son, 1900).

Besant, Annie. *An Autobiography* (London: T. Fisher Unwin, 1893).

Caird, Mona. *The Daughters of Danaus* (London: Bliss, Sands & Co., 1894).

Campbell, Harry. *Differences in the Nervous Organisation of Man and Woman: Physiological and Pathological* (London: H. K. Lewis, 1891).

Dangerfield, George. *The Strange Death of Liberal England* (London: Constable, 1936).

Davenport, B. R. *Anglo-Saxons, Onward!: A Romance of the Future* (Cleveland, Ohio: Hubbell Publishing Co., 1898).

Geddes, Patrick and J. Arthur Thompson. *The Evolution of Sex* (London: Walter Scott, 1890).

George, Henry. *Progress and Poverty* (1879; repr. London: J. M. Dent, 1911).

Gissing, George. *New Grub Street* (3 vols. 1889; repr. Harmondsworth: Penguin, 1968).

  The Crown of Life (1899; repr. Brighton: Harvester Press, 1979).

  Our Friend the Charlatan (London: Chapman & Hall, 1901).

Goodman, Godfrey. *The Fall of Man* (London: 1616).

Guyau, J. M. *Éducation et hérédité. Étude sociologique* (1889) trans. as *Education and Heredity* (London: Walter Scott, 1891).

Haeckel, Ernst. *The Riddle of the Universe at the Close of the Nineteenth Century* (1900; repr. Thinkers's Library London: Watts & Co, 1929).

Hakewill, George. *An Apologie of the Power and Providence of God in the Government of the World* (London: 1627).

Hall, G. Stanley. *Adolescence: Its Psychology and its Relationship to Physiology etc.* 2 vols. (New York: D. Appleton & Co., 1904).

Huxley, T. H. and Julian Huxley. *Evolution and Ethics 1893–1943* (London: Pilot Press, 1947).

James, Henry. *The Tragic Muse* (3 vols. 1890; repr. Harmondsworth: Penguin, 1980).

Johnson, Lionel. *The Art of Thomas Hardy* (London: Elkin Mathews, 1894).

Le Bon, Gustave. *La psychologie des foules* (Paris, 1895), trans. as *The Crowd: A Study of the Popular Mind* (London: T. Fisher Unwin, 1896).

Lecky, W. E. H. *Democracy and Liberty* (2 vols. London: Longmans & Co., 1896).

Linton, E. Lynn. 'Our Illusions', *Fortnightly Review* n. s. 49 (April 1891): 584–97.

London, Jack. *'The Call of the Wild' and 'The Game'* (London: New English Library, 1972).

Masterman, C. F. G. *From the Abyss* (London: R. B. Johnson, 1902).

[Masterman, C. F. G. (ed.)] *The Heart of Empire. Discussions of Problems of Modern City Life in England* (London: T. Fisher Unwin, 1901).

Maugham, Somerset, *Liza of Lambeth* (London: T. Fisher Unwin, 1897).

Morrison, Arthur. *A Child of the Jago* (London: Methuen, 1896).

Park, Robert E. *et al. The City* (1925; repr. Chicago: University of Chicago Press, 1967).

Parry, Hubert. Inaugural Address, *Journal of the Folk Lore Society* 1 (1899).

Pearson, Karl. 'Politics and Science', *Fortnightly Review* n. s. 56 (September 1894): 334–51.

Romanes, George J. 'Weismann's Theory of Heredity', *Contemporary Review* 57 (May 1890): 686–99.

'On Spencer on Natural Selection', *Contemporary Review* 63 (April 1893): 499–517.

'A Note on Panmixia', *Contemporary Review* 64 (October 1893): 611–2.

Rook, Clarence. *The Hooligan Nights*, (1899; repr. Oxford University Press, 1979).

Saleeby, C. W. *Worry: The Disease of the Age* (London: Cassell & Co., 1909).

Schopenhauer, Arthur. *Studies in Pessimism: A Series of Essays* (Selected from Schopenhauer's *Parerga*) (London: Swan Sonnenschein & Co., 1891).

Seeley, J. R. *The Expansion of England* (London: Macmillan, 1883).

Shaw, George Bernard. *The Philanderer* (1893); repr. in *The Bodley Head Bernard Shaw* Vol. 1 (London: Bodley Head, 1970).

Man and Superman (1905); repr. in *The Bodley Head Bernard Shaw* Vol. 2 London: Bodley Head, 1971).

Major Barbara (1907); repr. in *The Bodley Head Bernard Shaw* Vol. 3 (London: Bodley Head, 1971).

Spencer, Herbert. *The Man versus the State* (1884; repr. The Thinker's Library, London: Watts & Co., 1940).

'The Inadequacy of Natural Selection', *Contemporary Review* 63 (February 1893): 153–66.

Strachey, Ray. *The Cause: A Short History of the Women's Movement in Great Britain* (1928; repr. London: Virago, 1978).

Strahan, S. A. K. *Suicide and Insanity. A Physiological and Sociological Study* (London: Swan Sonneschein, 1893).

Sully, James. *Studies of Childhood* (London: Longman & Co., 1895).

Symonds, J. A. *Essays – Speculative and Suggestive* (2 vols. London: Chapman & Hall, 1890).

Thomson, William, Baron Kelvin. *Popular Lectures and Addresses* (3 vols. London: Macmillan, 1889–94).

Wallace, A. R. 'Are Individually Acquired Characters Inherited?', *Fortnightly Review* n. s. 13 (April 1893): 490–8; (May 1893): 655–68.

Wallas, Graham. *Human Nature in Politics* (1908; 3rd edn London: Constable & Co., 1938).

Weber, Adna Ferrin. *The Growth of Cities in the Nineteenth Century: A Study of Statistics*. (New York: Columbia College, 1899).

Weismann, August. 'The All-Sufficiency of Natural Selection', *Contemporary Review* 64 (September 1893): 309–38.

Wells, H. G. *The Island of Dr Moreau* (London: Heinemann, 1896).
'The Novels of Mr George Gissing', *Contemporary Review* 72 (August 1897): 192–201.

White, Arnold. *Problems of a Great City* (London: Remington, 1886).
Tries at Truth (London: Isbister & Co., 1891).

Wilde, Oscar. *The Picture of Dorian Gray* (1891; repr. Harmondsworth: Penguin, 1985).

Wilson, Andrew. 'Degeneration', *Gentleman's Magazine* 250 (April 1881): 470–94.

Zola, Emile. *La Faute de L'Abbé Mouret* (1874) trans. as *Abbe Mouret's Transgressions* (1886); repr. as *The Abbe Mouret's Sin* (London: Elek, 1957).

SECONDARY SOURCES FROM 1940

Abrams, Philip. *The Origins of British Sociology 1834–1914* (University of Chicago Press, 1968).

Batchelor, John. *H.G.Wells* (Cambridge University Press, 1985).

Beckett, Jane and Deborah Cherry (eds.). *The Edwardian Era* (London: Phaidon, 1987).

Bellamy, William. *The Novels of Wells, Bennett and Galsworthy 1890–1910* (London: Routledge & Kegan Paul, 1971).

Bergonzi, Bernard, *The Turn of a Century: Essays on Victorian and Modern English Literature* (London: Macmillan, 1973).
H. G. Wells: A Collection of Critical Essays (Englefield Cliffs, NJ: Prentice Hall, 1976).

Biddiss, Michael D. *The Age of the Masses* (Harmondsworth: Penguin, 1977).

Bloom, Harold. *Selected Writings of Walter Pater* (New York: New American Library, 1974).

Bradbury, Malcolm and James McFarlane (eds.). *Modernism 1890–1930* (Harmondsworth: Penguin, 1976).

Briggs, Asa. *William Morris. Selected Writings and Designs* (Harmondsworth: Penguin, 1962).

Victorian Cities (1963; repr. Harmondsworth: Penguin, 1968).

Brooks, Jean R. *Thomas Hardy: The Poetic Structure* (London: Elek, 1971).

Brownlow, Kevin. *Behind the Mask of Innocence* (London: Jonathan Cape, 1990).

Budd, Susan. *Varieties of Unbelief: Atheists and Agnostics in English Society 1850–1960* (London: Heinemann, 1977).

Burke, Peter. 'Tradition and Experience: The Idea of Decline from Bruni to Gibbon', *Daedalus* 105 (Summer 1976): 137–52.

Churchill, F. B. 'August Weismann and the Break from Tradition', *Journal of the History of Biology* 1 (1968): 91–112.

Clarke, I. F. *The Pattern of Expectation: 1644–2001* (London: Jonathan Cape, 1979).

Collini, Stefan. *Liberalism and Sociology: L. T. Hobhouse and Political Argument in England 1880–1914* (Cambridge University Press, 1979).

Coustillas, Pierre. *George Gissing: Essays and Fiction* (Baltimore: Johns Hopkins University Press, 1970).

Cowan, Ruth S. 'Nature and Nurture: The Interplay of Biology and Politics in the Work of Francis Galton', *Studies in the History of Biology* 1 (1977): 133–207.

Crossick, Geoffrey (ed.). *The Lower Middle Class in Britain 1870–1914* (London: Croom Helm, 1977).

Cunningham, A. R. 'The "New-Woman Fiction" of the 1890s', *Victorian Studies* 17 (December 1973): 177–86.

Denning, Michael. *Cover Stories: Narrative and Ideology in the British Spy Thriller* (London: Routledge & Kegan Paul, 1987).

Dickie, John. Review of D. Pick *Faces of Degeneration* (1989), *History Workshop Journal* no. 30 (Autumn 1990): 194–6.

Donzelot, Jacques. *La Police des familles* (1977) trans. as *The Policing of Families* (London: Hutchinson, 1979).

Draper, Michael. *H.G.Wells* (London: Macmillan, 1987).

Eby, Cecil, Degrotte. *The Road to Armageddon: The Martial Spirit in English Popular Literature 1870–1914* (Durham, NC: Duke University Press, 1987).

Ellenberger, Henri. *The Discovery of the Unconscious* (London: Allen Lane, 1970).

Ellmann, Richard. *Oscar Wilde* (London: Hamish Hamilton, 1987).

Elwin, Malcolm. (ed.). *The Essays of R. L. Stevenson: A Selection* (London: MacDonald, 1950).

Figlio, Karl. 'Chlorosis and Chronic Disease in Nineteenth Century Britain: The Social Constitution of Somatic Illness in a Capitalist Society', *Social History* 3 (May 1978): 167–97.

First, Ruth and Ann Scott. *Olive Schreiner* (London: Andre Deutsch, 1980).

Fisher, Joe. *The Hidden Hardy* (London: Macmillan, 1992).

Frayling, Christopher. *Vampyres: Lord Byron to Count Dracula* (London: Faber, 1991).

Gammon, Vic. 'Folk Song Collecting in Sussex and Surrey 1843–1914', *History Workshop Journal* no. 10 (Autumn 1980): 61–89.

Gordon, Linda. *Woman's Body, Woman's Right; A Social History of Birth Control in America* (1976; repr. Harmondsworth: Penguin, 1977).

Gould, Stephen Jay. *Ever Since Darwin* (New York: W. W. Norton, 1977).

Green, Martin. *Dreams of Adventure: Deeds of Empire* (London: Routledge & Kegan Paul, 1980).

Greist, Guinevere. *Mudie's Circulating Library and the Victorian Novel* (Newton Abbot: David Charles, 1970).

Gross, John. *The Rise and Fall of the Man of Letters* (Harmondsworth: Penguin, 1969).

Hamer, D. A. (ed.). *The Radical Programme* (1885; repr. Brighton: Harvester Press, 1971).

Harpham, G. G. 'Time Running Out: The Edwardian Sense of Cultural Degeneration', *Clio* 5 (1976): 283–301.

Harris, Ruth. 'Melodrama, Hysteria and Feminine Crimes of Passion in the Fin de Siècle', *History Workshop* 25 (Spring 1988): 31–63.

Harris, Victor. *All Coherence Gone* (London: Frank Cass & Co., 1966).

Harrison, John. *The Reactionaries: Yeats, Pound, Eliot, Lawrence: A Study of the Anti-Democratic Intelligentsia* (New York: Schocken, 1967).

Haynes, Roslynn. *H.G.Wells: Discoverer of the Future* (London: Macmillan, 1980).

Helfand, Michael S. 'T. H. Huxley's "Evolution and Ethics": The Politics of Evolution and the Evolution of Politics', *Victorian Studies* 20 (Winter 1977): 159–77.

Hennock, E. P. 'Poverty and Social Theory in England: the Experience of the Eighteen-Eighties', *Social History* 1 (1) (January 1976): 67–91.

Herz, Judith Scherer and Robert K. Martin (eds.). *E.M.Forster: Centenary Revaluations* (London: Macmillan, 1982).

Heywood, Christopher (ed.). *D.H.Lawrence: New Studies* (London: Macmillan, 1987).

Himmelfarb, Gertrude. *Victorian Minds* (London: Weidenfeld & Nicolson, 1968).

Hobsbawm, E. J. *The Age of Empire 1875–1914* (London: Weidenfeld & Nicholson, 1987).

Howard, David, John Lucas and John Goode (eds.). *Tradition and Tolerance in Nineteenth-Century Fiction: Critical Essays on some English and American Novels* (London: Routledge & Kegan Paul, 1966).

Hughes, H. Stuart. *Consciousness and Society: The Reorientation of European Social Thought 1890–1930* (Brighton: Harvester Press, 1979).

Huxley, Julian. *Evolution: The Modern Synthesis* (London: G. Allen & Unwin 1942).

Hynes, Samuel. *Edwardian Occasions* (London: Routledge & Kegan Paul, 1972).

Johnson, Richard. 'Barrington Moore, Perry Anderson and English Social Development', *Working Papers in Cultural Studies* 9 (1976): 7–28.

Kearney, Anthony. 'Savage and Barbaric Themes in Victorian Children's Writing', *Children's Literature in Education* 17 (4) (1986): 233–40.

Keating, P. J. (ed.). *Working-Class Stories of the 1890s* (1971; repr. London: Routledge & Kegan Paul, 1975).

Keating, Peter (ed.). *Into Unknown England 1866–1913: Selections from the Social Explorers* (London: Fontana, 1976).

Kemp, Peter. *H.G.Wells and the Culminating Ape: Biological Themes and Imaginative Obsessions* (London: Macmillan, 1982).

Kent, Christopher. *Brains and Numbers: Elitism, Comtism and Democracy in Mid-Victorian England* (University of Toronto Press, 1978).

Kern, Stephen. *The Culture of Space and Time* (London: Weidenfeld & Nicholson, 1983).

Korg, Jacob (ed.). *George Gissing: Notes on Social Democracy* (London: Enitharmon Press, 1968).

Kuhn, Annette. *Cinema, Censorship and Sexuality 1909–1925* (London: Routledge, 1988).

Ledbetter, Rosanna. *A History of the Malthusian League* (Ohio State University Press, 1976).

Lerner, Laurence. (ed.). *The Victorians* (London: Methuen, 1980).

Lester, John A. *Journey through Despair: Transformation in British Literary Culture 1880–1914* (Princeton University Press, 1968).

Levine, George. *Darwin and the Novelists: Patterns of Science in Victorian Fiction* (Cambridge, Mass.: Harvard University Press, 1988).

Lodge, David. *Language of Fiction* (London: Routledge & Kegan Paul, 1966).

Lynd, Helen M. *England in the 1880s: Towards a Social Basis for Freedom* (London: Oxford University Press, 1945).

Maik, Linda L. 'Nordau's *Degeneration*: The American Controversy', *Journal of the History of Ideas* 50 (1989): 607–23.

Mallett, Phillip (ed.). *Kipling Considered* (London: Macmillan, 1989).

Maxwell, J. C. 'The "Sociological" Approach to *The Mayor of Casterbridge*', in Maynard Mack and Ian Gregor (eds.). *Imagined Worlds: Essays on Some English Novels and Novelists in Honour of John Butt* (London: Methuen, 1968).

Miller, Jonathan. *The Body in Question* (London: Jonathan Cape, 1978).

Millgate, Michael. *Thomas Hardy: His Career as Novelist* (London: Bodley Head, 1971).

344   *Bibliography*

Nelson, Claudia. *Boys Will Be Girls: The Feminine Ethic and British Children's Fiction 1857–1917* (New Brunswick, NJ: Rutgers University Press, 1991).

O'Hanlon, Redmond. *Joseph Conrad and Charles Darwin: The Influence of Scientific Thought on Conrad's Fiction* (Edinburgh: Salamander Press, 1984).

Parrinder, Patrick. *H.G.Wells* (Edinbugh: Oliver & Boyd, 1970).

Parrinder, Patrick and R. M. Philmus. *The Literary Criticism of H. G. Wells* (Brighton: Harvester Press, 1980).

Parrinder, Patrick (ed.). *Science Fiction: A Critical Guide* (London: Longman, 1979).

Pickens, D. K. *Eugenics and the Progressives* (Nashville, Tennessee: Vanderbilt University Press, 1968).

Robb, J. H. *The Primrose League 1883–1906* (New York: Columbia University Press, 1942).

Rogers, J. A. 'Darwinism amd Social Darwinism', *Journal of the History of Ideas* 33 (April-June 1972): 265–80.

Rowbotham, Sheila and Jeffrey Weeks. *Socialism and the New Life: The Personal and Sexual Politics of Edward Carpenter and Havelock Ellis* (London: Pluto Press, 1977).

Said, Edward. *Orientalism* (London: Routledge, 1978).

Shannon, Richard. *The Crisis of Imperialism 1865–1915* (1974; repr. London: Paladin, 1976).

Shewan, Rodney. *Oscar Wilde; Art and Egotism* (London: Macmillan, 1977).

Simon, W. M. *European Positivism in the Nineteenth Century* (Ithaca, NY: Cornell University Press, 1963).

Smith, Anne. (ed.). *The Novels of Thomas Hardy* (London: Vision Press, 1979).

Soloway, Richard Allen. *Birth Control and the Population Question in England, 1877–1939* (Chapel Hill: North Carolina University Press, 1982).

Stokes, John. *Resistable Theatres* (London: Elek, 1972).

Suvin, Darko. *Metamorphoses of Science Fiction: On the Poetics and History of a Literary Genre* (New Haven: Yale University Press, 1979).

Swart, K. W. *The Sense of Decadence in Nineteenth Century France* (The Hague: Martinus Nijhoff, 1964).

Taylor, Richard H. *The Personal Notebooks of Thomas Hardy* (London: Macmillan, 1978).

Thompson, E. P. *The Poverty of Theory and Other Essays* (London: Merlin Press, 1978).

Tye, J. R. *Periodicals of the Nineties* (Oxford: Oxford Bibliographical Society, 1974).

Urlaub, Werner G. *Der spatviktorianische Sozialroman von 1880 bis 1890* (Bonn: Bouvier Verlag Herber Grundmann, 1977).

Vicinus, Martha (ed.). *Suffer and Be Still: Women in the Victorian Age* (Bloomington: Indiana University Press, 1972).

A Widening Sphere: Changing Roles of Victorian Women (Bloomington: Indiana University Press, 1977).

Walkowitz, Judith R. *Prostitition and Victorian Society* (New York: Cambridge University Press, 1980).

'Jack the Ripper and the Myth of Male Violence', *Feminist Studies* 8 (1982): 543–74.

Watt, Donald. (ed.). *Aldous Huxley: The Critical Heritage* (London: Routledge, 1975).

Weeks, Jeffrey. *Coming Out: Homosexual Politics from the Nineteenth Century to the Present* (London: Quartet Books, 1977).

Whyte, L. L. *The Unconscious before Freud* (London: Tavistock Publications, 1962).

Widdowson, Peter. *E.M.Forster's 'Howards End'* (London: Sussex University Press, 1975).

Williams, Raymond. *The English Novel from Dickens to Lawrence* (London: Chatto & Windus, 1970).

Politics and Letters (London: New Left Books, 1979).

Wright, Anne. *Literature of Crisis, 1910–22* (London: Routledge, 1984).

Yeo, Stephen. 'A New Life: The Religion of Socialism in Britain 1883–1896', *History Workshop Journal* no. 4 (1977): 5–56.

Index